Washington, DC

Laura Harger

LONELY PLANET PUBLICATIONS
Melbourne • Oakland • London • Paris

Washington, DC
1st edition – February 2001

Published by
Lonely Planet Publications Pty Ltd A.C.N. 005 607 983
90 Maribyrnong St, Footscray, Victoria 3011, Australia

Lonely Planet Offices
Australia Locked Bag 1, Footscray, Victoria 3011
USA 150 Linden St, Oakland, CA 94607
UK 10a Spring Place, London NW5 3BH
France 1 rue du Dahomey, 75011 Paris

Photographs
All of the images in this guide are available for licensing from
Lonely Planet Images.
email: lpi@lonelyplanet.com.au

Front cover photograph
US Capitol Dome (Dennis Johnson)

ISBN 1 86450 244 4

text & maps © Lonely Planet 2001
photos © photographers as indicated 2001

Printed by The Bookmaker International Ltd
Printed in China

Contents

3

4   Contents

The Author

Laura Harger

Laura was born in Takoma Park and grew up on DC's outskirts, in Maryland. After earning a BA at the University of Michigan, she returned to the capital for two years' sojourn in Adams-Morgan and Mount Pleasant. She then received an MFA from the Iowa Writers' Workshop, hopped across the country again, and worked in publishing in the Bay Area for several years before joining the Lonely Planet posse, where she was a senior editor for a couple of years. She's now a senior editor at the University of California Press and lives in Berkeley with her husband, Matt Campbell, but she still misses DC's *injera*, summertime humidity, and seismic stability.

FROM THE AUTHOR

Thanks go first to Mariah 'Nine Fingers' Bear and Kate Hoffman for letting me out of the kennel to romp around my favorite town. Tips of the stein also to the helpful staff of the DC Convention & Visitors Association and all the wonderfully knowledgeable volunteer mentors who keep the capital's museums and historic sites in working order; to Randy Peffer, Jeff Williams, and Kap Stann for their fine work on *Virginia & the Capital Region* 1, which informed my work on this book; to David Zingarelli for his tireless bar research and insights into DC's gay and lesbian scene; to Justin Marler for punk stuff; to my gracious bipartisan hosts, Rebecca Orman, Mark Brasher, and Ira and George, for pop-culture education, Hill-rat tips, and letting me be their basement troll; to Robert Harger and Rosemary Harger-Ruffieux for many good meals; to the Lonely Planet Caucus, consisting of Tullan Spitz, Michele Posner, Robert Reid, Valerie Sinzdak, Wade Fox, Monica Lepe, Kimra McAfee, and Herman So, for their undying patience, hard work, and fearless slaying of errant metaphors; and most especially to Matt for kindness and nest maintenance in my absence.

This Book

Washington, DC, was written by Laura Harger, with David Zingarelli, Justin Marler and Tullan Spitz contributing.

FROM THE PUBLISHER

This book was produced in Lonely Planet's Oakland office by a veritable congress of talented people. On its way to the printer, Laura Harger's impeccable manuscript passed through the capable hands of editors Tullan Spitz, Valerie Sinzdak, Wade Fox, and Elaine Merrill, overseen by senior Robert Reid and seniors Tom Downs and Michele Posner.

Herman So drew the maps, with Tessa Rottiers, Patrick Phelan and Matt DeMartini assisting. Monica Lepe, Kimra McAfee, and Alex Guilbert oversaw the cartographers. Shelley Firth designed the book under the guidance of Susan Rimerman, who also designed the cover. Beca Lafore did the sidebar trim and coordinated the illustrations, enlisting the talents of artists Hugh D'Andrade, Hayden Foell, Justin Marler, Hannah Reineck, and Jenn Steffey. Ken DellaPenta created the index.

Foreword

ABOUT LONELY PLANET GUIDEBOOKS

The story begins with a classic travel adventure: Tony and Maureen Wheeler's 1972 journey across Europe and Asia to Australia. Useful information about the overland trail did not exist at that time, so Tony and Maureen published the first Lonely Planet guidebook to meet a growing need.

From a kitchen table, then from a tiny office in Melbourne (Australia), Lonely Planet has become the largest independent travel publisher in the world, an international company with offices in Melbourne, Oakland (USA), London (UK) and Paris (France).

Today Lonely Planet guidebooks cover the globe. There is an ever-growing list of books, and there's information in a variety of forms and media. Some things haven't changed. The main aim is still to help make it possible for adventurous travelers to get out there – to explore and better understand the world.

At Lonely Planet we believe travelers can make a positive contribution to the countries they visit – if they respect their host communities and spend their money wisely. Since 1986 a percentage of the income from each book has been donated to aid projects and human-rights campaigns.

Updates Lonely Planet thoroughly updates each guidebook as often as possible. This usually means there are around two years between editions, although for more unusual or more stable destinations the gap can be longer. Check the imprint page (following the color map at the beginning of the book) for publication dates.

Between editions, up-to-date information is available in two free newsletters – the paper *Planet Talk* and email *Comet* (to subscribe, contact any Lonely Planet office) – and on our website at www.lonelyplanet.com. The *Upgrades* section of the website covers a number of important and volatile destinations and is regularly updated by Lonely Planet authors. *Scoop* covers news and current affairs relevant to travelers. And, lastly, the *Thorn Tree* bulletin board and *Postcards* section of the site carry unverified, but fascinating, reports from travelers.

Correspondence The process of creating new editions begins with the letters, postcards and emails received from travelers. This correspondence often includes suggestions, criticisms and comments about the current editions. Interesting excerpts are immediately passed on via newsletters and the website, and everything goes to our authors to be verified when they're researching on the road. We're keen to get more feedback from organizations or individuals who represent communities visited by travelers.

Lonely Planet gathers information for everyone who's curious about the planet – and especially for those who explore it firsthand. Through guidebooks, phrasebooks, activity guides, maps, literature, newsletters, image library, TV series and website, we act as an information exchange for a worldwide community of travelers.

Research Authors aim to gather sufficient practical information to enable travelers to make informed choices and to make the mechanics of a journey run smoothly. They also research historical and cultural background to help enrich the travel experience and allow travelers to understand and respond appropriately to cultural and environmental issues.

Authors don't stay in every hotel because that would mean spending a couple of months in each medium-size city and, no, they don't eat at every restaurant because that would mean stretching belts beyond capacity. They do visit hotels and restaurants to check standards and prices, but feedback based on readers' direct experiences can be very helpful.

Many of our authors work undercover; others aren't so secretive. None of them accept freebies in exchange for positive write-ups. And none of our guidebooks contain any advertising.

Production Authors submit their raw manuscripts and maps to offices in Australia, the USA, the UK or France. Editors and cartographers – all experienced travelers themselves – then begin the process of assembling the pieces. When the book finally hits the shops, some things are already out of date, we start getting feedback from readers and the process begins again....

WARNING & REQUEST

Things change – prices go up, schedules change, good places go bad and bad places go bankrupt – nothing stays the same. So, if you find things better or worse, recently opened or long since closed, please tell us and help make the next edition even more accurate and useful. We genuinely value all the feedback we receive. Julie Young coordinates a well-traveled team that reads and acknowledges every letter, postcard and email and ensures that every morsel of information finds its way to the appropriate authors, editors and cartographers for verification.

Everyone who writes to us will find their name in the next edition of the appropriate guidebook. They will also receive the latest issue of *Planet Talk*, our quarterly printed newsletter, or *Comet*, our monthly email newsletter. Subscriptions to both newsletters are free. The very best contributions will be rewarded with a free guidebook.

Excerpts from your correspondence may appear in new editions of Lonely Planet guidebooks, the Lonely Planet website, *Planet Talk* or *Comet*, so please let us know if you *don't* want your letter published or your name acknowledged.

Send all correspondence to the Lonely Planet office closest to you:

Australia: Locked Bag 1, Footscray, Victoria 3011
USA: 150 Linden St, Oakland, CA 94607
UK: 10a Spring Place, London NW5 3BH
France: 1 rue du Dahomey, 75011 Paris

Or email us at: talk2us@lonelyplanet.com.au

For news, views and updates, see our website: www.lonelyplanet.com

HOW TO USE A LONELY PLANET GUIDEBOOK

The best way to use a Lonely Planet guidebook is any way you choose. At Lonely Planet, we believe the most memorable travel experiences are often those that are unexpected, and the finest discoveries are those you make yourself. Guidebooks are not intended to be used as if they provided a detailed set of infallible instructions!

Contents All Lonely Planet guidebooks follow the same format. The Facts about the Country chapters or sections give background information ranging from history to weather. Facts for the Visitor gives practical information on issues like visas and health. Getting There & Away gives a brief starting point for researching travel to and from the destination. Getting Around gives an overview of the transport options available when you arrive.

The peculiar demands of each destination determine how subsequent chapters are broken up, but some things remain constant. We always start with background, then proceed to sights, places to stay, places to eat, entertainment, getting there and away, and getting around information – in that order.

Heading Hierarchy Lonely Planet headings are used in a strict hierarchical structure that can be visualized as a set of Russian dolls. Each heading (and its following text) is encompassed by any preceding heading that is higher on the hierarchical ladder.

Entry Points We do not assume guidebooks will be read from beginning to end, but that people will dip into them. The traditional entry points are the list of contents and the index. In addition, however, some books have a complete list of maps and an index map illustrating map coverage.

There may also be a color map that shows highlights. These highlights are dealt with in greater detail later in the book, along with planning questions and suggested itineraries. Each chapter covering a geographical region usually begins with a locator map and another list of highlights. Once you find something of interest in a list of highlights, turn to the index.

Maps Maps play a crucial role in Lonely Planet guidebooks and include a huge amount of information. A legend is printed on the back page. We seek to have complete consistency between maps and text, and to have every important place in the text captured on a map. Map key numbers usually start in the top left corner.

Although inclusion in a guidebook usually implies a recommendation, we cannot list every good place. Exclusion does not necessarily imply criticism. In fact, there are a number of reasons why we might exclude a place – sometimes it is simply inappropriate to encourage an influx of travelers.

Introduction

DENNIS JOHNSON

The name 'Washington' conjures up a host of images for people around the world. To some, Washington means white marble, verdant lawns, and the colorful, ritualistic pageantry of American politics: the Capitol dome gleaming against the azure sky of a hot summer's day while lawmakers broker deals and schmooze below it; the slow, limousine-filled Inauguration Day procession up Pennsylvania Ave from the Capitol to the White House; the mournful, somber, stately changing of the guard at Arlington National Cemetery. To others, Washington means power, pure and simple: Deep Throat divulging Nixon's dirty secrets to Bob Woodward in a downtown parking garage; legislators and lobbyists logrolling, back-scratching, and digging happily into each other's pockets; CIA spooks and G-men ferreting out foreign intelligence agents and hatching cryptic schemes of their own.

Washington is indeed all these things, and the very names of its physical features and buildings – the Hill, the Beltway, the Potomac, Watergate, the Supreme Court – have all become symbols of the power, intrigues, and corruptions of the American political system. Visitors to the city can revel in exploring these iconic sites firsthand and glimpsing the images and people usually seen only on the evening news. Indeed, Washington is almost unique as a major world capital: its monumental government buildings, from the Capitol to the White House to the Pentagon, are almost all open for casual visits by anyone who cares to take a peek inside them.

Yet Washington is no mere political ornament. It is also a *city*, a city where ordinary and extraordinary people live, work, and play, a city of vibrant and beautiful neighborhoods where the federal government and its machinery are merely backdrops to life, not the main-stage drama. After visitors have explored the wonders of the Smithsonian Institution's 14 museums (always free!), strolled through the halls of power, and played spot-the-senator in famous eateries, delightful districts like Dupont Circle, Adams-Morgan, and Georgetown offer opportunities to meet ordinary folks, tour lovely historic buildings, and dive into fabulous world cuisine. This little city (only about a half-million people live here) is also a polyglot wonderland, among the country's most international towns. American visitors can meet lots of folks from overseas, and visitors from abroad can find lots of compatriots to chase away the lonely-traveler blues. Because the town attracts flocks of well-educated, well-informed professionals, most people you'll meet here are as smart as all get-out, which means even casual bar conversations are a lot of fun.

Once upon a time, John Kennedy famously derided his temporary hometown as a city of 'Northern charm and Southern efficiency.' Others have delivered similarly pithy backhand slaps to the capital over the years, and, indeed, Washington has had its troubles. Although Washington is rich in African American history and is among the USA's few metropolises with a black majority, its black neighborhoods also have long suffered from profound poverty and street crime. Washington's city government has been, until recently, a parade of woes (topped off by the 1990 arrest of Mayor Marion Barry for smoking crack), and Washington, like many great American cities, has watched large chunks of its population move out to the suburbs over the last several decades.

Yet better days came to the capital at last in the 1990s. A booming economy, both nationwide and in the suburbs around Washington, permitted the downtown core, north of the Mall, to blossom with new restaurants, bars, sports venues, and clubs. Fewer residents abandoned the city for the 'burbs. Crime rates fell dramatically, and the city government cleaned up its act. Many of the Smithsonian museums (which were pretty cool to start with) have undergone major renovations and added new wings and displays. All this adds up to an even more compelling city for visitors.

If you spend time in Washington, exploring its neighborhoods as well as its famous sites, you'll find that new images of the capital have joined your old ones: swarms of colorful kites in the skies over the National Mall on a windy spring day; a hot summer's night spent with wine, food, and friends in an open-air rooftop bar in Adams-Morgan; the sound of birdsong and the wind in the leaves as you stroll through Rock Creek Park or along the upper reaches of the C&O Canal towpath in northwest DC; a Georgetown garden in spring, awash in rare roses and cherry blossom. It's a great little town.

Facts about Washington, DC

HISTORY
The First Washingtonians

Before the first European colonists sailed up the Potomac River from Chesapeake Bay, several groups of Native Americans, primarily Piscataway of the Algonquin language group, made their home near the confluence of the Potomac and Anacostia Rivers. The Potomac's waters below Great Falls were thick with seasonal runs of shad, rockfish, and other species, and Indian villages lined the banks, fishing, growing corn and tobacco, and trading with one another.

The Piscataway may have encountered Europeans as early as the late 16th century, when Spanish explorers made forays into the lands around the Chesapeake, but the first recorded contact was made in 1608 by the English Captain John Smith, who sailed the Potomac up to the site of today's Georgetown.

Smith was pleased by what he found, writing, 'The fourth river is called [by the Indians] Patawomeke, 6 or 7 myles in breadth. It is navigable 140 myles, and fed as the rest with many sweet rivers and springs, which fall from the bordering hills. These hills many of them are planted, and yeeld no lesse plentie and varietie of fruit. than the river exceedeth with abundance of fish. It is inhabited on both sides….'

Given that kind of press, European traders soon descended on the area, trading for furs trapped beyond the Allegheny Mountains and aided in their work by local Algonquin Indians. English settlers followed in their wake, and expansive agricultural estates sprang up along both sides of the Potomac, displacing the Indians in the process. (George Washington's family claimed over 8000 acres on the Virginia shore, the estate called Mount Vernon.) By 1697, few Piscataway were left on the Maryland side of the river. Most migrated to Virginia, and thence to Pennsylvania and far western New York.

The new plantations' most lucrative crop was the precious sotweed – tobacco – which was tended by increasing numbers of African indentured servants and slaves. In the mid-18th century, the river ports of Alexandria (on the Virginia bank) and Georgetown (on the Maryland bank) were established to ship tobacco to a smoke-hungry world. Garrison's Landing, on the Anacostia River, also prospered on the tobacco trade.

The Founding of the Federal City

After the 13 colonies had defeated their English masters in the Revolutionary War, the fledgling US Congress launched a search for a permanent home. For several years, Congress seemed to be rather a moveable feast, meeting in various cities – including New York, Philadelphia, Princeton, and Annapolis – as the new states vied among themselves for power. Southern states didn't want the capital in the North, because they feared wealthy urban Northerners would dominate it. Northerners didn't want the capital in the geographically

George Washington, the city's namesake

inconvenient South. The regional tensions that would eventually fuel the Civil War were already apparent in the debate over the siting of the capital city.

Towns from Germantown, Pennsylvania, to St Mary's City, Maryland, competed to become the capital. The squabbling continued until 1790, when Congress charged President George Washington with the selection of a site 'not exceeding 10 miles square.' Washington naturally gravitated toward the lands along the Potomac River, where he owned the estate of Mount Vernon. The site was a natural midpoint that satisfied the interests of both North and South, and it was at a point on the Potomac that positioned it well for river commerce (see Geography, later).

Maryland and Virginia agreed to cede land to the new capital, and in March 1791

the African American mathematician Benjamin Banneker and surveyor Andrew Ellicott surveyed and mapped a diamond-shaped territory that spanned the Potomac and Anacostia Rivers. Its four corners were at the cardinal points of the compass, and it embraced the river ports of Georgetown and Alexandria (the latter eventually returned to Virginia's control). In the same month, the French Major Pierre Charles L'Enfant – an American supporter in the Revolutionary War – began to sketch plans for the new city, which was named the 'Territory of Columbia' (to honor Christopher Columbus) and 'The City of Washington' (to honor George).

L'Enfant's sweepingly ambitious city plan, based on those of European capitals, featured majestic orthogonal boulevards and grand roundabouts. He selected the

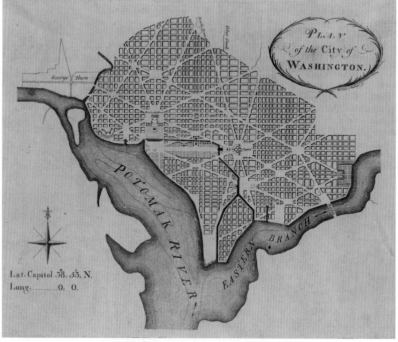

Pierre L'Enfant's original plan for Washington, DC

President's House and the Capitol itself as the two geographic centerpoints of his city, which he envisioned as a grand showcase for public buildings and monuments. But L'Enfant was a diva, squabbling with city commissioners, running afoul of local politicians, and doing unpopular things like knocking down people's houses while they were out of town. President Washington fired him in 1792, and his plans were only partly realized.

Land speculators arrived in Washington starting in 1791, buying up land particularly in the southwest quadrant, at the juncture of the two rivers. Buildings sprang up, and construction started on the two main seats of power – the President's House and the Capitol – in 1793. But despite this progress (and in mockery of L'Enfant's high hopes), the early city was a disorderly tangle of swampland and muddy streets. Gouverneur Morris, a wealthy New Yorker who visited in 1801, acidly observed, 'We only need here houses, cellars, kitchens, scholarly men, amiable women, and a few other trifles, to possess a perfect city.'

War of 1812: Washington Burns

Poor Washington – it was only finding its feet and getting the streets laid properly when it had to start all over. Work was barely complete on the Capitol in 1814 when British troops sailed up the Patuxent River, thrashed American forces at Bladensburg, and marched into Washington.

The victorious British embarked on a night of looting and arson throughout the capital. When it was over, most of the city's public buildings had been torched and President and Dolly Madison had fled to the Virginia suburbs, with the Declaration of Independence and Constitution in hand. The new Capitol and the President's House were sacked and burned. Although the British were soon expelled and Washington soon rebuilt, the city entered a slump from which it didn't recover for decades. A congressional vote to abandon the dispirited capital lost by just nine votes.

Until the Civil War, Washington grew only slowly, and the Mall and its public buildings

were plagued by Potomac floods and overgrown with scrub. Charles Dickens, visiting in 1842, dismissed DC thus: 'It is sometimes called the City of Magnificent Distances, but it might with greater propriety be called the City of Magnificent Intentions....Spacious avenues, that begin in nothing, and lead nowhere; streets, mile-long, that only want houses, roads, and inhabitants; public buildings that need but a public.'

Slavery in the Federal City

When Congress first convened in Washington, in 1800, the city had about 14,000 residents. It was, even then, a heavily African American town: 29% of the population were slaves or 'free blacks.' Most free blacks lived in the port of Georgetown, where a vibrant African American community emerged, and they frequently worked alongside and even socialized with the city's slaves.

Despite the significant numbers of free blacks in Washington, the capital also sheltered a shameful number of slave markets in the early 19th century. Among the most infamous was Robey's Slave Pen, in southwest Washington (on the site where the Federal Aviation Administration now sits), which was a holding tank for black slaves traded by Neal & Company. Neal and other slavers did good business in the capital, especially in Alexandria, selling slaves bought in Maryland or Virginia to Southern plantations for many times their purchase price. As one abolitionist wrote at the time, '…in no part of the earth was there so great, so infamous a slave market, as in…the seat of government of this nation which prides itself on freedom.'

Nonetheless, the number of slaves in Washington steadily dropped throughout the first half of the 19th century, while the number of free blacks rose. Slaveholders found it lucrative to 'rent out' their slaves as laborers, and these quasi-slaves often kept some profit for themselves, enabling them to buy freedom for themselves or relatives. Meanwhile, the relatively flexible nature of Washington slavery encouraged free blacks to migrate to the city to work as laborers and in other trades. Among the

FACTS ABOUT DC

From Slave to Statesman: Frederick Douglass

Born a slave in 1818 on a plantation on Maryland's Eastern Shore, Frederick Douglass is remembered as one of the country's most outstanding black 19th-century leaders.

When he was 21, he escaped wretched treatment at the hands of Maryland planters and established himself as a freeman in the booming whaling port of New Bedford, Massachusetts. Largely self-educated, Douglass had a natural gift of eloquence. In 1841 he won the admiration of New England abolitionists with an impromptu speech at an antislavery convention, introducing himself as 'a recent graduate from the institution of slavery, with his diploma [ie, whip marks] on his back.' The Massachusetts Anti-Slavery Society hired Douglass, and he traveled the free states as an energetic spokesman for abolition and the Underground Railroad, the network that shepherded escaping slaves to freedom. He also founded an antislavery newspaper.

Douglass' effectiveness so angered proslavery forces that his friends urged him to flee to England to escape seizure and punishment under the Fugitive Slave Law. But he kept lecturing in England, and admirers contributed enough money to enable him to purchase his freedom and return home in 1847.

Douglass then became the self-proclaimed 'station master and conductor' of the Underground Railroad in Rochester, New York, working with other famed abolitionists like Harriet Tubman and John Brown. In 1860, Douglass campaigned for Abraham Lincoln, and when the Civil War broke out, Douglass helped raise two regiments of black soldiers, the Massachusetts 54th and 55th, to fight for the Union.

After the war, Douglass went to Washington to lend his support to the 13th, 14th, and 15th Constitutional Amendments, which abolished slavery, granted citizenship to former slaves, and guaranteed citizens the right to vote. He later became US marshal for Washington and the US minister to Haiti (the country's first black ambassador).

Douglass died at Cedar Hill, his Anacostia home, in 1895. His funeral was held at DC's historic Metropolitan AME Church, 1518 M St NW, where one speaker mourned him in words that illustrated what Douglass had meant to black Washington: 'Howl, fir tree, for the Cedar of Lebanon has fallen.'

The Park Service now preserves Cedar Hill as a museum (see Things to See & Do for details).

most renowned of these emigrants was Benjamin Banneker, the black astronomer and mathematician who surveyed the original District boundaries in 1791. Free blacks established churches and schools for themselves throughout Washington, and the city became a key stop on the Underground Railroad, which shuttled escaped slaves to freedom in the northern states.

Yet Washington was by no means a haven for free blacks. Most lived in miserable conditions, often in back-alley shacks, and free blacks were sometimes kidnapped by slavers and sold back into bondage. In 1835, the white-led Snow Riots intimidated and attacked black Washingtonians. But at last, in 1850, Congress outlawed the slave trade in Washington, and slaves flooded into the District, fleeing their owners in Virginia and Maryland. In 1862, the District Emancipation Act abolished slavery within city limits.

Civil War & Its Aftermath

Washington might be called a city made by war – from the Civil War to WWII, major American wars have helped to develop the District. Wartime bureaucracy draws new workers, who require new houses and new office buildings in which to work, and after the war has ended, many of these temporary workers become permanent residents. During and after the Civil War, this dynamic caused the city's population to jump 75%, up to 131,175.

The Civil War brought bivouacs, temporary hospitals, and thousands of soldiers to Washington. The capital's site was selected, in 1790, as a compromise between North and South, but that compromise meant that Washington was on the front lines of battle throughout the Civil War. A ring of earthwork forts was hastily erected around the city to protect it from attack, but Washington saw only one battle on its soil: Confederate General Jubal Early's unsuccessful attack on Fort Stevens, in northern DC, in July 1864. Washingtonians lived in constant anxiety, however, as enormous and bloody battles raged nearby at Antietam, Gettysburg, and Manassas.

The war's chaos and expense led Washingtonians to wonder whether construction of the elaborate Capitol dome should be suspended. President Lincoln responded, 'If people see the Capitol going on, it is a sign we intend the Union shall go on.' Only five days after Confederate General Robert E Lee surrendered to Union General Ulysses S Grant at Appomattox, the Great Emancipator was assassinated in downtown Washington at Ford's Theatre (a memorial flag remains draped over the presidential box there today).

After the war, thousands of freed African Americans emigrated to the growing capital, seeking work and fleeing the depressed, chaotic South of the Reconstruction era. Howard University was founded in 1867 to educate black residents; by this time, blacks comprised nearly half the city's population.

In 1871, Congress appointed a new Board of Public Works to oversee Washington, independent of city government. It was led by the infamous Alexander R 'Boss' Shepherd, who overhauled the city's ailing infrastructure and filled in the swampy canal on the National Mall. Yet Shepherd's extravagant hand with federal funds and penchant for steamrolling his opposition led Congress to crack down, appointing a new commission to run Washington and robbing the city of self-government for another century. For the citizenry, such disenfranchisement was a high price to pay for a Washington that had finally begun to resemble L'Enfant's dream of a world-class capital.

The McMillan Plan

By the beginning of the 20th century, Washington had begun to assume its modern form. It was home to over a quarter-million residents, the new Smithsonian Institution and National Zoological Park had opened, and Rock Creek Park had been established, granting the city a permanent green corridor from its northern boundary to the Potomac. New 'suburbs' such as Woodley Park and Mount Pleasant offered wealthy Washingtonians a respite from the hot inner city, and electric trolleys plied the streets.

In 1900, Sen James McMillan, chairman of the Senate District Committee, appointed a commission to study Washington's city plan. Although the city was growing, the American government (just beginning to flex its muscles on the world stage) was unhappy with its ragamuffin capital, where scrubby trees covered the National Mall, coal-fired locomotives belched black smoke near the marble walls of Capitol Hill, and impoverished slums like Murder Bay and Swamppoodle stood near government buildings. The senator appointed Frederick Law Olmsted Jr, and Daniel H Burnham – son of the famed landscape architect and director of the 1893 Chicago Columbian Exposition, respectively – to formulate the so-called McMillan Plan for reshaping downtown Washington.

Implemented in 1902, the plan moved the railroads off the National Mall (replacing them with Burnham's majestic Union Station on Capitol Hill), straightened and tidied the Mall into the expansive green-sward of today, and spurred the construction of new, magnificent public buildings, many in the Beaux-Arts style popularized by the Columbian Exposition. Finally, the US could boast a capital that was a match for its political ambitions.

Of course, the daily life of many Washingtonians continued to be less than splendid. In 1904, social reformer Jacob Riis, famed for his work in the tenements of New York, came to Washington to document the squalid alleyways where about 20,000 poor black city residents still lived. His photographs of and reportage on alley dwellers' desperate circumstances demonstrated that the capital still had much work to do.

The World Wars

The two great wars of the early 20th century helped to turn Washington from a relatively sleepy town, profoundly Southern in mood, into an international capital. Wartime bureaucracy, with its unquenchable thirst for clerks, soldiers, nurses, and all manner of military support staff, drew 100,000 new residents to Washington during WWI; by the war's end, the population stood at just under a half-million. Meanwhile, the US's pivotal role in the war brought new world attention to the city and drew new visitors from abroad.

But that was nothing compared to WWII. Franklin Roosevelt's New Deal programs had, in the 1930s, expanded federal agencies throughout the city, but the agencies were nonetheless thrown into a panic by the overwhelming need for new hands that WWII created. 'Tempos' (temporary office buildings) were thrown onto the Mall. Workmen hastily constructed the enormous Pentagon across the river in Virginia. The US Army's DC civilian employee roll grew from 7000 to 41,000 in just the first year of the war. National Airport opened for passenger flights in the early '40s to accommodate the city's growing population and to enable military brass to easily access the Pentagon, just north of the airport. By the end of 1941, city population had soared to over a million. 'If the war lasts much longer, Washington is going to bust right out of its pants,' wrote a *Life* magazine reporter.

Of course, some workers pulled up stakes and returned home after V-E and V-J Days. But many newcomers stayed on in Washington, working for the permanently expanded federal bureaucracy that had now become the region's economic dynamo.

The Civil-Rights Struggle

In the early 20th century, Washington had begun to adopt the racial-segregation policies of the rest of the US South. Its restaurants, theaters, hotels, hospitals, schools, and other public spaces became, in practice if not in law, 'whites only.' The WWI-era administration of President Woodrow Wilson stoked the fires of Jim Crow by refusing to hire black government workers and insisting on segregated government offices. Poet Langston Hughes visited DC in 1924, by which time, he observed, 'I could not get a cup of coffee anywhere within sight of the Capitol on a cold day, because no "white" restaurant would serve a Negro.' The next year, the federal government permitted a Ku Klux Klan march on the National Mall.

Nonetheless, Washington was a black cultural capital in the early 20th century. Shaw and LeDroit Park, near Howard University, sheltered a lively black-owned business district, and black theater and music flourished along U St NW. And despite DC's active Jim Crow mood, Southern blacks continued to move to the city in search of better economic opportunities. Between 1920 and 1930, Washington's black population jumped 20%.

Citywide segregation eased somewhat with the advent of Franklin D Roosevelt's New Deal (which brought new black federal workers to the capital) and WWII (which brought lots more). In 1939, the DC-based Daughters of the American Revolution barred the black contralto Marian Anderson from singing at their segregated Constitution Hall. With Eleanor Roosevelt's assistance, Anderson instead sang at the Lincoln Memorial before a huge audience – and that iconic moment highlighted a new era of black-led demonstrations, sit-ins, boycotts,

Martin Luther King Jr led the
March on Washington in 1963.

and lawsuits that finally desegregated Washington's public spaces. Parks and recreational facilities were legally desegregated in 1954; schools followed soon thereafter.

With President John Kennedy's appointment of DC's first black federal commissioner, in 1961, and the election, in the subsequent decade, of Washington's first black mayors (Walter Washington and Marion Barry), Washington became one of the country's most powerful African American–governed cities.

Washington also played host to key events in the national civil-rights struggle. In 1963, Martin Luther King Jr led the March on Washington to lobby for passage of the Civil Rights Act, and his 'I Have a Dream' speech, delivered before 200,000 people on the steps of the Lincoln Memorial, became the movement's most stirring moment. In 1968, after King's murder, his successor at the helm of the Southern Christian Leadership Council, Dr Ralph Abernathy, spearheaded an encampment known as 'Resurrection City' on the National Mall. Here 2400 people camped for a month and a half in plywood shanties to dramatize the plight of the nation's poor.

The Home Rule Struggle

Alongside the political gains of Washington's black community, the city itself began to win some victories in the latter half of the 20th century. The capital had been under complete federal rule since the era of Boss Shepherd in the 1870s, when Congress threw out the city's locally elected officials and replaced them with federally appointed commissioners.

Ninety years later, in 1961, Washingtonians won a basic political right: they were permitted to vote in presidential elections. On the heels of this victory came another: in 1967, President Lyndon Johnson agreed to replace the federally appointed commission with a presidentially appointed mayor and city council.

In 1973, President Richard M Nixon decided to permit Washingtonians to vote on a 'home rule' charter. The charter would enable them to elect their own mayors and council and run their own city agencies, but Nixon and Congress would firmly retain the right of the federal government to approve parts of Washington's budget and intervene in city policy. Home rule passed in 1974, while Nixon's own administration crumbled under the Watergate scandal.

The next year, the 20th century's first DC mayoral election was held amid an atmosphere of hope and optimism for the city's fresh potential under home rule. Walter Washington (who was previously the District's presidentially appointed mayor) won the race handily and took office in 1975.

DC Today

In the 1960s, Washington – like many American cities – began to watch its population abandon downtown for the suburbs. Several factors contributed to the outflow, from fraying city infrastructure to 'white flight' after Washington's housing and public schools were desegregated.

In 1968, Washington was dealt a staggering blow: after the assassination of Martin Luther King Jr, riots (centered on 14th and U Sts NW in the Shaw district) enflamed the city for two nights. Hundreds of businesses were damaged or destroyed (many of them black-owned), and 12 people were killed. Still more jumpy white residents fled the city, and downtown Washington north of the

Mall, especially the Shaw district, fell into years of economic slump. By 1970, DC's population had fallen to around 750,000, while the suburbs boomed, reaching nearly 3 million people. The I-495 Beltway opened in 1964, and Metrorail, the sleek, federally funded city subway system, began to open its stations in 1976. Both developments made it easier still for people employed in Washington to move outside the city limits.

In 1980, when city population stood at just over 600,000, one of the saddest periods of Washington's history began. Mayor Marion Barry, a civil-rights leader and city council member in the 1960s and '70s, had won the mayorship from Walter Washington in 1978. Walter Washington's style had been fairly low-key and policy-oriented. Barry, on the other hand, was a scrappy political street fighter. He had been a member

Touring Washington's Sites of Scandal, Seduction & Skulduggery

You can hardly fling a brick in this town without hitting the site of some wrongdoing, be it a spy scandal or a politico's wrong-side-of-the-sheets snoggery. Whole books are dedicated to the topic of DC scandal, in fact, so we offer here only a brief primer on some of the city's best-known scandal sites.

Scandal Central: The Watergate Its snaggletoothed balconies towering like Olympus over the Potomac banks and the sites of other, lesser scandals, this chi-chi apartment/hotel complex has lent its name to generations of political crime. Here CREEP (Committee to Re-Elect the President) operatives were found hiding under a desk after trying to bug Democratic National Committee headquarters in the scandal that toppled Nixon, and here Monica Lewinsky pined for her presidential stud in the scandal that nearly toppled Clinton. Look at the building's exterior, but don't toddle in and ask staff to show you the rooms in question (unless you like frosty glares).

What's Your Position, Congressman?: The Capitol Steps John Jenrette was a little-known South Carolina representative until he embroiled himself in the ABSCAM bribery scandal of the early 1980s. His troubles were compounded, however, when his ex-wife, *Playboy* model Rita Jenrette, revealed that she and her erstwhile husband used to slip out during dull late-night congressional sessions for an alfresco quickie on the Capitol's hallowed marble steps. The revelations sure didn't help Jenrette's political fortunes, but it did give the fabulous Capitol Steps political-satire troupe a name.

Stool Pigeon Sushi: Pentagon City Food Court It was by the humble sushi bar on this mall's 1st floor that Monica Lewinsky awaited Linda Tripp, her lunch date (and betrayer) who led Ken Starr's agents down the mall escalators to snag her up for questioning in the nearby Ritz-Carlton Hotel.

Swimming for It: The Tidal Basin In October 1974, Rep Wilbur Mills (D-AR) was stopped by US Park Police here for speeding, whereupon his companion – the stripper Fanne Foxe, the 'Argentine Firecracker' – leapt into the Basin to escape. Mills, the 65-year-old chairman of the House Ways and of the Student Non-Violent Coordinating Committee, the civil-rights group that led protests throughout the South in the 1960s and registered thousands of African Americans to vote. As a DC councilman, Barry was nearly killed by black Muslim terrorists who attacked the District Building in 1977. Washington had high hopes for its glamorous and ambitious new mayor, who drew political support from black Anacostia as well as from the white power-broker elite of northwest DC.

But in the early 1980s, after his initially successful first term, rumors of corruption, mismanagement, womanizing, and drug abuse began to swirl around Barry and his advisors. Meanwhile, his city descended into the gang-war violence of the crack-cocaine years, earning it the 'Murder Capital' epithet that it never since has been able to shed.

Touring Washington's Sites of Scandal, Seduction & Skulduggery

Means Committee, and Foxe, 38, were both several sheets to the wind, and, unfortunately for Mills' political career, a TV cameraman was there to film the fun.

Swimming for It, Part Two: The White House Pool JFK often used the White House indoor pool for relaxing nude swims with 'Fiddle' and 'Faddle,' two obliging young female aides, according to Seymour Hersh's *The Dark Side of Camelot*, generally while Jackie was out of town. The priapic JFK reportedly fiddled at many other DC sites, too, including the Mayflower Hotel and his pre-presidential Georgetown home.

Smoking Gun: The Vista Hotel, 1400 M St NW – It was in room No 727 that former DC Mayor Marion Barry uttered his timeless sobriquet, 'Bitch set me up!' when the FBI caught him taking a friendly puff of crack in the company of ex-model (and police informant) Rasheeda Moore. The FBI video of his toke – and his chivalrous words for Moore – was broadcast, horrifying a city lacerated by crack violence. Barry was convicted of cocaine possession, served time in jail (where he was accused of receiving public fellatio from a female visitor), and, clothed in repentance, romped to re-election in 1994. (The Vista has since changed its name to the Wyndham Washington Hotel.)

The Third Man House, 4100 Nebraska Ave NW – This house was the DC base of Harold (Kim) Philby, famed Soviet double agent, assigned to the British Embassy in the early '50s. Here, in 1951, Philby ordered fellow spy Guy Burgess to travel to London and tell Donald McLean, another accomplice, that British and American intelligence were circling the trio. Philby, dubbed the 'Third Man' of the spy scandal, eventually fled to the USSR.

Love & Bullets: The Treasury Annex, Pennsylvania Ave and 15th St NW – The annex stands on the site of an infamous 1859 murder that proves the 20th century didn't invent the political-sexual scandal. Here Philip Barton Key, son of composer Francis Scott Key, was gunned down by Rep Daniel Sickles after Sickles' wife admitted her love affair with Key. Sickles avoided prison by pleading temporary insanity. Later, he got his leg shot off at Gettysburg. He packed the limb into a little coffin and sent it to the National Museum of Health & Medicine in DC, where it's still on view today.

My Dinner with Vitaly: Au Pied de Cochon, 1335 Wisconsin Ave NW – This Georgetown bistro was the scene of a major CIA flub-up in 1985. After dining on lobster with his CIA escort, Soviet defector Vitaly Yurchenko slipped off to the bathroom and through the restaurant's back door. Yurchenko, who had defected in Rome and supplied much inside intelligence to the CIA, later turned up at a Russian Embassy press conference, claiming he'd been kidnapped by the Americans, drugged, and forced to defect. The bistro, not one to miss a marketing opportunity, promptly created the 'Yurchenko shooter' (vodka and Grand Marnier) to celebrate the event.

Nonetheless, DC elected Barry to second and third terms.

In January 1990, Barry's political career seemed to come to a halt. The FBI set up a sting operation for him at DC's Vista Hotel, luring him there with a young woman named Rasheeda Moore, who was Barry's former lover. There, Barry was videotaped puffing on a crack pipe. Barry was sentenced to six months in prison – but the old street fighter didn't hit the mat so easily. He served his time and, in 1994, just two years out of prison, he ran for mayor again. Astoundingly, he trounced his opposition.

Four months later, Congress did what the FBI couldn't: ended Barry's career. Congress stripped Barry of financial control of the city, citing his 'scandalously corrupt and hopelessly incompetent' administration and effectively ending home rule for a time. In 1997, Congress took control of the city's failing agencies. Soon afterward, Barry declared that he would not seek a fifth term.

In 1999, DC's chief financial officer, Anthony A Williams, became the city's fourth elected mayor. A quiet technocrat who had never previously run for public office, Williams is in many ways Barry's political opposite, and Congress has recognized that fact by handing most city controls back to Williams shortly after his inauguration. Although Williams' low-key persona has already been banged around and bruised a bit by Washington's take-no-prisoners political battles, the mayor has fared extraordinarily well to date. City population outflow has stabilized; unemployment levels are low; infant mortality and homicide rates have dropped significantly; city budgets have been in surplus; and downtown DC is at last starting to flourish. Some of Williams' successes are due, at least in part, to nationwide boom times, but his first few years bode well for the future of a city too long scarred by political misfortune.

GEOGRAPHY

The topography of the 61-sq-mile District is both subtle and complex, although the visitor who sees only the downtown monuments around the Mall can be excused for perceiving the US capital as simply a low, level city at the juncture of two rivers. The truth is, however, that DC stands at a pivotal place: upon the fall line, the exact point where the Coastal Plain and higher, rockier Piedmont Plateau intersect.

Most of downtown and southeast DC lie on the delta formed by the joining of the Potomac River and its smaller tributary, the Anacostia River. A boater sailing from this juncture up the Potomac can see the fall line rising along the Arlington, Virginia, shore northwest of National Airport. This line of hills reaches the Potomac opposite Washington, and north of this point the river is full of boulders and swift currents.

The federal city was sited here precisely because of this geographic anomaly: Washington represents the last navigable point on the Potomac before Great Falls, where the river tangles itself in a series of cliffs and crags. George Washington and other city fathers thought that seagoing ships could serve the city and facilitate shipment of the Capital region's essential crop, tobacco. The C&O Canal, which begins on the Potomac's east bank in DC, was later built to bypass the rocky upper Potomac, thus facilitating water travel and commercial shipping from DC through the Allegheny Mountains to the western frontier.

On the east side of the Potomac, the fall line defines the high ground of Georgetown University's campus and the surrounding district of Georgetown. Farther east, the fall line runs through Adams-Morgan, roughly tracing the course of Kalorama Rd NW, and runs east just north of U St toward Shaw. Meridian Hill Park, just north of Florida Ave NW, is a great place to observe the fall line – the waterfall cascade here was designed to echo its course.

The southern, monumental part of Washington, around the Mall, consists mostly of coastal lowlands smoothed out by the last ice age and the seasonal flooding of the Potomac and Anacostia Rivers. To control this flooding, which in the 19th century occasionally sent foul waters sweeping up to the White House door, fill lands, such as West Potomac Park, were created on the Potomac's east bank, and the Washington Channel was dredged. It's likely that Capitol Hill, the gently sloping focal point on these lowlands, was once the actual meeting point of the Potomac and Anacostia before the rivers eroded new courses farther west and south.

CLIMATE

DC's summertime is famously awful (featuring days-long stretches over 90° F and lead-blanket humidity) and its winter little more beloved (freezing rain and the persistent inability of city services to cope with snow). But DC wins your heart with its long, gorgeous springs and falls, the best seasons to visit. Temperatures are mild; in spring, wildflowers and blossoming trees burst into color, and in fall, warm weather lasts well into October and foliage assumes beautiful hues. (Be prepared for rain and changeable weather in all seasons, however.)

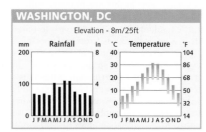

Summertime travelers should wear light clothing and a hat, carry water if they'll be outside for a while, and save visits to outdoor attractions – like the zoo – for cooler, cloudy days. In winter, the heaviest snowfalls (which really aren't very heavy; usually a few inches, max) come in late January and February. DC is notorious for its overreaction to snow: even an inch or two may prompt the government to send its workers home early and some attractions to close, so call ahead if you're touring on a snowy day. It doesn't get very cold here, however. Winter days are usually in the 20s or 30s°F.

ECOLOGY & ENVIRONMENT

Washington has little heavy industry, so it has few of industry's associated problems. Its main environmental troubles are exploding suburban sprawl and attendant automobile pollution. DC's suburbs are among the nation's fastest-growing, and the city's street and highway system cannot adequately handle the increased number of cars. As a result, visitors might encounter the occasional 'smog-alert' day in summer.

Chemical contamination, sewage, sedimentation, and garbage have long plagued DC's second major river, the Anacostia. In recent years, cleanup projects solved some problems, but much work remains to be done. In 2000, Mayor Anthony Williams announced a major riverfront redevelopment and cleanup effort that will, hopefully, spur revitalization of the Anacostia as a recreational resource. The Potomac has suffered similar, albeit less severe, problems, and protection efforts are occasionally hampered by the river's odd jurisdiction: it's officially owned by Maryland but traces Virginia's eastern border. The two states occasionally squabble over water rights and cleanup responsibilities.

FLORA & FAUNA

Washington has a lot of wild critters for a dense urban area, due to the abundant parkland within city limits. Hundreds of acres of protected, well-maintained gardens,

Great blue herons can be seen at Kenilworth Aquatic Gardens.

National Cherry Blossom Festival

A fluttering gauze scarf of the palest pink encircles the Tidal Basin, at the west end of the National Mall, each spring in late March or early April, as 1300 Japanese cherry trees explode into bloom. In 1912, the Japanese government presented the forerunners of these trees to President Taft as a goodwill gift. They are mostly of the Yoshino variety, whose blooms are nearly pure-white, but a handful of pink-blooming Akebono trees add a shimmer of dawn-like rose to the scene.

Washingtonians immediately adopted the trees as a symbol of their city. When the Tidal Basin was chosen as the site of the Jefferson Memorial, protestors even chained themselves to trees to prevent their removal. During WWII, the trees were occasionally vandalized, but they thrived anyway. In 1965, the Japanese government provided the US with 3800 more trees, which were planted along the Mall and near the Washington Monument. Later-blooming Kwanzan cherry trees were planted in East Potomac Park.

The city's biggest annual festival, the National Cherry Blossom Festival (www.gwjapan.com/cherryblossom), is held in late March or early April, timed to coincide with the trees' blossoming. However, because the blossoming time is somewhat unpredictable, and because Washington's quirky spring weather sometimes pelts the blossoms off the trees with icy rain and wind, the festival doesn't always get its flowers. Nonetheless, the parades, speeches, parties, and cultural events draw thousands of tourists and mark the official start of warm weather for Washington.

parks, riverfront, and wetlands permit animals and plants to make comfortable homes for themselves, and permit visitors to glimpse them, too.

Washington is a good place for bird-watching. Hundreds of bald eagles and ospreys nest along the Potomac south of Washington and the Patuxent River, to the east. Kenilworth Gardens, in northeast Washington DC, is thick with wading great blue herons, red-winged blackbirds, and bitterns. Ducks and geese bob in the shallows of the Potomac and the ornamental pools of the Mall. Cardinals, pileated woodpeckers, and woodthrushes flit around Rock Creek Park.

Among the best places in town to learn about local birds is the basement of the Smithsonian's National Museum of Natural History. Its little-visited 'Birds of DC' galleries display stuffed examples of Capital-region waterfowl, woodpeckers, raptors, and songbirds. Also check out the Audubon Naturalist Society (☎ 301-652-9188), 8940 Jones Mill Rd, Chevy Chase, Maryland; its 40 acres of grounds are home to all kinds of native birds, plus a bookstore with good local fauna guides.

Small woodland and aquatic animals are regularly seen in the city, too, especially in Rock Creek Park. These include raccoons, turtles, salamanders, beavers, white-tailed deer, weasels, muskrats, foxes, and opossums.

The mixed woodlands of DC parks are especially fetching in springtime, when fruit trees – especially cherries and crabapples – forsythia, and wildflowers (violets, bluebells, wild orchids, chicory, and trilliums) burst into a pale-pastel rainbow of blooms. Also native to the city, sometimes in near-virgin stands, are tulip poplars, red and white oaks, sycamore, elm, willow, dogwood, beech, hickory, and pine.

The most spectacular flora and fauna in DC aren't, of course, native to the city. In Kenilworth Aquatic Gardens, the National Botanic Gardens, and Dumbarton Oaks Garden, rare roses, water lilies, bonsai, tropical orchids, and bamboo flourish, enabling visitors to take a botanical world tour without ever leaving town. The National Zoo holds a similarly international cornucopia, from ball pythons to marmosets. Washington's most iconic plant – the cherry tree – and animal – the National Zoo pandas – are from Japan and China, respectively.

GOVERNMENT & POLITICS

Politically speaking, Washington is the oddest place in America. It's not a territory, reservation, or state, nor is it a part of any other state, yet its fortunes are intertwined with two states (Maryland and Virginia). It's the seat of federal government, but it does not fully govern itself or control its own destiny. It's a federal protectorate, and its budget is overseen by Congress. Although its residents pay federal income taxes, DC has only a nonvoting delegate to Congress.

City officials and District residents have made many pleas for statehood, but it seems a long way off, due in part to congressional intractability and in part to DC government's political and fiscal track record, which is mostly abysmal. Back in the 1870s, Mayor 'Boss' Shepherd so liberally disposed of federal funds that Congress revoked home rule for a century. After home rule was restored, in 1974, Mayor Marion Barry's several terms were rocked with scandals ranging from financial mismanagement to mayoral drug abuse to cronyism and kickbacks. Meanwhile, city services slid steadily downhill.

The FBI caught Barry smoking crack cocaine in 1990 and packed him off to jail. But he made his return to city politics and

A Little Colony on the Potomac: DC & Home Rule

Although the US was founded upon a principle barring 'taxation without representation,' there is still one American city that is both taxed by the federal government and denied voting representation in Congress. In fact, District residents gained the most basic political right of all – the right to vote in presidential elections – only in 1964. It gained limited home rule in 1974.

DC is an anomalous political entity that functions more like a colony or territory than a state, despite its population of a half-million people. A congressional committee oversees the District's budget and, according to its political whim, grants or restricts DC's ability to govern itself. The District has one nonvoting congressional delegate; at the time of writing, it is Eleanor Holmes Norton. Although there have been many efforts to gain Norton a vote, the Republican-controlled Congress has consistently stifled them. Norton is a Democrat, Washington is an overwhelmingly Democratic town, and the Republicans have no interest in admitting new Democrats to Congress.

Charges of paternalism and racism reverberate among DC residents whenever Congress interferes in local issues – in recent years, conservatives in Congress have tried to prevent the city from funding programs ranging from needle exchange to abortion services to domestic-partner benefits. Still more tension was created in 1997, when Sen Lauch Faircloth (R-NC) stripped day-to-day control of city government from troubled Mayor Marion Barry and handed it to a financial control board. Gradually, after Barry's successor, the less-controversial Anthony Williams, took office, Congress passed the power back.

But DC residents still lack a congressional vote. In March 2000, a federal court panel ruled that Washingtonians have no legal right to a vote in Congress, dealing a severe setback to community leaders and home-rule activists. (DC government cannot itself lobby for voting rights, because Congress forbids it to do so in riders on the city budget.) The court acknowledged the unfairness of the situation but claimed that no judicial precedent allowed voting rights for Washington. Mayor Anthony Williams summed up the city's disappointment: 'Over the last 200 years, residents of the District of Columbia have fought in nine wars and paid billions of dollars in federal taxes. Yet in our nation's capital – the epicenter of democracy – we lack the most fundamental right of all: the right to vote.'

Activists continue the struggle to gain DC voting rights. Check out DC Watch (www.dcwatch .com), an online magazine, for up-to-date information on the fight.

reclaimed the mayor's chair in 1994. In the wake of Barry's re-election, Congress systematically stripped away home rule and Barry's power until he was little more than a pathetic figurehead. Given Congress' hatred of Barry, it became clear that home rule would never be restored until he was out of office.

During the twilight of the Barry years, a new face entered city government as chief financial officer: Anthony Williams. During his three years in this post, he won general admiration for his intelligence, integrity, and his stabilization of the city's precarious financial situation. In the fall of 1998, Williams was elected mayor and brought a squeaky-clean, can-do image to city government. Tentatively hopeful, city residents are now looking forward to a more stable and prosperous – and, hopefully, more empowered – city government.

ECONOMY

The carriage of the DC economy is pulled by two horses: the government and service industries. In recent years, Washington's gross regional product has hovered near $50 billion. Revenues from federal, state, and local governments represent about 36% of that figure. Service businesses (tourism, legal services, education, management, and engineering) represent about 42% of the economy; this sector continues to grow, while the government sector has begun to shrink somewhat in recent years.

The Washington area – especially the northern Virginia suburbs – became a high-tech magnet in the 1990s, and tech industries are drawing even with the government in terms of economic importance to local workers. America Online, MicroStrategy, and a host of other booming tech firms now dominate the landscape around Dulles International Airport.

Washington's decreased dependence on government income and its increasingly diversified economic base probably will help the city in the long run. In the early 1990s, the nationwide economic recession hit the city very hard, vulnerable as it was to the vicissitudes of government monies. Rosy economic times at present have spurred a renaissance in Washington, evidenced in particular by the flourishing downtown business district, where a flock of crane booms eternally hovers overhead, and new restaurants and bars seem to open daily.

As of 2000, DC's unemployment rates were slightly below the national average, and it had begun to show annual budget surpluses – magnificent news for a city long plagued by joblessness and deficit. Taxation remains a chronic budget issue for the city, however. Two-thirds of income earned in

Weaving the World Wide Web

Sunny California and rainy Seattle always seem to get the credit for any advances in computer and Internet technology. But in truth, the idea of creating a network to link remote computers – the precursor to the modern World Wide Web – was born in Arlington, Virginia.

In the late 1960s, the US Advanced Research Projects Agency (ARPA), a think tank with heaps of government bucks, developed the idea of linking together scientists in remote locations. There was a touch of Cold War paranoia in the idea – if a network had multiple nodes, they couldn't all be knocked out simultaneously in a nuclear attack.

The brainpower of several universities around the country was eventually utilized to develop the protocols TCP/IP (transmission control protocol/internetworking protocol), the means by which computers talk to one another. But the original impetus came from ARPA, in Arlington.

Fittingly, the debut of ARPAnet happened in DC, in October 1972. Today, it's not surprising that America Online is headquartered in Reston, Virginia, near the birthplace of the network that made its fortunes possible.

DC isn't taxed by DC, because it is earned by suburbanites. Meanwhile, 41% of DC land can't be taxed by the city because it's owned by the federal government or foreign embassies. These factors force Washington to operate on a very narrow tax base.

POPULATION & PEOPLE

Washington itself is a relatively small city, with a population of about 525,000. But the metropolitan area as a whole, including the Virginia and Maryland suburbs, is home to 4.6 million people. More than most American cities, Washington is surrounded by sprawling 'edge cities,' such as Rockville, Tysons Corner, and the boomtowns of Loudoun County, where people both live and work. The old hub-and-spoke pattern of a city, with most people commuting to work downtown, doesn't really apply here. Many Washington-area residents commute among suburbs, not to the city. Three-quarters of area jobs are now in the suburbs. Even some of the bigger federal agencies have gone suburban – as they grew, they simply ran out of DC real estate.

Beginning in the 1960s, when there were about 764,000 Washingtonians, city population began to flow outward into the suburbs. The first immigrants were middle-class whites, but they were soon joined by middle-class blacks, both seeking to escape the increasing crime rates and failing schools and infrastructure of the capital. In the suburbs, the middle class also gained new political power: because Washingtonians have no voting congressional representation, they have no real control of how their tax monies are used. Quite recently, however, the outflow has slowed, as good economic times have enabled Washington to improve its downtown core, and new entertainment and dining venues have opened within city limits.

Washington itself is now among the most African American cities in the country. It's also among the most segregated. About 61% of the District is black. Only about 25% – mostly northwest DC – is white. The city's economic boundaries are as sharp as its racial ones. Two-thirds of its people earn under $32,000 annually, and most of these

are black. This racial and economic divide has defined city politics and social relations for decades – sadly, white and black Washingtonians rarely mix socially or professionally, and it's not uncommon to meet a black resident who has never visited Georgetown, or a white who has never seen Anacostia. These tensions are exacerbated by DC's odd political situation. Congress (mostly white and conservative) controls the budget of DC (mostly black and liberal), although most Congress members don't even live in the city. Congress also butts into city-level political debates over issues like needle-exchange programs.

Gentrification also increases racial tensions. In downtown, Shaw, and Adams-Morgan, among other neighborhoods, affluent, primarily white, homebuyers have moved in during recent years, pushing less affluent black renters farther east. The outflow of successful black families continues, too, particularly to Prince Georges County, Maryland.

Washington itself is a company town, the company being the federal government. About a third of its workers are employed by the government (either the federal or city bureaucracies). Ultimately, most businesses here are dependent, either directly or indirectly, upon government dollars. The dominance of the government and its related apparatus means that Washington draws many college-educated, highly skilled workers, but it also means that the city's population is transient. Many people 'do time' here, working for the course of a four-year presidential administration or perhaps spending a few years on the Hill or at a think tank, before moving to other parts of the country.

Finally, the District's population has two other distinctive qualities. DC has about 70,000 college students at 10 institutions of higher learning, making it the third-largest college town in the US (after Boston and New York). And in DC, females outnumber males by a ratio of more than five to four. Some estimates that focus on the city workforce place this ratio as high as two women for every man.

ARTS

Washington is the showcase of American art, but its arts scene is an unusual one. Because Washington is the country's political capital, and because it is home to the national museums – the Smithsonian – its most visible, best-known artworks were created by artists who weren't native to the city, or who spent only part of their lives here. The beautiful Vietnam Veterans Memorial by the Ohio-born Chinese American Maya Lin; the National Gallery's sprightly mobiles by New Yorker Alexander Calder; Frenchman Pierre L'Enfant's grand National Mall – all were crafted by non-Washingtonians. But DC does have a vibrant, albeit lesser-known, local arts scene that's well worth discovering. Good areas to look for art galleries are Gallery Place, along 7th St NW downtown, and Dupont Circle.

Architecture

The 18th- and 19th-century architecture of Washington, DC, was shaped by two major influences: first, the original city plan by Pierre L'Enfant, and, second, the desire of the infant nation to prove to European powers that its capital possessed political and artistic sophistication rivaling the ancient, majestic cities of the Continent.

L'Enfant's 1791 plan (see details in History, earlier) imposed a street grid filled with diagonal avenues, roundabouts, and grand vistas. He had in mind the magisterial boulevards of Europe, and in order to highlight the primacy of the city's political buildings, he intended that no building would rise higher than the Capitol. Although this rule rescued DC from the windy, dark, skyscraper-filled fate of most modern American cities, it also has resulted in many short, squat buildings, especially in modern times. The L'Enfant plan's trapezoidal blocks have given rise to interesting building shapes. Some, like the downtown Octagon, work quite well. Others, like the Canadian Embassy near the Mall, do not.

In an effort to rival European cities, Washington's early architects – many of them self-taught 'gentlemen architects' – depended heavily upon the classic revival and romantic revival styles, with their borrowed Roman and Grecian columns and marble facades (witness the Capitol, National Archives, and Lincoln Memorial). Domestic architecture was dominated by Federal-style row houses (which still fill the streets of Capitol Hill and Georgetown). In the later years of the 19th century, Victorian architecture lent a softening, playful hand to the cityscape, resulting in many beautiful mansions and magnificent creations such as the Smithsonian's Arts & Industries Building and the Old Pension Building (now the National Building Museum).

At the turn of the 20th century, the McMillan Plan for Washington revived many elements of the L'Enfant plan – it restored public spaces downtown, lent formal lines to the Mall and Capitol grounds, and added more classically inspired buildings (such as Daniel Burnham's Beaux-Arts Union Station). Classicism came to a screaming halt during and after WWII, when war workers flooded the city. Temporary offices were thrown onto the Mall, and new materials developed during wartime enabled the construction of huge homogenous office blocks. Slum clearance after the war, particularly in southwest DC, meant the wholesale loss of old neighborhoods in favor of modernist boxes, such as the monolithic government agencies that currently dominate the Federal Rectangle area. In other areas, such as Federal Triangle, historic buildings were preserved while modern ones were constructed nearby.

Washington architecture today is of uncertain identity. Many new major buildings,

Biking the Buildings

The DC-based American Institute of Architects offers great city-architecture biking tours through the Bike the Sites tour group (☎ 966-8662; $35). They'll provide the bike, and their guides take you around early DC historic sites, the famed Mall buildings, the waterfront, and other locales. The tour guides really know their stuff.

THE LIBRARY OF CONGRESS

The US Capitol, circa 1846

particularly those downtown, pay homage to their classical neighbors while striving toward a sleeker, postmodern monumentalism (check out the pillared facade of the huge Ronald Reagan Building near the Mall, an odd pairing with the soaring space-age atrium within). A handful of world-renowned architects have left examples of their work in the city: IM Pei's ethereal East Building of the National Gallery, Mies van der Rohe's Martin Luther King Jr Memorial Library, and Frank Gehry's new addition to the Corcoran Gallery.

To summarize, the architecture of Washington is not, and shall never be, an organic creature. Instead, it is a product of various city plans, federal mandates, clashing social agendas, and the ever-shifting national vision of what a capital – and government itself – should be. Wandering through the sometimes lovely, sometimes appalling architecture of this unique city gives visitors a chance to learn much about American political ideals and their often awkward application to reality. Exhibits at the National Building Museum offer insight into Washington's architectural choices.

Literature

Washington's literary legacy is, not surprisingly, deeply entwined with American political history. The city's best-known early literature consists of writings and books that hammered out the machinery of American democracy. From Thomas Jefferson's *Notes on the State of Virginia* to James Madison's *The Federalist Papers* and Abraham Lincoln's historic speeches and proclamations, this literature fascinates modern readers not only because it is the cornerstone of the US political system, but because of the grace and beauty of its prose. Skill with the pen is, alas, no longer a notable characteristic of US presidents.

Apart from politicians' writings, 19th-century Washington literature was created primarily by authors and journalists who resided here only temporarily, drawn to DC by circumstance, professional obligation, or wanderlust. (Washington was not, until the 20th century, a desirable residence for the artistic, what with its poor infrastructure and chaotic streets.) Walt Whitman's *The Wound Dresser* and *Specimen Days* and Louisa May Alcott's *Hospital Sketches* were based upon the authors' harrowing experiences as Civil War nurses at Washington's hospitals. The journalist Ambrose Bierce reported from DC for the Hearst papers before vanishing in Mexico in 1914. Poet Joaquin Miller, mostly known for his paeans to the California Sierra, wrote for many years in a studiedly rustic log cabin he constructed on 16th St NW. Mark Twain had an ill-starred (and short) career as a senator's speechwriter, memorialized in *Washington in 1868*.

Frederick Douglass (1818–95), the abolitionist, editor, memoirist, and former slave, is perhaps Washington's most revered writer. His *The Life & Times of Frederick Douglass* and *My Bondage & My Freedom*, seminal antislavery works, were written in DC, where Douglass lived on Capitol Hill and in Anacostia. Henry Adams (1838–1918) was another famed native Washington writer. His brilliant *Democracy* was the forerunner of many political-scandal novels of the 20th century. It and his later autobiography, *The Education of Henry Adams*, provide fascinating insights into 19th-century Washington and its high society. Adams, the grandson of President John Adams, was a millionaire whose mansion was the literary center of Lafayette Square.

Twentieth-century Washington literature remains a deeply political beast, defined by works such as Carl Bernstein and Bob Woodward's *All the President's Men* and John Kennedy's *Profiles in Courage*. Literary life in the city is populated by journalists and speechwriters, from William Safire to George Will to David Brinkley. But many more purely literary writers have appeared on the scene, too. Native Washingtonian Gore Vidal often aims his satirical pen at his hometown (pick up *Washington, DC* or *The Smithsonian Institution*). The literary novelists Richard Bausch, Alan Cheuse, and Elizabeth Benedict all live and work in or near DC today.

On a less elevated note, DC has also inspired thousands of potboilers. A representative sample is the oeuvre of Tom Clancy, northern Virginia resident and creator of innumerable right-wing thrillers that sometimes feature Washington's apocalyptic destruction (see *Debt of Honor* and *Executive Orders* for much president-and-Congress offing).

For a fine profile of the contemporary Washington literary scene, see David Cutler's *Literary Washington: A Complete Guide to the Literary Life in the Nation's Capital*.

Music

DC music has two faces. First, there are the big boys, weighty cultural landmarks like the National Symphony Orchestra and the Washington Opera (directed by Placido Domingo), which perform in the stately Kennedy Center. Then there are the ragamuffin, eclectic local scenes, which can be a lot more fun. Washington is not an American musical capital, but it has given birth to many interesting local interpretations of national musical trends.

Back in the late 19th century, military marching-band music reached its apotheosis (such as it was) in the work of John Phillip Sousa. Born and buried in southeast DC, he directed the Marine Corps Marching Band for many years. The band still performs his work today (see details in the 'Military Sights' section of Things to See & Do).

In the early 20th century, DC hosted a vibrant jazz, big-band, and swing scene, particularly in the Shaw district. Segregation of entertainment venues meant that black Washington had to create its own arts scene – so it created one far more vibrant than anything white Washington could boast. Greats such as Duke Ellington (see the boxed text), Pearl Bailey, Shirley Horne, Johnny Hodges, and Ben Webster all got their starts in the clubs of U St NW.

After WWII, DC also boasted a flourishing country-music scene, catering to emigrant Southerners and Appalachians drawn to the capital to work in wartime bureaucracy. Roy Clark, Patsy Cline, Charlie Daniels, and Jimmy Dean all played here frequently, particularly in the honky-tonks of Anacostia (which was then a working-class, primarily Southern white neighborhood). DC has spawned some folk and country stars of its own, too, from Mary Chapin Carpenter to John Fahey, who named his seminal folk record label, Takoma, for Takoma Park, his boyhood home.

In recent decades, DC music has been known for two things: go-go and punk. Go-go, an infectiously rhythmic dance music combining elements of funk, rap, soul, and Latin percussion, stomped onto the city scene in the 1970s (see a historical profile of it in the Entertainment chapter). DC's hardcore take on punk, as embodied by such

The Duke

'My road runs from Ward's Place to my grandmother's at Twentieth and R, to Seatan Street, around to Eighth Street, back up to T Street, through LeDroit Park to Sherman Avenue,' wrote DC's most famous musical son, jazz immortal Edward Kennedy 'Duke' Ellington (1899–1974), describing his childhood in Washington's Shaw district. In the segregated DC of the early 20th century, Shaw hosted one of the country's finest black arts scenes, drawing famed actors, musicians, and singers to perform at venues like the Howard Theatre and Bohemian Caverns, so the Duke took root in rich soil.

As a tot, Ellington purportedly first tackled the keyboard under the tutelage of a teacher by the name of Mrs Clinkscales, but he honed his chops by listening to local ragtime pianists like Doc Perry, Louis Thomas, and Louis Brown at Frank Holliday's T St poolroom. His first composition, written at 16, was the 'Soda Fountain Rag'; next came 'What You Gonna Do When the Bed Breaks Down?' The handsome, suave young Duke played hops and cabarets all over black Washington before decamping for New York in 1923.

There, Ellington started out as a Harlem stride pianist, performing at Barron's and the Hollywood Club, but he soon moved to the famed Cotton Club, where he matured into an innovative bandleader, composer, and arranger. He collaborated with innumerable artists – including Louis Armstrong and Ella Fitzgerald – but his most celebrated collaboration was with composer/arranger Billy Strayhorn, who gave the Ellington Orchestra their theme, 'Take the "A" Train,' in 1941. Strayhorn worked with Duke throughout his life, collaborating on later works like *Such Sweet Thunder* (1957) and *The Far East Suite* (1964).

Ellington's big-band compositions, with their infectious melodies, harmonic sophistication, and ever-present swing, made him one of the 20th century's most revered American composers, and his ability to craft arrangements highlighting the singular talents of his musicians made him the foremost bandleader of his time. His huge volume of work – more than 1500 pieces – is preserved in its entirety at the Smithsonian in his old hometown.

For more on the Duke, check out *Music Is My Mistress*, his witty memoir, which details his DC childhood and later accomplishments.

Minor Threat in the Nation's Capital

Washington, DC, has always been a birthplace for great music and musicians. Local heroes such as Duke Ellington, Pearl Bailey and Marvin Gaye became landmarks in music history for shaping jazz and soul. Few people, however, think of the US capital as a vital scene for the punk movement. Yet it is the birthplace of some of the most influential punk bands to date and is still the home of a thriving alternative music scene.

It all began with a group of young people in Washington, DC, in the late '70s and early '80s, who were frustrated with a government that seemed to be more about politics than about people and politicians who seemed to be only concerned with the wants of the rich and influential, ignoring the needs of the poor. Coming from various social classes and races, this group of young men and women banded together for change, and their choice medium for expressing themselves was nothing other than the hard-driving sound of punk rock.

In a matter of a few years, an entire underground music scene was born, which began to make an impression in Washington and the rest of the country. Bands such as Void, Marginal Man, Faith and Scream were loud megaphones to a deaf and intolerant world that surrounded them. With their unconventional, loud sound, these bands and the people whom they brought together became a voice for the country's youth.

One of the earliest icons of this new counterculture was (and still is) Ian MacKaye. From the very beginning MacKaye articulated a need for political and social change and challenged conventional society through his music. His first platform was a loud, aggressive band, ironically called Minor Threat, which to this day is one of the most influential punk bands of all time. After a three-year musical career, Minor Threat disbanded, and Ian went on to form the band he currently fronts, Fugazi. Ten years and well over a million records later, Fugazi still inspires listeners to face the challenging issues of our times, such as racism, sexism, and all the other -isms that plague the US.

But the keystone of Fugazi's effort rests in its love for Washington and its work in the local community. They're always playing free concerts and benefits to help local charities and outreach programs. For Ian Mackaye, it's all about community. In his own words: 'When I think back to those shows, to those times, I should say, I don't think about the bands. I think about the hang, about the community, and everyone was a part of that. The music was just a currency, just something people revolved around. The actual expression of all the bands was just part and parcel of the expression of everybody in one form or another.'

– Justin Marler

bands as Fugazi and Dag Nasty, combined super-fast guitar with a socially conscious mindset and flourished at venues like the now-defunct dc space. Arlington-based Dischord Records, one of the country's most successful small labels, grew out of the punk scene and remains a fierce promoter of local bands. Check out *Banned in DC*, a photo book by Cynthia Connolly that documents the Washington punk scene of the 1970s and '80s. In the past few years, the Washington-Baltimore area has become known as the

American rave-dance capital: one highlight is the traveling party, Buzz, where rave-dance troupes like Quixotica perform.

Cinema

Hollywood has a passionate love-hate relationship with Washington, portraying it alternately as a citadel of sternly chivalrous god-kings (think Henry Fonda in *Fail-Safe)* and a pit of unbelievable corruption and stupidity (think Peter Sellers in *Being There* and *Dr Strangelove*, and most of Oliver Stone's oeuvre). Directors just can't resist all the black limousines, white marble, counterintelligence subterfuges, and Oval Office sex that official Washington has to offer. Yet unofficial Washington – you know, the place where real people live – can go whistle as far as Hollywood is concerned. Few big-studio movies about DC are set anywhere other than Capitol Hill or the Mall.

Locally, there are a variety of good annual film festivals – occasionally featuring independent movies by Washingtonians – that visitors can check out. Try FilmFest DC/International Film Festival (☎ 628-3456; late April), Reel Affirmations/International Gay & Lesbian Film Festival (☎ 986-1119; October), and the Washington Jewish Film Festival (☎ 777-3248; late November/early December). And don't miss the films hosted by the Smithsonian during Black History Month (February) and Women's History Month (March); call ☎ 633-9884 for information on both.

SOCIETY & CONDUCT

Washington is sometimes described as a chilly, uptight town, full of type-A Maalox-chugging greyhounds too enmeshed in their political careers to befriend visitors. And if you spend all your time in 'official Washington' (Capitol Hill, Foggy Bottom), you'll probably agree with that assessment. But, happily, official Washington is a tiny part of the town. You'll have no problem meeting interesting, warm folks in most city neighborhoods, where all kinds of subcultures flourish that have nothing to do with government. And even those K St lawyers, once

you've poured them a martini or two, are pretty interesting – DC attracts a tremendous number of well-educated, highly articulate people, which makes conversation a lot of fun.

Although many Washingtonians make their livings from politics, visitors are often surprised by locals' dispassionate attitude toward political issues. Politics are really more of a sport than a heartfelt passion here, and political expediency often trumps political conviction. You'll witness few screaming inter-party arguments – even on the Senate floor – and you'll observe many bipartisan relationships and friendships. If you want to blend in, try gossiping about politicians rather than debating the issues.

Another good way to blend in is to dress down – or at least don't call attention to your clothes. Washington's lack of sartorial sense is famous. Professionals tend to favor dull gray or blue suits, adorned with those laminated government-ID neck tags that PJ O'Rourke wrote 'make Washington look like the City of Lost Dogs.' Slip on your loafers, cinch up your necktie, and you'll feel right at home.

RELIGION

DC is a profoundly secular town – the business of government doesn't exactly lend itself to spiritual contemplation. Nonetheless, it's also a profoundly international city, so most of the world's faiths are represented among its citizens. There are all brands of Christians (Protestant churches have long been a central social anchor in DC's black neighborhoods), a sizable, influential Jewish population, Muslims, Hindus, Mormons, Buddhists, and Baha'is.

Many faiths have their American headquarters in the city. A visitor can spend a couple of days touring Washington's plethora of beautiful churches, temples, and mosques, which include the Episcopals' National Cathedral, in Cleveland Park; the Islamic Center, the national mosque near Dupont Circle; the Catholic National Shrine of the Immaculate Conception, in upper northeast DC; Adas Israel Synagogue, downtown; and St John's Church (the

FACTS ABOUT DC

'church of the presidents'), across from the White House.

LANGUAGE

Washington's English is as varied as the city itself. You'll hear plenty of New York, Midwestern, and California accents and slang among the residents of this most transient US city, as well as the urban dialect of its African American neighborhoods. Occasionally, the soft Tidewater drawl (notable for its dropped 'r') that once predominated in the area is still heard, reminding visitors that Washington was once a true Southern town.

Diplomatic and immigrant communities add pockets of multilingualism to the city – you'll hear more Spanish than English in Mount Pleasant and lots of Amharic in Adams-Morgan's African restaurants; Vietnamese is the lingua franca in suburban Virginia's 'Little Saigon.'

Washington bureaucrats, who spend their days crafting acronyms, abbreviations, and neologisms, make their own peculiar contributions to the language. Only in this city can you hear gloriously baroque constructions like, 'If HR 3401 passes, everyone under GS-10 at HUD and HHS will be SOL' and po-mo phraseologies like 'non-means-tested entitlement,' 'soft money,' and 'what the meaning of *is* is.'

Washingtonspeak: A Glossary

Beltway bandits – Consultants who clean up on high-priced government contracts.

Camp Intern – The city in summer, when young students flood in for short stints on the Hill and at federal agencies and think tanks.

cave dweller – Old-money Washingtonians, many of whom can trace their ancestry in the city back to pre-Civil War days.

DC, the District – What locals call the place (never 'Washington, DC' – who has the time?).

doing a Barry – Embarrassing oneself profoundly in public (after former crack-puffing mayor Marion Barry).

Eye St – I St (to avoid confusion with 1st St).

GS – Government service level; a professional caste system. The higher the number (eg, GS-1 vs GS-15), the higher the salary and prestige.

Hill rat – Lifer congressional staffers; named for the book *Hill Rat*, by John Jackley.

Langley – Often synonymous with 'CIA'; Langley, Virginia, is that agency's home.

POTUS – Secret Service shorthand for President of the United States.

'Skins! – Redskins (DC's football team). Generally bellowed.

Facts for the Visitor

WHEN TO GO

There are no true 'high' and 'low' visitor seasons in DC. Travelers, both tourists and businesspeople, arrive year-round. However, spring and fall are the most temperate and scenic seasons in DC and thus draw the most visitors. The busiest tourist period runs from late March (when cherry blossoms attract crowds) to July (when the serious heat arrives). If you visit during these months, make lodging reservations well in advance, and expect to pay more for rooms. Make advance reservations at popular attractions whenever possible to avoid long lines.

DC business travel slumps during the late summer, when Congress is in recess, and vacationers who can tolerate the heat can find good lodging bargains. Bargains are also available in January and February, when some museums and attractions may partially close for exhibit installation or renovations.

ORIENTATION

At its founding, the federal city claimed a tidy diamond-shaped territory of 100 sq miles. The diamond spanned the Potomac and Anacostia Rivers and included land ceded by the states of Maryland and Virginia. Later, the diamond's southwestern edges returned to Virginia's possession, and the Potomac now bounds the city's western edge. The communities of Arlington and Alexandria dominate the river's western banks. To the north and east are Maryland's Montgomery and Prince Georges Counties, including major suburbs such as Bethesda, Silver Spring, and Rockville. The District itself now claims an area just over 61 sq miles.

The Grid

The Beltway (I-495), one of the country's most famous freeways, rings the city. Decades ago, the Beltway divided rural farmlands from the urban areas of the city proper. But today, tightly packed suburban housing extends at least 15 miles past the Beltway in all directions, up to and beyond Frederick, Maryland, and Reston, Virginia. The metropolitan area's population boom has made the Beltway painfully inadequate as a commuter artery – thus DC has some of the nation's worst traffic congestion.

Pierre L'Enfant's 18th-century city plan centered Washington upon two points: the Capitol and the White House. Broad avenues flare outward from both sites. The Capitol is the city's dividing point: from it proceed the axes of N Capitol St, S Capitol St, E Capitol St, and the National Mall, which divide DC into northwest, northeast, southeast, and southwest quadrants. All street names include a quadrant designation (14th St NW, 14th St SE).

The L'Enfant plan resulted in a city grid that is both logical and infuriatingly complex. Numbered streets run north to south across the city. They're numbered according to their distance from N and S Capitol Sts – eg, 1st St NW is just one block west of N Capitol St; 1st St NE is one block east of N Capitol St. Lettered streets run east to west, using E Capitol St and the Mall as their boundaries – A St NE is one block north of E Capitol St; A St SE is one block south of E Capitol St.

There are no B, J, X, Y, or Z Sts. A local urban legend holds that city planners deleted a planned J St from the grid because they hated Supreme Court Justice John Jay. But in truth, J and I simply look too similar on a map, so the grid jumps from I straight to K. Also note that I St is often written as 'Eye' St, to avoid confusion with the numeral 1. Addresses on lettered streets usually indicate the cross street: eg, Olives restaurant, 1600 K St NW, is at K and 16th Sts NW. Following the lettered streets are streets with two-syllable names, also arranged alphabetically (Adams, Bryant, etc). Then come three-syllable names; then streets named for plants and flowers.

That's all simple enough, but L'Enfant tossed a spanner in the works by overlaying his street grid with broad, Parisian-style diagonal avenues. These are named after states. Pennsylvania Ave, where presidents live, is the best-known – it connects the Capitol and White House. Other important avenues include the northwest thoroughfares of Connecticut and Wisconsin Aves NW, and New York Ave NE, the principal entryway into the northeast quadrant. The primary east-west arteries are K and M Sts NW; 16th St NW is a broad north-south route.

Traffic circles at major avenues' intersections add to the city's scenic appeal but also make DC a challenging place for visitors to navigate by car. They are useful, however, for turning around or changing direction without losing yourself in a confusing maze of back streets.

National Mall (Map 3)

Extending westward from the Capitol, the 3-mile-long Mall is the ceremonial heart of the city, lined with major museums, federal buildings, and national monuments.

Downtown (Map 3)

'Downtown' is a portmanteau term that describes the business district north of the Mall, between the White House and Union Station. It includes several smaller neighborhoods, such as Chinatown, Metro Center, and Federal Triangle.

For decades, downtown was one of DC's saddest areas. Although it was a thriving business district early in the 20th century, by the 1970s it featured block after block of empty storefronts. At night, when federal-government workers went home, it was more desolate still, its streets frequented by few but the homeless and guests scurrying between taxis and a clutch of hotels.

Now booming economic times have blessed the area. City government is pouring development money into downtown, and the MCI Center, a massive new sports arena, has attracted suburbanites and spurred new restaurants, clubs, and bars to open, some migrating here from traditionally popular

entertainment zones like Dupont Circle and Georgetown. The area is alive after dark once again, and downtown is now among the city's most interesting districts.

White House Area & Foggy Bottom (Map 3)

Streets around and west of the White House are big-government central, holding the State Dept, Interior Dept, and General Services Administration as well as important international organizations such as the World Bank and Organization of American States. Here too are George Washington University, upscale residential areas such as the infamous Watergate complex, and the K St NW 'lobbyists and lawyers' business corridor. Tourist attractions include a host of museums, such as the Renwick and Corcoran, top-end restaurants, and the Kennedy Center, which is Washington's premier cultural venue.

Capitol Hill & Southeast DC (Map 4)

The Capitol Hill district, at the Mall's east end, surrounds the Capitol itself and is one of DC's oldest neighborhoods, with some houses dating back to 1800. It sprawls across all four city quadrants, bounded (roughly) by the Washington Navy Yard, H St NW, 1st St SW, and 15th Sts NE and SE. Despite its name, there's no real 'hill' here, although the Capitol itself sits on a modest rise.

Near the Mall, Capitol Hill is the site of other monumental government buildings – the Supreme Court, Library of Congress, and House and Senate office buildings – and the beautifully restored Beaux-Arts Union Station. Upscale blocks of lovely old rowhouses cluster nearby, along with thriving bar-and-restaurant commercial districts along the Pennsylvania Ave SE and Massachusetts Ave NE corridors that cater to congressional staffers, professionals, and a large gay and lesbian community. Here too is Eastern Market, a Victorian-era crafts and farmers' market that is the central neighborhood gathering spot.

As one moves south and east from Capitol Hill, the neighborhoods become increasingly poorer. Across the Anacostia River lies **Anacostia**, one of Washington's most important black neighborhoods. Although poverty and crime have plagued it for several decades, and visitors should exercise caution here, it holds key attractions, including the Frederick Douglass National Historic Site and the Smithsonian's Anacostia Museum.

Upper Northeast DC (Map 5)

Northeast of the Capitol are residential and commercial districts such as Brookland, Fort Lincoln, and Petworth that range from middle-class to depressed. Northeast is terra incognita to many DC visitors – and even DC residents – and that's too bad, because there are some very cool things up here, including the little-visited US National Arboretum and Kenilworth Aquatic Gardens, the fabulous National Shrine of the Immaculate Conception, and the spooky-but-beautiful Franciscan Monastery. Accommodations are cheaper out here, too.

Southwest DC (Map 6)

Washington's smallest quadrant, with its boundary raggedly trimmed by the Washington Channel and Potomac River, is a mixed government and residential area. Just south of the Mall is Federal Rectangle, a district of block-long federal agencies such as the FAA and the Dept of Agriculture. Farther south, along the southwestern waterfront, are marinas, an open-air fish market, and big seafood restaurants; nearby is the broad expanse of East Potomac Park. Southwest attracts many residents and tourists out for a stroll or a bit of waterside dining.

Georgetown (Map 7)

This district, west of Foggy Bottom across Rock Creek Park, was a separate city until 1871, and its history stretches back well before the founding of the District (it was named for British King George II). A prosperous, scenic, and eminently walkable enclave, it's been home to some of DC's wealthiest residents since the mid-20th century. Its well-preserved historic streets feature hundreds of restaurants, bars, clubs, and shops, along with pristine Federal Period townhouses, the C&O Canal's southern stretch, and Georgetown University. Georgetown is generally seen as one of DC's more conservative areas, attracting upscale students, professionals, and flocks of Maryland and Virginia suburbanites on shopping and dining excursions.

Dupont Circle & Kalorama (Map 8)

A millionaires' enclave at the turn of the 20th century, the streets around Dupont Circle (at the intersections of Connecticut and Massachusetts Aves NW) are now home to a lively shopping, dining, and bar scene. The district's known for its progressive young residents (including a vibrant gay and lesbian community), the Embassy Row diplomatic enclave, and great small museums like the Phillips Collection and Textile Museum. With broad sidewalks and a myriad of outdoor cafés, Dupont Circle offers some of the best strolling and people-watching in the city. Adjacent Kalorama is upscale and residential.

Adams-Morgan (Map 9)

For the last couple of decades, this has been DC's own little Greenwich Village, where the bars and clubs and bistros are thick enough to cut with a knife and where DC's multicultural soul – black, white, Latino, Asian – is at its happy best. Its main business strips, 18th St NW and Columbia Rd, are chockablock with ethnic restaurants (Ethiopian to Cuban to Tex-Mex), and the surrounding blocks are filled with charming Victorian townhouses.

Shaw & the New U District (Map 10)

Just east of Adams-Morgan, this rapidly gentrifying but still edgy area is the historic heart of black DC. In the early and mid-20th century, Shaw was where the jazz played, black theater blossomed, and the city's civil-rights movement kicked into high gear. Smashed by the 1968 riots, it's rocking once again – its clubs are the best place to hear new music in DC, and its bars are low on attitude and high on fun. Howard University, the nation's first black university, anchors the district, which is also home to an eclectic new-theater scene.

Upper Northwest DC (Map 11)

Upper Northwest, the significant stretch of city land north of Adams-Morgan, Shaw, and Georgetown, primarily consists of wealthy residential areas such as Woodley Park, Cleveland Park, the Palisades, and Chevy Chase. Once upon a time, these neighborhoods were rural lands upon which the city's rich built country retreats. Now they're prime urban real estate for moneyed professionals. Sprinkled among the sleepy, fine homes are major attractions like the National Zoo, Washington National Cathedral, and the upper stretches of Rock Creek Park, plus fine little museums like the Kreeger Museum.

MAPS

Lonely Planet's *Washington, DC* street map is a laminated, pocket-size guide that shows all major DC attractions. Free pamphlet-size maps are offered by many DC museums and all the tourist offices, but these primarily show Mall-area attractions and aren't terribly useful for negotiating outlying areas. ADC's *Washington, DC* street atlas is a folio-size book that shows all city streets in detail.

The best place to buy maps is the Map Store (Map 3; ☎ 628-2608; Ⓜ Farragut West), 1636 I St NW, a wee downtown storefront packed with everything from DC activity guides to bus-route maps to huge foldout sheet maps of the District. Most city bookstores also sell a wide selection of city maps (see Shopping).

TOURIST OFFICES
Local Tourist Offices

The Washington, DC, Convention and Visitors Association (Map 3; ☎ 789-7000, www.washington.org; Ⓜ Metro Center), 1212 New York Ave NW, 6th floor, Washington, DC 20005-3992, distributes information on

lodging, restaurants, and attractions by mail and at its office; it's open 9 am to 5 pm weekdays.

More convenient visitors' centers are just east of the White House (Ⓜ Federal Triangle). The White House Visitor Center (Map 3; ☎ 456-7041, www.whitehouse.gov), in the Dept of Commerce Building, 1450 Pennsylvania Ave NW, has information on and maps of Mall-area attractions and distributes White House tour tickets; 7 am to 4 pm daily. The DC Chamber of Commerce Visitor Information Center (Map 3; 328-4748, www.dcchamber.org), 1300 Pennsylvania Ave NW in the Ronald Reagan Building, offers tours, maps, lodging brochures, and events listings and sells film, tickets, and souvenirs; 8 am to 6 pm Monday to Saturday.

The National Park Service, which operates most public federal sites in DC, has a Dial-a-Park recorded information line (☎ 619-7275) for details about events in and around Washington's parks and monuments. It also maintains the NPS Information Office (Map 3; ☎ 208-4747) inside the Interior Dept on C St NW, which supplies pamphlets on most NPS-managed DC sites and US national parks; 9 am to 3 pm weekdays only. You can also drop by the NPS Visitor Pavilion (Map 3) in the northeast corner of the Ellipse, south of the White House.

Smithsonian museum information is at ☎ 357-2700; the Smithsonian Visitors Center can be found on the Mall in the Smithsonian Castle (Map 3).

The multilingual International Visitors Information Service (☎ 703-572-2536) operates from the International Arrivals building at Dulles International Airport in Virginia. You can pick up brochures and maps here from 6:30 am to 10:30 pm daily.

Tourist Offices Abroad

The US lacks a well-developed overseas tourist-office system. Contact your local diplomatic office (see Embassies, below) for information from the US Travel & Tourism Administration (USTTA). Information on DC tourism can be obtained from the Convention and Visitors Association (see above) by phone, mail, or Web.

DOCUMENTS

With the exception of Canadians, who need only proper proof of Canadian citizenship, all foreign visitors to the USA must have a valid passport, and most must also have a US visa. Check current regulations with the US embassy in your home country before you depart. Keep photocopies of these documents, too; if stolen, they'll be easier to replace.

Your passport should be valid for at least six months longer than your intended stay in the USA. Documents of financial stability and/or guarantees from a US resident are sometimes required, particularly for visitors from Third World countries.

Visas

The reciprocal Visa Waiver Pilot Program applies to citizens of certain countries, who may enter the USA for stays of 90 days or less without a visa. Currently, these countries are Andorra, Austria, Belgium, Brunei, Denmark, Finland, France, Germany, Iceland, Italy, Japan, Liechtenstein, Luxembourg, Monaco, the Netherlands, New Zealand, Norway, San Marino, Spain, Sweden, Switzerland, and the UK. Under this program, you must have a round-trip ticket on an airline that participates in the program; you must have proof of financial solvency and sign a form waiving the right to a deportation hearing; and you cannot extend your stay beyond 90 days. Consult your travel agent or airline for more information.

Other travelers must obtain a visa from a US consulate or embassy. In most countries, this can be done by mail. Visa applicants may be required to demonstrate 'binding obligations' that ensure their return home. Because of this requirement, those planning to travel through other countries before arriving in the USA should apply for a US visa while still in their home countries, rather than doing so on the road.

HIV/AIDS & Entering the USA

All non-US citizens entering the USA are subject to the authority of the Immigration & Naturalization Service. The INS can bar people from entering or staying in the USA by excluding or deporting them. This is especially relevant to travelers with HIV (human immunodeficiency virus) or AIDS (acquired immune deficiency syndrome). Although HIV-positive status isn't a ground for deportation, it is a ground for exclusion, meaning that the INS can refuse to admit an HIV-positive visitor into the country.

Although INS officers don't test people for HIV/AIDS at the point of entry into the USA, they may try to exclude people who answer 'yes' to one question on the non-immigrant visa application form: 'Have you ever been afflicted with a communicable disease of public health significance?' The INS may also stop someone who looks sick, carries HIV/AIDS medication, or seems 'high-risk' (ie, gay), although sexual orientation isn't a legal ground for exclusion. Visitors can be deported if the INS later finds that they're HIV positive but didn't declare it, because failing to provide correct information on a visa application *is* a ground for deportation.

If you can prove to consular officials that you're the spouse, parent, or child of a US citizen or legal permanent resident (a green-card holder), you're exempt from the exclusionary law, even if you have HIV or AIDS.

Immigrants and visitors facing exclusion should discuss their rights and options with a trained immigration advocate in the USA before applying for a visa. For legal immigration information and referrals to advocates, contact the National Immigration Project of the National Lawyers Guild (☎ 617-227-9727), 14 Beacon St, Suite 602, Boston, MA 02108; or the Immigrant HIV Assistance Project, Bar Association of San Francisco (☎ 415-782-8995), 465 California St, Suite 1100, San Francisco, CA 94104.

The most common visa issued is a Non-Immigrant Visitors Visa: B1 for business purposes, B2 for tourism or visting friends or relatives. A visitor's visa is good for one or five years with multiple entries and specifically prohibits the visitor from taking paid employment while in the USA. The validity period for visitor visas varies depending on your citizenship. The length of time you're allowed to stay in the USA is ultimately determined by US immigration authorities at your port of entry.

Visa Extensions Tourist visitors are usually granted a six-month stay on first arrival. If you try to extend that time, immigration authorities' first assumption is that you're working illegally – so hang on to evidence that shows you've been a model tourist (like receipts to demonstrate that you've spent money in the USA or ticket stubs to show that you've traveled extensively). You must apply for an extension *before* the six months have expired. Visitors admitted under the Visa Waiver Pilot Program cannot apply for extensions.

To extend your stay, you must file Form I-539. Call ☎ 800-870-3676 to request the form. Mail it to the US Justice Dept's Immigration & Naturalization Service, Washington District Office, 4420 N Fairfax Drive, Arlington, VA 22203. Alternately, pick up a form at the office between 8 am and 2:30 pm weekdays (**M** Ballston).

Other Documents

Bring your driver's license or International Driver's Permit if you plan to drive in DC. Visitors from abroad can obtain IDPs from their auto clubs. Although your foreign driver's license *is* valid in the USA, and the major car-rental companies are used to seeing foreign licenses, local police are more likely to accept an IDP as valid identification than an unfamiliar document from another country. Note that an IDP is not itself a license but rather an official translation of your license, so you still need to bring your actual license.

Carry a picture ID (driver's license or passport will do) proving you're 21 or older if you plan to buy alcohol or go to nightclubs. A picture ID is also required to enter many federal buildings (although not to enter monuments or most museums).

No matter how you're traveling, take out travel insurance that covers you for medical expenses, luggage theft or loss, and unavoidable cancellation or delays in your travel arrangements. You should be covered for worst-case scenarios, too, like an accident requiring hospital treatment and a flight home. Coverage varies from policy to policy, so ask your insurer and your ticket-issuing agency to explain the finer points. STA Travel (www.sta-travel.com) offers a variety of travel-insurance options at reasonable prices. Keep a photocopy of your ticket separate from the original.

If you'll stay in youth hostels, bring your Hostelling International/American Youth Hostel membership card to get discount rates. Membership ($25) can be purchased at DC's HI/AYH hostel (Map 3; ☎ 737-2333, 800-909-4776; **M** Metro Center), downtown at 1009 11th St NW, at K St.

People over 65 are eligible for a range of discounts at DC-area attractions; a driver's license showing your birth date suffices. If you're a student, get an ISIC (International Student Identification Card) from your college, which can get you discounted admission to concerts and a number of other cultural events.

EMBASSIES
US Embassies

US diplomatic offices abroad include the following:

Australia (☎ 02-6214-5600) Moonah Place, Yarralumla ACT 2600; consulates in Melbourne, Perth, and Sydney

Canada (☎ 613-238-5335) 490 Sussex Drive, Ottawa, Ontario K1N 1G8; consulates in Calgary, Halifax, Montréal, Toronto, and Vancouver

China (☎ 86-10-6532-3431) 3 Xiu Shui Bei Jie, Beijing 100600; consulates in Hong Kong and Shenyang

France (☎ 01 43 12 22 22) 2 ave Gabriel, 75008 Paris; consulates in Lyon, Marseille, Rennes, Strasbourg, and Toulouse

Germany (☎ 0190-88 22 11) Neustädtische Kirchstrasse 4-5, 10117 Berlin; consulates in Düsseldorf, Frankfurt, Hamburg, Leipzig, and Munich

India (☎ 11-419-8000) Shantipath, Chanakyapuri, New Delhi 110021; consulates in Calcutta, Madras, and Mumbai

Ireland (☎ 353-1-668-8777) 42 Elgin Rd, Ballsbridge, Dublin 4

Israel (☎ 972-03-519-7341) 71 Hayarkon St, Tel Aviv

Japan (☎ 03-3224-5000) 1-10-5 Akasaka 1-Chome, Minato-ku, Tokyo 107-8420; consulates in Fukuoka, Nagoya, Naha, Osaka, and Sapporo

Mexico (☎ 01-5209-9100) Paseo de la Reforma 305, Colonia Cuauhtémoc, 06500 México, DF; consulates in Guadalajara, Juárez, Monterrey, and Tijuana

The Netherlands (☎ 31 70 310-9209) Lange Voorhout 102, 2514 EJ The Hague; consulate in Amsterdam

New Zealand (☎ 644-472-2068) 29 Fitzherbert Terrace, Thorndon, Wellington; consulate in Auckland

Russia (☎ 7-095-728-5599) Novinskiy Bul'var 19/21, Moscow 121099; consulates in St Petersburg, Vladivostok, and Yekaterinburg

South Africa (☎ 27-12-342-1048) 877 Pretorius St, Arcadia, Pretoria; consulates in Cape Town, Durban, and Johannesburg

Spain (☎ 91587-2200) Serrano 75, 28006 Madrid; consulate in Barcelona

UK (☎ 020-7499-9000) 24 Grosvenor Square, London, W1A 1AE; consulates in Belfast and Edinburgh

Embassies in Washington, DC

Nearly every country in the world has an embassy in DC, making this one of the US's most vibrant multinational cities. If your embassy isn't listed below, find its phone number through Information (☎ 411 in DC, 202-555-1212 outside DC). Embassies cluster in DC's northwest quadrant, particularly Dupont Circle, Kalorama, and Foggy Bottom. Weekday hours below are those during which embassies handle visa business.

Many embassies host films, art exhibits, concerts, and receptions, which are nice ways for lonely travelers to meet compatriots. Ask your embassy what's on, or check its Web site. The handy Electronic Embassy (www.embassy.org) offers links to all DC embassy homepages.

Australia (Map 8; ☎ 797-3000; Ⓜ Dupont Circle) 1601 Massachusetts Ave NW; 8:30 am to 12:30 pm

Canada (Map 3; ☎ 682-1740; Ⓜ Archives) 501 Pennsylvania Ave NW; 9 am to 12 pm

China (Map 8; ☎ 328-2500; Ⓜ Woodley Park-Zoo) 2300 Connecticut Ave NW; visa office (Map 11; 338-6688; Metrobus No 30, 32, 34, or 36 from Tenleytown station) 2201 Wisconsin Ave NW, Suite 110; 10 am to 12:30 pm and 1 to 3 pm

France (Map 7; ☎ 944-6000; Metrobus D6 from K St NW downtown) 4101 Reservoir Rd NW; 8:45 am 12:45 pm

Germany (Map 7; ☎ 298-4393; Metrobus D6) 4645 Reservoir Rd NW; 8:30 to 11:30 am

India (Map 8; ☎ 939-7000; Ⓜ Dupont Circle) 2107 Massachusetts Ave NW; visa office 2536 Massachusetts Ave NW; 9:30 am to 12:30 pm

Ireland (Map 8; ☎ 462-3939; Ⓜ Dupont Circle) 2234 Massachusetts Ave NW; 9 am to 1 pm and 2 to 4 pm

Israel (Map 11; ☎ 364-5500; Ⓜ Van Ness-UDC) 3514 International Drive NW; 9:30 am to 1 pm

Japan (Map 8; ☎ 238-6700; Ⓜ Dupont Circle) 2520 Massachusetts Ave NW; 10 am to noon and 2 to 4 pm

Mexico (Map 3; ☎ 728-1600; Ⓜ Farragut West) 1911 Pennsylvania Ave NW; 8 am to 1 pm

The Netherlands (Map 11; ☎ 244-5300; Ⓜ Van Ness-UDC) 4200 Linnean Ave NW; 10 am to noon

New Zealand (Map 11; ☎ 328-4800; Metrobus N6 from Farragut Square downtown) 37 Observatory Circle; 9 am to 5 pm

Russia (Map 11; ☎ 298-5700; Metrobus No 30, 32, 34, or 36) 2650 Wisconsin Ave NW; visa office 2650 Tunlaw Rd NW; 9 am to 12:15 pm

South Africa (Map 11; ☎ 232-4400; Metrobus N6) 3051 Massachusetts Ave NW; 9 am to 12:30 pm

Spain (Map 3; ☎ 452-0100; Ⓜ Foggy Bottom) 2375 Pennsylvania Ave NW; 9 am to 12:30 pm

UK (Map 11; ☎ 588-7800; Metrobus N6) 3100 Massachusetts Ave NW; visa office 19 Observatory Circle NW; 8 to 11:30 am

Your Own Embassy

It's important to know what your embassy – the embassy of the country of which you're a citizen – can and cannot do for you while you're in the US.

In emergencies, your embassy usually won't offer much help if your troubles are remotely your own fault. Remember that you're bound by the laws of the country you're visiting – your embassy won't be sympathetic if you're jailed for committing a crime in the US, even if the action is legal in your own country.

In other emergencies, you might get some assistance, but only if you've exhausted other channels. For example, if your money and documents are stolen, it might help you get a new passport, but a loan for onward travel is impossible. If you must return home urgently, the embassy won't give you a free ticket; it expects you to have insurance.

Embassies once kept letters for travelers and maintained reading rooms with home newspapers, but currently the mail-holding services have ceased and even newspapers are usually out of date.

CUSTOMS

On your flight to the US, you'll fill out a Customs declaration form. Visitors older than 21 can bring in 200 cigarettes and 1 liter of alcohol. US citizens are allowed a $400 duty-free exemption; non-US citizens are allowed $100. Strict rules apply to fruit, flowers, and animals (see www.aphis.usda.gov/oa/travel.html for details). There's no limit on the amount of cash, traveler's checks, etc that you can bring in, but you must declare any amount over $10,000.

MONEY

You've got three basic choices for handling money: cash, credit and debit cards, and traveler's checks. Most DC businesses accept all these options, but for convenience and security, it's best to travel with a mix of the three. Note that a credit card is required by most car-rental agencies and many hotels.

Currency

The only currency accepted in DC is the US dollar ($), consisting of 100 cents (¢). Coins are the penny (1¢), nickel (5¢), dime (10¢), quarter (25¢), half-dollar, and dollar (the

new, gold-colored 'Sacajawea' coin). Keep a stash of quarters for use in vending machines, parking meters, and Laundromats.

US bills can confuse the foreign visitor – they're all the same color and size – and exist in denominations of $1, $2 (rare), $5, $10, $20 (the only bills dispensed by ATMs), $50, and $100.

Exchange Rates

Exchange rates fluctuate daily. At press time, rates were as follows:

country	unit		dollars
Australia	A$1	=	$0.56
Canada	C$1	=	$0.68
EEC (euro)	€1	=	$0.86
France	FF10	=	$1.31
Germany	DM1	=	$0.44
Japan	¥100	=	$0.94
New Zealand	NZ$1	=	$0.43
UK	UK£1	=	$1.40

Exchanging Money

During business hours, major banks throughout DC exchange money and cash traveler's checks. Also try American Express, with several DC locations, including 1150 Connecticut Ave NW in the Dupont Circle district (Map 8; ☎ 457-1300; Ⓜ Farragut North), and 5300 Wisconsin Ave NW (☎ 362-4000; Ⓜ Friendship Heights), on the lower level of the Mazza Gallerie mall (Map 11). Both are open during business hours weekdays; the mall office is open till 6 pm weeknights and 10 am to 5 pm Saturday.

Another reliable exchange is Thomas Cook (☎ 800-287-7362), with offices at 1800 K St NW (Map 3; weekday business hours only; Ⓜ Farragut West) and in Union Station across from Gate G (weekend service available, too). Cook also has two counters at Reagan National Airport (both 7 am to 9 pm daily) and three at Dulles (hours vary, but one is open at all times between 7 am and 9 pm daily).

At BWI airport, go to Travelex (☎ 410-859-5997), on the upper level; open 6:30 am to 8:30 pm daily.

Cash & Traveler's Checks Traveler's checks are generally as good as cash in the US – you don't even have to visit a bank to cash them, as many businesses in the DC area accept them just like cash. Their major advantage over cash is that they are replaceable if stolen. American Express and Thomas Cook (see office locations above) have efficient replacement policies. A record of the check numbers is vital should you need to replace them – note them carefully and keep the record separate from the checks themselves.

Buying traveler's checks in US dollars saves you both trouble and expense. Traveler's checks denominated in non-US currency can be exchanged in DC, but it's not very conveninent or economical.

Buy the checks in large denominations ($100); changing smaller checks is a pain. Banks often charge service fees – generally 1% of the check value – for exchange.

ATMs With your bank-issued ATM card or a MasterCard or Visa, you can easily obtain cash at ATMs all over the DC area (you can't spit downtown without hitting a few dozen ATMs). All you need is your PIN, or personal identification number. ATMs obviate the need to buy traveler's checks in advance or pay commission when exchanging them; if you're visiting from abroad, you'll often get a better exchange rate, too. If you use a credit card, however, you probably will be charged a small fee and incur interest on the withdrawal until you pay it back.

Most DC ATMs are linked to Plus and Cirrus, the two biggest US ATM networks, which makes withdrawing money easy. If you use an ATM that doesn't belong to your own bank, however, you'll be charged $1.50 per withdrawal. These fees add up fast, so make a few large withdrawals during your stay rather than lots of small ones. Call your bank or credit-card company for exact information about using its cards at ATMs in the USA. If you will rely on ATMs, bring a couple of cards and keep them separate. Contact your bank if you lose your card.

Conveniently located ATMs in popular tourist districts include Crestar Bank at 18th St NW and Columbia Rd in Adams-Morgan (Map 9); Riggs Bank on the north side of Dupont Circle (Map 8); and Riggs Bank at Wisconsin Ave and M St NW in Georgetown (Map 7). You'll also find ATMs inside some Mall museums, near their gift shops.

Credit Cards Major credit cards are accepted at hotels, restaurants, gas stations, shops, and car-rental agencies throughout DC – in fact, it's almost impossible to rent a car or make phone reservations without one. Even if you rely on traveler's checks and ATMs, carry a credit card for emergencies, rentals, and reservations. If you rely primarily upon credit cards, bring more than one and include a Visa or MasterCard in your deck, as other cards aren't as widely accepted.

Places that accept Visa and MasterCard are also likely to accept debit cards, which deduct payment directly from users' bank accounts (you're charged a small transaction fee). Call your bank to confirm that your debit card is accepted in the USA.

Carry copies of your credit-card numbers separately from the cards. If you lose a card or it's stolen, contact the company immediately. Following are the main companies' toll-free numbers:

American Express	☎ 800-528-4800
Diners Club	☎ 800-234-6377
Discover	☎ 800-347-2683
MasterCard	☎ 800-826-2181
Visa	☎ 800-336-8472

Security

Despite DC's 'crime-capital' press, its heavily touristed areas are really quite safe, so leave the paranoia at home. Common-sense measures apply: leave excess cash in your hotel safe; carry money and credit cards in a pouch kept *under* your clothing; and if club-hopping, tuck money in a front pocket or in a purse that's small enough to sling on your shoulder when you're dancing.

Costs

DC is a surprisingly affordable travel destination compared to other US metropolises.

FACTS FOR THE VISITOR

There's so much free stuff to see and do, from the Smithsonian museums to federal sites to parks, that you needn't spend a penny to entertain yourself. The city's plethora of young (and often poorly paid) interns and government staffers means lots of inexpensive restaurants and happy hours (with free munchies and cheap drinks). And the city is negotiable without a car, so you don't need to rent one.

That said, it's easy to run up big credit-card balances in DC's expensive downtown hotels and high-end glamour eateries. To keep lodging costs low, consider a suburban hotel or the downtown hostels, and visit on weekends (when prices drop) rather than weekdays (when business travelers drive prices up).

A budget traveler staying in a hostel pays between $20 and $25 per night for a bed; eating in budget restaurants costs an additional $20 to $30 for all three meals. Getting around on Metro costs about $5 per day if you buy a daily pass.

Travelers wanting to live a bit higher on the hog pay between $70 to $120 for a double hotel room (the lower range applies mostly to weekends), about $30 to $50 for meals, drinks, and club cover charges, and $120 to $150 per week for car rental.

Tipping

Gratuities really aren't optional in the US. Waitstaff, hotel-room attendants, valet parkers, bellhops, etc receive minimum wage and depend on tips for their livelihoods. Service has to be pretty dreadful before you should consider *not* tipping.

In restaurants and bars, 15% is considered mandatory; 20% is the norm. Leave cash tips on the table, and add credit/debit-card tips to the signature slip. Don't tip at fast-food joints or cafeterias.

Hotel-room attendants should get $1 per guest per day: eg, $10 for two people who have stayed five days. Leave the tip in cash on the pillow. Tip taxi drivers about 10% of your fare. Airport baggage handlers get about $1 per bag. Hairdressers usually get tips, too (20%), as do coat-check staff ($1 is usually OK).

Taxes

Nearly everything you buy in the USA is taxed: accommodations, restaurant meals and drinks, clothing and other consumer goods, etc. Sometimes taxes are included in an item's advertised price (as with plane tickets). Usually, however, taxes are added onto advertised prices.

In DC, basic sales tax is 5.75%. In restaurants and bars, the tax is 10% (as it is for rental cars and liquor). Hotel tax is 14.5%, and you're charged an additional $1.50 per-night surcharge.

Maryland's sales tax is 5%; room tax is 10%. Virginia's sales tax is 4.5%; restaurant/bar tax is about 8% depending on the county. Virginia hotels combine the 4.5% sales tax with a 5% lodging tax (total about 10%).

When inquiring about lodging rates, always ask whether taxes are included. Unless otherwise stated, prices given in this book don't include taxes.

Special Deals

The USA is probably the most promotion-oriented society on Earth. Though the bargaining common in many other countries isn't usually done here, you can work angles to cut costs. Discount coupons are widely available – check circulars in Sunday papers, at supermarkets, tourist offices, and chambers of commerce.

If you're in DC on government, diplomatic, or military business, some hotel owners and car-rental agencies can offer you special rates. Ask when you make reservations. If you're not, and it's the off-season (late summer, early winter), casually mention a competitor's price: that often prompts management to lower the quoted rate. Seniors, kids, and students receive discounts at most area attractions.

POST & COMMUNICATIONS

DC's main post office (Map 5; ☎ 635-5300, Ⓜ Rhode Island Ave), where general-delivery mail is directed, is in northeast DC at 900 Brentwood Rd NE, Washington, DC 20066. Hours are 8 am to 6 pm weekdays, 7:30 am to 4 pm Saturday.

Far more convenient is the National Capitol Post Office (Map 4; ☎ 523-2628, Ⓜ Union Station), just across 1st St NE from Union Station, in the National Postal Museum building. It has the longest hours, too: 7 am to midnight weekdays, 7 am to 8 pm weekends. There's also a post office, appropriately, in the Old Post Office Pavilion (Map 3; Ⓜ Federal Triangle), downtown at Pennsylvania Ave and 12th St NW.

Throughout DC are branch post offices and post-office centers in supermarkets and drugstores – for the address of the nearest, just call ☎ 800-275-8777. Post offices are usually open 8:30 am to 4:30 pm weekdays, 8:30 am to noon Saturday.

You can also find numerous private mailing services (like Mail Boxes Etc) from which you can send faxes and packages via United Parcel Service or Federal Express. Both these overnight-mail services also maintain corner drop boxes downtown, especially in Foggy Bottom and the White House area.

To send a telegram, call Western Union (☎ 800-325-6000) and ask for the nearest office.

Postal Rates

US postal rates frequently increase, but at publication they were as follows: 33¢ for 1st-class mail within the USA for letters up to 1oz (22¢ each additional ounce), and 20¢ for postcards.

International airmail rates are 60¢ for a half-ounce letter, $1 for a 1oz letter, and 55¢ for a postcard sent anywhere in the world except Canada (to which it's 48¢ for a half-ounce letter, 45¢ for a postcard) and Mexico (40¢ for either). Aerogrammes cost 60¢.

The US Postal Service also offers priority mail service, which delivers letters and packages anywhere in the US in two or fewer days; $3.20 for 2lb or less; $6.50 for 5lb. In a hurry? Overnight express mail starts at $11.75. The Postal Service will even pick up your package, for $8.25.

For 24-hour postal information, call ☎ 800-275-8777 or check www.usps.com. They give postal codes for any given address, rules about parcel sizes, and locations and phone numbers of any post office.

Sending & Receiving Mail

If you have the correct postage, you can drop mail into any blue street mailbox. To buy stamps, weigh mail, or send a package 16oz or heavier, go to a post office. You can also purchase sheets of stamps from many ATMs in the city.

If your items require packaging, consider using the services of local packaging stores like Mail Boxes Etc: a convenient branch (Map 8; ☎ 986-4900) is near the Farragut North Metro at 17th and M Sts NW; open daily. In addition to fax, mailbox, and shipping services, these stores pack items and sell packaging materials.

General-delivery *(poste restante)* mail can be sent to you c/o General Delivery at the main DC post office (see above). Mail is usually held for 10 days before it's returned to the sender; ask your correspondents to write 'Hold for Arrival' on their letters. You need picture ID to collect general-delivery mail. Alternatively, have mail sent to the

The Old Post Office Pavilion

RICK GERHARTER

local representative of American Express or Thomas Cook, which provide mail services for their customers. Stores like Mail Boxes Etc also receive and hold mail for customers.

Telephone

The area code for Washington, DC is ☎ 202. The Maryland suburbs' code is ☎ 301; suburban Virginia is ☎ 703 or ☎ 571. When dialing another area code, you must dial ☎ 1 before the code – eg, to call an Alexandria number from DC, first dial ☎ 1-703.

At pay phones, local calls cost 35¢. Long-distance charges apply to 'non-local' calls within a single area code; this isn't a problem in DC, but you might incur such charges when calling in the suburbs. Watch out for hotel surcharges, too, which might be more than $1 for a local call – go down to the lobby to use a pay phone instead, or rely on a cell phone.

Toll-free numbers begin with ☎ 1-800 or 1-888 and allow you to call free within the USA – they're commonly offered by car-rental companies, bigger hotels, and the like. Dial ☎ 411 for directory assistance in DC, ☎ 1 + area code + 555-1212 for directory assistance outside DC, and ☎ 1-800-555-1212 for toll-free directory assistance. The operator is at ☎ 0.

International Calls When calling DC from abroad, first dial the US's international country code (☎ 1). To place an international call from DC, dial ☎ 011 + country code + area code (dropping the leading 0) + number. For international operator assistance, dial ☎ 00.

Generally it's cheaper to make international calls at night, but this varies with the country you're calling. The exact cost of an international call from a pay phone depends on the long-distance company and the country in question. Calls to Australia and Europe generally cost about $1.50 for the first minute and $1 for each additional minute. Calls to other continents usually cost twice as much or more.

To avoid feeding stacks of coins into a pay phone when calling long-distance, use a credit card, subscribe to a long-distance carrier, or purchase a phone-debit card (available at many copy shops and drugstores downtown). Long-distance debit cards allow purchasers to pay in advance and then access their account through a toll-free 800 number.

Phone Cards Lonely Planet's eKno Communication Card is aimed specifically at travelers and provides cheap international calls, a range of messaging services, and free email. (For local calls, you're usually better off using a local card.) You can join online at www.ekno.lonelyplanet.com or by phone from the USA (☎ 800-707-0031). To use eKno from the USA after you've joined, call ☎ 800-706-1333.

Fax

Fax machines are easy to find in the USA – at shipping outlets like Mail Boxes Etc, copy shops like Kinko's, and even corner drugstores. Be prepared to pay high prices, though (over $1 per page). Most top-end business hotels in downtown DC have fully equipped business centers for their guests, including fax machines.

Downtown, try any Mailboxes Etc location (see above) or Kinko's (see below). In Georgetown, there's Zap Copies & Communications (Map 7; ☎ 333-8877; Ⓜ Foggy Bottom), 1052 Thomas Jefferson St NW (8 am to 6 pm); on Capitol Hill, try Capitol Hill Fax Service (Map 4; ☎ 544-6400; Ⓜ Eastern Market), 607 Pennsylvania Ave SE (10 am to 5 pm).

Email & Internet Access

Getting online in DC is pretty easy – many copy shops and packaging services offer terminals with Web access. Generally they charge around $12 per hour.

If you bring along your own laptop, it's easiest just to sign up with a widespread ISP, like AOL, and then use its DC dial-up number. Earthlink is another good ISP for use in DC, with lots of reliable local dial-up numbers. When making hotel reservations, remember to ask if your room has a modem line or if the hotel has a business center that you can use.

If you don't have your own computer, you still have options. Several 24-hour Kinko's shops offer Web access for 20¢ a minute, including the Georgetown location (Map 7; ☎ 965-1414; Ⓜ Foggy Bottom), 3329 M St NW, and downtown (Map 3; ☎ 466-3777; Ⓜ Farragut North), 1612 K St NW.

Cybercafés in DC include the following:

Cafemyth.com (Map 7; ☎ 625-6984; Ⓜ Foggy Bottom) 3241 M St NW; $8/hour (coffee drinks, juice, light eats, gift boutique)

cyberSTOP Café (Map 8; ☎ 234-2470; Ⓜ Dupont Circle) 1513 17th St NW; $7/hour (teas, coffees, munchies)

Kramerbooks & Afterwords Café (Map 8; ☎ 387-1400; Ⓜ Dupont Circle) 1517 Connecticut Ave NW; email-checking is free (fabulous independent bookstore, with full café menu and booze)

The cheapest email access while traveling is via a free Web-based email account – from Hotmail (www.hotmail.com), Yahoo (www.yahoo.com), or Netscape (www.netscape.com), for example – that's accessible from any browser-equipped computer.

INTERNET RESOURCES

The *Washington Post* has an excellent Web site (www.washingtonpost.com) that provides daily news, restaurant reviews, events listings, and 'virtual tours' of DC neighborhoods. A reasonably thorough visitors' guide is on the Washington, DC, Convention and Visitors Association site (www.washington.org). At http://DCpages.com, you'll find links to hundreds of DC community Web sites – businesses, dining guides, parks, social organizations, you name it. Metro's site, www.wmata.com, gives information on subways and buses and features a handy route planner.

Folks interested in local politics should tune in to www.dcwatch.com, an online magazine covering City Hall and the District's ongoing struggle for full home rule and voting congressional representation. If national politics are your speed, check out www.whitehouse.gov, www.senate.gov, www.house.gov, or www.supremecourtus.gov. The Smithsonian site, www.si.edu, has links to all its museums and information on its

special events. For concert and events listings and snappy articles on city life, go to www.washingtoncitypaper.com.

BOOKS

If you're interested in learning more about DC, the many high quality local bookstores listed in the Shopping chapter are excellent resources. Most of them maintain special 'Washingtoniana' sections full of guidebooks, historical works, and books by local authors.

Lonely Planet

If you're exploring Virginia, Maryland, or Delaware, pick up Lonely Planet's *Virginia & the Capital Region* – the perfect companion to this book, it has all the details on the Shenandoah, Eastern Shore, colonial sites, and the attractions of Baltimore, Annapolis, and Richmond.

Guidebooks

Two excellent guides covering black and women's history sites are available at local bookstores. Jacci Duncan's and Lynn Page Whittaker's *The Women's History Guide to Washington* discusses key feminist landmarks throughout the city; Sandra Fitzpatrick's and Maria Goodwin's amazingly thorough *Black Washington* relates the history of DC's black neighborhoods and civil-rights sites.

If you're exploring the C&O towpath, get *The C&O Companion*, by Mike High, which relates the canal's history and provides a mile-by-mile sight guide. (See additional activity-guide suggestions in the Activities section of the Things to See & Do chapter.) The Smithsonian's little *Official Guide to the Smithsonian*, available at its gift shops, is a handy compendium of museum information.

No architecture buff should visit DC without two invaluable companions. The American Institute of Architects' *AIA Guide to Washington, DC* is a learned yet witty look at DC landmarks and the people who built them. EJ Applewhite's *Washington Itself* provides intensive histories and take-no-prisoners critiques of famed buildings and monuments (however, it's rather out of date). Bibliophiles will enjoy David Cutler's *Literary Washington*, a guide to bookstores and writers' groups and resources.

History

Although most general US-history books discuss the capital's founding, there are few thorough, up-to-date histories of the city. Constance McLaughlin Green's *Washington: A History of the Capital, 1800-1950* is an excellent scholarly exploration of the capital's early years; *Creating the Federal City, 1774-1800*, by Kenneth Bowling, offers an in-depth look at post-Revolution wrangling over where to place the US capital. Carl Abbott's *Political Terrain: Washington, DC* explores DC's symbolic identity, from its days as a sleepy Southern town to its present iconic status. Finally, there's *City of Magnificent Intentions*, edited by Keith Melder, a collection of essays on DC history.

Washington's black neighborhoods are given close attention in Constance McLaughlin Green's *The Secret City: A History of Race Relations in the Nation's Capital* and James Borchert's *Alley Life in Washington, 1850-1970*, which examines the impoverished 'substreets' where many DC blacks lived until quite recently. Francine Cary's *Urban Odyssey: A Multicultural History of Washington, DC* explores the contributions of DC's Latino, Asian, and African immigrants.

Wartime Washington – from the War of 1812 to the Vietnam War – is the subject of many tomes. Two fine ones are *The Burning of Washington*, by Anthony Pitch, which investigates the British invasion and destruction of the capital in 1814, and *Washington Goes to War*, by David Brinkley, a delightfully readable book about the sea change that WWII wrought upon DC as thousands of newcomers flooded in to town to fill government jobs. *Testament to Union: Civil War Monuments in Washington, DC*, by Kathryn Jacob, is a geographically organized guide to statuary commemorating heroes and battles of that war.

Politics

Push aside the hefty stack of US presidential biographies and you're still left with thousands of books written about the machinations of American politics. Start with a classic, *All the President's Men*, by Carl Bernstein and Bob Woodward, which is one of the best whodunits ever written – the two *Post* reporters who toppled Nixon spin a fascinating tale of off-the-record sources, death threats, and White House thuggery. Woodward's *The Brethren: Inside the Supreme Court* is another set-on-deep-background journalistic thriller.

Several good books cover local politics. *Marion Barry: The Politics of Race*, by Jonathan Agronsky, explores the tragic history of DC's most notorious mayor. Published in 1962 but still insightful is Martha Derthick's *City Politics in Washington*.

If you're curious about what goes on inside DC embassies (mostly parties, apparently), check out Gail Scott's *Diplomatic Dance: The New Embassy Life in America*, a fun, gossipy look at local diplomatic society.

Wanna know why they called LBJ 'Bull Nuts'? Nigel Cawthorne's *Sex Lives of the Presidents* gives you the answer, along with many other scraps of unwashed White House laundry. Recover with PJ O'Rourke's *Parliament of Whores*, a collection of satirical essays on Congress that's caustic enough to burn your eyeballs.

Natural History

Richard Berman and Deborah McBride's *Natural Washington* offers an excellent summary of local recreational resources and parks, including little-visited gems. *Birds of Washington, DC*, by Chris Fisher, is a slender handbook on feathered city residents and where to spot them, as is *Finding Birds in the National Capital Area*, by Claudia Wilds.

A small gem of local nature writing, *Spring in Washington DC*, was written in 1947 by State Dept official (and naturalist) Louis Halle. It narrates the arrival of DC's prettiest season in Rock Creek Park, on the Mall, and along the Potomac.

FILMS

DC's combination of scenic glory and political shenanigans has proved irresistible to Hollywood – hundreds of movies have been shot in and around the District. Back in 1939, Jimmy Stewart got all rumpled and morally outraged by the city in *Mr Smith Goes to Washington*; in 1951, much the same thing happened to aliens who landed downtown in *The Day the Earth Stood Still*.

In the 1970s, the District really hit its cinematic stride in *The Exorcist* – set in Georgetown, it detailed supernatural rather than political horrors. In 1976, the ultimate political scandal, Watergate, was dramatized by *All the President's Men*. *St Elmo's Fire* (1984), chronicling the heartaches and hangovers of a gaggle of pretty yuppies, is the über-Georgetown movie.

Various crappy White House dramas *(In the Line of Fire, The American President, Dick)* have made Oval Office life appear a nonstop series of shootouts and makeouts. Skip 'em and reach for Kubrick's *Dr Strangelove* (surely the Pentagon's least-favorite movie), *Wag the Dog* (a hilarious parody of presidential-election spin), or *No Way Out* (a thriller in which Navy officer Kevin Costner outraces Russian spies and paws Sean Young in a DC cab). Recently, parts – excuse the pun – of *Hannibal* were shot downtown, starring Anthony Hopkins as Hannibal Lecter.

NEWSPAPERS & MAGAZINES

The *Washington Post* (25¢) is the dominant local daily and one of the nation's best all-around newspapers. Its Friday 'Weekend' section is particularly useful for events listings. Its competitor, the *Washington Times* (25¢), owned by the Unification Church, is more conservative (and nowhere near as good). The *Washington Afro-American* is the city's black newspaper.

Washington City Paper, the alternative weekly, is distributed free in boxes throughout the city. It scrutinizes DC politics and trends and has great entertainment coverage: concerts, exhibits, readings, festivals, movies, etc. The very useful *Barstool* is

another freebie, providing the scoop on local watering holes.

DC neighborhoods have their own papers, too, which you can find in corner boxes and in heaps at shop and restaurant entryways. *The Georgetowner* weekly tabloid covers arts, entertainment, and real estate, with a focus on Georgetown events and personalities. Over on Capitol Hill, *Roll Call* is a semi-weekly that details congressional goings-on and dishes juicy political gossip. *Voice of the Hill* is a free monthly with neighborhood-oriented news.

Worthwhile magazines include *The Washingtonian*, a gossipy lifestyle monthly with the dirt on local celebrities, plus entertainment and dining reviews. There's also *The Smithsonian*, which has articles about the institution's research, exhibits, and special events – it's very enjoyable, a less slick *National Geographic*.

RADIO

You can find National Public Radio programs and classical music at WETA-FM 90.9; more NPR and talk shows are on WAMU-FM 88.5. Alternative plays on WHFS-FM 99.1, and album-oriented dinosaur rock is on the menu at WWDC-FM 101.1. News junkies like WTOP-FM 107.7 for round-the-clock local and national political coverage.

Radioheads will enjoy tours of DC-based National Public Radio and the Voice of America – see details in the Things to See & Do chapter.

TELEVISION

All of the national networks are represented on the DC dial: NBC is on Channel 4, Fox on Channel 5, ABC on Channel 7, and CBS on Channel 9. The federally supported Public Broadcasting System, based in DC, operates superior national news, arts, children's, and entertainment programming. (PBS is highly regarded but also hotly contested – conservative congressmen who consider it too liberal regularly try to axe its budget.) Find *The News Hour, Sesame Street*, and *Mr Rogers' Neighborhood* on

PBS's WETA Channel 26. C-SPAN broadcasts live from the floor of Congress (aired in offices and bars across Capitol Hill).

A couple of national TV dramas have been set in Washington. Notable is NBC's *The West Wing*, in which Martin Sheen plays an unrealistically thoughtful Chief Executive, and the WB's *DC*, a welterweight bit of fluff detailing the romantic foibles of young Hill staffers.

PHOTOGRAPHY & VIDEO

It's practically illegal to go outdoors in DC without a camera – on sunny days, even a simple stroll down the Mall becomes a lambada as you duck and weave out of other people's shots. It's tempting to spend all your film on famous buildings and monuments, but remember that those photos will look pretty generic once you get them home. If you include a few loved ones or fetching strangers in your photos, they'll mean more to you a few years hence.

Moto-Photo, a local chain with many city locations, offers reliable one-hour processing. Try 1819 H St NW in Foggy Bottom (Map 3; ☎ 822-9001; Ⓜ Farragut West) or 1601 Connecticut Ave NW (Map 8; ☎ 797-9035; Ⓜ Dupont Circle). For camera repair and gear, try Ritz Camera (Map 3; ☎ 861-7710; Ⓜ Farragut North), 1750 L St NW downtown.

Flash photography is banned in many museums and historic houses. Shooting pictures on or near DC's military sites may win you a scolding from MPs, but you can usually get away with it if you're sneaky.

Overseas visitors who purchase videos here should remember that the USA uses the National Television System Committee (NTSC) color TV standard, which isn't compatible with other standards like Phas Alternative Line (PAL). Unless you find worthwhile PAL-format videos (available in some DC shops), it's wise to avoid cheap movie purchases until you get home.

TIME

DC is on Eastern Standard Time, five hours behind Greenwich Mean Time. Daylight Saving Time is observed between April and October. When it's noon here, it's 5 pm in London, 6 am next day in Sydney, and 8 am next day in Auckland.

ELECTRICITY

Electric current in the USA is 110-115V, 60Hz AC. Outlets may accept flat two-prong or three-prong grounded plugs. If your appliance is designed for another electrical system, buy an adapter, readily available anywhere that sells hardware and at drugstores.

WEIGHTS & MEASURES

Like the rest of the country, DC is afraid of the metric system and uses the US measurement system instead. Distances are in feet, yards, and miles; weights are in ounces and pounds. There's a conversion chart inside the back cover of this book.

LAUNDRY

Pricier hotels will do your wash for you, but it usually isn't cheap. Some hostels and guesthouses have on-site wash-your-own laundry facilities; you can ask when you book a room.

Dry cleaners abound throughout DC (you'll find lots on the K St NW corridor), usually charging a few dollars to clean a shirt. Self-service Laundromats are less common. Most Laundromats charge $1 for a wash, 25¢ for 15 minutes of dryer time. The machines take quarters, and usually there's an on-site change machine. Convenient Laundromats include the following:

Evers Laundry (Map 9; ☎ 518-5884), 1730 Columbia Rd NW, Adams-Morgan

Super Clean Laundromat (Map 11; ☎ 965-0295), 2414 Wisconsin Ave NW, upper northwest

Washtub Laundromat (Map 8; ☎ 332-9455), 1511 17th St NW, Dupont Circle

HEALTH

Washington is like most American cities when it comes to health care: there are really no unexpected health dangers, excellent medical attention is readily available, and the only real concern is that a collision with the US medical system might injure your wallet. Remember to buy health insurance before you travel.

Most foreign visitors need no immunizations; cholera and yellow fever may be required for entrance if you're coming from areas with a history of those diseases.

George Washington University Hospital (Map 3; ☎ 994-1000; Ⓜ Foggy Bottom) is at 901 23rd St NW. Serving many State Dept types, it has the excellent Travelers' Clinic (☎ 994-4525), offering immunizations and health advice for travelers going anywhere on the planet. Most noninsured emergency patients are taken to DC General Hospital (Map 4; ☎ 675-5000, Ⓜ Stadium-Armory), 199 Massachusetts Ave SE, and lines can be very long.

Pharmacies open 24 hours include CVS at 6-7 Dupont Circle NW (Map 8; ☎ 833-5704; Ⓜ Dupont Circle) and 1199 Vermont Ave NW at Thomas Circle (Map 8; ☎ 737-3962; Ⓜ McPherson Square). Dial ☎ 911 (free from pay phones) for an ambulance.

WOMEN TRAVELERS

Washington is a safe destination for women travelers. It's also a fascinating destination for women – it offers innumerable monuments and historic sites that remember women's key roles in the nation and the city (the National Museum of Women in the Arts, the Women in Military Service to America Memorial, the Mary McLeod Bethune House, etc).

Street hassling isn't much of a problem, particularly in well-touristed areas like the Mall. You might encounter catcalls or whistles at night in party districts such as Georgetown, but even then they're easily ignored. Many American men think that women alone in a bar or club are looking for a pick-up – if you're not, a polite 'No, thank you' usually gets rid of them. If they persist, raise your voice, and staff or fellow patrons will help you give them the heave-ho.

Common-sense safety measures do apply, however: be careful in unfamiliar neighborhoods, bring cab fare when you go out at night, and choose a hotel in an area that makes you feel safe. Accommodations near the Mall and in upper northwest neighborhoods are usually just fine. There's an all-women hostel in town, Thompson-Markward Hall on Capitol Hill (see Places to Stay).

Women's clinics include Planned Parenthood (Map 8; ☎ 347-8512; Ⓜ Farragut North), 1108 16th St NW, offering obstetric, gynecological, and counseling services; and Columbia Hospital for Women (Map 3; ☎ 293-6500; Ⓜ Foggy Bottom), 2425 L St NW, with a range of health-care services.

Washington Women Outdoors (☎ 301-864-3070, http://patriot.net/~wwo/) has a full calendar of hikes, climbs, biking trips, etc that are a great way to befriend local women. The city's women's bookstore, Lammas (Map 8; ☎ 775-8218; Ⓜ Dupont Circle), 1607 17th St NW, is a good place to find out about women-oriented groups and events.

GAY & LESBIAN TRAVELERS

Home to more than 30 national gay and lesbian organizations and more than 300 social, athletic, religious, and political support groups, DC is one of the most gay-friendly cities in the US. The community is most visible in the Dupont Circle and Capitol Hill neighborhoods, where there are many gay-owned and gay-friendly businesses, including the landmark bookstore Lambda Rising (see the Shopping chapter). For a detailed overview of the city's gay nightlife scene, see the special section 'Out on the Town in Gay & Lesbian DC' in the Entertainment chapter.

The *Washington Blade*, the hometown gay and lesbian weekly newspaper, offers coverage of local politics, information about community resources, and lots and lots of nightlife and meeting-place listings. Other good sources include the *Metro Weekly* and *WOMO*, a monthly publication with information about a slew of women's organizations in the Washington area, from the DC Lesbian Avengers to OWLS (Older, Wiser Lesbians). You can also check out the Washington, DC, Convention and Visitors Association's free *Gay & Lesbian Guide to Washington, DC*, available at the organization's Web site (www.washington.org).

The Bi Women's Cultural Alliance (☎ 828-3065) organizes casual get-togethers for lesbians and bisexual women. Women in the Life (Map 8; ☎ 483-9818; Ⓜ Dupont Circle), 1611 Connecticut Ave NW, is an advocacy group for lesbians of color. It sponsors a variety of events during the summer, including poetry readings and monthly parties, at different venues throughout the city. For information, visit the group's Web site (www.womeninthelife.com) or stop by its Dupont Circle office, where local and visiting women can socialize, network, and find out what's going on in the community.

The Whitman-Walker Clinic (Map 8; ☎ 797-3500, www.wwc.org; Ⓜ U St-Cardozo), 1407 S St NW, serves gay and lesbian DC with general health care and HIV/AIDS care. Other useful resources include:

Gay and Lesbian Hotline (☎ 833-3234) – phone counseling; referrals

AIDS Hotline (☎ 800-342-2437) – 24-hour help line

DISABLED TRAVELERS

DC is an excellent destination for disabled visitors. Most museums and major sights are wheelchair-accessible, as are most large hotels and restaurants. The Smithsonian and many other museums arrange special tours for people with with visual, auditory, or other impairments; call the museum or the Smithsonian's main number (☎ 357-2700, TTY 357-1729) for details.

All Metrorail trains and 70% of Metrobuses are wheelchair-accessible. All Metro stations have elevators, and guide dogs are allowed on trains and buses. Disabled people who can't use public transit can use MetroAccess, a door-to-door transport provider – apply for a pass by calling ☎ 301-562-5361.

Out of doors, hindrances to wheelchair users include buckled brick sidewalks in the historic blocks of Georgetown and Capitol Hill, but sidewalks in most other parts of DC are in good shape and have dropped curbs. Unfortunately, only a handful of crosswalks, mostly near the Mall, have audible crossing signals.

Many large hotels have suites for disabled guests, but call the hotel itself – not the chain's 800 number – to check before you reserve. Larger car-rental agencies offer hand-controlled models at no extra charge. All major airlines, Greyhound buses, and Amtrak trains allow service animals on board and frequently sell two-for-one packages if you need an attendant to accompany you.

The Washington, DC, Convention and Visitors Association (Map 3; ☎ 789-7000) can send you a fact sheet with details about accessibility at local attractions, lodgings, and restaurants.

Many organizations and tour providers specialize in helping disabled travelers, including the following:

Mobility International USA (☎ 541-343-1284, fax 541-343-6812, www.miusa.org) PO Box 10767, Eugene, OR 97440

Society for the Advancement of Travel for the Handicapped (SATH; ☎ 212-447-7284, www.sath.org) 347 Fifth Ave, No 610, New York, NY 10016

Hearing-impaired visitors should check out Gallaudet University (TTY 651-5000) in northeast DC, which hosts many lectures and cultural events especially for the deaf.

SENIOR TRAVELERS

Many attractions in DC are free to everyone, but those attractions that do charge admission generally give discounts to seniors (62 or older). Bring a photo ID proving your age. Amtrak and Greyhound also offer senior discounts, as do some hotels and restaurants. The DC Office on Aging (☎ 724-5626; Ⓜ Judiciary Square), 441 4th St NW, distributes a free directory listing city businesses that cut seniors a break; 8:15 am to 4:45 pm weekdays.

Some national advocacy groups that can help you plan your travels include the following:

American Association of Retired Persons (Map 3; ☎ 800-424-3410, www.aarp.org) 601 E St NW, Washington, DC 20049 – an advocacy group for Americans 50 years and older and a good resource for travel bargains. US residents can get one-/three-year memberships for $8/20. Citizens of other countries can get the same memberships for $10/24.

Elderhostel (☎ 877-426-8056) 75 Federal St, Boston, MA 02110 – a nonprofit organization offering seniors the opportunity to attend academic college courses throughout the USA and Canada. Programs last one to three weeks, include meals and accommodations, and are open to people 55 years and older.

WASHINGTON FOR CHILDREN

Washington is a wonderful town to travel in with children. See details in the 'Washington, DC, for Kids' section, immediately following this chapter.

USEFUL ORGANIZATIONS

The American Automobile Association (AAA), with an office near the White House (Map 3), provides its members with maps, accommodations listings, and travel-planning services, plus emergency road and towing services. Call ☎ 800-222-4357 to enroll.

Hostelling International/American Youth Hostels, with its US headquarters in downtown DC (Map 3; ☎ 737-2333, 800-909-4776; Ⓜ Metro Center), 1009 11th St NW, provides a $25 yearlong membership that entitles you to pay some of the lowest bed rates in the USA.

LIBRARIES

DC is a haven for library junkies, with a seemingly endless number of private, public, university, specialty, and historic libraries. From the National Archives to the Folger Shakespeare Library, Historical Society of Washington, DC Library, Dumbarton Oaks Library, and Warren Robbins Library at the National Museum of African Art, the list goes on and on. Many major DC museums maintain public research libraries related to their topic areas, as do federal agencies.

And, of course, the venerable grandfather of US libraries is also here: the Library of Congress (Map 4; ☎ 707-5000; Ⓜ Capitol South), which stashes multiple millions of volumes inside its Capitol Hill buildings. Anyone can use the Library of Congress, but you must apply for a visitor's card first

(see Things to See & Do). Many other private libraries also restrict access – call to ensure you're welcome before you visit.

DC's main public library is Martin Luther King Jr Memorial Library (Map 3; ☎ 727-1221; Ⓜ Metro Center), 901 G St NW, an excellent resource for books, periodicals, and community-events calendars.

UNIVERSITIES

Several large campuses are within city limits, and their vibrant student populations loosen up DC's tie and generally rescue it from workaday stuffiness. Most offer low-cost cultural events, from concerts to films to plays, so they're a good resource for visitors on a budget.

Best known is Georgetown University (Map 7; ☎ 687-0100, www.georgetown.edu), a private Jesuit university at the west end of its namesake neighborhood. Founded in 1789, the school is noted for its politico alumni (a mixed bag including Bill and Hillary Clinton but also Patrick Buchanan and Rep Henry Hyde) and top-ranked law, medical, and foreign-service schools. Its shady campus holds several architecturally attractive 19th-century buildings. You'll see its students holding down barstools all over Georgetown and its crew teams skimming like water bugs down the Potomac.

Just across Rock Creek is George Washington University (Map 3; ☎ 994-1000, www.gwu.edu; Ⓜ Foggy Bottom), which offers heavy competition in the famous-alum department: Jackie O, Colin Powell, and J Edgar Hoover all went here. Its sprawling campus isn't particularly attractive, but its concerts and special events are great, particularly at Lisner Auditorium (☎ 994-6800).

In DC's Shaw district, just north of downtown, is famed Howard University (Map 10; ☎ 806-6100, www.howard.edu; Ⓜ Shaw-Howard U), established in 1867 to educate African Americans freed during the Civil War. This traditionally black university has educated notables such as Toni Morrison and Thurgood Marshall. A major attraction here is the Moorland-Spingarn Research Center (☎ 806-7239), which owns the largest collection of black literature in the US.

Northeast DC has several big campuses, including Gallaudet University (Map 5; ☎ 651-5505, www2.gallaudet.edu), 800 Florida Ave NE, the world's only accredited college for the deaf and hearing-impaired. Here too is sprawling Catholic University of America (Map 5; ☎ 319-5000, www.cua.edu; Ⓜ CUA-Brookland), whose claims to fame include the massive National Shrine of the Immaculate Conception, the Western Hemisphere's biggest (and perhaps its strangest-looking) Catholic church.

In upper northwest DC is American University (☎ 885-1000, www.american.edu; Ⓜ Tenleytown-AU), off Massachusetts Ave. Its Bender Arena (a big concert venue) and hopping calendar of cheap theater, dance performances, and recitals make it a worthwhile stop for travelers.

CULTURAL CENTERS

Washington's cultural centers range from embassies to international arts associations to groups serving the city's diplomatic community. You'll find more cultural centers listed in the Things to See & Do chapter, but here are a few highlights. Most host events such as concerts and art shows as well as social gatherings.

The Meridian International Center (Map 9; ☎ 667-6800; Ⓜ U St-Cardozo), on a gorgeous estate at 1630 Crescent Place NW, is an educational and cultural institution that hosts art exhibitions from abroad and offers services to international visitors and the diplomatic community.

The French Embassy's Maison Française (Map 7; ☎ 944-6090; Metrobus D6), 4101 Reservoir Rd NW, serves as both a gathering place for DC's French community and a major cultural center, hosting fine films, concerts, exhibitions, and lectures year-round. The Mexican Cultural Institute (Map 9; ☎ 728-1628; Ⓜ Columbia Heights), 2829 16th St NW, has a calendar of excellent art exhibits and concerts by Mexican musicians, plus talks on Mexican culture. A similar menu of cultural events is hosted by the Japanese Embassy's Information and Culture Center (Map 8; ☎ 238-6900; Ⓜ Farragut West), 1155 21st St NW.

The Goethe-Institut (Map 3; ☎ 289-1200; Ⓜ Gallery Place), 814 7th St NW, primarily a German-language school, also has a film series, lectures, art exhibits, and the like. The Italian-American Foundation (Map 8; ☎ 387-0600; Ⓜ Dupont Circle), 1860 19th St NW, sponsors lectures and symposia and offers courses on Italian history and culture in conjunction with the Smithsonian. The Irish Center of Washington, DC (Map 5; ☎ 756-2756; Ⓜ Brookland-CUA), 415 Michigan Ave NE, offers cultural programs and services for the public, Irish Americans in particular.

DANGERS & ANNOYANCES
Crime

Washington, DC, has a reputation for drug crimes and violence (44 murders per 100,000 residents as of 1999, more than twice the rate of any comparably sized US city). A lot of that reputation was won during the terrible crack years of the 1980s and '90s, and matters have started to improve: homicides fell 12% in 1999.

Should visitors worry about violent crime, then? Not really. Most violent crime happens between acquaintances, not strangers. Also, most touristed areas of the city are very safe. In fact, the Mall and streets around the Capitol are among the world's most heavily policed areas: several separate forces, from the US Park Police to the DC Metropolitan Police Dept, patrol here. In Dupont Circle, Adams-Morgan, Georgetown, Foggy Bottom, and most of downtown you are also quite safe.

However, several sections of DC are home to people living in desperate circumstances, and you could be at risk there. These areas include all of Anacostia (southeast of the Anacostia River); southeast and northeast DC east of about 15th Sts SE and NE; and the southeastern waterfront near the Navy Yard. These areas have attractions of their own, but use extra caution when visiting them.

Other dodgy areas are pockets within otherwise safe districts or on their fringes.

Travelers should avoid streets east of 13th St NW at night when visiting the Shaw district, and be cautious on 14th St NW between U and M Sts. East of Columbia Rd and 16th St NW, on Adams-Morgan's northwest edge, is another unsafe area. Many residents prefer to take a cab after dark from Dupont Circle to the restaurants and clubs of Adams-Morgan instead of making the short, six-block walk that goes uphill along dark streets.

Standard urban common sense applies: leave valuables at home; store identification and cash securely in a money belt or neck pouch; avoid walking alone through poorly lit areas at night; and if you're lost and confused, try not to look lost and confused.

Heat

DC has very hot, humid summer weather, especially in July and August. It won't fuss visitors coming from the US South or Latin America, but if you're unaccustomed to heat, take a few precautions to avoid sunburn and dehydration. This is particularly important if you plan to visit attractions such as the National Bureau of Printing & Engraving or the Washington Monument, where you must wait in outside lines, or if you're attending a political rally or street fair. Plan your travel for the cooler mornings and late afternoons (advance planning can also reduce your time in line); aim to be inside in air-conditioning during the midday heat; carry water; and wear hats, sunblock, and loose, light clothing.

Street People

The USA has a lamentable record in dealing with its most unfortunate citizens, who often roam the streets of DC and other large cities in the daytime and sleep by storefronts or in alleyways and abandoned buildings. Homeless people may approach you, but nearly all of them are harmless. It's an individual judgment call whether it's appropriate to offer them money or anything else.

EMERGENCIES

To summon an ambulance or police anywhere in the DC area, call ☎ 911 (free from pay phones). Specify your city quadrant; otherwise emergency services might go to the wrong side of town. In nonemergencies, call ☎ 727-1010 to reach DC Metropolitan Police.

The Travelers Aid Society offers information, referral, and assistance to stranded travelers or those in need – hotline service is at ☎ 546-3120; drop-in service is available at its information and referral desks in Union Station (☎ 371-1937), National Airport (☎ 703-417-3975), and Dulles airport (☎ 703-572-8296).

Other useful numbers include the DC Rape Crisis Center (☎ 333-7273) and Poison Control (☎ 362-3867).

LEGAL MATTERS

You must be 21 to buy or drink alcohol in DC. Club and bar bouncers are generally picky about seeing photo ID for proof of age, but in university districts like Georgetown, they might look the other way. Stiff fines, jail time, and loss of your driver's license are the usual penalties for driving while intoxicated.

If you are stopped by the police for any reason, remember that you can't pay fines on the spot (that might be considered bribery). Traffic police will explain your options to you. Usually, you have 30 days to pay a traffic fine.

If you are arrested for more serious offenses, you have the right to remain silent and the right to a lawyer. There is no legal reason to speak to a police officer if you don't want to, but never walk away from an officer until given permission.

If you're arrested, you are legally allowed one phone call. If you don't have a lawyer or relative to help you, call your embassy. The police will give you the phone number upon request.

DC imposes a youth curfew: kids under 17 cannot be in public places any time between 11 pm and 6 am Monday to Thursday and midnight to 6 am Friday to Sunday without a parent or guardian.

For information about driving and car-insurance laws, see the Getting Around chapter.

BUSINESS HOURS

Generally speaking, hours for most businesses and government agencies are 9 to 5 pm weekdays. There are no hard and fast rules, however.

Most major DC museums and tourist attractions are open daily except major holidays, from about 10 am to 5 pm. Some are open shorter hours; a few only open a few days a week. Call ahead if you're unsure.

Restaurants are generally open from 11 or 11:30 am until 2 or 3 pm for lunch and from 5 to 10 or 11 pm for dinner. Clubs usually stay open until 2 am. Shops are usually open from 9 or 10 am to 5 or 6 pm, but in malls they're often open until 9 pm, except on Sunday, when hours are noon to 5 pm.

Post offices are open 8 am to 4 or 5:30 pm weekdays, and some are open 8 am to 3 pm Saturday. Banks are usually open from 9 or 10 am to 5 pm weekdays. A few banks are open on Saturday morning, too (check with the branch).

PUBLIC HOLIDAYS & SPECIAL EVENTS

Washington's biggest annual events are the Cherry Blossom Festival, the Smithsonian Folklife Festival, and Independence Day celebrations. But there are dozens of smaller special events throughout the year. For a full calendar, contact the Washington Convention and Visitors Association (☎ 789-7000). Some highlights are listed below.

Banks, schools, government offices, and some attractions close on national holidays. Transportation runs on a Sunday schedule. Holidays falling on Sunday are usually celebrated on the following Monday. In the list below, national holidays are marked by an asterisk.

January

*New Year's Day – the 1st.

*Martin Luther King Jr Day – 3rd Monday. Celebrates the Civil Rights–movement leader's birthday. Orators recite King's 'I Have a Dream' speech at the Lincoln Memorial.

Presidential Inauguration – the 20th, every four years. DC's ultimate social-political event involves a whole string of balls, receptions, parties, and, for ordinary folk, gathering at the Capitol to watch a tiny guy, far away, say something over a Bible.

February

Black History Month – February's a big deal in DC, with many special black-history programs at museums throughout the city. Pick up a calendar at the Smithsonian.

*Presidents' Day – 3rd Monday. Celebrates the birthdays of Abraham Lincoln and George Washington. Lincoln's Gettysburg Address is read at his memorial. Special events at Mount Vernon (see the Excursions chapter).

Chinese New Year's Parade – mid-month. Dances and firecrackers abound, lighting up Chinatown (☎ 724-4091).

March

St Patrick's Day – the 17th. DC's Irish and wanna-be Irish whoop it up at a parade down Constitution Ave, a 10K race, and Irish pubs across the city.

Smithsonian Kite Festival – last Saturday. Fly your colors at this annual celebration (see the boxed text).

National Cherry Blossom Festival – late March to early April. This two-week arts and culture fest celebrates the blooming of DC's cherry trees and culminates in a parade extravaganza. See the boxed text in the Facts about Washington, DC chapter, and www.gwjapan.com/cherryblossom.

April

Easter – 1st spring Sunday after a full moon, usually in April. Americans dye eggs and nosh on chocolate bunnies. The White House Easter Egg Roll, on the South Lawn, is a special Easter-Monday treat for kiddies three to six, hosted by the first lady. Enter at the East Gate on E Executive Ave (see www .whitehouse.gov).

Shakespeare's Birthday – the 23rd. The Folger Shakespeare Library (☎ 544-4600) hosts kids' events and Renaissance-themed concerts and opens its beautiful reading rooms to the public.

Smithsonian Craft Show – late April. Hundreds of artists sell their work at the National Building Museum (☎ 357-4000).

FilmFest DC – late April/early May. Cutting-edge film at venues all over the city (☎ 628-3456).

May

Annual Georgetown Garden Tour – variable dates. Private gardens of historic houses are opened to the public, with hostesses at each. Call ☎ 333-4953 for details; $15 each.

*Memorial Day – last Monday. Honors war dead (and marks the unofficial start of the summer tourist season). Wreaths are laid at Arlington National Cemetery and the Vietnam Veterans Memorial.

Gay Black Pride – Memorial Day weekend. The nation's largest annual Gay Black Pride celebration draws participants from across the country.

June

Gay Pride Day – early June. 'Capital Pride,' DC's version of the international holiday, draws thousands of marchers to the Mall, and many bars and clubs host special events.

Smithsonian Folklife Festival – 10 days before July 4. The Smithsonian sponsors a rollicking music, food, and cultural festival on the Mall that celebrates a US state and a foreign country (www.folklife.si.edu).

July

*Independence Day – the 4th. Commemorates the adoption of the Declaration of Independence, in 1776. Huge crowds gather on the National Mall to watch fireworks, listen to free concerts, and picnic in the sunshine. The Declaration is read from the National Archives' steps.

August

National Frisbee Festival – late August or early September. Crowded annual competition outside the National Museum of Air and Space features many leaping humans and canines (☎ 800-786-9240).

September

*Labor Day – 1st Monday. Honors working people; on the preceding Sunday, the National Symphony Orchestra closes its summer season with a free concert on the West Lawn of the Capitol.

DC Blues Festival – early September. A lineup of top local blues acts at Rock Creek Park's Carter Barron Ampitheater; free. Call ☎ 828-3028 for information.

Adams-Morgan Days – variable weekend in mid-September. DC's biggest neighborhood festival takes over 18th St NW with live music, vendors, and food stalls (www.adamsmorganday.org).

Flying Your Colors

On the last Saturday of each March, the skies near the Washington Monument come alive with banners and streamers of many colors, along with strange creatures not usually allowed in DC airspace: flying frogs, enormous space aliens, dragons, even the occasional Pokémon. It's the Smithsonian's annual Kite Festival, sponsored by the National Museum of Air and Space.

The festival – celebrating its 35th anniversary in 2001 – includes competitions in kite design, speed, and performance, not to mention beauty and humor. Local kitemakers display their works, kite clubs from around the country compete, and vendors sell unique kites. The festival is popular with small kids and usually begins around 10 am. For information, contact the Smithsonian at ☎ 357-2700 or see www.si.edu/tsa/rap/kitefest.htm.

Hispanic Heritage Month – September 15 to October 15. Cultural, entertainment, and educational events celebrating Hispanic life in DC.

October

*Columbus Day – 2nd Monday.

Marine Corps Marathon – final week. This popular road race starts at the Iwo Jima Memorial, circles around DC, and ends up where it started (☎ 703-784-2225, www.marinemarathon.com).

Halloween – the 31st. Trick-or-treating in quiet neighborhoods; a big bar night in Adams-Morgan and Georgetown.

November

*Veterans Day – the 11th. Special memorial services honor military veterans at Arlington Cemetery and the Vietnam Veterans Memorial.

*Thanksgiving – 4th Thursday in November. The day that Americans stuff turkeys, and then stuff themselves.

December

Kennedy Center Holiday Celebration – all month. Free seasonal music and activities, including gospel and a festive *Messiah* sing-along (tickets available at ☎ 467-4600).

National Christmas Tree & Menorah Lighting – 2nd Thursday. The president does the honors on the Ellipse.

*Christmas – the 25th. Candlelight tours of the White House; Christmas services at the National Cathedral.

New Year's Eve – the 31st. Much drinking and ballyhoo in the bars of Georgetown, Adams-Morgan, and Dupont Circle.

WORK

Foreign visitors are not legally allowed to work in the USA without the appropriate working visa. But US citizens – especially young ones – flock here in summer to take up internships on Capitol Hill, at federal agencies, and in think tanks. If you want an internship, it's important to start looking early – the fall of the preceding year is a good time to start.

Find your congressional representatives' office addresses via the Capitol switchboard (☎ 224-3121). You should remember that most internships are unpaid or involve only small stipends that probably won't cover your expenses.

Washington, DC, for Kids

Washington may be the best big city in the US to travel with children. There are endless things to do: all the major museums are oriented (in part or in total) toward kids; all the monuments and historical sites are child-friendly; and there's plenty of parkland and green space where kids can romp. In addition, a vacation to Washington is usually educational – kids come away having learned something about history, art, or science, which is more than can be said of the average beach vacation. And, best of all, most attractions here are absolutely free.

Planning with Kids

When planning a day of sightseeing with kids, follow commonsense rules. Make sure everyone's wearing comfortable clothes and shoes, because lots of walking is necessary on the National Mall and in museums. Carry snacks and water and, in summertime, put sunblock and hats on the kids. It's wise to bring a comfortable baby carrier or stroller for small ones, too. Visit popular attractions, such as the Washington Monument, early in the day so that you needn't wait in long lines. Finally, don't do too much in one day. The downtown museums are quite large and often crowded, so you can easily spend a full day seeing just one.

If you're unsure what to do in DC, try Children's Concierge (☎ 301-948-3312, www.kidsgotoo.com), 15757 Crabbs Branch Way, Rockville, MD 20855, which arranges family-friendly itineraries and outdoor activities customized to your interests.

There's a children's curfew in DC. Unless accompanied by a parent or guardian, kids under 17 cannot be in public places between 11 pm and 6 am Monday to Thursday and midnight to 6 am Friday to Sunday.

Right: Getting dirty on the 'National Lawn'

Books & Informational Resources The *Washington Post*'s Weekend section, published each Friday, features the Saturday's Child pages, which detail upcoming family- and kid-oriented activities, exhibits, and cultural events. See also the great 'Our Kids' Web site (www.our-kids.com) for event listings and local kid-related news.

Available in local bookshops, Pamela McDermott's *Going Places with Children in Washington, DC* ($15) provides a kid's-eye view of capital attractions. For general advice on traveling with kids anywhere in the world, see *Travel with Children*, by Lonely Planet cofounder Maureen Wheeler.

Childcare Some larger hotels help arrange babysitting, usually through outside providers rather than an on-site daycare center. Ask when you make reservations. Usually, rates are $12 to $15 per hour.

If the hotel doesn't have a favored agency, WeeSit (☎ 703-764-1542) is a reliable choice for day or overnight care. This agency works with hotels all over DC and can send sitters to your lodging. Rates are $13/12 per hour for kids/babies under 12 months, with a four-hour minimum and $12 transportation charge. Each additional sibling costs $1 per hour.

Discounts Children receive discounts on many things in DC, ranging from theater tickets to hotel rooms. The definition of 'child' varies widely – some places consider anyone under 18 a child and thus eligible for discounts. Other places include only children under six.

Things to See & Do with Kids

Listed here are some lesser-known options for keeping kids busy and happy in Washington. See the Things to See & Do chapter for details on well-known attractions like the Smithsonian's National Museum of Natural History and the National Air & Space Museum, as well as the National Zoo.

VERONICA GARBUTT

Left: These kids don't know they're learning.

Museums The **Capital Children's Museum** (Map 4; ☎ 675-4120; Ⓜ Union Station), 800 3rd St NE, features inviting hands-on exhibits for kids, including a do-it-yourself television studio, dolls, a cave, miniature Mexican village, fire station, hands-on chemistry lab, a what's-under-the-street exhibit, games and puppet playrooms, and maze and bubble rooms. Outside is a 'Fantasy Garden' of mosaic sculptures. Weekends are filled with hands-on craft classes and demonstrations. Open 10 am to 5 pm daily; $6 for everyone over age two.

The **Washington Dolls' House & Toy Museum** (Map 11; ☎ 244-0024; Ⓜ Friendship Heights), 5236 44th St NW, displays a marvelous collection of Victorian dollhouses and toys: a teeny Capitol, mansions complete with tiny china and linens, amazingly detailed castles, etc. The museum's miniatures shop sells dolls, accessories, and dollhouse-building kits. Open 10 am to 5 pm Monday to Saturday; $4/2 adults/kids under 12.

National Geographic Explorers' Hall (Map 8; ☎ 857-7588; Ⓜ Farragut North), 17th and M Sts NW, features interactive exhibits on natural history, dinosaurs, weather, animals, and space exploration (see details in the Things to See & Do chapter). In Arlington, the **Newseum** (see the Arlington map; ☎ 888-639-7386; Ⓜ Rosslyn), 1101 Wilson Blvd, includes state-of-the-art newsrooms and TV studios where kids can write and tape their own news broadcasts (see details in the Excursions chapter).

Outdoor Attractions After the kids tire of museums, take them outdoors to air them out. In addition to the beloved National Zoo, here are other options for al fresco fun.

The **antique carousel** on the Mall's Jefferson Drive (Map 3) offers rides on old-fashioned colorful ponies; across the Mall, kids climb on sculptures made by famous artists in the funky, child-friendly **National Sculpture Garden**. To the west, children can't stay away from the **Einstein statue**,

RICK GERHARTER

Right: Kids can't stay off the world's cuddliest genius.

behind the National Academy of Sciences on Constitution Ave. The grandfatherly scientist sits on a bench, and tots crawl into his lap (you'll never find a better photo opportunity).

Rock Creek Park has several kids' attractions. The **Nature Center & Planetarium** (see the Rock Creek Park map in the Things to See & Do chapter; ☎ 426-6829), off Military Rd in upper northwest DC, features hands-on ecological displays, kids' nature hikes, and planetarium shows. Farther south at **Pierce Mill** (☎ 426-6908), Tilden St, kids can watch rangers demonstrate the circa-1820 mill and try it themselves.

If you're up for a drive, the DC area's best playground is **Cabin John Regional Park** (☎ 301-299-0024), 7140 Tuckerman Lane, north of DC in Rockville, Maryland, accessed via Hwy 270 from the Beltway. Its great playground equipment includes a rocket and plane-shaped slides, a huge wooden climbing structure, mazes, playhouses, and swings. In town, drive to East Potomac Park's **Hains Point** (Map 6) in southwest DC – near the point's tip, you'll find a good playground with lovely river views. In the heart of Adams-Morgan is **Kalorama Park Playground** (Map 9), on Columbia Rd NW.

In quaint Leesburg, Virginia, the **Animal Park** (☎ 703-433-0002), 19270 James Monroe Hwy, is a petting zoo with all things fuzzy and snuggly – see details in the Excursions chapter.

Kids' Performances & Programs The Smithsonian's Arts & Industries Building, on the Mall, holds **Discovery Theater** (☎ 357-1500; Ⓜ Smithsonian), which stages performances and puppet shows that delight kids. In Vienna, Virginia, at Wolf Trap Farm Park (☎ 703-255-1860), 1624 Trap Rd, the **Theatre-in-the-Woods** presents dance, music, theater, storytelling, and clown performances all summer long in a charming woodland setting (see details in the Excursions chapter).

Glen Echo Park (☎ 301-492-6229), just over the border in Maryland, includes a theater and puppet theater for kids (not to mention a historic

carousel and a great kids' ecological museum). Performances run all year, and kids can also take theater, dance, and art classes here (see details in the Excursions chapter).

The **Hirshhorn Museum** (Map 3; ☎ 357-3235; Ⓜ L'Enfant Plaza), Independence Ave and 7th St SW, offers great art programs for kids six to nine. At 10 am on Saturday, 'Young at Art' programs introduce children to artistic study; the regularly scheduled 'Improv Art' classes give kids the chance to

RICK GERHARTER

make their own artworks. The museum runs special tours for kids, too, on topics like 'Animals in Art.'

Children interested in crafts will enjoy the **Textile Museum**'s Learning Center (Map 8; ☎ 667-0441; Ⓜ Dupont Circle), 2320 S St NW, with hands-on interactive exhibits that teach you about weaving, dyeing, embroidering, and patterning fabrics.

The Washington National Cathedral (Map 11; ☎ 537-2934), Massachusetts and Wisconsin Aves NW, offers its family-oriented **Medieval Workshop** ($4), where kids can make gargoyles or stained-glass windows, from 10 am to 2 pm each Saturday. The Historical Society of Washington, DC, based at Dupont Circle's Heurich Mansion (Map 8; ☎ 785-2068; Ⓜ Dupont Circle), offers 'Samantha' programs for kids seven to 12; these explore Washington life in 1904 through the eyes of a fictional little girl ($25).

Events for Kids

Late March/early April: White House Easter Egg Roll – Kiddies three to six get to romp around the South Lawn, see the First Lady, and hunt for sweets and prizes. See details at www.whitehouse.gov; free.

Late March: Kite Festival – on the last Saturday of the month near the Washington Monument; see the boxed text in the Facts for the Visitor chapter.

June: Children's Festival – Concerts, plays, and interactive programs are featured at this festival sponsored by the Park Service and Capital Children's Museum at Carter Barron Amphitheater, Rock Creek Park. Call ☎ 619-7222 for details; $10.

Right: The Sculpture Garden at the Hirshhorn Museum

TONY WHEELER

Kid-Friendly Places to Stay

Many DC hotels, especially national chains, allow children under 16 to share a room with their parents for free. Some add a fee for an extra cot or rollaway bed. Small hotels and B&Bs might not cut you the same deal – indeed, some upscale B&Bs bar children altogether. Ask about rules and discounts when you book.

An all-suite hotel, such as **Doubletree Guest Suites** (*Map 3; ☎ 333-8060, 2500 Pennsylvania Ave NW;* Ⓜ *Foggy Bottom*), is a good family choice – kids have room to run around, and you can make meals in the attached kitchenette. 'Kids' clubs,' which are featured at some upscale DC hotels, include activities, bedtime goodies, and discount passes to local attractions.

The mid-range **Hotel Harrington** (*Map 3; ☎ 800-424-8532;* Ⓜ *Federal Triangle*), just north of the Mall at 11th and E Sts NW, is a family favorite where deluxe family rooms cost $119 to $125. A top-end family-friendly downtown hotel is **Loews L'Enfant Plaza Hotel** (*Map 5; ☎ 484-1000, 480 L'Enfant Plaza SW*), a few blocks south of the Mall and atop the L'Enfant Plaza Metro. Kids under 18 stay free; cribs and rollaways are free. There are recreation programs, kids' menus, a 'Back House' hotel tour for kids, and a 'Bark Ball' for pets. Rates are $189 to $309, but seasonal specials drop as low as $129.

Kid-Friendly Places to Eat

Many restaurants, particularly those close to the Mall, offer inexpensive entrées like burgers and peanut-butter-and-jelly sandwiches to diners under 12. But most families visiting downtown attractions find that food courts – especially the big ones at the **Old Post Office Pavilion** and **Union Station** – are the best option. Picky kids can choose among a variety of cuisines, no one gripes if they make noise, and prices are reasonable (see the boxed text 'Food Courts' in the Places to Eat chapter).

Another fine downtown choice, **Sholl's Colonial Cafeteria** (*Map 3; ☎ 296-3065, 1990 K St NW;* Ⓜ *Farragut West*) offers low-cost cafeteria standards and a family-friendly atmosphere. Adventurous little diners will like eating with their hands in Adams-Morgan's plentiful Ethiopian restaurants (see the Places to Eat chapter).

For dessert, good children are taken to the National Museum of American History's **Ice Cream Parlor** (Ⓜ *Federal Triangle*), with its old-fashioned setting and big hot-fudge sundaes; **Gifford's Ice Cream** (*☎ 301-907-3426, 7720 Wisconsin Ave NW;* Ⓜ *Bethesda*), in business since 1938; and **Max's Ice Cream** (*Map 11; ☎ 333-3111, 2416 Wisconsin Ave*), where 200 flavors are made on-site.

Shopping with Kids

Most Smithsonian museums and the National Zoo have large gift shops, many of them aimed primarily at small children. These stores sell educational toys and games, books, stuffed animals, dolls, kites, model-airplane

RICK GERHARTER

and build-your-own-dinosaur kits, and all kinds of other kid-friendly stuff (see details in the Shopping chapter).

Washington also has a handful of great independent toy shops. In Union Station, check out the **Great Train Store** (☎ 371-2881), jumping with both tykes and adult hobbyists. You can get Thomas the Tank Engine choo-choos as well as sophisticated Lionel railway sets. Union Station's main hall features seasonal displays of toy trains, especially at Christmas.

Sullivan's Toy Store (Map 11; ☎ 362-1343; Metrobus Nos 30, 32, 34, or 36), 3412 Wisconsin Ave NW, specializes in European and educational toys that are a nice antidote to the video-games fare of many kids' stores. If you're in the mood for a serious romp in toyland, however, set the kids free in **FAO Schwarz** (Map 7; ☎ 965-7000; Ⓜ Foggy Bottom), in the Georgetown Park mall at M St NW and Wisconsin Ave.

The **Discovery Channel Store** (Map 3; ☎ 639-0908; Ⓜ Gallery Place), 601 F St NW in the MCI Center, is a museum/toy store that sprinkles educational displays on flight, fossils, weather, animals, and other scientific subjects among its several floors of toys, games, and clothing. The store's overwhelming for adults, what with all the video displays and excited children, but kids themselves adore it.

Right: The Great Train Store at Union Station

The **Left Bank** (Map 8; ☎ 518-4000; Ⓜ Dupont Circle), 1627 Connecticut Ave NW, is ostensibly an art and book shop for adults, but its focus is on French and European cartoon stars. Sophisticated kiddies love its posters, books, and toys featuring Babar, Madeleine, and Tintin.

Getting There & Away

AIR
Departure Tax

Airport departure taxes are usually included in the price of tickets bought in the US, but they may not be included with tickets bought abroad. A US$6 airport departure tax is charged to all passengers bound for any foreign destination from a US city. A US$6.50 North American Free Trade Agreement tax is charged to foreigners entering the US from abroad. Both fees are essentially 'hidden' taxes added to the purchase price of your ticket.

Airports

A trio of large airports serves DC: Ronald Reagan Washington National (across the river from downtown), Dulles International (26 miles from DC in the Virginia suburbs), and Baltimore-Washington International (in Maryland). National mainly handles short-range domestic flights. If you're coming from

across the country or over the sea, you'll likely land at Dulles (the largest airport) or BWI. Flights to National often cost more than those to Dulles or BWI.

See the Getting Around chapter for information on ground transportation serving the three airports.

Ronald Reagan Washington National Airport National (Map 6; ☎ 703-417-8000, www.metwashairports.com), on the Potomac's west bank, is very convenient to DC. But because it's in a dense urban region, it's subject to slot restrictions and a perimeter rule that limit its flights. As of 2000, Congress, which partially controls National's budget, was maneuvering to increase the airport's flights, so more and cheaper flights may be available here in coming years (to the distress of Washingtonians concerned about airport noise). Flights here are exclusively domestic except for service to Canada.

National has three terminals: Terminal A is the little-used original airport; Terminals B and C are new, busy, and attached to a big shopping mall and Metrorail, DC's subway system. TWA, Northwest, and Midway serve Terminal A. Terminals B and C house US Airways (and its East Coast shuttle), Air Canada, American, United, Delta (and its shuttle), and America West. (See Major Airlines, later in this chapter, for airline phone numbers.)

Three information desks, one in the center of each terminal, provide local maps and pamphlets describing tourist attractions and lodging. ATMs, Thomas Cook currency exchange, the Traveler's Aid Society (☎ 703-417-3972), a mail drop, and many shops and restaurants are all inside the airport. Smoking is not permitted.

Should you have any time on your hands, be sure to check out the Exhibit Hall in lonely Terminal A, which displays artifacts found in archaeological digs on airport property.

Dulles International Airport

RICK GERHARTER

Dulles International Airport Dulles International Airport (Map 1; ☎ 703-572-2700, www.metwashairports.com) is the area's largest airport and is the one you'll likely use. A beautiful Eero Saarinen–designed building that looms like a space-age castle in the Virginia suburbs, west of DC, the airport is served by many international and national carriers, including US Airways (and its East Coast shuttle), United, American, Delta, TWA, British Airways, Air Canada, Air France, Lufthansa, and KLM. Dulles International Airport's flights are easier to obtain and cheaper than National's, and both domestic and international flights (to Asia, Europe, South America, the Middle East, and Africa) depart here.

In the main terminal are the ticketing counters, baggage claim, information desk, ATMs, shops, Thomas Cook currency exchange, and Travelers' Aid (☎ 703-661-8636). A few airlines depart from this terminal, but most depart from midfield concourses, to which you're taken by lumbering transport vehicles that resemble lunar landers. Smoking is banned except in designated lounges.

Baltimore-Washington International Airport BWI (☎ 800-435-9294, www.bwiairport.com) is in Maryland, near Baltimore. It too offers abundant domestic and long-distance services (Europe, South America, Canada, and the Middle East) and its terminals offer a complete range of traveler services. Often, you can obtain cheaper fares to BWI than to either National or Dulles, so despite its geographic inconvenience, this is a handy airport for those on a budget.

Other Parts of the USA

Nonstop flights link nearly all major US cities to at least one DC airport. A dozen US carriers offer service to National, and most major carriers are at Dulles and BWI, too. However, National is allowed to receive flights only from destinations within a 1250-mile perimeter – so if you're coming from the western states, you must fly into either Dulles or BWI, or change planes along the way.

A good place to begin the hunt for the cheapest fare is the Sunday 'Travel' section of the *Washington Post* and similar sections in the *New York Times, Chicago Tribune*, and *Los Angeles Times*, in which there are many

Air Travel Glossary

Baggage Allowance This is written on your ticket and usually includes one 20kg item for the aircraft's hold and one item of hand luggage.

Bucket Shops These unbonded travel agencies specialize in discounted airline tickets.

Bumped Even if you have a confirmed seat, that doesn't mean you're going to get on the plane (see Overbooking).

Cancellation Penalties If you have to cancel or change a discounted ticket, heavy penalties are often involved; sometimes, you can take out insurance against such penalties. Some airlines impose penalties on regular tickets, too, particularly against 'no-show' passengers.

Check-In Airlines ask you to check in a certain time period before your scheduled departure (usually one to two hours for international flights). If you check in late and the flight's overbooked, the airline can cancel your reservation and give away your seat.

Confirmation Even if you have a ticket showing a certain flight and departure date, this doesn't mean you have a seat until an agent has checked with the airline that your status is 'OK' or confirmed. Meanwhile, you could be just 'on request.'

Lost Tickets If you lose your ticket, an airline usually treats it like a traveler's check and, after inquiries, issues you another. Legally, however, an airline is entitled to treat it like cash; if you lose the ticket, it's gone forever. Take good care of your tickets.

No-Shows These passengers fail to show up for their flight. Full-fare passengers who don't turn up are sometimes entitled to travel on a later flight. The rest are penalized (see Cancellation Penalties).

On Request This is an unconfirmed flight reservation.

Onward Tickets An entry requirement in many countries is a ticket out of the country. If you're unsure of your next move, the easiest solution is to buy the cheapest onward ticket to a neighboring country or a ticket from a reliable airline that can later be refunded if you don't use it.

Open Jaw Tickets These return tickets allow you to fly out to one place but return from another; thus you don't have to backtrack to your arrival point.

Overbooking Airlines hate flying with empty seats. Since a few passengers fail to show up for most flights, airlines often overbook their planes. Usually excess passengers make up for no-shows, but occasionally somebody is bumped – usually passengers who check in late.

Point-to-Point Tickets These discount tickets can be bought on some routes if passengers waive their rights to a stopover.

Reconfirmation At least 72 hours prior to departure time of an onward or return flight, you must contact the airline and 'reconfirm' that you'll be on the flight. If you don't, the airline can delete you from the passenger list, and you could lose your seat.

Restrictions Discounted tickets often have various restrictions – such as advance payment, minimum and maximum periods you must be away (eg, a minimum of two weeks or a maximum of one year), and penalties for changes.

Stand-By This is a discounted ticket on which you only fly if there is a seat free at the last moment. Stand-by fares are usually available only on domestic routes.

Travel Periods Fares vary with the season. There are low (off-peak), high (peak), and often low-shoulder and high shoulder seasons. Usually, fares depend on the date of your outbound flight – if you depart in high season and return in low, you pay high-season fare.

travel agents' ads. Friday's *Wall Street Journal* travel section offers useful tips for business travelers. The Washington office of Council Travel and the HI/AYH Travel Center at the DC hostel (see Travel Agencies, below) are good places to go for competitive fares and air-travel information. Council has offices in other US cities, too.

Fares change constantly, but nearly all the cheapest ones require an advance purchase of seven to 21 days. When buying tickets, especially if changing planes to reach National, remember that most big airlines work on the hub-and-spoke system. Booking flights through an airline's hub gets you cheaper fares and more frequent flights than booking nonstop service between two 'spoke' points.

At the time of writing, high-season (late spring/early summer), economy-class, round-trip fares from major US cities to DC included the following:

Chicago	US$195
Los Angeles	US$435
Miami	US$179
Seattle	US$470

Use these fares as a benchmark only; fares change frequently and your travel agent can apprise you of the best current prices.

From New York's La Guardia Airport, Delta's and US Airways' shuttles offer frequent weekday flights, mainly catering to business travelers. (If you've a bit of extra time, however, Amtrak service between DC and New York is cheaper; see Train, below.)

Delta's shuttle leaves National every hour on the half hour; roundtrip fare is US$174. US Airways' shuttle, leaving every hour on the hour, costs a bit less. Note that in spring 2000, US Airways was in the process of being acquired by United, and its National shuttles were expected to be sold to a new airline, DC Air. Travel agents can apprise you of the shuttles' current status and fares.

Canada
Canada is the only foreign country with direct flights to National. From Ottawa, Toronto, and Montréal, United and Air Canada fly daily to both National and Dulles. Fares fluctuate dramatically with season and airline whim, but they're usually between US$250 and US$350 (C$370 and C$520) for roundtrip economy-class tickets in high season.

From other Canadian cities, you'll likely fly into Dulles. United and Air Canada also serve Halifax (Nova Scotia) with daily Dulles-bound flights. Travel CUTS in Canada (www.travelcuts.com) offers good prices to DC and most other US destinations.

Australia & New Zealand
There are no direct flights from Down Under to DC. You must fly to the USA's West Coast and change planes there. But Qantas and Air New Zealand make the process easy with code-sharing connections to Dulles or BWI on domestic flights from San Francisco or Los Angeles.

An Auckland–Los Angeles flight takes about 13 hours; a Sydney–Los Angeles flight takes about 14 hours. Typical roundtrip economy fares from Australia (Melbourne or Sydney) are between A$1400 to A$1800; fares from Auckland are about NZ$1800 to NZ$2000.

From Australia, Qantas, British Airways, and American Airlines have a Global Explorer pass that enables you to fly from Sydney to the US to Europe to Asia and back to Australia for A$1880 to A$2400. From New Zealand, a similar ticket via North America, Europe, and Asia on Air New Zealand (and some other airlines) costs about NZ$2300.

Weekend newspaper travel sections in both countries' major cities have ads for travel agents specializing in cheap fares. In Australia, Flight Centre and STA agencies offer competitively priced tickets. STA operates in New Zealand, too.

The UK & Continental Europe
There are abundant nonstop flights, particularly with United, from European capitals to Dulles. British Airways and Virgin Atlantic fly daily from London. Summer is the peak time to travel, so fares will be higher then. They may also rise on weekends. London is an excellent place to find discounted tickets; you will be able to get heavily discounted

1st-class and business tickets as well as cheap economy tickets. The weekly magazine *Time Out* and the *Evening Standard* are good sources for ads touting cheap fares. Good agents for low fares in London include:

Campus Travel (☎ 020-7938-2188) 174 Kensington High St, London W8 7RG; and (☎ 020-7437-7767) 28A Poland St, London W1V 3DB

STA (☎ 020-7581-4132) 86 Old Brompton Rd, London SW7 3LQ

Trailfinders (☎ 020-7938-3939) 194 Kensington High St, London W8 7RG

Travel Cuts (☎ 020-7637-3161) 295A Regent St, London W1

London usually offers the best deals for flying across the pond, but there are numerous direct connections from continental cities, too. KLM flies daily from Amsterdam; Air France flies daily from Paris; Lufthansa flies daily from Frankfurt and Munich; Sabena flies daily from Brussels; and Spanair flies from Madrid several times weekly. United flies several times weekly from all these cities, too, plus Milan.

At press time, sample fares for economy-class roundtrip tickets in high season (spring/summer) included the following:

London   US$825 (UK£560)
Paris   US$940 (FF6835)
Frankfurt   US$955 (DM2070)

Central America & Mexico

United and Mexicana fly to Dulles from Mexico City daily. You can expect to pay about US$500 (4615 pesos) for an economy-class roundtrip ticket in summer. Several airlines provide direct Dulles flights from the Caribbean (Puerto Rico, the Virgin Islands, Barbados, and Trinidad, among other destinations) and Central America (Costa Rica, El Salvador, and Belize).

Asia

There are limited direct flights from Asian capitals to Dulles: Northwest flies thrice weekly from Delhi; Korean Air flies thrice weekly from Seoul; and United and All Nippon fly daily from Tokyo. As a benchmark, you can expect to pay about US$1360

(¥145,488) for an economy-class roundtrip ticket in summer from Tokyo.

From other Asian cities, you're best off flying to San Francisco or Los Angeles and jumping onto a transcontinental domestic flight there.

Africa

DC's East African community ensures good service to that side of the continent: Ethiopian Airlines flies thrice weekly to Dulles from Addis Ababa. From most other African countries, however, including South Africa, it's easiest – and cheapest – to fly to New York's Kennedy Airport and connect with a domestic flight for the short hop down to DC.

Major Airlines

Most major airlines offer service to DC. Here's a partial list of those with toll-free telephone numbers (free within the US). Major domestic carriers are noted with an asterisk.

Air Canada	☎ 888-247-2262
Air France	☎ 800-237-2747
Air New Zealand	☎ 800-262-1234
All Nippon (ANA)	☎ 800-235-9262
American Airlines*	☎ 800-433-7300
British Airways	☎ 800-247-9297
Canadian Airlines	☎ 800-426-7000
Continental Airlines*	☎ 800-525-0280
Delta Air Lines (& Shuttle)*	☎ 800-221-1212
Ethiopian Airlines	☎ 877-389-6753
KLM Royal Dutch Airlines	☎ 800-374-7747
Korean Air	☎ 800-438-5000
Lufthansa	☎ 800-645-3880
Mexicana	☎ 800-531-7921
Northwest Airlines*	☎ 800-225-2525
Qantas Airways	☎ 800-227-4500
Sabena	☎ 800-955-2000
Southwest Airlines*	☎ 800-435-9792
Spanair	☎ 888-545-5757
TACA	☎ 800-535-8780
TWA*	☎ 800-221-2000
United Airlines*	☎ 800-241-6522
US Airways (& Shuttle)*	☎ 800-428-4322
Virgin Atlantic	☎ 800-862-8621

In addition to their desks at local airports, many airlines maintain downtown offices in the K St NW corridor, clustered near the intersection with 16th St NW, including American, United, US Airways, and TWA. If you need to talk to an airline representative in person, these offices can save you a trip to the airport.

Travel Agencies

Two convenient agencies specializing in low-budget and student-oriented travel are Council Travel (Map 7; ☎ 337-6464, www .counciltravel.com), 3301 M St NW in Georgetown, and Hostelling International/ American Youth Hostel Travel Center (Map 3; ☎ 737-2333, 800-909-4776), on the 1st floor of its central DC hostel headquarters, downtown at 1009 11th St NW, at K St. They help find airfare discounts and sell Eurail passes; the Travel Center hosts travel seminars and maintains a small library and bookstore as well. Both are closed Sunday.

BUS

Intercity bus service in the US is an option of last resort: it's cheap but it sure isn't pleasant. But it's useful if you're on a tight budget or bound to DC from a small town that lacks air or rail service.

Greyhound (☎ 800-231-2222 for fares and schedules, 214-849-8966 for customer service, www.greyhound.com), which provides nationwide service, arrives and departs the Greyhound Terminal at 1005 1st St NE, at L St (Map 4). Peter Pan Trailways (☎ 800-343-9999), with northeastern US service, uses a terminal just opposite Greyhound's. This run-down neighborhood is deserted after dark, and the nearest Metro station is several blocks south (via 1st St NE), at Union Station. Cabs are usually available at the terminal, and you should hail or call one; don't walk across town from the terminal at night.

Greyhound's services include several buses daily to and from New York ($56 roundtrip in summer with seven-day advance purchase), Boston ($79), Philadelphia ($33), Miami ($99), and other cities all over the US. You'll save money if you book

a few weeks in advance. Children, seniors, disabled people, and military personnel qualify for discounted fares; inquire when you purchase your ticket.

TRAIN

Passenger trains from around the USA arrive directly downtown at magnificent Union Station, the flagship terminal of the national Amtrak system (☎ 800-872-7245, www.amtrak.com). It's the most enjoyable way to arrive in DC. At 50 Massachusetts Ave NE on Capitol Hill, a few blocks from the Mall, Union Station (Map 4; ☎ 371-9441) has a Metro station in its basement, which makes getting to your lodgings easy.

Amtrak's ticketing counter is on the station's ground floor near the main staircases. You can pick up timetables here. Departure gates are behind the counter, on the station's north side. Currency exchange, ATMs, pay phones, restrooms, and abundant shops and restaurants are inside the station.

Detail of Union Station

RICHARD CUMMINS

GETTING THERE & AWAY

Amtrak has a complex fare system, and its Web site doesn't provide general route fares. You must select a date and route and pretend to book – then it gives you a fare only for that time and route. If you buy at Union Station, the actual fare will probably be a bit different from the amount quoted on the Web site.

Most trains departing Union Station are bound for other East Coast destinations. The station is the southern terminus of the rail corridor from DC to New York to Boston that earns Amtrak most of its income. Trains also depart for Virginia destinations (Richmond, Williamsburg, Virginia Beach); southern destinations including Florida and New Orleans; Montréal, Canada; and Amtrak's national hub, Chicago, where you can connect to Midwest- and West Coast–bound trains.

MARC and VRE commuter trains connect Union Station to Virginia and Maryland. See the Getting Around chapter for details on fares and routes.

Northeast Corridor Trains

Service on the Northeast corridor – stopping at Baltimore, Philadelphia, New York, New Haven (Connecticut), Boston, and intermediate points – departs DC all day long. There's usually at least one departure per hour on weekdays. Regular (unreserved) trains are cheapest, but pokey. Express Metroliners (reserved) to New York are faster, and fastest of all are the new, superfast Acela trains that zing to New York (and then to Boston) at speeds in excess of 150mph. It's an extremely civilized way for visitors to travel from downtown Manhattan to downtown DC.

One-way weekday sample fares include $67 for unreserved (3½ hours), $118 for Metroliner or Acela. The old Metroliners take three hours, the Acelas 2¾ hours. Weekend fares are often a bit lower.

International Gateway Fares are discount fares that can be purchased overseas in conjunction with an international air ticket for specific one-way trips in the Northeast,

RICK GERHARTER

Union Station's Grand Concourse

including New York to DC ($50) and Metro-liner express service ($60).

Trains from Elsewhere in the USA

If you're traveling to DC from outside the Northeast corridor, reserve early. Reservations can be made any time from 11 months in advance to the day of departure and give you the best chance at a discount fare. One-way, roundtrip, and touring fares are available, with discounts of 15% for seniors 62 and over, 50% for children ages two to 15, 25% for military, and 15% for disabled travelers.

Fares vary according to type of seating (coach seats or sleeping compartments). Low-season fares are offered on tickets from early January to mid-June and late August to mid-December. Amtrak also offers a variety of all-inclusive holiday tour packages and rail passes, including a 30-day USA Rail Pass for unlimited coach-class East Coast travel for $320/265 in high/low season.

CAR & MOTORCYCLE

Interstate 95, the East Coast's central artery, runs north-south to DC, merging into the I-495 Beltway surrounding the metro region. Approaching from the northeast, Hwy 1 leads into Rhode Island Ave NE, and the Baltimore-Washington Expressway (I-295) leads to Route 50 and then to New York Ave NE.

From the south, I-395 takes you downtown, near the Mall's west end, via either the 14th St or Rochambeau Bridges. From the west, I-66 runs from Virginia to the Mall area, but you should avoid this route during congested rush hours unless you have at least two passengers. This permits you to use the zippy carpool lane (you'll get a ticket for using it unless you have at least three people in your car).

From the Maryland suburbs to the north, take the Beltway's Connecticut Ave exit, marked 'Chevy Chase,' to reach Adams-Morgan and Dupont Circle, or the Wisconsin Ave exit to reach Georgetown.

See the Getting Around chapter for information on traffic regulations and car rental.

Taking a Bicycle on Amtrak

It's a well-kept secret that Amtrak is a great way to bring your bicycle with you when you travel. A few Amtrak routes have cars with a designated spot for bicycles, but most require that you check two-wheelers with the luggage. When making a reservation, mention that you'll be bringing a bike, and the agent will tell you if you'll need to box it up. If so, arrive at the station early and head to the baggage area, where you can buy a bicycle box ($10 to $15). Bring your tool kit and pump and be prepared to deflate tires, drop the saddle all the way down in the seat post, and remove the pedals and handlebars (which can then be secured to the frame and shipped with the bike). Give yourself enough time to fuss with extra cardboard, bubble wrap, or other padding (it's a good idea to bring your own) to protect delicate parts of the bike, such as derailleurs, forks, and top tube: Amtrak insists it stores bicycles upright, but this isn't always the case. If, like many cyclists, your bike is the most important or expensive item you own, it's wise to buy extra insurance at the baggage counter; rates are reasonable and Amtrak is quick to process claims.

– Tullan Spitz

HITCHHIKING

Don't plan on thumbing your way to or around the DC area. Almost nobody hitchhikes here (or in other US urban regions), and with good reason – there are far too many horror stories about criminals preying on hitchhikers. Although some stories are urban myths, hitchhiking remains unsafe and rare here, and travelers who attempt it should know that they're taking a risk.

If you do choose to hitch, always travel in pairs, let someone know where you're going, and take time to chat with and assess drivers before hopping into their cars. Remember that hitchhiking is illegal on highways and ramps, and you should expect hassles from police even on minor roads. Pony up the Metro fare instead.

Getting Around

DC's confusing street grid and fearsome commuter traffic make driving a real hassle. Fortunately, the city also boasts a superior public transportation system, so you can forgo a car altogether (or leave it in an outlying area). The reliable, safe, clean subway system, the Metrorail ('Metro'), serves most major sites and hotel districts, and you can easily reach areas it doesn't go to via Metrobus or taxi. Walking and biking are other excellent methods for getting around this level-terrained, scenic city.

Cabs are plentiful and relatively cheap options for daytime or evening travel – for groups of three or four, taxis can be nearly comparable in price to taking Metro. All three major airports can be reached by taxi or public transportation.

TO/FROM THE AIRPORTS
Ronald Reagan Washington National Airport

National Airport (Map 6; ☎ 703-417-8000, www.metwashairports.com), rechristened a few years back after the former Gipper in Chief, is on the Virginia side of the Potomac River, just a few miles from downtown DC. If you're driving from the city, take I-395 south across the Potomac, then drive south on the George Washington Memorial Parkway and take the 'National Airport' exit. In rush hour, this trip can take about 20 minutes, but the trip is shorter at most other times. Both hourly and long-term parking areas are available; call ☎ 703-417-4311 for rates and details.

There are three main information desks, in the centers of Terminals A, B, and C. Staff here can direct you to ground transportation pick-up areas and rental-car offices.

Metrorail is a very easy option for reaching DC and major suburban locations from National. Simply cross the walkway that connects Terminals B and C to the National Airport Metro station. (Signs throughout the airport direct you.) From here, the Blue and Yellow Lines will whisk you downtown

in 20 minutes. The fare to downtown's Metro Center is $1.35 one way (non-rush hour). The station closes at 2 am Friday and Saturday, midnight on other days. Metrobuses serving local Virginia destinations stop at the station, too; one-way fare is $1.10.

If you don't want to schlep your own baggage, SuperShuttle (☎ 800-258-3826) provides door-to-door van transportation between National and any destination in DC or its immediately surrounding suburbs, 5:30 am to 12:30 am daily. A ride from National to a Capitol Hill or downtown hotel costs around $9 one way (drivers should be tipped a couple dollars, too). SuperShuttles pick up passengers at curbside on the lower levels of all three terminals.

Rental-car companies are in Parking Garage A and do business from 6 am to 11 pm daily; shuttle buses take passengers from all three terminals to the garage. See Car, below, for a listing of rental agencies at National.

Taxis from downtown to National charge about $12 to $15, depending on your pick-up point. Taxis departing National for downtown often tack on an additional $1.

The Washington Flyer Express Bus (☎ 888-927-4359), operated by the three local airports, provides transportation between National and Dulles Airports for $16 one way. Buses run daily (on the hour from 5 am to 11 pm weekdays; on Saturday and Sunday, every two hours from 5 am to 1 pm and then hourly until 11 pm).

Dulles International Airport

Dulles International Airport (Map 1; ☎ 703-572-2700, www.metwashairports.com) is the DC area's major transport hub. It's many miles away from the city center, however (near Reston, Virginia), and thus harder to reach than National. Metrorail does not serve it.

If driving from downtown DC, head west on I-66 to exit 67 (Dulles Access Rd) and continue 16 miles to the airport. Allow yourself plenty of lead time if you're driving this congested route in rush hour. Hourly and long-term parking lots are available; call ☎ 703-572-4546 for details.

Washington Flyer Express Bus (☎ 888-927-4359) provides transportation between Dulles and National (see above); between Dulles and the DC Convention Center at 900 9th St NW; and between Dulles and several major downtown hotels. Buses run to the Convention Center from 5:20 am to 11 pm on weekdays (at 20 minutes and 50 minutes past the hour). On weekends, service runs hourly 5:20 am to 12:20 pm; thereafter service continues as on weekdays, at 20 minutes and 50 minutes past the hour. Return buses from the Convention Center depart each half hour (call for exact schedule). The fare is $16/26 one way/roundtrip. Buses also shuttle between Dulles and the West Falls Church Metro station in suburban Virginia at least every half hour from 6 am to 10:30 pm weekdays, 7:30 am to 10:30 pm weekends ($8/14 one way/roundtrip). Washington Flyer picks up passengers on the lower level of the main airport terminal.

Washington Flyer also operates a 24-hour airport taxi fleet; call ☎ 703-661-6655 to schedule pickups from your hotel. Its fares to downtown DC run between $35 and $47 plus tip, one way, depending on your destination.

SuperShuttle (☎ 800-258-3826) offers door-to-door vans from 5:30 am to 12:30 am daily. One-way fares to downtown DC run $20 to $24, plus tip.

Rental-car agencies here do business 24 hours a day. To contact the companies, use the courtesy phones in the lower level of the main terminal. Shuttle buses will take you to the companies' counters; from baggage claim, exit the terminal's lower level and go out to the second curbside. See Car, below, for a list of companies at the airport.

Baltimore-Washington International Airport

BWI (☎ 800-435-9294, www.bwiairport.com) is in Maryland, 10 miles south of downtown Baltimore and 30 miles northeast of Wash-

ington. Shuttle, taxi, train, and buses from BWI serve DC and points beyond.

BWI is 30 miles, or about 45 minutes' drive from the freeway, from DC. Get onto the Baltimore-Washington Parkway via New York Ave NE, follow the Parkway until you see the I-195/BWI sign, and then take I-195 to the airport.

On weekdays only, you can take the MARC commuter train (☎ 800-325-7245) between DC's Union Station and a terminal near BWI; once there, you'll be shuttled to and from the airport free of charge. The fare is $6 one way. Amtrak also stops at BWI, but the fare from the airport to DC can be as high as $15.

SuperShuttle vans (see above) run 24 hours a day between DC and BWI. Call 24 hours in advance for reservations and pickup at your lodging. The fare is $28/56 one way/roundtrip.

A taxi between BWI and downtown Washington costs about $60 plus tip.

TO/FROM THE TRAIN STATION

The Metro's Union Station stop is conveniently located in the basement of the train station itself: from your arrival gate, simply turn right and follow signs through the station to the subway entrance (it's just past the liquor store).

Cabs wait outside Union Station's Massachusetts Ave NE entrance night and day. From the same entrance, several Metrobus routes serve the Mall, downtown, and Capitol Hill ($1.10 one way).

Union Station also has a large parking garage (☎ 898-1950), which costs $5/12 per hour/day. Two-hour parking is free if you get your ticket validated at the station's central information desk. Car-rental counters are in the station itself (see Car, below).

METRORAIL

DC boasts a sleek modern subway network called the Metro, which is managed by DC, Maryland, Virginia, and the federal government. It runs to most major sights, hotel and business districts, and the Maryland and Virginia suburbs (see the Washington Metrorail map). Thanks to ample federal

The morning commute on the Metro

funding, its trains and stations are well marked, well maintained, well lit, climate controlled, reasonably priced, decently staffed, reliable, and safe. Metro is among history's most expensive public-works projects – over $3 billion spent in the past three decades – and its grand, barrel-vaulted architecture and efficient trains suggest the money was well spent.

Call ☎ 637-7000 (☎ 638-3780 TDD) for route and fare information from 6 am to 10:30 pm weekdays, 8 am to 10:30 pm weekends, or check www.wmata.com. Each station has payphones and an information kiosk providing system and fare information, route maps, and local bus timetables.

As of June 2000, trains run daily – from 5:30 am to midnight Monday to Thursday, 5:30 am to 2 am Friday, 8 am to 2 am Saturday, and 8 am to midnight Sunday. Note that the last train may depart your station before the official system closing time: to ensure you don't miss it, get the *Metrorail Last Train Departure Times* pamphlet from a kiosk.

The network consists of five color-coded lines – Blue, Yellow, Orange, Green, and Red – that intersect at nine transfer points. Trains are identified by their line color and final destination point: eg, an Orange Line train to Vienna is heading west; an Orange Line train to New Carrollton is eastbound. Carefully check the destination and color designation before boarding.

Plentiful parking is available at certain outlying stations. The time limit for parking

is 24 hours, and there's a $2.25 charge between 2 and 10:30 pm (no charge if you arrive before or leave after these times).

Trains get dreadfully jammed during big events such as the Cherry Blossom Festival and Fourth of July. At such times, buy a roundtrip ticket at your departure point and consider hopping off and on at a station before your destination to avoid the shuffling herds (eg, use Federal Triangle station rather than Smithsonian when heading to the Mall).

The system is still a-building: the federal government has committed to a new Red Line station at Florida and New York Aves NE (due to open 2004) in hopes of revitalizing that depressed city quadrant. The Blue Line will eventually extend to Largo, Maryland, and the Green Line to Suitland, Maryland.

A final note: the city likes to append the names of local attractions to its subway stops (thus monstrosities like 'U Street-Cardozo-African-American Civil War Memorial'). Keep in mind that some attractions aren't right at the stops that bear their names – for example, you must walk several blocks to reach Adams-Morgan from the 'Woodley Park-Zoo-Adams-Morgan' station.

Fares & Farecards

To ride Metro, buy a computerized paper farecard from the self-service machines inside the station entrance. Printed instructions on the machines and nearby posters talk you through this simple process. Each passenger, except kids under five, needs a farecard.

You must use the farecard to enter *and* exit station turnstiles. Upon exit, if the card's value is the same as the fare, the turnstile keeps the card and the gates open. If the card's value is greater, the turnstile returns the card to you with the remaining value printed on it, and the gates open. If the card's value is less than the fare, the turnstile returns the card and the gates don't open; if this happens, you need to use

A Long Way Down

Metro's escalators are an acrophobe's nightmare – they're among the world's tallest. Riding these vertiginous monsters, such as the 200-foot escalator at Dupont Circle station's north entrance, is like being swallowed by a giant, concrete version of a Dune sandworm.

Because the Metro was excavated deep underground to avoid mushy topsoil and subterranean infrastructure (sewerage lines, telephone cables, etc), huge escalators are needed to shuttle passengers between street level and platforms. In fact, the Western Hemisphere's longest escalator is at Wheaton station: 230 feet long, it's powered by six 60hp engines.

Occasionally Metro puts its titanic escalators to artistic use – for example, in 2000 Finnish artists created a light-and-music show in a Dupont escalator well, delighting the normally jaded commuter crowds.

RICK GERHARTER

an 'Addfare' machine, which tells you how much money to add. Other machines inside the gates dispense free bus transfers that enable you to pay just 25¢ on connecting bus routes – remember to get these before exiting if you need a bus connection.

Fares are sort of byzantine compared to those of other cities' subways: they're determined by both distance traveled and time of day. The higher, so-called 'regular' (ie, rush hour) fares are in effect from 5:30 to 9:30 am and 3 to 7 pm weekdays. At other times,

'reduced' fares are charged. The minimum one-way fare is $1.10, but it's wisest to buy a high-value card to avoid repeated trips to the farecard machine. If you're hopelessly confused by all this, simply consult the station-to-station fare chart posted prominently in each Metro station.

A variety of passes are available. A one-day pass costs $5 and permits unlimited travel after 9:30 am weekdays and all day weekends. A weekly FAST pass ($17.50) allows unlimited rides for a week. For $30 you get a FAST pass that's good on both Metrorail and Metrobus. Senior discounts are available to holders of the free Metro Senior Citizen ID Card. All these special passes are available from the Sales & Information office in the Metro Center station at 12th and F Sts NW; Metro's Web site (see above); and Safeway and Giant grocery stores.

METROBUS

DC's Metrobus system provides relatively clean and efficient bus service throughout the city and to outlying suburbs. Call ☎ 637-7000 for route information, schedules, and fares. Stops are marked by red-white-and-blue signposts.

The fare is $1.10 ($2 on express routes), or 25¢ with a Metrorail transfer. Fortunately, buses don't fuss with special rush-hour fares the way the trains do. Kids under five ride free. Automatic fare machines accept paper dollars; you must have the exact fare or a FAST pass (see Metrorail, above).

Some handy routes are the L2, which runs along 18th St in the heart of Adams-Morgan (connecting to Metro stations at Woodley Park and Foggy Bottom) and up Connecticut Ave NW; the D2, connecting Dupont Circle and Georgetown; the D6, which runs from Union Station across downtown to Georgetown; and the 30 and 32 lines, serving Georgetown and upper Wisconsin Ave NW.

A good route for clubhoppers is No 98 ('The Link'), connecting the Green Line's U St-Cardozo Metro station to the Red Line's Woodley Park-Zoo station, traversing the central bar districts of Adams-Morgan and

GETTING AROUND

U St. It runs every 15 minutes 6 pm to midnight Sunday to Thursday, 6 pm to 1 am Friday, and 10 am to 1 am Saturday.

You can buy the handy, color-coded *Metro System Route Maps* ($1.50 each), which display both bus and subway routes and timetables, at the transit store in the Metro Center station, from Metro's Web site, and at local shops, including the Map Store (Map 3; ☎ 628-2608; Ⓜ Farragut West), 1636 I St NW. One map covers DC and Maryland; the other covers DC and Virginia.

TRAIN

In addition to the city's own Metrorail, two commuter train systems serve downtown DC from the Maryland and Virginia suburbs. If you're saving money by staying at a suburban hotel, you'll find them very useful for accessing city sights. However, remember that they're *commuter* lines: most trains run weekdays only, going to the city in the morning and returning to the 'burbs during evening rush hour.

Maryland Rail Commuter (MARC; ☎ 800-325-7245, www.mtamaryland.com) is a 40-station, 187-mile system connecting DC, the northern Maryland suburbs, Baltimore, and eastern West Virginia. Its Brunswick Line runs from Martinsburg, West Virginia to DC; the Camden Line runs from Baltimore's Camden Station; and the Penn Line runs from Perryville, Maryland, stopping at BWI Airport. All three lines converge on MARC's sole DC stop: Union Station, where you can connect to Metro. Trains run 5 am to midnight weekdays. Fares vary depending on where you board; the Baltimore-DC one-way fare is about $6.

From downtown DC, Virginia Railway Express (VRE; ☎ 703-684-1001, 800-RIDE-VRE, www.vre.org) serves northern Virginia's suburbs with lines to Manassas (stops include Fairfax and Alexandria) and Fredericksburg (stops include Quantico, Franconia/Springfield, and Crystal City). VRE has only two stops in DC itself: Union Station and, in the city's southwestern quadrant, L'Enfant Plaza. Metro is directly accessed from both. Trains run about every half hour during weekday rush hours (see the Web site for the schedule). Fares vary with trip length.

CAR & MOTORCYCLE

A car is largely unnecessary in downtown DC, but it's useful for day trips to surrounding attractions that public transportation doesn't serve.

Road Rules

Many visitors are surprised to learn that DC has some of the nation's worst traffic congestion – as of 2000, it was second only to Los Angeles'. The worst bottlenecks are in the suburbs, where the Beltway (I-495) meets interstates: Maryland's I-270 and I-95 and Virginia's I-66 and I-95. Avoid the Beltway in early-morning and late-afternoon rush hours (about 6 to 9 am and 3 to 6 pm). Clogged rush-hour streets in DC include the main access arteries from the suburbs: Massachusetts, Wisconsin, Connecticut, and Georgia Aves NW, among others.

Besides congestion, the major challenges drivers face in DC are a confusing street grid and numerous traffic circles. Keep a map handy, and watch for directional signs at the roundabouts – Dupont Circle is particularly tricky for newbies to negotiate.

Certain lanes of some major traffic arteries (such as Connecticut Ave NW) change direction during rush hour, and some two-way streets become one-way. Signs indicate hours of these changes, so keep your eyes peeled. Motorcades are occasional hassles in Foggy Bottom and the White House area; treat them as you would a fire engine, pulling to the side and waiting until the vehicles are out of sight. While you wait, feel free to gawk at the passing nabobs.

Except where otherwise posted, the speed limit on DC surface streets is 25mph (15mph in alleys and school zones). You must wear your seat belt and restrain kids under three in child-safety seats.

For emergency road service and towing, the American Automobile Association's members can call ☎ 800-222-4357. The AAA has a downtown office (Map 3; ☎ 942-2050) near the White House at 1440 New

Plate Spotting

Want to spot local bigwigs? Start looking at license plates. Both congressional representatives and the diplomatic corps have special plates – and special driving and parking privileges that occasion some grumbling among DC's automotive hoi polloi, whose city plates don't get them any perks.

Embassy staffers' red-white-and-blue plates are issued by the State Dept and emblazoned with 'S' (staff) or 'D' (diplomat). Because diplomatic immunity sometimes protects embassy staff against tickets for traffic violations, some wags suggest that the D actually stands for 'Dammit, I'll drive however I want.' In 1997, a drunken Georgian diplomat killed a teenager in a spectacular Dupont Circle crash, but he wasn't charged for many weeks, provoking a major debate in DC over immunity. (Eventually, his immunity was revoked, and he was prosecuted.) Numeric codes on the plates tell police officers which embassy drivers are connected to. US senators and representatives also have numerically coded plates, which indicate their state. Their privileges include getting to park for free in lots close to the terminals at National and Dulles Airports.

The city itself sports some unusual plates these days: in 2000, Mayor Anthony Williams and the city council approved new city license plates sporting the slogan 'Taxation Without Representation,' bemoaning Washington's lack of voting representation in the US Congress.

York Ave NW, No 200, open weekday business hours.

Conveniently located gas stations include the Capitol Hill Exxon (Map 4), 339 Pennsylvania Ave SE on the corner of 4th St SE, and Georgetown Exxon (Map 7), 1601 Wisconsin Ave NW. For road conditions in DC, call ☎ 727-5745, or check the *Post*'s Traffic page, updated constantly throughout the day, at www.washingtonpost.com.

Parking

Finding street parking is difficult in popular neighborhoods (Georgetown and Adams-Morgan are particularly heinous), but it's reasonably easy in less congested districts. Hucksters sometimes 'find' parking spaces for you in crowded neighborhoods at night; they stand in empty spaces, beckon you in, and then hit you for a tip (a buck usually makes them happy).

It's often easier just to pay to park. Carr Park (☎ 333-5091) maintains strings of lots throughout northwest DC; you can also try Colonial Parking (☎ 295-8100) and Diplomat Parking (☎ 496-4200). There are paid lots in the Georgetown Park mall on M St NW and at Union Station (useful for Capitol Hill visitors).

You must park at least 3 feet from other cars, 5 feet from private driveways and alleys, 10 feet from fire hydrants, and 25 feet from the corner of one-way streets. You can leave a car on the street for only 72 hours before moving it. Parking police are picky about these rules.

If you get towed, first pay your fine ($75 plus $10 daily storage fee) at the Dept of Motor Vehicles/Adjudication Services, 65 K St NE (Map 4); then take a cab from the Rhode Island Ave Metro station (don't walk) to the Brentwood Impoundment Lot (Map 5) off Brentwood Rd NE, which is open 7 am to 8 pm weekdays only.

Rental

All the major car-rental agencies and many small local ones are present in Washington,

GETTING AROUND

DC, especially at the airports. Many big agencies maintain downtown offices, too, and there are counters at Union Station. Airport rates are often better than those at downtown offices.

Weekly rates are often the best deal. An economy-size car typically costs around $120 to $150 per week. Expect to pay more during peak visitor times, such as the Cherry Blossom Festival, and when big conventions and political demonstrations are in town.

On top of the rental price, add 5.75% sales tax in DC (but you might pay up to 8% at the airports). There's also insurance to consider. Basic liability insurance, required by US law, is generally included in the rental price, but check the contract carefully. You can also purchase loss/damage waiver (LDW) insurance, usually about $8 to $12 per day. Some credit-card companies provide LDW insurance if you rent the car using their card, but confirm this with the company. Your personal auto-insurance policy may also automatically cover rental-car insurance (if so, bring along a photocopy of your policy as proof). Most rates include unlimited mileage: if a rate seems super cheap, that may be because you'll get hit for a mileage charge upon returning the car. Return the car with a full tank of gas, or the agency will charge you more.

Booking well in advance of your visit usually yields the best rate. If you're in town on government or diplomatic business, agencies often slash their rates for you.

Unfortunately for young drivers, most major agencies in DC won't rent to anyone under 25. Some local companies rent to drivers over 21 who have a major credit card, but their rates generally aren't competitive.

Agencies in DC include the following:

Alamo – ☎ 800-327-9633; 703-260-0182 (Dulles Airport)

Avis – ☎ 800-331-1212; 202-467-6585 (Map 8; 1722 M St NW); 703-419-5815 (National Airport); 703-661-3505 (Dulles)

Budget – ☎ 800-527-0700; 202-289-5373 (Map 4; 50 Massachusetts Ave NW); 703-920-3360 (National)

Dollar – ☎ 800-800-4000; 703-519-8700 (National); 703-661-6630 (Dulles)

Enterprise – ☎ 800-325-8007; 202-393-0900 (Map 3; 1029 Vermont Ave NW); 703-553-7744 (National); 703-661-8800 (Dulles)

Hertz – ☎ 800-654-3131; 202-628-6174 (Map 3; 901 11th St NW); 703-979-6300 (National); 703-471-6020 (Dulles)

National – ☎ 800-328-4567; 202-842-7454 (opposite Gate J in Union Station); 202-783-1590 (National); 703-471-5278 (Dulles)

Thrifty – ☎ 800-367-2277; 202-783-0400 (Map 3; 1001 12th St NW); 703-658-2200 (National); 703-481-3599 (Dulles)

Rent-A-Wreck (☎ 800-421-7253) offers older vehicles at lower prices.

TAXI

Taxicabs are plentiful in central DC and generally easy to find; hail them with a wave of the hand. Diamond (☎ 387-6200), Yellow (☎ 544-1212), and Capitol (☎ 546-2400) are three major companies.

The fare structure works on a zone system rather than by the traditional metered system. DC consists of eight concentric zones (zone maps are posted in cabs), and rates are determined by how many zones you cross, the number of passengers, and time of day (there's a $1 rush-hour surcharge). You pay the base fare, $4, to travel within one zone. Each additional zone costs $1.50. Each additional passenger costs $1.50. More fees are added for extra services (large bags, ordering a cab by phone, traveling during snow emergencies, etc). Taxis in the Virginia and Maryland suburbs use the usual metering method. Taxi drivers are usually tipped about 10% of the total fare.

You can hire Yellow Cab and Diamond drivers for guided sightseeing drives around the city.

BICYCLE & BOAT

Washington (a low, flat city with lots of parkland) is a great town for bicycling. The adjacent Potomac provides recreational boating options, too. See the Activities section of the Things to See & Do chapter for information on rentals, costs and recommended routes.

WALKING

Walking is the best way to get around central Washington, and most visitors do a lot more of it than they might expect. The monuments and museums downtown are separated by lots of lovely, regal lawn, and the only way to cross it is on foot. Wear comfortable shoes: this is not the place to strut your new Manolo Blahniks. On the bright side, there are hardly any hills.

Particularly nice hiking paths are discussed in Things to See & Do, where you'll also find maps and descriptions of several recommended neighborhood walking tours.

ORGANIZED TOURS
Bus Tours
The big boy on the local narrated bus-tour scene is Tourmobile (☎ 554-5100, 888-868-7707). Its primary tour runs around the National Mall (it's the only tour bus permitted there), Capitol, White House, and out to Arlington National Cemetery. You can hop off and reboard for free at any of its 24 stops, which is nice for those who aren't able to walk long distances. It costs $16/7 adults/kids ages three to 11. Tourmobile also does separate tours of Arlington National Cemetery ($4.75/2.25) and Mount Vernon ($22/11).

Gray Line (☎ 289-1995) competes with a more varied menu of downtown and Ar-lington tours. It will pick you up at your hotel. Costs range between $25 and $42.

Those visitors unafraid of silly transportation will enjoy DC Ducks (☎ 966-3825), amphibious land/water vehicles that waddle around on daily city tours beginning at Union Station ($24/12 adults/kids ages five to 12).

Walking Tours
Tour DC (☎ 301-588-8999, www.tourdc.com) offers a variety of excellent walking tours of DC neighborhoods, all led by the knowledgeable local travel writer Mary Kay Ricks. She focuses on Georgetown, Embassy Row (both $12), and Dupont Circle ($18).

DC Heritage Tours (☎ 639-0908), working out of the Discovery Channel Store in the MCI Center at 601 F St NW, offers informative daily walking tours of the surrounding downtown, hitting all the highlights from Chinatown to important Civil Rights–movement sites. The 1½-hour tours cost $7.50/5 adults/children and seniors.

Another good choice is Washington Walks (☎ 484-1565, washingtonwalks.com), which does two-hour jaunts that include Embassy Row, 'artful Thursdays,' a 'haunted DC' walk, and the Waterfront. Tours start at a nearby Metro station and cost $10/5 adults/kids under 12.

GETTING AROUND

Things to See & Do

Washington is a small but dense town, and there are enough museums, monuments, and memorials in its several dozen square miles to keep you busy for years. Most traditional tourist sights, from the Smithsonian to the Capitol, are clustered along the long greensward of the National Mall. Yet DC is also a city of neighborhoods, and smaller museums and historic sites hidden away in less famous districts are great destinations as well. Best of all, most attractions are free, so you can see a lot without spending anything. This chapter discusses visitor attractions and places of interest first; recreational activities are at its end.

National Mall (Map 3)

The 400-foot-wide green expanse stretching 3 miles from the Potomac to Capitol Hill is known as the National Mall. Lined with gravel paths and bordered by tree-shaded avenues (Constitution Ave to the north, Independence Ave to the south), the Mall is fringed by museums, dotted with monuments, and hosts festivals, demonstrations, sunning tourists, Frisbee-catching dogs, jogging bureaucrats, and hawkers selling souvenirs.

It assumed the role of 'national lawn' only recently. In 1791, Pierre L'Enfant planned the Mall as the heart of his DC scheme, a grand mansion-lined promenade that would be an American Champs-Élysées. But until the 20th century it languished, home to a railway station, marsh, rubbish dump, open sewers, fish-breeding ponds, and other urban detritus. In 1902, Congress' McMillan Commission resuscitated L'Enfant's plans and began to transform the Mall into the welcoming grassy avenue that is the heart of modern Washington. It's now a national park, its memorials and grounds maintained by the Park Service.

The Smithsonian's Kite Festival in late March and Folklife Festival in June are two of many popular annual public events on the Mall. But the Mall is best known for its political gatherings. From suffragettes to victorious soldiers, from Inauguration Day crowds to antiwar rallies, generations of protestors and celebrants have made the Mall their own. Protestors demonstrated against the Vietnam War during the 1960s, and in 1963, Martin Luther King delivered his 'I Have a Dream' speech on the Lincoln Memorial steps. Today gun-control advocates, pro-lifers, pro-choicers, and anti-globalization ralliers are as common as tourists on the Mall.

The Mall's monuments are similarly eclectic. When the Vietnam Veterans Memorial opened in 1982, it generated tremendous controversy, but its popularity sparked a monument binge in Washington. New Congressionally approved monuments (in various stages of

Protest on the National Mall

RICK GERHARTER

completion) include ones to WWII, the Korean War, women in Vietnam, black Revolutionary War patriots, and Japanese-American patriots. (An Army canine-corps monument didn't win Congressional approval.)

All these memorials, as well as the jumbled architectural styles of the museums and buildings fringing the Mall, might be taken as evidence of chaotic planning or federal ego. Perhaps so, but the Mall's strange mixture of statuary and buildings also offers a fascinating glimpse of the debate over what a national capital – and democracy itself – should be. If you look carefully, you'll see a history lesson in sod and stone.

SMITHSONIAN INSTITUTION

More than 150 years old, the massive, 16-museum Smithsonian is DC's premier attraction. Far more than a complex of museums, the Smithsonian is also a vast research and educational institution and cares for approximately 140 million artworks, scientific specimens, artifacts, and other objects – a collection so huge that only a tiny percentage of it is on display at any time. Its 14 DC museums and the Smithsonian-run National Zoo together draw millions of visitors each year, and they also offer year-round calendars of films, lectures, kids' activities, and other programs, most free.

The Whippersnapper Vagabond

The Smithsonian Institution owes its existence to a single mysterious line in the 1826 will of a British chemist who never visited the USA. Should his heir, a nephew, die childless, James Smithson wrote, 'I then bequeath the whole of my property…to the United States of America, to found at Washington, under the name of the Smithsonian Institution, an establishment for the increase & diffusion of knowledge among men.'

JOHN NEUBAUER

Smithson was born in 1765, the illegitimate result of an affair between Elizabeth Macie (a wealthy widow) and the first Duke of Northumberland. After distinguishing himself at Oxford, Smithson had an illustrious career as a chemist and mineralogist: he was best known for his discovery that zinc carbonates are minerals rather than zinc oxides. (A zinc carbonate, smithsonite, is named for him.) He undertook more fanciful research as well, on such topics as the chemical composition of a woman's teardrop and the ideal method for making coffee. He had no children, and his nephew died heirless, leaving the Smithson fortune in American hands.

Given Smithson's political views – he slammed the British monarchy as a 'contemptible encumbrance' and publicly embraced the infant US democracy's ideals – his $508,318 bequest wasn't much of a surprise to anyone but the US Congress, which promptly looked his gift horse in the mouth. 'Every whippersnapper vagabond…might think it proper to have his name distinguished in the same way,' grumped Sen William Preston, and Sen John C Calhoun argued that Congress wasn't authorized to accept the money and that it was 'beneath [American] dignity to accept presents from anyone.' Anti-British sentiment informed some of this debate: the 1814 British torching of Washington remained fresh in many American minds. Finally, in 1846, Congress deigned to accept the gift and used it to build a museum and research center, the seed of today's sprawling Smithsonian.

Smithson is now literally a part of the Smithsonian – his remains lie in a marble bier in the Castle's Crypt Room, just inside the entrance. Wave to him as you pass by.

The nine Smithsonian museums on the Mall are described below. For Smithsonian museums in other districts – such as the Renwick Gallery near the White House and the Zoo in northwest DC – see the relevant neighborhood sections, later. In 2002, the Smithsonian will open the **Museum of the American Indian** on the Mall's southeast corner.

Information All Smithsonian museums, except where noted below, are open 10 am to 5:30 pm daily except Christmas. Entrance to all is free.

For current exhibit and program information, call ☎ 357-2700 (TTY 357-1729) 9 am to 5 pm weekdays, 10 am to 4 pm weekends; check the Web at www.si.edu; or email info@info.si.edu. Dial-a-Museum (☎ 357-2020) offers 24-hour recorded information.

The Smithsonian Visitors Center, in the Castle (see below), offers informational pamphlets – including a free guide and map – an orientation film, multilingual touch-screen displays, and the excellent *Official Guide to the Smithsonian* ($8.95). The free *Exploring African American Heritage at the Smithsonian* pamphlet is another great resource. The center is open 9:45 am to 4 pm daily.

Each museum has a shop, and eight restaurants and cafés of varying quality are scattered throughout the Smithsonian – because their food is usually costly, you may be better off going to a nearby food court. See Places to Eat for suggestions.

Getting There & Around The Smithsonian provides no public parking, and the nearby street-parking situation is nightmarish. Take Metro to any Mall-area station: Smithsonian, Federal Triangle, Archives, or L'Enfant Plaza. Tourmobile (☎ 888-868-7707) offers inexpensive narrated bus tours of the Mall daily, stopping at various museums.

The Castle

This is the Smithsonian's iconic building, the turreted, red-sandstone fairytale castle that housed the original museum, designed in 1855 by James Renwick. Its official name is the Smithsonian Institution Building (Ⓜ Smithsonian), 1000 Jefferson Drive SW, and it now houses the central information office, a logical first stop for the Mall visitor (see Information, above).

The small round building directly west of the Castle is the aboveground entrance to the subterranean **Ripley Center**. Public lectures, classes, and temporary exhibits take place in the center's classrooms and meeting spaces. To the east is the **Folger Rose Garden**, awash in blossom throughout summer.

Arts & Industries Building

An exquisite Victorian dream of red brick, multicolored tiles, and fanciful ironwork, the 1881 Arts & Industries Building (Ⓜ Smithsonian), 900 Jefferson Drive SW, was built to

---

Smithsonian Folklife Festival

The most popular annual Mall festival is this Smithsonian-sponsored fair, held during the 10 days before July 4. The extravaganza, which celebrates international as well as American cultures, brings arts, crafts, concerts, food stalls, workshops, craft demonstrations, and dance performances to the Mall lawns in front of the Smithsonian Castle. Each year a foreign country and a US state are celebrated (in 2000, it was Tibet and DC – neither's an official state, but so what?). It's all free, except the food and crafts. Call ☎ 633-9884 for information during the festival; at other times, check www.folklife.si.edu.

JOHN NEUBAUER

THINGS TO SEE & DO

hold items from the 1876 Centennial Exposition. Most of its eclectic collection of scientific and industrial artifacts and artworks was later distributed to other Mall museums, but it still displays remnants: steam-driven dynamos, an old locomotive, antique jewelry, tools, etc, all wreathed in a ghostly carnival ambience. The bunting-draped central rotunda, with an ornate central fountain, is illuminated by clerestory windows and features beautiful stencilwork on its walls.

The building's **Discovery Theater** (☎ 357-1500) hosts performances and puppet shows for kids – see the Entertainment chapter. Another kid favorite is outside, across Jefferson Drive: an **antique carousel** offering rides for $1.25.

National Museum of African Art

One of twin 'bookends' behind the Castle (the other is the Sackler Gallery), the Museum of African Art (Ⓜ Smithsonian), 950 Independence Ave SW, starts to entertain before you even see its collection. When you enter the foyer, you discover that the museum is underground (built to conserve open space), and tunnels connect it to the Sackler, Freer, and Ripley galleries. (Kids enjoy tossing pennies three stories down its stairwell into the fountain.) Devoted to

DENNIS JOHNSON

The Castle

ancient and modern sub-Saharan African art, its dimly lit, peaceful galleries display masks, textiles, ceramics, ritual objects, and other examples of the visual traditions of a continent of 900 distinct cultures. A fine shop offers books and African crafts, and the excellent research library opens weekdays

RICHARD CUMMINS

Smithsonian Arts & Industries Building

THINGS TO SEE & DO

(call ☎ 357-4600). Educational workshops and lectures are held frequently; pick up a calendar in the foyer.

Enter the museum's ground-level pavilion via the beautiful **Enid A Haupt Memorial Garden**, with its geometric flowerbeds and Asian moongates – it's on the garden's southeast side.

Arthur M Sackler Gallery

Dedicated to Asian artwork, the Sackler (Ⓜ Smithsonian), 1050 Independence Ave SW, is underground at the southwest corner of the Haupt garden. Its collection of paintings, sculpture, sacred objects, and crafts ranges from the Mediterranean shores to South India to Southeast Asia. Particularly noteworthy are its temple sculptures, Chinese lacquerware and jades, and Persian and Indian calligraphy. Free lectures, films, gallery talks, and tours round out its offerings – get a bimonthly calendar at the information desk.

Freer Gallery of Art

Named for founder Charles Lang Freer, the Freer Gallery (Ⓜ Smithsonian), just west of the Castle, was built in 1923 to hold Freer's collection of American and Asian art. On the Asian side of things are ancient ceramics, screen paintings, sculpture, and musical instruments from China, Japan, Southeast Asia and the Near East; the 19th- and 20th-century American artworks include an extensive collection of paintings by James McNeill Whistler. The museum's famed **Peacock Room**, originally designed by Whistler for a London shipowner, features gilded wall murals and an elaborate system of wood shelving that displays prized Chinese porcelains. The Freer also offers an eventful calendar of free tours, concerts, and lectures.

Hirshhorn Museum & Sculpture Garden

Uncharitable observers say that this modern-art museum (Ⓜ L'Enfant Plaza) resembles a gun turret; nicer ones say it resembles New York's Guggenheim. The cylindrical museum, at Independence Ave

and 7th St SW, is certainly a contrast to the Mall's mainly neoclassical buildings, but its collection is among the country's best.

The museum was founded to house the extensive collections of Latvian-American millionaire Joseph Hirshhorn. On its two main exhibit floors, concentric gallery spaces exhibit 19th- and 20th-century sculpture and canvases in chronological fashion, from Modernism's early days to the millennium. Highlights include sculpture by Rodin, Brancusi, Calder, and Moore, plus canvases by Bacon, Miró, O'Keeffe, Warhol, Stella, and Kiefer.

Outside, massive sculptures dot the courtyard and plaza; across Jefferson Drive is the sunken **Sculpture Garden**, presenting a rich collection of works in a beautifully landscaped setting, including Rodin's *The Burghers of Calais*. An outdoor café opens nearby in summer.

The Hirshhorn's entrance is on Independence Ave, not the Mall side. Free tours of the collection are offered at 10:30 am and noon weekdays, noon and 2 pm weekends. The museum has an excellent calendar of free lectures, workshops, and special tours; from September to June, it also screens independent films and art documentaries. Call ☎ 357-3235 for special events.

National Air & Space Museum

The Air & Space Museum (Ⓜ L'Enfant Plaza) is no longer the world's most popular museum – as of 2000, the nearby Museum of Natural History had grabbed that crown – but 8 million people, many of them children, still visit annually. Its cavernous halls exhibit airplanes and spacecraft, including the Wright Brothers' *Flyer*, Charles Lindbergh's *Spirit of St Louis*, and the Apollo 11 command module; its 23 galleries trace the history of aviation and space exploration through interactive displays and historic artifacts. It's not just for kids, though; adults too like touching the moon rock, walking through the DC-7 cockpit, checking out the enormous Pratt & Whitney and Rolls-Royce aircraft engines, and joining volunteer-led tours to hear the stories behind the impressive flying machines on display. Special

Dogfight at the Air & Space Museum

exhibits examine topics like airborne warfare and black aviators.

The **Langley IMAX Theater** is a major draw, featuring all-day rotating films ($5.50/4.25 adults/kids). *To Fly*, the grizzled granddaddy of in-your-face IMAX films, still plays here daily, along with newer offerings. The museum also holds the **Einstein Planetarium**, offering an alternating menu of three shows daily ($3.75): 'The Stars Tonight,' 'Sky Quest,' and 'And a Star to Steer Her By.'

If the kids get hungry, the Flight Line Café and The Wright Place Restaurant are here, in a spacious greenhouselike setting overlooking the Mall. If the urge to shop strikes, check out the massive museum store (see the Shopping chapter for details). Many special programs and lectures are offered year-round; see www.nasm.si.edu for listings.

But wait, there's more. In Suitland, Maryland, the museum's **Paul E Garber Facility** offers free tours of its 150 craft; call ☎ 357-1400 to reserve a spot at least two weeks in advance. Out at Dulles International Airport in Virginia, the massive new **Dulles Center** will open in 2003 to display 300 more craft, including the *Enola Gay*, SR-71 Blackbird, and space shuttle *Enterprise*.

National Gallery of Art

The National Gallery (☎ 737-4215, www.nga.gov; Ⓜ Archives) comprises two buildings: the original neoclassical building across the Mall from the Air & Space Museum, now called the West Building, and the modern, angular East Building, across 4th St NW. The two are connected by an underground tunnel.

The **West Building** exhibits primarily European works, from the Middle Ages to the early 20th century, including masterpieces by El Greco, Renoir, Monet, and Cézanne. It's the only gallery in America that owns a da Vinci painting *(Ginevra di' Benci)*, and it hosts big-time touring exhibitions that draw lines round the block – Vermeer, Titian, etc. Customize your own tour in the 'Micro Gallery,' using its interactive computers. The spacious **East Building**, designed by IM Pei, features a Calder mobile as the centerpiece of its four-story atrium. Downstairs, you'll find abstract and modern works. Smaller upstairs galleries hold special exhibits and permanent items like Picasso's *Family of Saltimbanques*. A small Matisse cut-outs gallery on the 3rd floor opens during limited hours.

Although it's affiliated with the Smithsonian, the National Gallery isn't officially part of it. Note the different hours: 10 am to 5 pm Monday to Saturday, 11 am to 6 pm Sunday. The West Building operates the Terrace Café; a buffet cafeteria and espresso bar are in the tunnel linking the wings. There are large book and souvenir shops, too. Check at information desks for an events calendar (free concerts, lectures, and films).

National Gallery of Art, East Building

National Sculpture Garden

Set between the National Gallery's West Building and the National Museum of Natural History, this delightful 6-acre garden (... Archives) opened in 1999. It's studded with whimsical sculptures like Roy Lichtenstein's *House*, a giant Claes Oldenburg typewriter eraser, and Louise Bourgeois' leggy *Spider*. Kids love this place.

In winter, the garden's central fountain becomes the **Sculpture Garden Ice Rink**. It offers a homey ice-skating scene from November to March (weather depending), generally open 10 am to 11 pm. Admission costs $5/4 adults/children. Skate rental costs $2.50 per two-hour session.

National Museum of Natural History

The world's most-visited museum (Ⓜ Federal Triangle) recently spent $80 million to bring its turn-of-the-century building up to modern standards. In addition to its dinosaur bones, Gems & Mineral Hall, and Orkin Insect Zoo, the museum now sports a new Discovery Center (with a giant IMAX theater and hands-on science exhibits), the African Voices hall (examining the cultures of that continent), and the Mammals Hall. Even 'Henry,' the beloved stuffed African elephant in the museum rotunda, has received a fluff-up.

Exhibits at the museum trace Earth's history from its birth to the complex life systems of today and examine human cultures both ancient and modern. On the 1st floor, visit halls exploring the beginnings of life; the Dinosaur Hall, with its gigantic Diplodocus and Tyrannosaurus skeletons and Burgess Shale fossils, is always crowded with eager visitors.

Other 1st-floor halls explore the cultures of the Americas, Asia, and Africa. Upstairs are the Insect Zoo (live tarantula feedings!) and the Gems & Minerals Hall, famed for its 45-carat blue Hope Diamond. Free tours run at 10:30 am and 1:30 pm weekdays from the rotunda.

The hands-on **Discovery Center** enables children to examine shells, bones, geodes, costumes, and much more. It's open noon to 2:30 pm Tuesday to Friday, 10:30 am to 3:30 pm weekends. You need a timed pass, so show up when it opens for the widest choice of times.

The **Johnson IMAX Theater** shows nature extravaganzas like *Galapagos 3D* daily; tickets cost $6.50/5.50 adults/kids and seniors. Buy tickets at the theater or in advance by calling ☎ 633-7400 (extra $3 per ticket). Downstairs, the Baird Auditorium offers free films and lectures; an annual highlight is the Wildlife Film Festival in March. Check the events calendar at www.mnh.si.edu/cal_events.html.

The museum's two cafeterias (one for Smithsonian members only) are among the least tasty of the institution's restaurants – instead, wander over to the Museum of American History or up to the Old Post Office Pavilion. Shopping, by contrast, is great: the Gallery Shop sells books, CDs, and jewelry, and the Family Shop sells toys and kids' books.

RICHARD CUMMINS

National Museum of Natural History

National Museum of American History

From venerated historic touchstones like the original American flag to kitschy icons like Dorothy's ruby slippers, the original Kermit the Frog, and Fonzie's *(Happy Days)* jacket, the collection of the Museum of American History (Ⓜ Federal Triangle) celebrates US culture. Don't be misled by the museum's name: it offers no comprehensive survey of American history. Instead, it's a delightful hodge-podge of artifacts, founded in 1858 to house objects from the 'National Cabinet of Curiosities.' It's also enormous – you might visit twice and still not see everything.

The original whites-only lunch counter from the Woolworth's in Greensboro, North Carolina, tells the story of the sit-ins that led to desegregation; the poignant Vietnam Memorial collection exhibits the touching mementos left at 'the Wall' over the years. The first ladies' ball gowns, loaded with sequins and froo-froo, are another perennial favorite. Downstairs are celebrations of American technology: old autos, locomotives, Latino 'lowriders,' printing presses, steamship memorabilia, engines, turbines, and pumps.

There are hands-on kids' science and history centers, and a lively gift shop sells specialty items from around the US: Vermont maple syrup, Appalachian quilts, Charleston tea, Navajo jewelry, books, toys, and trinkets. The remodeled cafeteria has an updated menu; the Palm Court ice-cream parlor offers sit-down service in an ice-cream parlor.

WASHINGTON MONUMENT

This pale obelisk needling the sky near the Mall's west end honors the country's first president and the city's namesake. At 555 feet, it's also the tallest thing in the District.

The beautifully simple monument has a tangled history. Construction began in 1848 but wasn't completed until 37 years later. The first glitch occurred when a stone contributed by Pope Pius IX was stolen by antipapists, who then undermined fundraising efforts. A sorry-looking 152-foot stub sat un-

Washington Monument

finished during the Civil War – inspiring some jokes about federal impotence – but building resumed after the war (the two construction phases are evident in the monument's two shades of stone). Its capstone was set in 1884 amid a fierce storm. It survived an attempted terrorist attack in 1982. Recently, an 18-month renovation refurbished the aging structure.

An elevator takes you to an observation landing inside, where you may admire the spectacular views. Then you can descend the 897 steps – the shaft's interior is decorated with stones inscribed by various states and organizations.

It's open daily except Christmas, 9 am to 5 pm September to March, 8 am to midnight April to August. Admission is free, but expect long lines. You can get advance tickets through TicketMaster (☎ 800-505-5040) for a 'convenience charge' of $1.50 per ticket.

West of the monument is the small **Jefferson Pier**, a stone marking the axes of L'Enfant's original city plan. Southeast, the **Sylvan Theater** (☎ 426-6841) features free military and big-band concerts at 8 pm Tuesday to Friday and Sunday from June to August.

WEST POTOMAC PARK

The National Mall's western extension is officially called West Potomac Park; it incorporates the Reflecting Pool and the monuments surrounding it, plus the Tidal Basin and its monuments. To the south, East Potomac Park extends downward toward the confluence of the Potomac and Anacostia Rivers. In the late 19th century, the western part of the Mall was a malodorous swamp/sewage dump that sometimes flooded right up to the White House gates. Congress eventually had the area cleaned, filled, and decorated with memorials and grand avenues.

Smithsonian Metro station is the closest stop to the sites described in this section, but you'll do lots of walking while seeing the West Potomac Park sites. (East Potomac Park and the Tidal Basin are discussed in the Southwest DC section, later in this chapter.)

Constitution Gardens

Extending along Constitution Ave, these gardens were originally planned as a Tivoli-style amusement park, but that idea soon died. The gardens – really just a grove of trees – are now a quiet place for a stroll. In their midst is a small, kidney-shaped pool punctuated by a tiny island holding the **Signers' Memorial**, a plaza honoring the Declaration of Independence's signers. At their northeast corner squats an intriguing, aged stone cottage – the 1835 **C&O Canal Gatehouse**, a lockkeepers' house that is a remnant of the days when the Washington City Canal flowed through this area. The lock transferred boats from the City Canal onto the C&O Canal, which begins in Georgetown.

Vietnam Veterans Memorial

This somber arrow of black stone, striking the earth northeast of the Lincoln Memorial, is an American pilgrimage site. Designed by a 21-year-old Yale architecture student, Maya Lin, and dedicated in 1982, it was initially highly controversial but has since become the most-visited monument in DC.

Its two walls of polished Indian granite meet in a 10-foot apex and are inscribed with the names of the 58,209 soldiers killed in the war, arranged chronologically by date of death. It's an eloquent inversion of the Mall's other monuments: rather than a pale, ornate structure reaching skyward, it's dark, austere, and burrows into the earth, symbolizing the war's wound to the national psyche.

Visitors – there are crowds of them, night and day – move past the walls on a walkway. Paper indices at both ends help you locate individual names. Upon request, volunteers help you get rubbings of names from the Wall. The most moving remembrances are the notes, medals, and mementos left by survivors, family, and friends; these items are gathered up by park rangers, and some are displayed at the nearby Museum of American History. In 1984, opponents of Maya Lin's design insisted that a more traditional (and far

RICK GERHARTER

Vietnam Veterans Memorial

The Great Emancipator

less interesting) sculpture of soldiers be added nearby.

Also nearby is the **Women in Vietnam Memorial**, to the southeast. Here a group of women soldiers aid a fallen man; they're encircled by eight yellowwood trees that honor the eight women killed in action.

The memorials are open 24 hours, and rangers staff the information kiosk from 8 am to midnight daily, answering questions and giving talks about the Wall.

Lincoln Memorial

The Lincoln Memorial, at the Mall's west end, is more than a monument to the 16th president – its symbolic power became apparent immediately upon its completion, in 1922. Dr Robert Moten, president of historically black Tuskegee Institute, was invited to speak at the dedication, yet officials sat him in a segregated section of the audience. Outraged African Americans protested, and the memorial to the author of the Emancipation Proclamation became a symbol of the struggle for civil rights.

In 1939, black contralto Marian Anderson, barred from the DAR's Constitution Hall, sang from the memorial's steps instead; in 1963, the historic March on Washington reached its zenith here when Martin Luther King Jr delivered his 'I Have a Dream' speech.

Designed by Henry Bacon to resemble a Doric temple, the monument is a visual symbol of national unity: it balances the long axis of the Mall, a counterpoint to the Capitol at the eastern end. Its 36 columns represent the 36 states in Lincoln's union. Within, the seated statue of Lincoln, sculpted by Daniel Chester French, is framed by the carved text of the Gettysburg Address and Lincoln's Second Inaugural.

Inside the entrance is a National Park Service information desk and bookshop; rangers are around from 8 am to midnight daily to answer questions.

Behind the monument, paired statues called *The Arts of Peace* and *The Arts of War* flank the western approach from the Potomac. Before the monument, the 2000-foot

Reflecting Pool stretches away toward 17th St, its shallow, duck-speckled waters reflecting both the Lincoln and Washington memorials. At the pool's east end, the new **World War II Memorial** began construction in late 2000.

Korean War Veterans Memorial

Dedicated in 1995, this memorial, on the Reflecting Pool's south side, depicts a troop of heavily cloaked soldiers on night patrol. The life-size statues are shown mid-stride, heroic yet realistically exhausted and anxious. One local writer relates how 'walking among the soldiers early on a rainy morning is spooky…like being in a cinéma vérité before the talkies were invented.' Park Service rangers staff the nearby information kiosk from 8 am to midnight daily to answer questions and show you around.

Nearby is the small **District of Columbia War Memorial**, commemorating local soldiers killed in WWI. This circular temple, set amid a grove, is a nice place to escape Mall crowds.

Ghostly soldiers patrol at the
Korean War Veterans Memorial.

DENNIS JOHNSON

Downtown (Map 3)

'Downtown' is a portmanteau name loosely applied to the area between 3rd and 15th Sts NW and Constitution Ave and L St NW, comprising the Federal Triangle, Metro Center, Chinatown, Gallery Place, and Judiciary Square areas.

Downtown Washington, DC, has, like the rest of DC, seen its ups and downs. It began in the area now called Federal Triangle, east of the White House and bordered by Pennsylvania and Constitution Aves. In the 19th century, this area was a busy marketplace district that also had its share of vice: its first nickname was Murder Bay. The Civil War drew thousands of soldiers to the nation's capital, who in turn attracted thousands of prostitutes. (A persistent urban myth traces the nickname 'hooker' to General Joseph Hooker, commander of the DC troops, who ineffectually tried to limit prostitutes' working areas.)

In the 1920s, the federal government bought 'Federal Triangle' and built large office complexes for its workers. By this time, downtown had spread north and east and was a central commercial area. It began to decline, however, after WWII, when residents started moving to the suburbs. President Kennedy encouraged a revitalization effort in the 1960s, which resulted in the renovation of the Old Post Office, among other buildings. Yet downtown languished until quite recently.

Now, improved economic times have allowed the DC government to dump serious money into resuscitating the downtown area, and efforts are beginning to pay off. Housing, nightlife, galleries, restaurants, shops: all have made a comeback. The MCI Center sports arena has attracted many new visitors, and DC is building itself a new convention center north of Mt Vernon Square. Other visible signs of this downtown revitalization include the patrols of so-called SAMs, city employees in red jackets who can give visitors directions and help to tidy the streets.

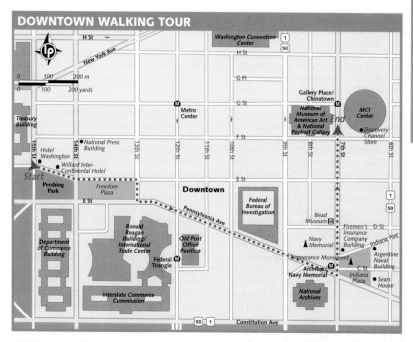

DOWNTOWN WALKING TOUR

Walking Tour

A fine place to start a downtown stroll is the corner of 15th St and Pennsylvania Ave, east of the White House. Pennsylvania Ave was originally planned to provide a straight line of sight between the White House and Capitol, but parks and the large Treasury Building have since blocked the view. (Note that some sights given a cursory description here are examined in detail later in this section.)

Walking east along Pennsylvania, you'll pass a power-broker block of historic hotels. The ultra-plush 1901 **Willard Inter-Continental**, at 14th St, is the newest in a series of hotels that have stood on this site since 1816. Something about it inspires the pen – here Julia Ward Howe wrote 'The Battle Hymn of the Republic' during the Civil War, and here Martin Luther King polished his famed 'I Have a Dream' oratory in 1963. The word 'lobbyist' was invented to describe guys who

slinked around its halls hunting political quarry (they still do). Its neighbor, the **Hotel Washington**, 515 15th St, is the oldest hotel in continuous use in DC.

Here, too, **Pershing Park** and **Freedom Plaza** attract brown-bag lunchtime crowds, and there's an outdoor café in summer (plenty of nearby carts offer fast food). Swing north on 14th St to see the **National Press Building**, at F St NW, housing journalists from around the world. The building holds the National Place complex of shops and a food court.

Back on Pennsylvania, you'll pass the grand **Old Post Office Pavilion**, another great place to stop and snack. The Dept of Justice is down at 10th St, and across Pennsylvania from it is the **FBI Building**, J Edgar's old digs, with free tours.

At 9th St, the **National Archives** display the Constitution, Declaration of Independence, and other famed documents. After seeing them, cool your heels in Indiana Plaza, at the junction of Pennsylvania Ave and 7th St.

This little plaza, ringed by historic buildings and centered upon the 19th-century Temperance Monument, offers a cross-section of Washington's downtown building styles, from the palatial neoclassicism of the Archives to the modern Market Square complex. On the plaza's east side, the twin-towered 1860 **Sears House** houses the National Council of Negro Women, founded by Mary McLeod Bethune; near it is the manorial white-marble 1889 **Argentine Naval Building**. Across Indiana Ave is the charming 1883 **Firemen's Insurance Company Building**, topped by a gilt onion dome.

Up 7th St, you'll find many art galleries to browse (see details in the Shopping chapter). The **Bead Museum** (☎ 624-4500), 400 7th St NW, Suite 202, displays ethnic beads and local beadwork; open 11 am to 4 pm Monday, Wednesday, and Saturday, 1 to 4 pm Sunday. Local artists lead free gallery walking tours at 6:30 pm on the third Thursday of each month, starting at the Discovery Channel Store, 601 F St NW (☎ 661-7582 for details).

Continuing north on 7th St takes you past the **National Portrait Gallery**, **National Museum of American Art**, and the **MCI Center**, where you can hop onto the Gallery Place Metro.

Old Post Office Pavilion

The landmark 1899 Old Post Office Pavilion (Ⓜ Federal Triangle) – nicknamed 'Old Tooth' for its spiky clock tower – is a downtown success story. Threatened with demolition during much of the 20th century, the Romanesque building was restored in 1978 and became a key attraction. Now its beautiful, bunting-draped, 10-story central atrium holds shops, a large food court, a discount-ticket counter, and government agencies.

The Park Service operates a glass elevator that takes visitors to the 270-foot **observation deck** for a broad view of downtown. The free tour starts from the northwest corner of the pavilion's ground floor. Tours run 10 am to 5:45 pm daily (8 am to 10:45 pm in summer).

RICHARD CUMMINS

National Archives Building & National Gallery of Art Sculpture Garden

Across 12th St is the **Ronald Reagan Building/International Trade Center**, a gigantic complex designed by James Ingo Freed. It's mostly office and conference space, but you can visit its downstairs food court and the DC Chamber of Commerce Visitor Information Center (☎ 328-4748) on the ground floor, and check out the huge, light-flooded central atrium. Behind it, near Federal Triangle Metro station, is a circular sculpture garden that's a great, quiet place to eat lunch.

RICK GERHARTER

Ronald Reagan Building/International Trade Center

National Aquarium

In the massive Dept of Commerce Building is the National Aquarium (☎ 482-2825; Ⓜ Federal Triangle), with its entrance on 14th St NW. It has a touch tank, displays on various marine ecosystems (the Chesapeake Bay, marshes), and a few rooms of aquariums, but with its small tanks, outdated signs, and faded photos, it's in desperate need of a makeover. Visit at 2 pm, when staff feed piranhas and sharks. Open 9 am to 5 pm daily; $3/75¢ adults/kids.

Federal Bureau of Investigation

The nation's G-men (and G-women) are based in a massive, neo-brutalist concrete building (☎ 324-3447; Ⓜ Archives) at 10th St and Pennsylvania Ave. It's officially named the J Edgar Hoover FBI Building in honor of the notorious director who led the bureau for 48 years (1924–72) and transformed the FBI into a huge crime-fighting bureaucracy.

Free tours are offered 9 am to 4:30 pm weekdays only. Enter from E St, and expect big lines, especially in summer, when people sometimes queue up by 7:30 am.

Visitors are admitted in groups of 30 for the hourlong, closely guarded tour (they don't let you straggle behind or even use the bathroom during the tour). Downstairs, you're shown some pretty simplistic exhibits about crimefighting – eg, a display on Asian gangs mostly discusses their tattoos.

Upstairs, you see the more interesting crime labs, forfeiture unit, and gun-ID room (with thousands of types, including a one-shot gun shaped like a cane). The real highlight comes at tour's end, when you're ushered into an auditorium to watch an FBI agent shoot at practice targets. Later the agent emerges to chat with the audience. Now's your chance to get answers to all your burning *X-Files* questions.

Navy Memorial

On Market Square, the Navy Memorial (☎ 737-2300; Ⓜ Archives) is a circular plaza bordered by masts sporting semaphore flags. On its western side, a sculpted seaman hunches down in his peacoat. Inside the eastern Market Square building, the visitors' center displays naval artifacts and ship

RICK GERHARTER

FBI Headquarters

JOHN NEUBAUER

The Declaration of Independence and Bill of Rights on display at the National Archives

models and has a small shop selling souvenirs and books. At 2 pm daily, its theater screens the gung-ho *At Sea*, which dramatically depicts battle-group maneuvers ($3/10/12 military/seniors/everyone else). Open 9:30 am to 5 pm Monday to Saturday; free.

National Archives

A grand neoclassical building on Constitution Ave between 7th and 9th Sts NW houses the National Archives (☎ 501-5400; Ⓜ Archives). Inside, a dimly lit rotunda displays the three original documents upon which the US government is based – the Declaration of Independence, Constitution, and Bill of Rights. Also here is the 1297 version of the Magna Carta, courtesy of Texas billionaire (and erstwhile presidential candidate) H Ross Perot. These precious documents are sealed in airtight, helium-filled cases that sink nightly into an underground vault to protect them from attack or theft.

Expect long lines, and don't expect to linger over the Big Three – guards make you keep moving even as you pass them, but you can study the Magna Carta and other documents at your leisure. Open 10 am to 5:30 pm daily (till 9 pm April 1 to Labor Day); free. Enter the Rotunda from the Mall side of the building; you'll pass through X-ray security. *Note:* the Rotunda plans to close for renovation from July 2001 until summer 2003.

The Archives themselves preserve reams of essential government documents, from the Louisiana Purchase Treaty to the Emancipation Proclamation. Researchers can access documents 8:45 am to 5 pm Monday to Saturday; enter on the Pennsylvania Ave side and go to room No 403 to register.

After visiting the Rotunda, go to the Archives' Pennsylvania Ave side to see the **first memorial to Franklin Delano Roosevelt**, a small stone at the corner of 9th St. A bigger memorial on the Tidal Basin also honors FDR (see the Southwest DC section, later in this chapter).

National Museum of American Art & National Portrait Gallery

These Smithsonian museums are roommates in the 19th-century US Patent Office building at 9th and F Sts NW (Ⓜ Gallery Place), a neoclassical quadrangle that hosted Lincoln's second inaugural ball and a Civil War hospital. Walt Whitman based 'The Wound-Dresser' upon his experiences as a volunteer nurse here. ('The hurt and wounded I pacify with soothing hand/I sit by the restless all the dark night…')

Note, however, that both museums are closed for renovation until 2003. For information on reopening dates, call the Smithsonian at ☎ 357-2700. The Portrait Gallery's works include portraits of important Americans and biographical exhibits. The Museum of American Art's holdings include a spirited collection of American folk art, such as James Hampton's *Throne of the Third Heaven of the Nations Millennium General Assembly*. This funky room-size tinfoil shrine was constructed in a DC garage by a government janitor and discovered after his death.

MCI Center

This 20,000-seat sports arena (☎ 628-3200; ⓜ Gallery Place), 601 F St NW, opened in Chinatown in 1997 to become the new home of the NHL Capitols, NBA Wizards, and WNBA Washington Mystics. The arena also includes the **Sports Gallery** (☎ 661-5133), with interactive sports displays and memorabilia from Babe Ruth to Mark McGwire to Sammy Sosa. Closed Mondays; $5.

Another big attraction is the **Discovery Channel Store** (☎ 639-0908), on the F St side, offering a truly postmodern shopping experience: a museum store without the museum. Run by the Discovery TV network, the four-floor complex has educational displays on dinosaurs, weather, astronomy, etc, among its shelves of toys, puzzles, stuffed animals, nature books, and jewelry. You can also watch a 15-minute film, *Destination DC*, that profiles the capital. Guided walking tours of downtown leave from here daily; see the Getting Around chapter for details. Open daily.

Chinatown

You enter DC's small Chinatown under **Friendship Arch**, the ornate golden gate on H St at 7th St NW – it's the largest of its kind outside China and was until recently Chinatown's most appealing feature. The area was in decay for years, but the MCI Center brought more visitors and nightlife to the area. Now Chinatown's booming, with new eateries, bars, and clubs springing up like mushrooms in the blocks around the 7th and H St intersection. The mood's no longer particularly Chinese, however ('MCItown,' anyone?).

At 604 H St is the **Surratt House** (now Go-Los Restaurant), where the Lincoln-assassination conspirators met in 1865. Its owner, Mary Surratt, was eventually hung at Fort McNair for her part in the plot. Chinatown also boasts a passel of beautiful churches, such as the Calvary Baptist Church at 9th and H Sts, the Gothic-style New Hope Baptist Church across the street, and, down

at 5th and H Sts, the 1890 St Mary's Catholic Church.

Martin Luther King Jr Memorial Library

DC's main library (☎ 727-1221; ⓜ Metro Center), 901 G St NW, is Mies van der Rohe's only Washington building, a low, sleek black-glass structure. It holds a popular mural portraying the Civil Rights Movement, and it's an important community and cultural center, sponsoring many readings, concerts, films, and children's activities. There's a gift kiosk as well, with specialty periodicals. Open daily.

National Building Museum

This museum (☎ 272-2448; ⓜ Judiciary Square), 401 F St NW, occupies an entire city block. Devoted to the architectural arts, it's appropriately housed in an architectural jewel: the 1887 Old Pension Building. Designed by Civil War Quartermaster General Montgomery Meigs, it's a massive red-brick variation on Rome's Farnese Palace. In its atrium (the Great Hall), rows of Corinthian columns – among the world's largest – rise 75 feet high. Four stories of ornately ornamented balconies flank the dramatic 316-foot-wide atrium, a grand setting for inaugural balls since the Cleveland Administration.

The showy space easily overshadows the exhibits, but they're good nonetheless – 'Washington: City and Symbol' examines

Chinatown's Friendship Arch

Atrium of the National Building Museum

the deeper significance and symbolism of DC architecture. Changing exhibits focus on American suburban growth, emerging architects, and contemporary planning issues. Concerts here make the most of the natural acoustics, and there's also a coffee bar. The museum shop has great crafts and rich coffee-table books. Open 10 am to 4 pm Monday to Saturday, noon to 4 pm Sunday; free.

National Law Enforcement Officers Memorial

This memorial, on Judiciary Square across F St from the Building Museum (Ⓜ Judiciary Square), commemorates the 14,500 US police officers killed on duty since 1794. In the style of the Vietnam memorial, names of the dead are carved on two marble walls curving around a plaza, and paper indices help you locate names. The memorial is saved from visual dullness by bronze lion statues that peek over the walls, guarding their sleeping cubs. The visitors' center, nearby at 605 E St NW, displays more information about the fallen officers; open daily.

Adas Israel Synagogue

Housing the Jewish Historical Society of Greater Washington (☎ 789-0900; Ⓜ Judiciary Square), 701 3rd St NW, this tiny brick 1876 synagogue is DC's oldest. Ring the doorbell and society staff let you into the upstairs sanctuary, which displays its original ark, antique ritual objects, and photos of DC's 19th-century Jewish community. The temple once sat at 6th and G Sts NW but was trucked to its current address in the 1970s. Open 10 am to 4 pm Monday to Thursday; donations welcome.

National Museum of Women in the Arts

The only American museum exclusively devoted to women's artwork, Women in the Arts (☎ 783-5000; Ⓜ Metro Center) is in a magnificent Beaux-Arts mansion at 1250 New York Ave NW. Its collection – 2600 works by almost 700 women artists from 28 countries – moves from Renaissance artists like Lavinia Fontana to 20th-century works by Kahlo, O'Keeffe, Frankenthaler, and Chicago. Works are largely paintings, and mostly portraits at that – not as rich a range as one might hope. But its special exhibits are extraordinary, gathering works from around the world by such artists as Camille Claudel, Sofonisba Anguissola, and Remedios Varo and introducing them to a wider audience. A fine shop, café, and research library are located here, and the museum hosts literary readings, lectures, concerts, and films by women. Open 10 am to 5 pm Monday to Saturday, noon to 5 pm Sunday; suggested donation $3.

RICK GERHARTER

National Museum of Women in the Arts

Ford's Theatre

On April 14, 1865, John Wilkes Booth, actor and Confederate sympathizer, assassinated Abraham Lincoln as President and Mrs Lincoln watched *Our American Cousin* in the Presidential Box of Ford's Theatre

PHILIP GAME

Ford's Theatre, where John Wilkes Booth shot Lincoln

(☎ 347-4833; Ⓜ Metro Center), 511 10th St NW. The box remains draped with a period flag to this day. You can look around on your own, catch a tour, or, to fully enjoy the beautifully restored theater, attend one of its performances. The basement **Lincoln Museum** maps out the assassination's details and displays related artifacts.

The unconscious president was carried across the street to **Petersen House**, today immortalized as the 'house where Lincoln died.' Its tiny, unassuming rooms create a movingly personal portrait of that slow death. The national historic area encompassing both sites is open 9 am to 5 pm daily (the theater occasionally closes for rehearsals or matinees); free. It's popular, so expect lines.

Other Downtown Attractions

Folks who listen to Scott Simon and Bob Edwards every day will enjoy a tour of **National Public Radio** headquarters (Ⓜ Mt Vernon Square), 635 Massachusetts Ave NW. They run at 11 am each Thursday; free.

The **Inter-American Development Bank**, 1300 New York Ave NW, houses the excellent, under-visited Cultural Center (☎ 623-3774; Ⓜ Metro Center), which hosts art exhibitions, concerts, and lectures focusing upon artists from the bank's 46 member countries, especially Latin America. Open 11 am to 6 pm weekdays; free.

White House Area & Foggy Bottom (Map 3)

The site of the White House was selected by George Washington and Pierre L'Enfant in 1791. The mansion balances the long axis of Pennsylvania Ave, heading northwest from the Capitol, in a visual metaphor of the power balance between the executive and legislative branches of the US government. Originally called the President's House, the White House was painted white after being burned in the War of 1812. Teddy Roosevelt later gave official sanction to the executive mansion's popular name.

The White House originally sat in a rather rural, orchard-covered area, but like the magnet it was, it soon drew the wealthy and powerful around it. Lafayette Square, to its north, became DC's first really fash-ionable area, filled with the sweeping skirts of wealthy ladies calling on one another at lovely mansions bordering the square. By the 20th century, bureaucracy swamped the area, and the White House neighbors are now mostly federal office buildings.

West of the White House is the district known as Foggy Bottom. The nickname probably derived from the district's original inhabitants (a gasworks, brewery, cement factory, and other smoggy industries), but modern wits say the name describes the bureaucratic hot air arising from the area's numerous federal agencies.

Before it was foggy, though, it was funky – its first settlers, Germans from Hamburg who arrived in the mid-18th century, called their home Funkstown. (Some church services are still read in German here.) Laborers lived close to the riverside industries, and wealthier folks lived north of K St. After the Civil War, many new black residents settled south of K St as well.

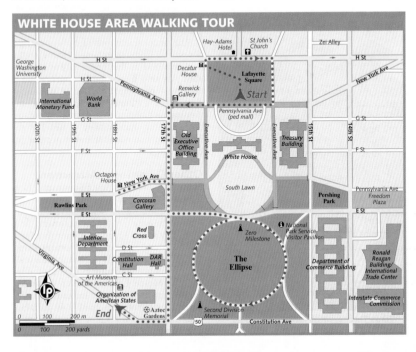

WHITE HOUSE AREA WALKING TOUR

THINGS TO SEE & DO

In 1912, the campus of George Washington University was built here, and its students and their nightlife rescue this workaday district from terminal stuffiness.

Walking Tour

A stroll through this neighborhood can begin where the nightly network news always seems to begin: on the north side of the White House, the nation's best-known private home.

Old Executive Office Building

RICHARD CUMMINS

Here, **Lafayette Square** (named for the Marquis de Lafayette, the Revolutionary War hero) is a grassy park studded with statues of foreigners who have aided the US in its wars. It's a nice spot to walk around, play at chessboard tables, or observe tourists, undercover security police, and placard-carrying demonstrators (a near-constant presence here). Once an orchard, the square was lined in the 19th century with the mansions of the rich and powerful. The writer Henry Adams, who lived in a mansion on its northern edge, described it thus: 'Lafayette Square was society…Beyond the square, the country began.'

Among the square's remaining Victorian homes is **Decatur House**, where tour guides tell stories of the square's high society. In the 1960s, the government proposed tearing down these historic houses to erect government buildings, but Jacqueline Kennedy's

The Hay-Adams Hotel, on Lafayette Square

RICK GERHARTER

appeals spared them. Modern government monoliths now loom directly behind the square, lending it a somewhat poignant mood.

On the west side of 16th St, just north of the square, is the **Hay-Adams Hotel**, an exclusive, quietly luxurious hostelry that gained a whiff of notoriety in the mid-'80s when Colonel Oliver North solicited illegal contributions for the Nicaraguan contras here. It was built on the site of Henry Adams' old mansion. To the east is little **St John's Church**, where a pew is permanently reserved for presidential families.

Pennsylvania Ave NW runs between Lafayette Square and the White House. Until recently, it was a central thoroughfare, but after two threatening incidents in 1994 (a stolen airplane crashed into White House grounds, and a man fired a semiautomatic at the mansion), the portion by the White House was closed to car traffic. Now concrete blockades and a heightened security presence add an imposing imperial air to the White House, but they also make the area a more pleasant pedestrian walkway.

West of the square on Pennsylvania Ave, you'll find the national crafts museum, the **Renwick Gallery**, in a historic mansion at the corner of 17th St. Across from it, there's no missing the wonderfully baroque **Old Executive Office Building**, where White House staff work.

Head south on 17th St to find the **Ellipse**, the expansive park just south of the White House. Bordering the National Mall, it's surrounded by more sights, and its northernmost point provides you the classic photo opportunity: the White House facade, in dignified remove across its private South Lawn.

Also on the Ellipse's north edge is the **Zero Milestone**, a stone marker from which all US highway distances are measured (in case you ever wondered). The National Christmas Tree is illuminated nearby in December, and whimsical urban visionaries have proposed installing a 'national sofa' here, before a large screen allowing two-way communication with White House residents. The Park Service operates a **visitor pavilion** in the Ellipse's northeast corner (snacks and restrooms available). Another good backdrop for a photo is the **Second Division Memorial** at the Ellipse's southern edge – its centerpiece is a giant golden hand thrusting forth a flaming sword.

The elegant row of monumental buildings on 17th St at the Ellipse's west side, from New York Ave NW south to the Mall, includes the wonderful Corcoran Gallery (with the Octagon House directly behind it), the Red Cross, Daughters of the American Revolution, and the Organization of American States, at the corner of Constitution Ave. All have exhibits open to the public, so you can end your tour with a stroll through art galleries and historic rooms.

White House

Every US president since John Adams has lived in this 132-room mansion (**M** McPherson Square), 1600 Pennsylvania Ave NW, and its stature has grown through the years. No longer a mere residence, it's now the central icon of the American presidency.

It was torched by the British in 1814 and reopened in 1818. An overhaul in 1950 gutted almost the entire interior, and Jacqueline Kennedy's extensive redecoration campaign in the 1960s replaced the previous hodgepodge with more tasteful furnishings. Presidents have customized the property over time: Grant put in a personal zoo; FDR added a pool; Truman a balcony; Bush a horseshoe-throwing lane; and Clinton a jogging track. Some residents never leave: it's said that Eleanor Roosevelt and Harry Truman both sighted Lincoln's ghost in Abe's old study.

Touring the White House Back before Herbert Hoover's era, presidents used to open the doors at noon each day to shake visitors' hands. Alas, no longer.

Now, 20-minute self-guided free tours are offered from 10 am to noon Tuesday to Saturday only. From late March to early September, you must get a free ticket at the White House Visitors Center (**☎** 456-7041; **M** Federal Triangle), in the Dept of Commerce Building at Pennsylvania Ave and 15th St NW. Tickets are distributed for that day only and distribution starts at 7:30 am. Get here *early*, especially in spring and summer. The visitors' center is open 7 am to 4 pm daily. At other times of year, you don't need a ticket – go to the White House's southeast gate for first-come, first-served entry.

Tours may be cancelled because of official events, so call the visitors' center before you visit.

For US citizens, free guided tours are also available. Contact your congressional representative or senator and request free guided-tour tickets at least two months before you plan to visit (call the Capitol switchboard at **☎** 224-3121).

Self-guided tours show you parts of the 1st and 2nd floors, including the East, Blue, Red, and Green Rooms. A pamphlet highlights details on decor and history, but you'll enjoy the tour more if you read a bit about the presidents beforehand, so that you can personalize the house by imagining the powerful personalities who shaped it.

Special **House & Garden Tours** are offered on selected weekends in April and October; **Candlelit Tours** run in December. The **Easter Egg Roll**, for kids three to six, happens on the South Lawn each Easter Monday (the only time the grounds are open to the public). See www.whitehouse .gov for details.

LEE FOSTER

1600 Pennsylvania Ave

St John's Church

On the square's north side, at 16th and H Sts NW, St John's (☎ 347-8766; Ⓜ McPherson Square) is the 'Church of the Presidents' – every president since Madison has attended its services at least once. Lyndon Johnson prayed here on the first morning of his presidency, after JFK was killed.

Designed in 1815 by Capitol architect Benjamin Henry Latrobe, the church reserves a pew (No 54, purchased by Madison) for presidential families. The church bell was made from a British cannon captured in the War of 1812. A small, butter-colored building, St John's isn't DC's most imposing church, but it's among the most charming. You can enter to see the sanctuary's lovely stained glass from 9 am to 3 pm daily, or take a tour after the 11 am service on the first Sunday of each month.

Decatur House

At Lafayette Square's northwest corner, Decatur House (☎ 842-0920; Ⓜ Farragut West), 748 Jackson Place NW, was designed in 1818 by Benjamin Latrobe for the naval hero Stephen Decatur (who got himself

killed in a duel just a year later). A tour shows you the house's austere architectural charms and details the lives of not only its famous tenants – including Martin Van Buren and Henry Clay – but of the slaves who waited upon them. Buy tour tickets in the H St gift shop, which also sells souvenirs like reproductions of presidential china. Open 10 am to 3 pm Tuesday to Friday, noon to 4 pm weekends; $4/2.50 adults/kids.

Treasury Building

This squat monolith (☎ 622-0896; Ⓜ McPherson Square) occupies a city block by the White House, at Pennsylvania Ave and 15th St NW. To end the debate on where to build it (planners didn't want to block the White House's view of Congress), President Andrew Jackson stuck his cane in the ground and declared, 'Build it here!'

The 1836 Greek Revival colossus (each of its 30 36-foot columns were carved from a single granite block) is decorated as befits a treasury, with golden eagles, ornate balustrades, and a two-story Cash Room, constructed with eight types of marble. US currency was printed in the basement from

1863 to 1880. This building no longer prints any money, but it is often confused with the present 'money factory,' the Bureau of Printing & Engraving, south of the Mall.

Free 1½-hour guided tours are offered at 10, 10:20, 10:40, and 11 am Saturday only. Call for reservations (a complicated process in which you leave a message and a tour representative calls you back). The tours are popular, so book a few weeks ahead. It's worth the bother, for the interiors are very impressive.

Blair & Lee Houses

The 1824 Blair House (**Ⓜ** Farragut West), 1653 Pennsylvania Ave, has been the official presidential guesthouse since 1942, when Eleanor Roosevelt got sick of tripping over dignitaries in her White House. A plaque on the front fence commemorates the bodyguard killed here while protecting President Truman from a 1950 assassination attempt by Puerto Rican pro-independence terrorists. The neighboring 1858 Lee House was built by the famous general's family. Here scion Robert E declined command of the Union Army when the Civil War erupted. Both houses are private.

Renwick Gallery

The Smithsonian's Renwick (**☎** 357-2531; **Ⓜ** Farragut West), on Pennsylvania Ave at 17th St, next to Blair House, invites you up the stairs of its regal 1859 mansion and then startles you with some really wild pieces of artistic whimsy. This is the national crafts

The elegant Renwick Gallery

RICK GERHARTER

museum, displaying woodwork, ceramics, sculpture, metalwork, furniture, and the like, but 'crafts' doesn't really describe these pieces – they're wonderfully creative artworks.

The many playful pieces make it a wonderful place to introduce kids to art. They especially love Larry Fuentes' *Game Fish*, a sailfish trophy meticulously adorned with beads, buttons, badminton birdies, Scrabble tiles, dominoes, yo-yos, Pez dispensers, and more. Grownups like the Grand Salon and Octagon Room, recently restored in the grand Gilded-Age styles of the 1870s and 1880s. There's a great museum store downstairs (see the Shopping chapter). Open 10 am to 5:30 pm daily; free.

Old Executive Office Building

Truman called it 'the greatest monstrosity in America'; Hoover griped that it was an 'architectural orgy.' Yet the ornate OEOB (**☎** 395-5895; **Ⓜ** Farragut West) delights most visitors today. With its 900 columns and wiggy marble loop-de-loops, this exuberantly excessive French Second Empire building resembles something designed by Monty Python.

Actually, it was designed by Alfred Mullet in the 1870s to house State, War, and Navy Dept staff. His design was roundly blasted, and poor old Mullet killed himself two years after its completion. Today it houses White House staff; in the 1980s, Ollie North ran his illegal fundraising for the contras from basement room No 392.

Extremely popular free Saturdaymorning tours must be reserved by calling 9 am to noon Tuesday to Friday; call several weeks ahead. The Indian Treaty Rooms are particularly noteworthy.

The Octagon

This historic house (**☎** 638-3105; **Ⓜ** Farragut West), 1799 New York Ave NW at 18th St, was built in 1800 and now houses the American Institute of Architects' museum. Designed by William Thornton (the Capitol's first architect) for the

RICK GERHARTER

The Octagon

wealthy Tayloe family, the Octagon housed President and Dolly Madison after the Brits burned the White House in 1814. Madison signed the Treaty of Ghent, which ended that war, in its 2nd-floor drawing room.

The house is a symmetrically winged Federal structure designed to fit an odd triangular lot. Behind it, the AIA's large modern offices wrap around the little house like a protective older brother. Knowledgeable docents show you the Octagon's hidden doorways, twin staircases, and period furniture; upstairs galleries host topnotch exhibits on architecture and design. Downstairs, exhibits explain the careful archaeological work required to restore this and other old houses. Open 10 am to 4 pm Tuesday to Sunday; $5/3 adults/kids.

The AIA building itself has more fine exhibits on historic and modern architecture on its 1st and 2nd floors, along with an excellent architectural bookshop. Open 8:30 am to 5 pm weekdays; free. The AIA also offers tours and workshops – get a calendar at the Octagon.

Corcoran Gallery

In a beautiful 1897 Beaux-Arts building overlooking the Ellipse, the Corcoran (☎ 639-1700; Ⓜ Farragust West), 500 17th St NW, exhibits American and European masterworks alongside contemporary paintings, photography, and sculpture. Its esteemed American collection includes examples of the Hudson River, ashcan, pop, and abstract expressionist schools. The Corcoran also houses an art school and mounts intriguing exhibits of its students' work. In 1999 the Corcoran selected Frank Gehry (famed architect of the Bilbao Guggenheim) to design a new wing that will double its gallery space.

Café des Artistes, on the 1st floor, has an unusually good menu for a museum restaurant; there's a gospel brunch some Sundays, and jazz musicians play at the museum weekly. The front desk has calendars. Open 10 am to 5 pm daily except Tuesday (till 9 pm Thursday); admission by donation of $3 for adults and kids over 12.

Behind the Corcoran, on E St NW between 18th and 20th Sts, is pretty **Rawlins Park**, named for US Grant's Secretary of War. With goldfish in its little pond and blooming magnolias in spring and summer, it's among downtown DC's most charming oases.

Red Cross

Three pillared marble mansions on 17th St NW between D and E Sts house the national headquarters of the 150-year-old Red Cross. Tiffany windows in its main building depict nurses tending swooning soldiers. At 1730 E St is the **American Red Cross Museum** (☎ 639-3300; Ⓜ Farragut West), displaying cool old Red Cross posters by Norman Rockwell and NC Wyeth and exhibits on disaster relief and the organization's history. Open 9 am to 4 pm weekdays; free.

DAR Constitution Hall

The Daughters of the American Revolution (☎ 628-1776; Ⓜ Farragut West), a patriotic organization, make their home at, appropriately, 1776 D St NW. Its Memorial Continental Building contains the DAR Museum (consisting of 33 period-decorated 'State Rooms') and the DAR Library (holding a wealth of genealogical information dating back to the Revolution). Both are open 8:30 am to 4:30 pm weekdays, 1 to 5 pm Sunday; the museum's free but the library charges a small fee. State Room tours are offered 10 am to 3 pm weekdays, 1 to 5 pm Sunday.

Adjacent is 3200-seat Constitution Hall (☎ 628-4780), a popular concert/performance venue designed by the neoclassicist John Russell Pope. In 1939, the DAR barred Marian Anderson, a black singer, from performing at Constitution; instead Anderson sang to a crowd of 75,000 at the Lincoln Memorial in an iconic civil-rights moment.

Organization of American States

The OAS (☎ 458-3000; Ⓜ Farragut West), 17th St NW at Constitution Ave, was sort of a forerunner to the UN: an international organization founded in 1890 to promote cooperation among Western Hemisphere nations. Its main building is a marble palazzo surrounded by the sculpture-studded **Aztec Gardens**. They are punctuated by a decorative pool (designed by Gertrude Vanderbilt Whitney) that's presided over by a squatting Xochipilli, the Aztec flower god.

In a small building on 18th St behind the OAS is the **Art Museum of the Americas** (☎ 458-6016), featuring modern Latin American art. Open 10 am to 5 pm Tuesday to Sunday; free.

Department of the Interior

This department (Ⓜ Farragut West), on C St NW at 19th St, responsible for managing the US's natural resources, is in a mammoth neoclassical office block designed by the marvelously named Waddy B Wood (no relation to Wascally Wabbit). On its 1st floor, the small **Dept of the Interior Museum** (☎ 208-4743) displays landscape art, Indian artifacts and historical photos of Indian life, and exhibits on wildlife and resource management. The museum is little-visited, and that's a shame; its exhibits are limited but excellent. Museum hours are 8:30 am to 4:30 pm weekdays, 1 to 4 pm the third Saturday of the month. Admission is free.

The 1st floor also holds the National Park Service Information office (☎ 208-4747), with pamphlets on all the country's parks and most DC historic sites; a library; and the Indian Crafts Shop (see Shopping). Show photo ID to enter the building.

Federal Reserve

The Federal Reserve (☎ 452-3000; Ⓜ Foggy Bottom), on C St between 20th and 21st Sts

NW, is as close to a central bank as the US possesses. It offers free tours – no, you don't see Greenspan – at 2:30 pm Thursday. Alternately, see the **Federal Reserve Board Gallery** (☎ 452-3686), another of those little-known but excellent galleries hidden in the bowels of DC's federal office buildings. It shows 19th- and 20th-century paintings, sculptures, and drawings, plus more idiosyncratic exhibitions – the recent 'Moneymaking' focused on the art of currency design. Open 11 am to 2 pm weekdays; free.

National Academy of Sciences

The academy (☎ 334-2436; Ⓜ Foggy Bottom), on Constitution Ave between 21st and 22nd Sts NW, which advises the government on scientific and technical issues, hosts scientific and art exhibitions, concerts, and symposia. Recent exhibitions have included deep-space and Antarctic photography and historic maps. Open 9 am to 5 pm weekdays; free.

Its nicely landscaped grounds along Constitution feature DC's most huggable monument: the **Albert Einstein statue**. The larger-than-life, sandal-shod, chubby bronze reclines on a bench, and little kids crawl all over him. He's elevated on a 'star map' pedestal that depicts the heavens that his theories reshaped for humanity.

State Department

Across C St is the US State Dept (☎ 647-3241; Ⓜ Foggy Bottom), covering two blocks between 21st and 23rd Sts NW. It's a forbidding, well-guarded edifice, but you can tour its grand Diplomatic Reception Rooms, where Cabinet members and the Secretary of State entertain visiting potentates amid ornate 18th-century American antiques. Call at least a month beforehand to reserve a tour spot; tours run at 9:30 and 10:30 am and 2:45 pm weekdays; free. Bring photo ID; no kids under 12. Enter at C and 22nd Sts.

The Watergate

The riverfront Watergate complex, 2650 Virginia Ave NW (Ⓜ Foggy Bottom), is a posh private community encompassing apartments, designer boutiques, and a deluxe hotel. Its name is a synonym for American political scandal: in 1972, a break-in at Democratic National Committee headquarters here was linked to CREEP – the Committee to Re-elect the President – leading to the unprecedented resignation of a sitting president, Richard Nixon. Later, Monica Lewinsky, famed White House pizza gal, lived here during her affair with President Clinton.

Its curious name derives from a never-realized 1930s plan to build a ceremonial water gate in the Potomac, a stairway onto which visiting dignitaries could disembark. With its undulating facade and dragon-tooth balconies, it's among DC's most recognizable landmarks, and it houses swank shops from Valentino to Vera Wang, plus the upscale Aquarelle restaurant. The hotel's lobby lounge is a good place to have a drink and look at the Potomac.

Kennedy Center
Overlooking the Potomac, the Kennedy Center (☎ 467-4600; Ⓜ Foggy Bottom), 2700 F St NW, was dedicated in 1964 as a 'living memorial' to JFK. The center's theaters, concert hall, opera house, and cinema almost single-handedly reversed Washington's former reputation as a cultural desert. Its site once housed the Christian Heurich Brewery, makers of Senate-brand beer until 1956.

There are nice river views from the greenery-shaded terrace (particularly at sunset), several shops, a café, and the Roof Terrace restaurant. You may look around on your own or take a tour (offered by appointment 10 am to 1 pm), but the best way to see the center is at one of the many performances, festivals, films, and concerts held here year-round. See more details in the Entertainment chapter.

Other Attractions
The **Arts Club of Washington** (☎ 331-7282; Ⓜ Farragut West), 2017 I St NW, has two galleries that feature paintings and photography by local artists, plus a good Friday-night concert series. Open 10 am to 5 pm Tuesday to Friday; 10 am to 2 pm Saturday; free.

The 1887 **St Mary's Episcopal Church** (Ⓜ Foggy Bottom), 730 23rd St NW, sheltered the first black Episcopal congregation in DC. It's a beautiful red-brick building designed by James Renwick (designer of the Mall's Smithsonian Castle) especially for the congregation.

In spring 2000, anti-globalization protestors jammed Foggy Bottom streets during the annual meeting of the **World Bank**. The controversial multilateral lender is housed in a fiercely security-conscious rampart at 1818 H St NW, and it runs the excellent World Bank InfoShop just across 18th St NW. It sells a vast collection of books and documents on all aspects of development and economics; open weekdays.

Capitol Hill & Southeast DC (Map 4)

Three years after Jefferson and Hamilton decided upon Washington as the site of the federal city, construction began on the grand Capitol gracing the rise east of the Potomac. Thus was born 'the Hill,' the district whose name is synonymous with American politics.

During the Civil War, Capitol Hill was nicknamed 'Bloody Hill' for all the injured soldiers who moved into legislative buildings that served as temporary hospitals. Today the residential areas east of the Capitol are home to a cross-section of Washingtonians, poor living near rich, longtime residents next to transplanted staffers, in a neighborhood that combines both beautiful historic-district rowhouses – among the city's most charming – and rundown areas.

Visitors should remember this mixture when they are walking around: crime is a problem east of 8th St and south of I-395. Keep your eyes open and only go where you feel comfortable.

Walking Tour
The Hill is Washington's epicenter – all city avenues intersect at an imaginary point

under the Capitol dome. Strolling the Hill shows you many famed federal landmarks, but it also offers insights into the city's history, glimpses of gorgeous old houses, and visits to historic sites. After following this tour, you're encouraged to wander through other areas of the Hill.

The best place to begin your tour is, of course, the **US Capitol** itself. If you approach it from the Mall side, you're actually looking at the building's back. On the front (east) side, a small plaza opens outward, surrounded by monolithic government landmarks. If Congress is in session, you'll encounter a hectic scene of neckpass-wearing government staffers, pods of well-dressed school groups, and the occasional clump of journalists jockeying for position at an outdoor press conference.

After touring the Capitol's grand interiors and seeing the Mall views from its western terraces, cross the plaza and 1st St to climb the marble steps of the **Supreme Court**. Then head southward on 1st St to see the elaborate Jefferson Building of the **Library of Congress**.

For a quiet walk through the Hill's historic residential district, follow E Capitol St past the **Folger Shakespeare Library**, to your right. You can cut a bit north to see the **Frederick Douglass Museum** (☎ 544-6130), 320 A St NE. Housed in the abolitionist's first DC home, it has exhibits on Douglass' life and achievements. Open for tours noon to 2 pm Monday, Wednesday, and Friday.

Among the 19th-century rowhouses, brownstones, and old corner shops on E Capitol is **Lincoln Park**, a lively neighborhood center with two historic statues and a nice Capitol view (unobstructed by trees in winter). Its **Emancipation Memorial** (1876) portrays a kneeling man (modeled upon the last man captured under the Fugitive Slave Law) who snaps slavery's chains as Lincoln proffers the Emancipation Proclamation to him. Freed black slaves raised all the funds

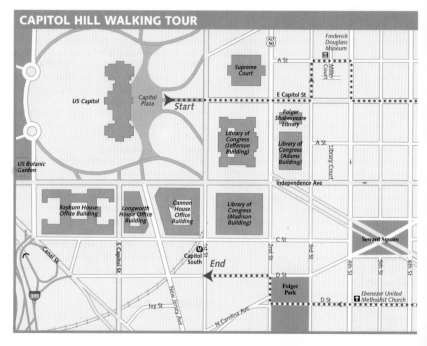

to erect it. The **Mary McLeod Bethune Memorial** (1974) honors the black educator and founder of the National Council of Negro Women. It was DC's first statue of a black woman.

Around Lincoln Park are many beautiful rowhouses. Particularly noteworthy are the granite houses at **1111–1119 E Capitol St**, built in 1892 just south of the park. East, at 14th and E Capitol Sts, is the **Car Barn**, DC's 19th-century trolley turnaround (now private housing). Return to 11th St SE and walk south to see more lovely homes, including **Philadelphia Row** (124–154 11th St SE), constructed in the 1860s by a builder with a homesick Philadelphia-born wife.

Turn right on Independence Ave and walk to North Carolina Ave to find **Eastern Market**, at 7th St SE. This lively farmers'/artists' market, with a great seafood lunch counter inside, is a good stop for a sandwich. Once fortified, you can hop the Eastern Market Metro or continue your walk.

RICHARD CUMMINS

US Supreme Court

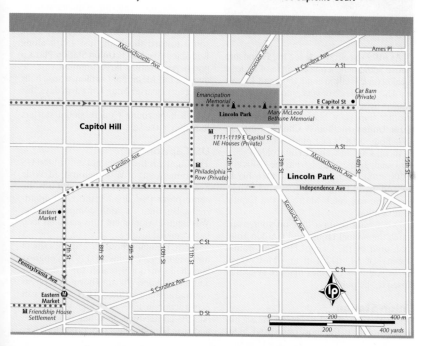

Philadelphia Row

At 619 D St SE, you'll see the **Friendship House Settlement**, a fine example of Federal architecture. Built around 1800 and known as 'The Maples,' it was once owned by Francis Scott Key. At 4th and D Sts SE is another important black-history site: **Ebenezer United Methodist Church**, which in 1864 housed DC's first public black school. Both sites are in Capitol Hill's oldest area, with many homes dating from the 1840s and 1850s; stroll around and look at their black-iron stoops and charming brickwork. Afterward, you can catch Metro at the Capitol South station.

Don't want to do a tour on your own? Catch the annual House and Garden Tour, sponsored by the Capitol Hill Restoration Society (☎ 543-0425) in mid-May, which shows you lovely homes that are generally closed to the public.

Union Station

Union Station (☎ 371-9441), 50 Massachusetts Ave NE, is the most impressive gateway into Washington. The massive 1908 Beaux-Arts depot was beautifully restored in 1988 (after years of neglect) and transformed into a contemporary city center and transit hub, with Amtrak connections to destinations throughout the East. There's also a Metro station, cinema, and 200,000-sq-foot complex of shops and restaurants. Many travelers' services are here: Travelers' Aid, transit information, currency exchange, and ATMs.

The huge main hall – the 'Grand Concourse' – is patterned after the Roman Baths of Diocletian. The legionnaire statues lining its 2nd-floor balconies hold strategically placed shields across their waists – the station's designers added them so ladies wouldn't be offended by unsightly bulges. In the station's east wing, the old Presidential Waiting Room, where dignitaries and celebrities once alighted when they traveled to DC, is now a restaurant, but it retains its high ceilings and lush detailing.

The station's exterior, with its Beaux-Arts Columbia Memorial Fountain, offers vistas of the Capitol and avenues radiating south toward the Mall. Just south along Louisiana Ave NW is **Union Station Plaza**, a grassy park with a large fountain cascade and the Taft Memorial Carillon, whose bells ring every quarter-hour. On warm days, this is a nice place to rest your feet and listen to the yack of young Congressional staffers lunching in the sun.

US Capitol

The Capitol is the center not only of the US government but of Washington itself. Wide avenues flare outward from it, and it is the centerpoint that divides the city's quadrants. But like its Mall companion, the Washington Monument, this national icon has a tangled history.

Pierre L'Enfant chose the Capitol's site in his original city plans of 1791. Congress launched a national search for a designer and selected one William Thornton, a physician and amateur architect. His Capitol began construction in 1793 as George Washington laid the cornerstone, anointing it with wine and oil in Masonic style. The cornerstone was promptly lost, and its whereabouts remain among DC's abiding mysteries.

Later, Jefferson added Benjamin Henry Latrobe to the design team, producing years of squabbles between the two architects. Then the British marched into DC in 1814 and burnt the half-finished construction. The dispiriting destruction tempted people to abandon the DC experiment altogether, but the government finally rebuilt the Capitol under the direction of a third architect, Charles Bulfinch. In 1855 the 9-million-pound iron dome was designed, replacing a smaller one; the House and Senate wings were added in 1857. Everyone breathed a sigh of relief when the final touch, the 19-foot *Freedom* sculpture, was placed atop the dome in 1863. The modern Capitol is more than twice as large as the original building and bears little resemblance to its predecessor.

The House of Representatives meets in the south wing, the Senate in the north wing. When either body is in session, a flag is raised above the appropriate wing. A light in the dome at night means one group is working late. Most presidents have been inaugurated on the East Terrace (Reagan preferred the West Terrace).

You enter from the east side *(not the Mall side)* into the dramatic **Rotunda**. Here many presidents, from Lincoln to Kennedy, have lain in state. The dome's fresco, Constantino Brumidi's *Apotheosis of Washington*, depicts the president greeted in heaven by 13 angels representing the 13 original states. (Some claim that Brumidi used local prostitutes as models for the angels.) Brumidi and his successors also painted the murals in the hallways, which depict various American heroes and their deeds (the *Challenger* astronauts, among others). Bare spaces await future heroes; similarly, a marble statue of suffragettes has a blank space, awaiting the first woman president.

South of the Rotunda is **Statuary Hall**, where the House convened

until 1857. In 1864, each state contributed statues of two distinguished citizens to this room, but their weight was eventually deemed too much for the floor, so several statues now grace other parts of the Capitol. Yet an impressive assemblage of giant stone figures remains here.

The Supreme Court originally met in the Capitol's **Old Supreme Court Chamber** and later in the **Old Senate Chamber**. Here the great Senate debates over slavery took place before the Civil War. Downstairs, in the **Crypt**, you can see exhibits narrating the Capitol's history. It's not really a crypt, by the way – Congress once considered stashing George and Martha Washington's bodies down here, but they're buried at Mount Vernon instead.

US Capitol

Congressional sessions vary by year but generally run from about late January to October, with time off for holidays and district work. Representatives and senators do business in six office buildings surrounding the Capitol. The Senate buildings – Hart, Dirksen, and Russell (its Senate Caucus Room hosted the Watergate hearings) – are on Constitution Ave. House buildings – Rayburn, Longworth, and Cannon – are on Independence Ave.

Tours The Capitol (☎ 225-6827; Ⓜ Capitol South) is open 9 am to 4:30 pm daily (to 6 pm March through August) for guided and self-guided tours.

Enter from the east (1st St) side. Guided tours depart each half-hour from 9:30 am to 3:30 pm (until 5 pm March through August); line up on the south side of E Capitol St. For self-guided tours, line up on the north side (you're admitted in groups of 15 every five minutes).

If you don't feel like waiting in line, there's another option. The Capitol subway – it's separate from Metro – connects the Capitol to all three Senate office buildings and the Rayburn House building. Simply enter the office building, walk down to the basement, hop the subway to the Capitol, walk upstairs, and wander around on your own. The subway is especially entertaining for kids, with its open, rollercoaster-style cars.

Congress Watching If you want to see the Capitol's legislative floors, you have two choices. Daily Capitol tours (see above) stop at visitors' galleries overlooking the House and Senate floors, but only when Congress is *not* in session.

To watch floor action when Congress *is* in session, you need a pass to the galleries. US citizens: call or visit your senator's or representative's office to request passes (find numbers through the Capitol switchboard, ☎ 224-3121). Foreign visitors: request passes from the House or Senate appointment desks on the Capitol's 1st floor. Committee hearings are often more interesting than open session, and some are open to the public. Before your visit, check the *Post*'s 'Today in Congress' listing, in the A section, for details on current hearings and votes (or else you might wind up watching a thrilling grain-subsidies debate). Also check www .house.gov and www.senate.gov.

US citizens can request appointments with their senators and representatives by calling or writing (as early as three months beforehand).

Capitol Grounds The Capitol's wide lawns are an attraction in themselves, criss-crossed with paths and lush with trees and flowers. They owe their charm to famed landscape architect Frederick Law Olmsted, who, in 1874, was commissioned by Congress to refashion its grounds. Soldiers had camped in Capitol halls and stomped around its lawns during the Civil War, and spring cleaning was in order. Olmsted added greenery and majestic terraces and generally softened and tidied up the place.

Olmsted's planting schemes gave rise to the over 4000 trees that now adorn the lawns, which are especially pretty in spring. Trees from all 50 states and many countries are here – look for labels on their trunks. Northwest of the Capitol is Olmsted's charming 1879 **grotto**, a red-brick hexagon with black-iron gates and an interior well. (Its gates are often locked, but you can peek in.)

At the base of Capitol Hill, the **Capitol Reflecting Pool** echoes the larger, rectangular Reflecting Pool at the other end of the Mall, before the Lincoln Memorial. This pool is actually a 'lid' capping the I-395

JOHN NEUBAUER

US Capitol dome

Supreme Justice

The US Supreme Court, the country's highest judicial body, consists of nine justices appointed for life terms. It's referred to by the name of its presiding chief justice (the 'Warren Court,' the 'Rehnquist Court'). The image of stately justices cloaked in black robes is a familiar one, but only recently have the faces of women and African Americans appeared.

The court's high stature began with the appointment of John Marshall as chief justice in 1801. Previously, justices gave separate opinions, but Marshall established the single 'opinion of the court,' which carried much more weight. The Marshall Court issued a number of decisions that upheld Congress' power over the states and affirmed the court's right to declare other governmental branches' actions unconstitutional.

The court's most notorious 19th-century case, in 1857, was *Dred Scott v Sandford*, a major catalyst to the Civil War. Here the Taney Court ruled that blacks couldn't be US citizens and that Congress couldn't prevent territories in the American West from permitting slavery. In 1896 in *Plessy v Ferguson*, the court upheld the segregation of the 'white and colored races' under the doctrine of 'separate but equal.' In dissent, Associate Justice John Marshall Harlan wrote that the Constitution recognizes 'no superior, dominant, ruling class of citizens….all citizens are equal before the law.' Not until almost 60 years later did the court say, in *Brown v Board of Education of Topeka*, that 'separate but equal' was not, in fact, equal.

Perhaps the most controversial 20th-century ruling was the 1973 *Roe v Wade* decision, which negated state laws denying a woman's right to abortion in early pregnancy. The opinions of prospective Supreme Court justices on *Roe v Wade* are invariably an essential factor in their selection. This case, in addition to many others, draws protestors and advocates alike to the court's marble steps, where they try to sway judicial and public opinion.

freeway, which dips under the Mall here. The ornate **Ulysses S Grant Monument** dominates its eastern side, showing the general in horseback action.

Supreme Court

The Supreme Court (☎ 479-3030; Ⓜ Union Station), directly opposite the Capitol at 1 1st St NE, convenes in an imposing 1935 all-marble building designed by Cass Gilbert. Gilbert used himself and friends as models for the justices carved into the building's pediment. Other statues represent Confucius, Moses, and other wise folks. Panels on the 13,000lb bronze front doors depict the history of jurisprudence.

The court is open 9 am to 4:30 pm weekdays, and you can see exhibits on its ground floor. On days when court's not sitting, you can hear lectures about the Supreme Court in the courtroom (and check out its lofty architecture) on the half hour from 9:30 am to 3:30 pm.

The court is in session from the first Monday in October through June. Justices usually hear arguments at 10 am Monday to Wednesday for two weeks every month until April, but the schedule varies considerably. Check the *Post*'s 'Supreme Court Calendar' listing (A section) or www.supremecourtus.gov to see what cases are being heard. Arrive by 8 am to snag a seat: first-come, first-served.

Library of Congress

East of the Capitol are the three buildings of the Library of Congress (☎ 707-5000; Ⓜ Capitol South). The world's largest library, it contains approximately 120 million items, including 22 million books, plus manuscripts, maps, photographs, films, and prints. Its smallest book is 1/25 inch tall, its largest a 3-foot 'elephant folio.' The library was founded in 1800 but destroyed by the British in 1814. Thomas Jefferson then sold his collection to the library to replenish it.

JOHN NEUBAUER

The Main Reading Room, Library of Congress

Your first stop should be the library's visitors' center in the historic 1897 **Jefferson Building**, on 1st St SE (use the carriageway entrance). Here you can see the spectacular Great Hall, with ornate stained glass and marble and a Gutenberg Bible, and the three-story Main Reading Room, with arched marble galleries, statuary, and gilt trim. Several very worthwhile free tours run here daily, and the 'American Treasures' exhibit on the 1st floor displays rare books. Open 10 am to 5 pm Monday to Saturday; free.

The library has two modern annexes. The **Adams Building** is between 2nd and 3rd Sts SE. The **Madison Building**, between Independence Ave and C St SE, holds another visitors' center and a low-cost public cafeteria. If you wish to use the reading rooms – open to everybody over 17 – get a card from room No LM140 of the Madison Building. For reading-room hours, call ☎ 707-6400.

The library hosts concerts and screens classic films. Call ☎ 707-8000 for events information or check www.loc.gov/today.

US Botanic Garden

The conservatory (☎ 225-8333; Ⓜ Capitol South), on the Mall's far eastern end (downhill from the Capitol), dates from 1933 and resembles London's Crystal Palace. Iron-and-glass greenhouse rooms provide a beautiful setting for displays of exotic and local plants, including cycad trees that produce 50lb cones. Behind the conservatory, across Independence Ave, is the grand **Bartholdi Fountain**. After a complete three-year overhaul, the garden reopened in late 2000. It's a great place to relax and cool off. Open 9 am to 5 pm daily (to 9 pm in summer); free.

Folger Shakespeare Library & Theater

The world's largest collection of the Bard's works is housed at the Folger Library (☎ 544-4600; Ⓜ Union Station), 201 E Capitol St, including seven First Folios. Its 'Great Hall' exhibits Shakespeare artifacts and other rare Renaissance manuscripts (books of hours, illuminated manuscripts, etc) to the public.

RICK GERHARTER

Elizabethan Theatre at Folger Shakespeare Library

Most of the rarities are housed in the library's reading rooms, closed to all but scholars except on Shakespeare's birthday (April 23). But you can take a peek – electronically – via the multimedia computers in the Shakespeare Gallery. The gorgeous **Elizabethan Theatre** (☎ 544-7077) replicates a theater of Shakespeare's time. With its wood carvings and sky canopy, the castle is an intimate setting for plays, readings, and performances, including the stellar annual PEN/Faulkner readings. (See listings at www.folger.edu.) East of the building is the Elizabethan Garden, full of flowers and herbs that were cultivated during Shakespeare's time.

The Folger is open 10 am to 4 pm Monday through Saturday; free. Tours are offered at 11 am Monday to Saturday.

Sewall-Belmont House
This historic home (☎ 546-1210; Ⓜ Union Station), 144 Constitution Ave NE, is a feminist landmark: the National Woman's Party, founded by legendary suffragette Alice Paul, has been based here since 1929. Paul spearheaded efforts to gain the vote for women – enshrined in the 19th Amendment – and wrote the Equal Rights Amendment. Docents show you historical exhibits, portraits, sculpture, and a library that celebrate feminist heroines. Tours run 11 am to 2 pm Tuesday to Friday, noon to 3 pm Saturday; donations welcome.

National Postal Museum
The idea of a postal museum might not excite you. But put your skepticism aside – this place is pretty cool. In the National Capitol Post Office Building, just west of Union Station, the newest Smithsonian museum (☎ 357-2991) features kid-friendly exhibits on postal history from the Pony Express to modern times. Also here are antique mail planes, beautiful old stamps, Cliff Clavin's postal carrier uniform (from the television sitcom *Cheers*), and great special exhibits of old letters (from soldiers, pioneers, etc). It's open 10 am to 5:30 pm daily; free.

Eastern Market
Delightful Eastern Market, at 7th St and North Carolina Ave SE, is the heart of the Capitol Hill community. The last of the 19th-century covered markets that once supplied most food to DC, Eastern Market was built in 1873. Its South Hall has food stands, bakeries, flower stands, and delis. North Hall is an arts center where craftspeople sell handmade wares. Both are open daily except Monday. Weekends are when Eastern Market bursts into full bloom, though, as craftspeople, food vendors, and a flea market spill over the sidewalks outside the market. (See more details in the Places to Eat and Shopping chapters.)

Military Sights
The southeastern waterfront is dominated by the **Washington Navy Yard** (Ⓜ Navy Yard), stretching along the Anacostia River from 1st to 11th Sts SE.

Alice Paul, crusader for equal rights

Capitol Hill isn't all monumental buildings.

Established in 1799, the Yard holds the **Navy Museum** (☎ 433-4882), Building 76, with displays of ship models, gun turrets, uniforms, and artifacts. Outside, tour the decommissioned destroyer USS *Barry*. Open 9 am to 4 pm weekdays, 10 am to 5 pm weekends. Here too is the less-extensive **Marine Corps Museum** (☎ 433-3534), open 10 am to 4 pm daily except Tuesday, noon to 5 pm Sunday. Both museums are free. From the Navy Yard Metro, exit onto M St and walk east to 9th St to enter.

Nearby is an oddball sight: Ulric Dahlgren's entombed leg. Dahlgren lost the leg at Gettysburg, but his father, the Navy Yard commandant, had it interred with full honors. A plaque marks the site on Isaac Hull Ave. (From the Navy Museum exit, turn right, walk three blocks, turn right on Isaac Hull, and walk to the fire hydrant.) Another Civil War–era site is at 921 Pennsylvania Ave SE: the 1865 **Old Naval Hospital**. There's talk of turning this rundown but still grand building into DC's mayoral mansion.

The Eighth & I St **Marine Corps Barracks** (☎ 433-6060; Ⓜ Eastern Market) are home to the Marine Corps commandant. The Marine Corps Band practices here; their most famed bandmaster, John Philip Sousa, king of the rousing military march, was born nearby at 636 G St SE. He's buried in southeast DC's Congressional Cemetery. You can catch a two-hour parade drill here in summer at 8:45 pm Fridays; call at least three weeks beforehand for reservations, or just show up for general-admission seats at 7 pm.

Anacostia

Separated from the rest of DC by the Anacostia River, Anacostia was originally inhabited by Indians who did a brisk trading business from this site at the confluence of two rivers. European explorers such as John Smith were drawn here as early as 1608.

Before the Civil War, Anacostia was the home of a small free black community, and after the war, freed slaves settled here. Anacostia was incorporated into DC in 1854, and in 1877 abolitionist Frederick Douglass moved in. For the next century, Anacostia was a middle-class, mixed-race community, but whites began to leave in the 1960s. The '68 riots sent Anacostia into a tailspin from which it has not yet recovered, and subsequent years of decline earned the area a reputation for violent crime. Now Anacostia is often seen as 'the other DC,' poor, desperate, and almost entirely black. All of this makes Anacostia a renowned boogeyman for suburbanites (many of whom have never set foot here), even though recent development is starting to slightly improve the neighborhood's fortunes.

Visitors here shouldn't be paranoid. But this isn't the neighborhood for a stroll, especially if you don't know where you're going. Take a cab from the Metro station, or drive.

Anacostia Museum This Smithsonian museum (☎ 357-2700; Ⓜ Anacostia), 1901 Fort Place SE, began as a neighborhood museum and expanded into a regional heritage center celebrating black history and culture in DC and the mid-Atlantic states. It's recently undergone renovation but will re-open in spring 2001. Rotating exhibits explore topics like the history of Anacostia and churches' roles in black communities. Sculpture, paintings, and photography by black artists are displayed. Black History Month (February) is a great time to visit, with many free concerts, kids' workshops, and films. The museum also hosts exhibits at the Arts & Industries Building on the Mall. Open 10 am to 5 pm daily; free.

From the Anacostia Metro, you can take a taxi or the W1 or W2 bus to the museum.

Frederick Douglass National Historic Site The great abolitionist's Anacostia home, Cedar Hill (☎ 426-5961), 1411 W St SE, is maintained by the Park Service as a museum honoring his life. Diplomat, author, and former slave, Douglass lived here from 1877 until his death in 1895. Here Douglass wrote *Narrative of the Life of Frederick Douglass*, and the house still contains most of his original furnishings, down to his wire-rim eyeglasses on his rolltop desk. The hilltop home has a commanding view of DC.

You can see the house on your own or via a tour (offered 10 am to 3 pm). Start at the visitors' center embedded in the foot of the hill; here you can see a short biographical film. Open 9 am to 4 pm daily; $3/1.50 adults and kids/seniors for admission and tour. For reservations, call ☎ 800-967-2283.

From the Anacostia Metro, you can take a B2 or B4 bus right to the house, but the bus stop and route for the return trip are less convenient; consider a cab.

RICK GERHARTER

Frederick Douglass National Historic Site

Upper Northeast DC (Map 5)

The upper northeast district of Washington is mostly a residential area, and its neighborhoods range from peaceful to dangerous. It's dominated by the large campuses of Gallaudet University, to the south, and Catholic University, farther north. Trinity College is also here. Northeast is well off the beaten tourist track, but it has many rewards for the adventurous visitor – scattered across this large stretch of the city are numerous fascinating sites, from religious shrines to lush gardens.

Gallaudet University

Established in 1864, Gallaudet University (☎ 651-5505, TDD 651-5359), 800 Florida Ave NE, is the world's only accredited liberal-arts school for the hearing-impaired. Student protests here in 1989 led to the appointment of the college's first

THINGS TO SEE & DO

RICHARD CUMMINS

National Shrine of the Immaculate Conception

hearing-impaired president. Few sports fans know that in 1894, Gallaudet football players invented the American football huddle to prevent their opponents from reading the sign language used to call the plays. Tours of the campus are available by advance reservation. No Metro station is nearby, so you'll need to drive.

RICHARD CUMMINS

Altar of the National Shrine of the Immaculate Conception

National Shrine of the Immaculate Conception

This huge, strange church (☎ 526-8300; Ⓜ Brookland), on the grounds of Catholic University at Michigan Ave and 4th St NE, accommodates 6000 worshipers: it's the largest Catholic church in the Western Hemisphere. In addition to its unearthly size, the Marian shrine sports an eclectic mix of Romanesque and Byzantine motifs, from classical towers to a mosquelike dome, all anchored by a 329-foot minaret-shaped campanile. Yet taken singly, its mosaics, stained glass, and carvings are lovely.

Downstairs is the Eastern-style crypt church, with low, mosaic-covered vaulted ceilings lit by votives and chandeliers. Upstairs, the main sanctuary is lined with elaborate saints' chapels, lit by rose windows, and fronted by a dazzling mosaic of a stern Christ. A large gift shop sells religious literature, rosaries, statues, and the like.

The shrine's open 7 am to 7 pm daily and holds seven Sunday masses, as well as hosting acclaimed choral performances. Admission's free. From Brookland Metro, walk west onto campus and up the hill to the shrine – there's no missing it.

The new **John Paul II Center** should be open on Harwood Rd NE, near the Basilica, in early 2001 to exhibit papal memorabilia and art from the Vatican.

Franciscan Monastery

The Franciscan order maintains its DC monastery, known as Mount St Sepulchre (☎ 526-6800; Ⓜ Brookland), at 1400 Quincy St NE. It's set amid 44 beautifully landscaped acres of gardens that, in spring, explode into a riot of color as tulips, dogwoods, cherry trees, and roses bloom.

This place isn't just about flowers, however. The Order of St Francis is charged with guardianship of the Holy Land's sacred sites by the Catholic Church. The DC monastery has interpreted that task in a unique way, constructing replicas of those sites for the faithful who are unable to visit the Holy Land. Among the glorious blooms are life-size fake-granite reproductions of the Tomb of Mary, the Grotto at Lourdes, and other subterranean sacred places.

More oddities await inside Mount St Sepulchre itself, including reproductions of

Franciscan monastery and gardens

JOHN NEUBAUER

Henry Adams' Grief

In Rock Creek Cemetery on Rock Creek Church Rd NW (just west of Catholic University, off New Hampshire Ave) is one of DC's most poignant monuments: the **Adams Memorial**, or **Grief**. Commissioned in 1890 by the historian and novelist Henry Adams after the suicide of his wife, Marian (who killed herself by drinking photographic chemicals), the seated, shrouded figure was sculpted by Augustus Saint-Gaudens. Often, you'll see solitary visitors sitting on the bench across from it, studying its exhausted yet strangely peaceful face. Adams never remarried, and when he died, in 1918, he was buried here next to Marian.

the Roman Catacombs under the sanctuary floor. These dark, narrow passages wind past fake tombs and the actual remains of Sts Innocent and Benignus. It's all very creepy and fascinating, like a holy Disneyland.

Resident monks lead hourly free tours 9 am to 4 pm Monday to Saturday and 1 to 4 pm Sunday. Donations are welcome. From Brookland station, walk east on Michigan Ave NE, then turn right on Quincy. The monastery is located on the east side of 14th St NE.

US National Arboretum

Way out in northeast DC are 446 acres of blooming trees, ornamental plants, and verdant meadows. But because it's hard to access the national gardens (☎ 245-2726), 3501 New York Ave NE – they're in a gritty area far from the Metro – they remain among DC's hidden treasures. Most visitors are locals, not tourists, so it's a wonderful place to stroll and flower-peep in peace.

Stop at the Administration Building near the R St gate for a map and information. Highlights include the **Bonsai and Penjing Museum**; the **Capitol Columns Garden**, studded with Corinthian pillars removed from the US Capitol in the 1950s; an herb garden; and a native-plants garden. The best

JOHN NEUBAUER

Azaleas at the US National Arboretum

Southwest DC (Map 6)

In 1790, the confluence of the Potomac and Anacostia Rivers was chosen as the site of the new federal city. Land speculators hopped on the area immediately, and Jefferson chose southwest Greenleaf Point to house the new Navy Yard. The area – DC's smallest quadrant – did well until the early 20th century, by which time it had become a depressed slum that urban-renewal activists used as a key symbol of DC's ills.

In response, Congress and DC government launched one of the city's most sweeping urban-renewal clearances. The largely black, poor residents were moved aside in favor of office blocks and apartment complexes, and decrepit rowhouses were replaced with stern modern constructions. Now Southwest has an uncertain identity, comprising gigantic federal agencies in the 'Federal Rectangle' area south of the Mall, big national museums and monuments, parkland, and a riverfront marina area. Nonetheless, visitors will find many appealing attractions here.

Tidal Basin

The amoeba-shaped Tidal Basin, southwest of the Lincoln Memorial, serves both practical and ceremonial functions. It flushes the adjacent Washington Channel – at high tide, river waters fill the basin through gates under the Inlet Bridge, and at low tide, gates under the Outlet Bridge open and water streams into the channel. The basin is beloved for the magnificent Yoshino cherry trees that ring it, a 1912 gift from Japan. In late March and early April, the banks shimmer with pale-pink blossoms. The Cherry Blossom Festival celebrates this event – the first two weeks of April draw 100,000 visitors to DC for the festivities, which climax with the Cherry Blossom Parade.

A paved walkway rings the basin's perimeter and offers lovely strolling possibilities. Mind the kiddies – some stretches aren't fenced. You'll pass the **Japanese Lantern** at the Kutz Bridge's west end, lit

times to visit are spring (when azaleas bloom) and fall (autumn leaves). Tram tours ($3) run spring and summer weekends. No direct buses serve the gardens and it's hard to negotiate them on foot, so drive or bike. Open 8 am to 5 pm daily; free.

Kenilworth Aquatic Gardens

Across the Anacostia River from the National Arboretum are these aquatic gardens (☎ 426-6905; Ⓜ Deanwood), 900 Anacostia Drive NE, the only national park devoted to water plants. Aquatic flora from around the world grow here. The best times to visit are June (when day-blooming water lilies hit their peak), July, and August (for nighttime lilies). In summertime rangers lead nature walks.

From Deanwood Metro, walk along Douglas St to the pedestrian overpass, continue to Anacostia Ave, and turn right. By car, take New York Ave (US-50) east across the Anacostia River; at the highway split, stay right, toward Annapolis. Exit at Kenilworth Ave south (I-295), turn right on Douglas, and follow signs. Open 8 am to 4 pm daily; free.

The Gnawers

During the 1999 Cherry Blossom Festival, the Park Service was horrified to discover an ambitious beaver family chomping on the Tidal Basin's famed cherry trees. The beasts' intentions weren't clear – perhaps they hoped to dam the Potomac – but their hubris was admirable, and they eventually felled four trees. Many locals cheered on the plucky animals, but rangers trapped the beavers and exiled them to less scenic hinterlands.

during the festival, and, at its east end, the **Tulip Library** garden. The Tidal Basin **boathouse** (☎ 484-0206), on the east bank, rents paddleboats 10 am to 6 pm daily from March to September: $7/14 per hour for a two/four-seat boat.

Franklin Delano Roosevelt Memorial

FDR didn't want a grand memorial. In fact, during his presidency he requested that a slab no larger than his desk be placed outside the Archives. His wishes were followed; you can still see that modest stone there today. Planners later felt the stone wasn't grand enough, however, so this second, 7.5-acre memorial opened in 1997.

It's an intriguing place. On the Tidal Basin's west bank, it is composed of four red-granite 'rooms' that narrate FDR's presidency through statuary and inscriptions, punctuated with cascades and peaceful alcoves. Strolling through it, you're told a story about the 32nd president, rather than simply seeing a single monumental image as you do at most DC memorials.

The first and second rooms narrate the New Deal and the Depression's aftermath through inscriptions and George Segal's sculpted breadline. The third room shows Roosevelt in the WWII years, seated with his dog Fala at his feet (there's something pretty silly about a Scottie in bronze). The last room shows Eleanor, and FDR's funeral cortege. As of May 2000, an additional sculpture was in the works, depicting FDR in his wheelchair – something he concealed from the public.

Rangers staff the memorial 8 am to midnight daily; a bookstore and information kiosk are near the first room.

Thomas Jefferson Memorial

This memorial, on the Tidal Basin's south bank, honors Thomas Jefferson, the third US president, political philosopher, drafter of the Declaration of Independence, and founder of the University of Virginia. Designed by John Russell Pope to resemble Jefferson's library at the university, the rounded, domed monument was initially derided by critics as 'the Jefferson Muffin.' Inside is a 19-foot bronze likeness, and excerpts from Jefferson's writings etch the walls. In spring, you can sit on the steps and

THEY (WHO) SEEK TO ESTABLISH SYSTEMS OF GOVERNMENT BASED ON THE REGIMENTATION OF ALL HUMAN BEINGS BY A HANDFUL OF INDIVIDUAL RULERS... CALL THIS A NEW ORDER. IT IS NOT NEW AND IT IS NOT ORDER.

TONY WHEELER

FDR and Fala

DENNIS JOHNSON

Thomas Jefferson Memorial

admire the cherry blossoms; at night, the Tidal Basin offers lovely moonlit reflections.

Rangers staff the memorial from 8 am to midnight daily. A bookstore in the lobby sells Jeffersoniana, and rangers give talks and show visitors around.

East Potomac Park

East Potomac Park, extending southward from the Tidal Basin, offers myriad recreation possibilities. This artificial peninsula was created in the late 19th century, along with the adjacent Washington Channel, to ease the Potomac's occasional floods.

On foot, you can access the park by following trails that lead from the Jefferson Memorial under the George Mason, Rochambeau, and 14th St Bridges. A 5-mile paved waterside trail runs around the park's circumference, paralleling Ohio Drive – it's a fine place for a walk, run, or bike ride, and nearby cherry trees add color in spring. If you drive, you can park on Ohio Drive's shoulder. The center of the park is the East Potomac Park Golf Course (see Activities, later).

The park's southern tip, **Hains Point**, offers picnic tables, a playground, and the eerie *Awakening* sculpture, which portrays a massive giant emerging from the earth. Only his arms, legs, and roaring head are visible aboveground. Lean against a leg and watch jets thunder into National Airport, directly across the Potomac.

United States Holocaust Memorial Museum

The somber, soaring Holocaust Museum (☎ 488-0400; Ⓜ Smithsonian), 100 Raoul Wallenberg Place SW, memorializes the millions murdered by the Nazis in WWII. It's unlike any other DC museum – brutal, direct, impassioned, its exhibits leave many visitors in tears and few unmoved.

The extraordinary building was designed in 1993 by James Ingo Freed, and its stark facade and steel-and-glass interior echo the death camps themselves. It manages to be both ominous and lovely, frightening and elegiac.

The permanent exhibit, to which you must get a timed pass, begins on the 4th floor and winds down past exhibits of personal artifacts, photos, and voice and video recordings that move from the rise of the Nazis to the liberation of the camps. Apart from these exhibits, there's the candlelit Hall of Remembrance (for quiet reflection); the Wexner Learning Center, with text archives, photographs, films, and oral testimony available on touch-screen computers; a café; theater; and shop. If you have young children in tow, don't show them the

RICK GERHARTER

Hall of Rememberance at the United States Holocaust Memorial Museum

permanent exhibits, which are very graphic. Instead, there's 'Remember the Children,' a gentler kids' installation, on the 1st floor.

The free permanent-exhibition passes can run out well before closing, so arrive early or get a pass from ProTix (☎ 800-400-9373). The passes are timed, to prevent crowding. Thus you might arrive at 10 am but get a pass for noon. Hours are 10 am to 5:30 pm daily except Christmas and Yom Kippur.

National Bureau of Printing & Engraving

Often mistakenly called the 'Mint,' the bureau (☎ 874-3019; Ⓜ Smithsonian), at 14th and C Sts SW just south of the Holocaust Museum, is where all US paper currency is designed, engraved, and printed. Tour guides lead groups on raised walkways through what is, essentially, a big print shop. Nonetheless, kids love it, so many families wait hours in line for their turn. You do learn fun money trivia, though, and you can buy souvenirs like shredded money and uncut sheets of $1 or $2 bills.

Free tours run 9 am to 2 pm weekdays only. They're popular, so be prepared to wait a *looong* time. July through August, you must get tickets at the kiosk on 15th St, then go to the 14th St entrance for the tour (tickets are often gone by late morning).

Voice of America

The Voice of America (☎ 619-4700; Ⓜ Federal Center SW), inside the Health & Human Services Dept building, broadcasts US and world news in 44 languages from its studios at 330 Independence Ave SW. Free 45-minute tours are offered at 10:30 am and 1:30 and 2:30 pm weekdays. Reservations are required. Enter on C St.

Waterfront Walking Tour

A riverside promenade runs along the Washington Channel parallel to Maine Ave SW, from the vicinity of 6th St to 12th St SW. One side is lined with yachts, sailboats, and houseboats, the other with park benches (a great spot for sunset watching) and several big, popular seafood restaurants, a few with patio seating.

To reach the promenade and see more of southwest DC, start your tour at the L'Enfant Plaza Metro station. Exit onto 7th St SW and walk south across the I-395 bridge.

Turn left onto I St, then right on 6th, to reach the first interesting sight: IM Pei's **Town Center Plaza**, covering the 1100 block of 6th St, a sleekly modern apartment/commercial complex that epitomizes southwest DC's architecture since its urban-renewal clearance. Down 6th St at Maine Ave SW is one of DC's premier theaters and the cultural anchor of southwest DC, **Arena Stage** (☎ 488-3300). Founded in 1951, it welcomed

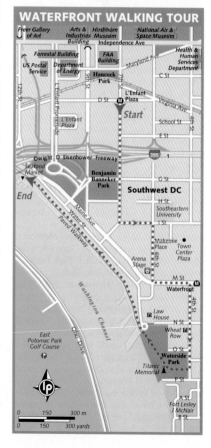

WATERFRONT WALKING TOUR

RICK GERHARTER

Get fresh fish at the seafood market.

racially integrated audiences from the start, a radical departure for a DC theater at the time. (See Entertainment for more details.)

Two nearby survivors of the 1950s urban clearance date back to DC's founding. The 1796 **Law House**, 1252 6th St SW, a Federal-style rowhouse that's among DC's oldest buildings, was built by one of the first DC land speculators. The 1795 **Wheat Row** houses, 1313–1321 4th St SW, south of N St, have charming, human-scale brick facades that add welcome warmth to the neighborhood.

From 4th St, turn right onto small Waterside Park, near the waterfront's south end, a pleasant plaza holding the *Titanic* Memorial, a 18-foot figure sculpted by Gertrude Vanderbilt Whitney. Just south is **Fort Lesley J McNair**, an Army post established in 1791 and burned by the British in 1814. The Lincoln-assassination conspirators were hung at McNair in 1865; it now houses the National Defense University and National War College (closed to the public).

From Waterside Park, walk north on the waterfront promenade. Along the waterfront, you'll pass the Gangplank, Capital Yacht Club, and Washington Marinas, along with several cruise companies (see Activities, later). Near the promenade's end, at Maine Ave and 11th St SW, is the **seafood market**, where fisherfolk hawk their daily

catch from barges. You can buy steamed blue crabs, spicy shrimp, and just about anything with fins here, then return to L'Enfant Plaza Metro via 7th St.

Georgetown (Map 7)

Georgetown was an established Maryland trading town well before the federal city existed. Its history stretches back even farther, in fact: it was an Indian settlement called Tohoga when the British fur trader Henry Fleet stopped here in 1632.

After the government set up shop nearby, Georgetown began to draw the gentry of the new city, and it thrived on the tobacco trade as well. In 1789, its prosperity was capped by the founding of Georgetown University, the country's first Roman Catholic university, at the neighborhood's western end. Many 18th-century buildings still remain throughout the campus and district.

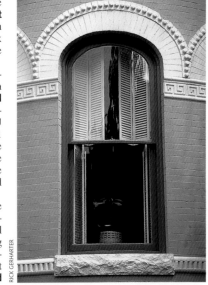

RICK GERHARTER

Architectural detail in Georgetown area

THINGS TO SEE & DO

JOHN NEUBAUER

Mules towing a barge up the C&O Canal

Although Georgetown was a Confederate bastion during the Civil War, it was also a stop on the Underground Railroad. An antebellum free black community arose in Herring Hill (between 29th St and Rock Creek Park, north of P St). Although these residents were later supplanted by Georgetown's expanding affluent white community, historic black churches remain, drawing worshippers from other parts of DC.

Georgetown remained independent of DC until 1871, by which point Georgetown was in a profound slump, its port trade fading away. The New Deal period in the 20th century brightened prospects again, as government employees began to snap up its charming rowhouses. The Kennedys moved into Marbury House, on N St, in the 1950s, and that was all she wrote – Georgetown's been insanely fashionable ever since, a wealthy district hopping with diners, bar-crawlers, shoppers, and folks in search of a little antebellum charm.

Georgetown stretches west from Rock Creek Park along the Potomac River and north past T St NW. Its heart is the intersection of M St and Wisconsin Ave, and both downtown streets are walled with popular

eateries, trendy clothing boutiques, bookstores, bars, and clubs. The community resisted a Metro station, so it isn't easily accessible by public transit; the closest stop is Foggy Bottom. Street parking can be near impossible (off-street parking is both limited and expensive). If you must drive, look for spots on O, P, or Q Sts NW near Dumbarton Oaks or the same streets by Georgetown University.

C&O Canal

From its Georgetown start, the historic Chesapeake & Ohio Canal runs 185 miles upriver to Cumberland, in western Maryland. A recreational gold mine for hikers, cyclists, and boaters, the canal and its towpath parallel M St in Georgetown's central zone and are crisscrossed by walkways and bridges. On either side, old warehouses and factory buildings have been made over into upscale retail and entertainment complexes, so you can mix a walk here with food, drink, and shopping if you like.

The Park Service operates a **visitors' center** (☎ 653-5190) on the lower back floor of 1057 Thomas Jefferson St, upon the canal's towpath. Walk south from M St to find it. It's open on weekends in winter and 10 am to 4 pm daily April to October. Buy tickets here for mule-pulled **barge rides** that carry passengers along the canal the old-fashioned way. Barges generally run from early April to November (depending on weather). Fares are $7.50/6/4 adults/seniors/children. You can do your own boating on the canal and nearby Potomac, too: rent boats from nearby Fletchers Boathouse or Thompson Boat Center (see Boating, later in this chapter).

The canal leaves central Georgetown under the Key Bridge. Just north of the towpath here, at 35th St, is small **Francis Scott Key Park**, honoring the Georgetown lawyer who wrote the 'Star-Spangled Banner' after witnessing the British assault on Baltimore's Fort McHenry in 1814.

Old Stone House

Sitting incongruously in the midst of the Georgetown shopping drag is DC's oldest surviving building (☎ 426-6851), 3051 M St. Built in 1765 by cabinetmaker Christopher Layman, it's since been a boardinghouse, tavern, brothel, and shop. It was almost de-

RICK GERHARTER

The Old Stone House is DC's oldest surviving building.

molished in the 1950s, but a persistent (albeit false) rumor that L'Enfant used it as a workshop while designing DC saved it for posterity.

The Park Service now maintains it as an example of 18th-century life. The outside appears old, but the inside has been renovated to accommodate sightseers. The small garden is a peaceful place to sit. Open noon to 5 pm Wednesday to Sunday; free.

Nearby, at 1230 30th St, is the site of another oddity, **Spite House**. Some claim that this 11-foot-wide house (Georgetown's narrowest) was the product of a neighborhood squabble, built only in order to block a neighboring house's view.

Georgetown University

Founded in 1789, America's first Roman Catholic college (☎ 687-6538), on 37th St NW, was originally directed by the country's first black Jesuit, Father Patrick Healy. Today, about 12,000 students pursue degrees here. Notable 'Hoyas' (the name's derived from the Latin *hoya saxa*, 'what rocks') include both Clintons. Enter at O and 37th Sts NW; you can pick up a campus map and information from the gatehouse here.

Its attractive, shaded campus retains some original 18th- and 19th-century buildings. In particular, check out the imposing, Flemish-style 1879 **Healy Building**, at the campus' east gate, with its tall clocktower, and, in the campus' northeast corner, the 1874 **Convent of the Visitation**, which is the second-oldest US convent.

Movie buffs will remember that the campus figured prominently in 1973's shockfest *The Exorcist*. You can compose your own little *Exorcist* tour on campus. Stop at the Healy Building, where the movie-star mom stood in the movie's early scenes, then visit the vertiginous *Exorcist Steps* at 3600 Prospect St NW, west of 36th St – two of little Regan's hapless victims met their fates here.

Tudor Place

This 1816 mansion (☎ 965-0400), 1644 31st St NW, was owned by Martha Washington's granddaughter, Martha Custis Peter. Her descendants retained the property until it was opened to the public in 1983. Well kept, with over 5 acres of garden-adorned grounds, the mansion now functions as a small museum and features furnishings from Mount Vernon. Guided tours run at 10 and 11:30 am and 1 and 2:30 pm Tuesday to Friday and on the hour from 10 am to 3 pm Saturday; $6/5/3 adults/seniors/students. Seeing just the gardens (open 10 am to 4 pm Monday to Saturday) costs $2.

Dumbarton Oaks

It was here, in 1944, that the agreement to create the United Nations was forged. On R St between 31st and 32nd Sts, this 19th-century mansion (☎ 339-6401), houses a fine art museum and research libraries and is set amid 16 acres of terraced gardens. Enter the museum from 32nd St, the gardens through the R St gate.

The gardens are the most beautiful in Washington. Slender brick paths wind down toward Rock Creek amid boxwood and wisteria; 19 pools and fountains add notes of coolness; and banks of cherries, crabapples, and forsythias explode with color in spring. A rose garden and 1810 orangery are other lovely touches. Although the gardens are popular, they hold many little nooks and corners that let you find a quiet bower of your own. Open 2 to 6 pm; $5/3 adults/children. November to March, the gardens close at 5 pm but admission's free.

The museum features renowned Byzantine and pre-Columbian collections, the latter housed in a light-flooded circular

Garden at Dumbarton Oaks

gallery designed by Philip Johnson. The main house's Music Room has European antiques, an intricately painted beamed ceiling, and El Greco's *The Visitation*. Open 2 to 5 pm daily except Monday; donations welcome.

Oak Hill Cemetery

This 24-acre, obelisk-studded cemetery (☎ 337-2835) contains 19th-century gravestones (enter at R and 30th Sts NW). Several

Georgetown's Black History Sites

Three sites recall the history of Georgetown's 19th-century free black community, who lived in an area known as Herring Hill. Founded in 1816, **Mount Zion United Methodist Church** (☎ 234-0148), 1334 29th St NW, is DC's oldest black congregation. Its original site, on 27th St, was a stop on the Underground Railroad.

Nearby, at **Mount Zion Cemetery**, 2700 Q St, and the adjacent **Female Union Band Cemetery**, behind 2515–2531 Q St, are the overgrown headstones of many free black residents. The church hid escaping slaves in a vault here. You can reach the cemeteries from Wisconsin Ave by heading east on Q St and turning left at the path just before 2531 Q St.

THINGS TO SEE & DO

JOHN NEUBAUER

of Washington's descendants are buried here. Note the lovely gatehouse and the wee gneiss chapel designed by James Renwick (both circa 1850), and wander the winding walks to see tombs set into the hillsides of Rock Creek. Open 10 am to 4 pm weekdays; no photography, backpacks, bikes, or walking on graves, please.

Between the cemetery and Dumbarton Oaks is verdant **Montrose Park**, with Lover's Lane, a paved path, running along its western side. The lane hosted trysts back in the early 20th century, but it's a dog-and-baby scene these days, and it makes a nice stroll.

Dumbarton House

Often confused with Dumbarton *Oaks*, Dumbarton *House* (☎ 337-2288), 2715 Q St NW, is a modest Federal historic-house museum open for guided tours Tuesday to Saturday at 10:15 and 11:15 am and 12:15 pm; $3 donation. If you miss tour time, stroll its small, pretty garden at Q and 27th Sts, with peaceful benches and a view of Oak Hill Cemetery.

Constructed by a wealthy family in 1798, when the Federal City was first a-buildin', Dumbarton's now run by the Colonial Dames of America. The Dames' genteel but witty tours focus not only on the house – chockablock with antique china, silver, furnishings, rugs, gowns, and books – but on quaint Federal customs like passing round the chamber pot after formal dinners so gentlemen could have a group pee. The house closes in August.

Dupont Circle & Kalorama (Map 8)

The Dupont Circle area was once a marshland called the Slashes. In the early 1870s, a group of developers, the California Syndicate, bought most of the Slashes and renamed them Pacific Circle; by the early 1900s, the area was home to Washington's wealthiest citizens. Though some abandoned their mansions during the Depression, the area regained luster when many houses

were converted into elegant embassies along Massachusetts Ave. Nearby Sheridan Circle soon became the center of Washington's diplomatic community, Embassy Row.

Today the eclectic neighborhood ranges from plush ambassadorial estates and refined museums to gay bars, yuppie pool parlors, and secondhand bookstores, not to mention a wealth of restaurants, cafés, pubs, and trendy boutiques. Patio seating on wide sidewalks, window tables, and park benches offer some of DC's best people-watching roosts.

Meaning 'beautiful view' in Greek, the Kalorama neighborhood, adjoining Dupont to the northwest, was named after an estate built by Jefferson confidante Joel Barlow that dominated this hilly area in the 19th century. Now Kalorama is a sleepy enclave of embassies and the brick-and-stone mansions and deep gardens of DC's ultrarich. This is the 'hood of DC's storied 'cave dwellers' (old-money residents), and presidents from Wilson to Harding have lived here. The area's still thick with powerful politicos and ambassadors.

Walking Tour

This tour begins in the heart of Dupont Circle and moves northwest through Embassy Row and Kalorama.

Dupont Circle itself, a scenic park with a fountain, statues, slacking bicycle messengers, spooning lovers, and old guys playing chess at built-in tables, is at the intersection of Connecticut and Massachusetts Aves NW. Underneath the circle lie the abandoned

RICK GERHARTER

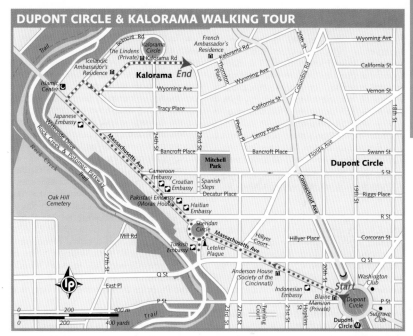

DUPONT CIRCLE & KALORAMA WALKING TOUR

tunnels of DC's old streetcar system (you'll see padlocked entryways around the circle). Closed in 1962 and since superannuated by Metro, the tunnels have generated much fanciful planning speculation: everything from fallout shelters to a crypt has been proposed for them. (Learn more about DC's old streetcars at the National Capital Trolley Museum; see the boxed text).

Spin in a circle to see three grand remnants of the days when Dupont was a millionaire's ghetto: the stately 1900 **Sulgrave** Club, 1801 Massachusetts Ave; the double-winged 1902 **Washington Club**, 15 Dupont Circle, designed by Stanford White; and the 1881 **Blaine Mansion**, 2000 Massachusetts Ave on the circle's west side. The latter is an ominous concoction of fanciful turrets and seven chimneys built by 'Slippery Jim' Blaine, a Republican Party founder.

For more majestic architecture, walk northwest on Massachusetts through **Embassy Row**. The embassies are the anchor of DC's prominent international community,

National Capital Trolley Museum

Transportation-history junkies take note: DC's old electric-trolley system shut down in the mid-20th century, but the cars roll on at the National Capital Trolley Museum (☎ 301-384-6088), 1313 Bonifant Rd, Silver Spring, Maryland. It preserves 17 streetcars that run on a demonstration track and exhibits historical photographs of the system. It's open noon to 5 pm weekends only (also 11 am to 2 pm Thursday and Friday from mid-March to mid-May); donations encouraged.

THINGS TO SEE & DO

Embassies from the Inside

Understandably, security at most embassies is tight, so visitors can't just wander around inside them. Too bad, because many are treasure-houses of national artworks. For a peek, check out Goodwill Industries' Annual Embassy Tour (☎ 636-4225 for details). Held on a mid-May Saturday, the daylong tour includes several of the Row's most beautiful embassies and chanceries. Make reservations several weeks in advance; $30 per person.

and here tongues of a hundred nations are heard; streets are crowded with sleek sedans sporting embassy plates; and diplomats' kids on study break from American University and Georgetown's School of Foreign Service preen in local clubs. The embassies are a cultural gold mine, too, hosting public art exhibits, concerts, and lectures year-round. For events listings, see *The Washington Diplomat*, a free monthly given away at Dupont shops and restaurants, or the *Post*'s Weekend section.

At 2020 Massachusetts is the **Indonesian Embassy**, in the Walsh-McLean House (1903). Commissioned by Thomas Walsh, a gold-mining magnate, this lavish home, with its gold-flecked marble pillars, was DC's costliest house of its era. Walsh embedded a gold nugget in its foundation (no one's found it) to honor his fortune, and his daughter Evalyn Walsh McLean owned the fantastic blue Hope Diamond. It's been said the house is 'cursed': after the Walshes moved in, they were beset by tragedies from mental illness to suicide. Nearby is the grand **Anderson House**, 2118 Massachusetts, once a private family mansion and now a museum of Revolutionary War–era artifacts.

Farther up Massachusetts is **Sheridan Circle**, wreathed in lavish embassies and centered on Gutzon Borglum's equestrian statue of Civil War General Philip Sheridan. (Borglum later sculpted Mt Rushmore.) On the circle's south side, at 23rd St, is a sadder memorial: a raised plaque noting the car-bomb assassination here, in 1976, of pro-Allende Chilean exile Orlando Letelier and his aide Ronni Moffitt. Agents of the Pinochet dictatorship were later tied to the murders.

At 1606 23rd St, south of the circle, is the **Turkish Embassy** (1914), nicknamed 'San Simeon on the Potomac.' Designed by architect-to-the-rich George Oakley Totten, it's noted for its interior fabulousness (gold doorknobs!) and the fact that its first owner, Edward Everett, made millions by inventing the prosaic fluted bottle cap.

The **Haitian Embassy** (1909), 2311 Massachusetts, is a little Beaux-Arts jewel: note its copper roof ornamentation and the pretty black-iron gate to its right. Next door at No 2315 is the **Pakistani Embassy** (1908), or Moran House, another Totten creation, with a limestone facade enlivened by classical water-bearer sculptures and an imposing tower.

Totten rides again up at No 2349, the **Cameroon Embassy**, frosted with fanciful stone-and-copper crosses and punctuated by a castlelike tower. At No 2343, a cross-legged sculpture

RICK GERHARTER

Indonesian Embassy

RICK GERHARTER

Monument to Orlando Letelier and Ronni Moffitt

of St Jerome dreams over his book before the **Croatian Embassy**.

The **Japanese Embassy**, No 2516, is an interesting blend of Georgian and Asian architectural styles. The beautifully landscaped grounds (which you can only glimpse through the fence) hold Ippakutei, a reconstruction of an antique teahouse. Nearby is the ethereal **Islamic Center**, No 2551, the national mosque.

If you like, continue over the Rock Creek Park bridge to view more embassies (see Upper Northwest DC, later). Alternately, you can turn right on Belmont Rd to explore Kalorama.

Many ambassadors' homes are in this neck of the woods. Among the most delightful is the **Icelandic ambassador's residence**, 2443 Kalorama Rd, a half-timbered brick mansion that looks as if it could survive an Arctic winter. At 2401 Kalorama Rd is **The Lindens** (private), DC's oldest extant building. The Georgian-style mansion was built in Massachusetts in 1754 and shipped to DC in 1934.

The **French ambassador's residence**, 2222 Kalorama Rd, Kalorama's largest home, is a Tudor-style mansion commanding an unparalleled view of Rock Creek Park. Check out the enormous French flag dangling before the house: it's big enough to shroud an elephant.

Phillips Collection

In this historic brownstone is the country's oldest modern-art museum (☎ 387-2151), 1600 21st St NW. Its intimate, comfortable galleries feature exceptional works from the mid-1800s onward; it's famed for its Impressionist and Post-Impressionist collections. Monet, Degas, Whistler, van Gogh, Ingres, Braque, Klee, Rothko, and Diebenkorn are all represented. Renoir's panoramic *Luncheon of the Boating Party* crowns its holdings.

Enter through the modern extension wing on 21st St and work your way back into the brownstone, which also houses a café and bookstore. Weekday admission's by donation; weekends it's $7.50/4 adults/students and seniors (kids under 18 free). Special exhibitions cost $10. Open 10 am to 5 pm Tuesday to Saturday, noon to 7 pm Sunday. Thursday, the museum stays open till 8:30 pm and offers live jazz and gallery talks. Sunday-afternoon concerts and lunchtime lectures are among other regular events.

Behind the Phillips, small Hillyer Ct holds two excellent commercial galleries. **The Foundry** (☎ 387-0203) shows contemporary art; the **Edwards Gallery** (☎ 232-5926) has 19th- and 20th-century photography.

RICK GERHARTER

St Jerome at the Croatian Embassy

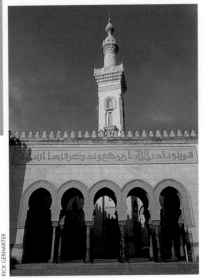

RICK GERHARTER

Islamic Center

Islamic Center

The serenely beautiful Islamic Center
(☎ 332-8343), 2551 Massachusetts Ave NW,
is the national mosque for American Muslims. Topped with a 160-foot minaret, the
pale limestone mosque (which faces Mecca)
is so delicately inscribed with Koranic verse
that it appears to float above Massachusetts
Ave. Inside, the mosque glows with bright
floral tiling, thick Persian rugs, and gilt-
trimmed ceilings detailed with more Koranic
verse. You can enter to look around; remove
your shoes, and women must bring scarves
to cover their hair.

Textile Museum

This gem (☎ 667-0441), 2320 S St NW, gets
our vote for DC's best non-Smithsonian
museum. In two historic mansions, its cool,
dimly lit galleries hold exquisite fabrics and
carpets dating from 3000 BC to the present.
Accompanying wall commentary explains
how the textiles mirror the social, spiritual,
economic, and aesthetic values of the so-
cieties that made them. Founded in 1925,
it's the country's only textile museum, and

its collection includes rare kimonos, pre-
Columbian weaving, American quilts, and
Ottoman embroidery. (Find the flaw: Traditional textile artists, from Islamic carpet-
makers to Appalachian quilters, often
weave intentional flaws into their work to
avoid mimicking God's perfection.)

A hands-on learning center (see the
Washington, DC for Kids section), public
research library, shop, and tranquil garden
round out its offerings. Open 10 am to 5 pm
Monday to Saturday, 1 to 5 pm Sunday; $5
suggested donation. Docent-led tours are
available daily; call for reservations.

Woodrow Wilson House

This Georgian Revival mansion (☎ 387-
4062), 2340 S St NW, offers guided hourlong
tours focusing on the 28th president's life
and legacy. Genteel elderly docents discuss
highlights of Wilson's career (WWI, the
League of Nations) and home, which has
been restored to the period of his residence
(1921-24). The tour features a lovely garden,
a stairwell conservatory, European bronzes,
1920s-era china, and Mrs Wilson's elegant
dresses, all of which offer a glamorous portrait of Roaring Twenties DC society. Open
10 am to 4 pm Tuesday to Sunday, $5/4/2.50
adults/seniors/kids eight to 18.

When you leave, stop at the garden-lined
Spanish Steps, a fanciful little stairway
running down the hillside from S St to
Decatur Place.

Historical Society of Washington, DC

Perhaps the country's only historical society
with a basement beer cellar, the Historical
Society of Washington, DC (☎ 785-2068),
1307 New Hampshire Ave NW, is headquartered in the ornate Victorian 1892 mansion
of German-American brewing magnate
Christian Heurich. You can wander through
14 rooms of Heurich House, a rococo treat
full of gilding and overstuffed furniture. A
pamphlet and wall signs guide you around,
telling you what the Heurichs did in each
room. Everything's written as if the
Heurichs are still alive, which is disconcert-
ing ('Mrs Heurich thanks you for not

smoking in her house,' says a restroom sign) but does help you get a sense of daily life in Victorian DC.

The breakfast room downstairs is designed to resemble a *rathskellar*, complete with beer-positive wall mottoes that must have exerted an interesting influence on the little Heurichs, like *'Wer niemals einen Rausch gehabt, Der ist kein braver Mann'* (He who has never been drunk is not a good man).

The society operates a small shop selling Washingtoniana and a public research library on DC history. It also offers fine children's programs (see Washington, DC for Kids), neighborhood walking tours, and lectures; call to request an events calendar. Open 10 am to 4 pm Monday to Saturday; $3/1.50 adults/seniors, free for those under 12.

National Geographic Explorers' Hall

This natural-science museum, at National Geographic Society headquarters (☎ 857-7588, www.nationalgeographic.com), 17th and M Sts NW, can't compete with the Smithsonian's offerings at their museums farther downtown, but the Explorers' Hall is a good stop if you have kids in tow. They'll enjoy its permanent exhibits on evolution, animals and plants, and environmental issues, plus 'Earth Station One' (a kinda lame multimedia theater simulating orbital flight).

Special exhibits are what really make this place worthwhile, however; past treats include Shackleton Antarctic-expedition photography and natural-history drawings from *National Geographic Magazine*'s early years. Check the Web to see what's on during your visit. Weekly 'Passport Fridays' feature free lectures and concerts at 10 am. Open 9 am to 5 pm Monday to Saturday, 10 am to 5 pm Sunday; free.

The society's year-round **Live...from National Geographic** series, at the Gilbert Grosvenor Auditorium, 1600 M St, includes films, concerts, and lectures by famed researchers and explorers; call ☎ 857-7700 for details.

Cathedral of St Matthew the Apostle

The sturdy red-brick exterior doesn't hint at the marvelous mosaics and gilding within this 1889 Catholic cathedral (☎ 347-3215), 1725 Rhode Island Ave NW, where JFK's funeral mass was held. Its vast central dome, altars, and chapels depict biblical saints and eminent New World personages – from Simón Bolívar to Elizabeth Ann Seton – in stained glass, murals, and scintillating Italianate mosaics; almost no surface is left undecorated.

Evening's the best time to visit, when flickering candles illuminate the sanctuary, but you can attend Latin mass at 10 am Sunday or slip in almost any time to look around. Guided tours run at 2:30 pm Sunday; donations welcome.

B'nai B'rith Klutznick Museum

One of the country's largest Judaica collections is inside this museum (☎ 857-6583), 1640 Rhode Island Ave NW, on the B'nai B'rith building's ground floor. In its quiet rooms are archaeological artifacts, folk art, and beautiful ritual objects, including silver Torah crowns, Kiddush cups, menorahs, Passover platters, and rarities like a 1556 Torah scroll. Here too are exhibits on subjects like early Jewish settlement in the US, the Holocaust, and Jews in American history and the arts. The **National Jewish American Sports Hall of Fame** is an intriguing recent addition.

A tranquil sculpture garden is behind the museum, and a delightful shop sells books and keepsakes (see Shopping). Open 10 am to 5 pm Sunday to Friday; donations welcome.

Washington Post

Want to see where Woodward and Bernstein toppled a president? Stop by the *Post*'s headquarters (☎ 334-7969; Ⓜ McPherson Square), 1150 15th St NW. Its free tours don't reveal much of the paper's operations but do show you the busy newsroom and explain how the paper is printed. They run at 10 and 11 am and 1, 2, and 3 pm Monday only. Call to reserve a spot.

Other Museums & Galleries

The **National Museum of American Jewish Military History** (☎ 265-6280), 1811 R St NW, showcases Jewish soldiers' contributions to the US Armed Forces with photographs and memorabilia of American wars from the Civil to the Gulf. Open 9 am to 5 pm weekdays, 1 to 5 pm Sunday; free.

A delightful artist-run community museum, the **Fondo del Sol Visual Arts Center** (☎ 483-2777), 2112 R St NW, promotes the Americas' cultural heritage and arts through exhibits of contemporary Latin-American artists' work, pre-Columbian artifacts, *santos* (carved wooden saints), and folk art. In late summer, the Caribbeana Festival features salsa and reggae music. Open 12:30 to 5:30 pm Wednesday to Saturday; donations encouraged.

Nearly two dozen **art galleries** throughout the district offer glimpses of works as varied as Tiffany glass, African masks, and Inuit carvings; there's a compact gallery row on R St between Florida and Connecticut Aves, clustered around Fondo del Sol. See the Shopping chapter for details. Find current exhibition listings in the monthly *Galleries* guide, available at most DC galleries, or see www.artline.com/plus. The 21-member Dupont gallery association holds a collective open house the first Friday of each month except August and September (☎ 232-3610 for information).

Historic Buildings

A stately example of Dupont Circle's turn-of-the-century grand manses, the 1902 Beaux-Arts **Anderson House** is now the headquarters of the Society of the Cincinnati (☎ 785-2040), 2118 Massachusetts Ave NW. Founded in 1783 by officers who served under Washington in the Continental Army, the society displays European and Asian art and fine furnishings acquired by the Anderson family, plus exhibits on the Revolution. Highlights include Revolutionary musketry and a pretty winter garden. Open 1 to 4 pm Tuesday to Saturday; free.

The full name of the **Scottish Rite Masonic Temple** (☎ 232-3579), 1733 16th St NW, the US Masonic headquarters, is 'The Supreme Council of the Inspectors General Knights Commanders of the House of the Temple of…' – well, it goes on like that for a while. Its architectural excesses echo its nomenclatural ones: patterned in 1911 by John Russell Pope after the Temple of Halicarnassus, it's lofted on a high pedestal of stairs, fronted by lion statues and grim bronze doors, and, inside, frosted with the ersatz Greek and Egyptian arcana beloved by Masons, all rich in numerological meaning. Docents lead tours. You'll see departed Masons' tombs, the downstairs 'J Edgar Hoover Room,' and tons of purple velvet. Open 8 am to 4 pm weekdays; free.

The **Washington Hilton & Towers**, 1919 Connecticut Ave NW, was the site of John Hinckley's assassination attempt on President Ronald Reagan, on March 30, 1981. Hoping to impress the actress Jodie Foster, the disturbed young man (now housed at St Elizabeth's mental hospital in southeast DC) shot Reagan, his press secretary, and an FBI agent near the T St NW entrance. The hotel has since constructed a big protective entryway.

The country's largest 19th-century black congregation worshiped at the 1886 **Metropolitan AME Church**, 1518 M St NW (Ⓜ Farragut North), a red-brick Gothic shrine that hosted Frederick Douglass' funeral in 1895. Developers have often tried to buy the valuable site, but the congregation remains loyal to its historic home.

Adams-Morgan (Map 9)

Funky, ethnic, bohemian Adams-Morgan – DC's liveliest entertainment district – is centered along 18th St NW and Columbia Rd NW. Before 1955, this area was called Lanier Heights, but after DC became the first big US city to voluntarily integrate its schools, residents renamed it for two local elementary schools: historically white Adams and black Morgan. Adding to this blend today are immigrants from Latin America, the Caribbean, East Africa, and Southeast Asia.

This is a great district for people-watching, hanging out, and clubbing. The long blocks of 18th St between Florida Ave and Columbia Rd are wallpapered with bars, clubs, new and secondhand bookstores, record stores, retro and nouveau clothing boutiques, sidewalk cafés, and rooftop restaurants. Just north is **Mount Pleasant**, DC's most Latino neighborhood, where the streets are lined with Salvadorean *pupuserías* and Central American groceries.

The neighborhood isn't very convenient to Metro, though in decent weather you can walk from Woodley Park-Zoo station along Calvert St. At night, take a cab to avoid gridlocked streets and parking hassles.

September, when the weekend-long Adams-Morgan Days street fair is held, is a nice time to visit (see Special Events in the Facts for the Visitor chapter).

Walking Tour

Adams-Morgan is mostly an area for hanging out with a coffee or beer and watching life move by you, but a stroll reveals more of the area's charms. This walk takes you through Adams-Morgan from the south side of the neighborhood.

Begin your walk at Columbia Rd and Connecticut Ave NW, where you'll see a tall, green-copper equestrian statue of Civil War General George McClellan looking ready to charge south and conquer Dupont Circle. Walk north along Columbia, a climbing, twisting road that began life centuries ago as a Native American trail.

You'll pass several luxurious apartment buildings constructed early in the 20th century, including the 1901 **Lothrop Mansion**, 2001 Connecticut Ave, now the Russian Trade Federation; the 1905 **Wyoming**, 2022 Columbia Rd, where the Eisenhowers lived for a time; and the 1916 **Altamont**, 1901 Wyoming Ave, with its stately towers and airy loggia.

Turn east on Wyoming and walk two blocks to 18th St NW, Adams-Morgan's main drag. Walk north on 18th, which is designed for summertime people-watching, with a plethora of rooftop bars and sidewalk

The Knickerbocker Disaster

The southwest corner of 18th St and Columbia Rd – where Crestar Bank now stands – was the site of DC's worst disaster, the Knickerbocker Theater collapse. On January 28, 1922, a crowd of 300 watched a screening of the comedy *Get-Rich Quick Wallingford* at the Knickerbocker, an elaborate cinema palace frequented by stylish Washingtonians in evening clothes. Meanwhile, a massive storm dumped 26 inches of snow on the capital.

As the film drew to its close, the flimsy theater roof buckled under the accumulated snowfall and collapsed onto the theater's balcony, which crushed the audience below. As the *Post* reported:

…a hearty peal of laughter preceded the falling of the roof. 'Great God!' [a witness] exclaimed. 'It was the most heart-rending thing I ever want to witness.'…When the crash first came, it was followed by the screams of women and the shouts of men. Agonizing cries pierced the air. One woman, in particular, shouted at the top of her voice – shouted not for help, or aid, or succor; because she was probably not conscious of what happened. Her shouts were the gasps of the dying…

Ninety-eight people died, and 136 were injured. (The toll surpasses DC's second-worst disaster, the 1982 crash of Air Florida Flight 90 into the 14th St Bridge, which killed 78 and also occurred in a freak blizzard.) The collapse of the theater's roof destroyed the career of the Knickerbocker's architect, Reginald Geare, who later killed himself, but it did prompt stricter building codes.

No plaque marks the site today, where the bank's small plaza fills on weekends with people shopping for produce and crafts at Adams-Morgan's farmers' market.

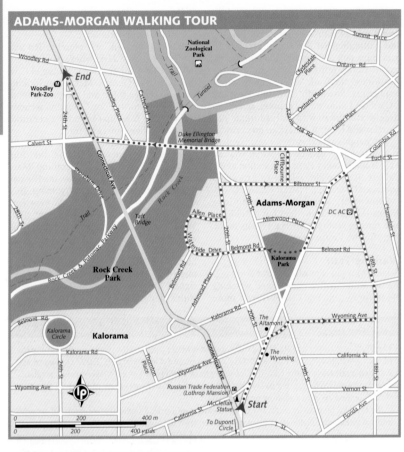

ADAMS-MORGAN WALKING TOUR

RICK GERHARTER

Rowhouses in the Adams-Morgan area

bistros. Hidden among the shops and restaurants is eclectic little **DC AC** (☎ 462-7833), 2438 18th St NW, a performance space/ theater that shows funky local artwork. It's open 2 to 6 pm Wednesday and Thursday, 2 to 10 pm Friday to Sunday; free.

The heart of Adams-Morgan is 18th St's intersection with Columbia Rd. Its most attractive residential streets lie west of the intersection, so turn left on Columbia and cut through Kalorama Park to reach them. Belmont Rd, Waterside Drive, Allen Place, and Biltmore St are all streets lined with

well-restored brick rowhouses and their landscaped pocket gardens.

From here, you can cross the lofty **Duke Ellington Memorial Bridge** (that famed jazzman was born in DC), which offers a view of Rock Creek Park 120 feet below and is, sadly, DC's favored suicide-jump spot. 'Spirit of Travel' figures, celebrating air, auto, water, and rail transport, decorate its piers. From here, you can continue into Woodley Park and hop onto Metro.

Meridian Hill Park

Unofficially dedicated to Malcolm X, this park scales a hillside from the Shaw neighborhood to Adams-Morgan's upper reaches and adds much-needed scenery to the area. (It's most easily reached from U St-Cardozo Metro station.) Built astraddle the fall line, the geologic boundary between the rocky Piedmont Plateau and softer Coastal Plain, the park emphasizes its odd locale with terraced walkways and a waterfall cascade. An eccentric mix of statuary, from Jeanne d'Arc to Dante, enlivens its contoured lawns. It's lovely in springtime, when the dogwoods and azaleas flower, but isn't safe to visit after dark.

The park was constructed in the early 20th century, when Meridian Hill was a very fashionable district. Just across 16th St lived the neighborhood's reigning social queen, Mary Henderson, wife of a Missouri senator, who built herself a grand old castle here. (The castle's been demolished, but its crenelated walls still stand on 16th St.) Her favorite architect, George Oakley Totten, built many ornate manses near her castle, some of which still exist. Check out his **Pink** Palace (1906), 2600 16th St, a Venetian-style palazzo now housing the Interamerican Defense Board.

Meridian International Center

Inside an elevated, walled compound on curving Crescent Place NW, near the park, the Meridian International Center (☎ 667-6800) is housed in two superb mansions designed by John Russell Pope. An educational and hospitality center for DC's international community, it hosts cultural events and holds the fine **Cafritz Galleries**, with exhibitions of international artwork. Gallery hours are 2 to 5 pm Wednesday to Sunday; free.

The International Visitors Information Service is here, too, providing traveler services like home-hospitality visits, multilingual Capitol tours, and an information line (☎ 939-5544).

Meridian International Center

Shaw & the New U District (Map 10)

Named for Robert Gould Shaw, a Civil War colonel mortally wounded while commanding the famed black 54th Massachusetts Regiment, Shaw stretches south to north from around Thomas Circle to Harvard St, and east to west from roughly 15th St NW to N Capitol St.

To walk through Shaw is to walk through the history of black Washington. Starting in the 1890s, Shaw became the political and cultural center of African American DC as

Pearl Bailey, jazz singer and one-time waitress

black families and opinion makers settled here, driven out of increasingly segregated downtown Washington. Civil-rights leaders Archibald and Francis Grimké and Calvin Chase, editor of the crusading *Washington Bee*, lived here; black lawyers, doctors, and tradesmen opened offices along U St, which blossomed into a separate downtown for those excluded by racism from DC's other shops. Civil-rights struggles were a constant feature of Shaw life: in the 1950s, Washington's Committee for School Desegregation first met at John Wesley AME Zion Church at 1615 14th St NW, and their work led to the landmark *Brown v Board of Education*, which mandated school desegregation.

In Shaw's theaters and music halls sprang up a vibrant arts scene known as 'Black Broadway,' which flourished from the 1920s to the '40s. Duke Ellington grew up on T St. Pearl Bailey waitressed and danced at U St's Republic Gardens. Ella Fitzgerald sang at Bohemian Caverns, the 11th St jazz club; Louis Armstrong played the Dance Hall at

V and 9th Sts; and the Lincoln and Howard Theatres presented Harlem's and DC's finest to black audiences. Shaw was a high point on the renowned 'chitlin circuit' of black entertainment districts.

By the '50s, segregation started to ease. Middle-class blacks could live elsewhere, so some moved. Shaw entered a decline that became a tailspin in April 1968, when riots exploded after the murder of Dr Martin Luther King, Jr. Centered upon 14th and U Sts, the violence destroyed many black-owned businesses and frightened others away.

Until the late '80s, Shaw languished. In 1991, the U St-Cardozo Metro station opened, drawing back businesses. Today Shaw's gradual renaissance continues, particularly in the 'New U' area along U and 14th Sts.

Walking Tour

Begin your Shaw stroll at Metro's U St-Cardozo station, with its lively murals of Shaw streetlife. Exit via the west escalator to 13th St; at street level, turn around to see a fine **mural of Duke Ellington** painted on a building facade.

Head east on U St, passing the restored historic **Lincoln Theatre** (☎ 328-6000), No 1215, which has regained its position as one of DC's preeminent black cultural institutions. It's best to see it during one of the many performances held here, from flamenco to hip-hop (see Entertainment).

Its neighbor, **Ben's Chili Bowl**, 1213 U St NW, is a down-home restaurant that not

RICK GERHARTER

Ben's Chili Bowl serves great dogs.

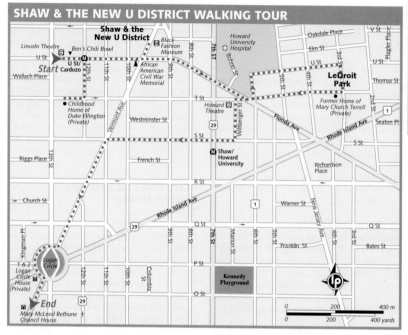

only serves great chili dogs (stop for lunch) but has been a gathering place for DC's black politicos and community leaders since its opening, in 1958. National celebs like Bill Cosby (who has a chili dog named after him) make the occasional appearance, too. From here, duck a block south to see the **childhood home of Duke Ellington**, 1212 T St (private).

At U St and Vermont Ave, outside the Metro station's east entrance, is the **African American Civil War Memorial**. Here the names of the 209,145 black soldiers who fought in the Union Army are engraved on two steel walls curving around statues of rifle-bearing troops. A paper index helps you locate names.

Turn north to see the eclectic little **Black Fashion Museum** (☎ 667-0744), 2007 Vermont Ave NW, showcasing the work of black designers past and present. Here you can see slaves' dresses, the dress Rosa Parks wore during her historic bus ride, the handi-

work of unsung seamstresses who costumed famous figures from Mary Todd Lincoln to Jackie Kennedy, and African artwork. Open by appointment; call one week in advance.

Turn right on Florida Ave, then cut a bit north and turn right on U St to see **LeDroit Park**, a small subdivision of fine Victorian homes built in the 1870s by architect James McGill, between 2nd and 7th Sts north of Rhode Island Ave. Once a fenced-off all-white enclave, it later housed Howard University scholars and DC's black elite. At 326 T St is the **former home of Mary Church Terrell** (private), the educator and civil-rights heroine who, after being refused service in whites-only Thompson's Restaurant, launched the campaign that led to desegregation of DC's public spaces.

A key fixture on 'Black Broadway' was the **Howard Theatre**, 620 T St, which still stands but is unused and in disrepair (although efforts to restore it are occasionally launched). Ella Fitzgerald, Billie Holiday, and Lena Horne sang here; later, James Brown and Motown bands performed. Next door was Frank Holliday's poolroom, where the young Ellington honed his keyboard chops.

Return to Vermont Ave and walk three blocks south to reach **Logan Circle**, another historic district of well-preserved Victorian homes. Once home to white socialites, then to black movers and shakers, it's now being rediscovered by wealthy folks. Note especially **1 & 2 Logan Circle** (private), an ornate cream-colored manse built in 1877 by Ulysses S Grant Jr. Finish your walk at the **Mary McLeod Bethune Council House**, the former home of the great black educator (see below).

Howard University

Anchoring the neighborhood is Howard University (☎ 806-6100; Ⓜ Shaw-Howard U), 2400 6th St NW, the country's oldest black college, founded in 1867. Distinguished alumni include the late Supreme Court Justice Thurgood Marshall (who enrolled after he was turned away from the

University of Maryland's then all-white law school), Ralph Bunche, Nobel laureate Toni Morrison, and former New York City Mayor David Dinkins. Today it has over 12,000 students in 18 schools.

Campus tours are available; call ☎ 806-2900. You may also wish to visit the **Moorland-Spingarn Research Center** (☎ 806-7239), in Founders' Library, with the nation's largest collection of African American literature, open 9 am to around 4:30 pm weekdays; and the **James Herring Gallery of Art** (☎ 806-7070), open 9:30 am to 4:30 pm weekdays; free.

Mary McLeod Bethune Council House

The Council House (☎ 673-2402), 1318 Vermont Ave NW, in the Logan Circle Historic District, is the former home of pioneer black educator and activist Mary McLeod Bethune and the first headquarters of the National Council of Negro Women. The Second Empire townhouse, now managed by the NPS, is an attractive setting for a collection of Bethune memorabilia and an important archive of black women's historical materials. Rangers lead you on tours here and show you videotapes about Bethune's life. Exhibits, lectures, and workshops on black history are held here as well. Open 10 am to 4 pm; donations welcome.

Upper Northwest DC (Map 11)

Northwest of Adams-Morgan and Georgetown lie affluent residential neighborhoods filled with large homes on quiet, tree-lined streets. Including the districts of Woodley Park, Cleveland Park, Chevy Chase, Foxhall, and the Palisades, this extensive area is studded with parks and served by Metro's Red Line. Three major attractions are here – the National Zoo, National Cathedral, and Rock Creek Park (see 'Rock Creek Park' following this chapter) – as well as small museums and historic sites.

RICK GERHARTER

Mary McLeod Bethune Council House

National Zoological Park

The Smithsonian-operated zoo (☎ 673-4800, http://web2.si.edu/natzoo; Ⓜ Woodley Park-Zoo), 3001 Connecticut Ave NW, is one of DC's crown jewels. Founded in 1889 and beautifully planned by Frederick Law Olmsted, designer of New York's Central Park, the zoo's 130 acres follow the natural contours of its woodland-canyon setting. Its enclosures and buildings, set along curving paths, hold cheetahs, lions, monkeys, gorillas, and other exotic beasties.

RICK GERHARTER

Signs at the zoo announce that it's actually a 'biopark' – ie, it's dedicated to conservation, research, and education, not just displaying cuddly animals. That's not mere PR blather: the zoo is intensively involved in worldwide ecological study and species-preservation work, and its exhibits are noted for natural-habitat settings. Tamarins scamper uncaged through the treetops, piranhas hunt in a simulated Amazon, and tigers snooze on their enclosures' terraced grass hillsides.

Plan to spend a full day at the zoo; seeing it all takes time. There's also a crowded calendar of daily special events, from lectures to films to elephant-training demonstrations. Guided tours are given weekend mornings by advance reservation.

Information The zoo's open daily except Christmas. May 1 to September 15, its grounds are open 6 am to 8 pm (to 6 pm the rest of the year). Zoo buildings are open 10 am to 6 pm May 1 to September 15 (to 4:30 pm the rest of the year). Admission's free.

Inside the Connecticut Ave NW entrance is the visitors' center, offering maps (25¢), program information, restrooms, an ATM, wheelchair and stroller rental, and a bookshop. Other information centers are at the zoo's Rock Creek Park entrance and near the Panda House. Numerous shops on the grounds sell souvenirs, stuffed animals, and toys. Several cafés serve fast food (overpriced and undertasty): cross Connecticut Ave to the Animal Crackers Café or Zoo Bar instead.

The limited parking fills up by early morning. Metro's closest station, Woodley Park-Zoo, is an easy 10-minute walk south on Connecticut Ave NW.

The zoo can be hellaciously crowded, especially on summer weekends. To beat the crowds, visit in early morning on a cloudy, cool, even slightly rainy day – such weather not only keeps human herds at bay but encourages heat-sensitive or shy big animals (wolves, bears, tigers) to venture outside their dens and into their enclosures, where you can easily see them.

Olmsted Walk The zoo's higher path passes the American prairie exhibit, Panda House (temporarily empty as of 2000; see the boxed text), elephant/giraffe house, primate and reptile houses. Nearby is **Think Tank**, a wonderful collection of interactive exhibits on animal intelligence and social structure aimed at the six-to-12 set. Down the trail a bit are open-air lion and tiger enclosures and the **Bat Cave**, a perennial kids' favorite.

Little ones acting up? Take them to the cheetah enclosure's 'What's for Dinner?' display. Here you weigh yourself and are told what sort of prey animal you'd be and what would eat you. ('100-150 pounds: You're a female warthog. A pack of lions could finish you off in an hour.')

Panda-monium

Once upon a time, the zoo was home to two furry super-stars: Ling-Ling and Hsing-Hsing the pandas, gifts from the Chinese government. For 20 years the two held Washington spellbound with their snuggling and squabbling and endless, fruitless efforts to make little pandas. Much like the British royal family – albeit cuter and lacking Buckingham Palace – the bears appeared in city headlines every time they laid a paw on each other. Zoo visitors adored them.

Ling-Ling padded off to that great zoo in the sky back in '92, and Hsing-Hsing followed her in '99 (after a last meal of his favorite food, a Starbucks blueberry muffin). Zoo administrators instantly launched a search for new pandas. Congressmen and cabinet secretaries helped with the negotiations, which ran into US-Chinese tensions over non-cute issues like human rights and Taiwan. But in May 2000 China agreed to loan a new pair to the zoo for 10 years (for $10 million). Any cubs produced will belong to China. Zoo director Michael Robinson declared himself 'happy as a tick on a mattress' at the result, and zoo visitors will no doubt agree.

Valley Trail This trail passes the Bird House (eagles, worldwide exotics) and wetlands displays (waterbirds, lilies). It also passes the tamarins' forest, where the little primates range free in warm weather, and seal tanks. At its eastern end is the zoo's most amazing exhibit, **Amazonia**. In this building is a mini-ecosystem, complete with downstairs aquariums – the 'river' – that open into an upstairs conservatory – the 'forest.' In the water swim piranhas and magnificent fish, and the trees (anchored by a massive kapok) are filled with epiphytes, ferns, birds, and monkeys. Impressive hands-on study rooms and a library complete the exhibit.

Hillwood Museum & Gardens

Housing the biggest collection of Russian imperial art outside Russia itself, Hillwood (☎ 686-5807; Ⓜ Van Ness/UDC), 4155 Linnean Ave NW, Cleveland Park, is the former estate of heiress Marjorie Merriweather Post (of Post Toasties fame), who was married to the ambassador to the USSR in the '30s. By all accounts a formidable woman, Post convinced Stalin and the Soviets to sell her lots of Czarist swag, and her collection includes furniture, paintings, and exquisite Fabergé eggs and jewelry. The 25-acre estate, reopened in fall 2000 after a 2½-year restoration, features lovely gardens (with notable azalea and orchid collections, and Post's dog cemetery), a greenhouse, and a museum shop. A café serves Russian treats (borscht, blintzes) and afternoon tea.

Tour guides show you around, and advance reservations are required; $10/5 adults/students. Kids under six can't visit the mansion, but they're OK in the gardens. Open 9 am to 5 pm Tuesday to Saturday; closed February.

Washington National Cathedral

A national cathedral in a country premised upon the separation of church and state is an unusual idea. So, by definition, the National Cathedral (☎ 537-6200), Massachusetts and Wisconsin Aves NW, is an unusual place, run by the Episcopal diocese but paying tribute to many faiths and peoples.

The cornerstone of this majestic Gothic cathedral (the world's sixth-largest) was laid by Teddy Roosevelt in 1908, and construction didn't stop until 1990. Its pale limestone walls, flying buttresses, intricate carving, and exquisite stained glass (all intended to rival Europe's great cathedrals) have won for the cathedral, in many critics' eyes, the title of the country's most beautiful church. Martin Luther King Jr gave his last Sunday sermon here; now it's the standard place for state funerals and other high-profile events. Each week prayers are devoted to a different state and religious tradition.

Take the elevator to the **tower overlook**, DC's highest point, for expansive city views; posted maps explain what you see. Downstairs in the main sanctuary, chapels honor the Apollo astronauts, MLK, Abe Lincoln, and abstract ideas like peace and justice. The endearing Children's Chapel is here as well, filled with images of real and imaginary animals. Downstairs in the **crypt** are more chapels; famous folks from Helen Keller to Woodrow Wilson are buried here.

Outside, walk through the charming **Bishop's Garden**, a small English-style garden with winding paths that lend a mood of solitude, and stop at the **Herb Cottage**, selling garden goods, herbs, and gifts. St Alban's School for Boys and the National Cathedral School for Girls are also on the grounds – these tony schools's alumni include Al Gore.

The shop located under the main sanctuary sells books on spirituality, cathedrals,

Beasties on the Buttresses: The National Cathedral Gargoyles

Gargoyles serve both a practical function (they're rainwater spouts, and their name derives from the French *gargouille*, to gargle) and numerous spiritual ones: they warn churchgoers of hell's terrors, ward off the devil's assaults on the holy, and represent pagan deities long ago assimilated by Christian monotheism. They reached their apotheosis on European churches like Notre Dame, but the National Cathedral has raised the gargoyle tradition to comical new heights.

On its southern facade perch dogs and cats, boars and donkeys, and beasts wholly imaginary (including a dragon skeleton with a snake lunging from its eye socket). On the western side loom the god Pan, a feasting glutton, and a reading elephant. Elsewhere are Darth Vader, a stonemason leering at the Cathedral School girls, a placard-toting hippie, a sobbing tortoise, and caricatures of craftspeople and clergy associated with the cathedral. Like everything else in the National Cathedral, each gargoyle is a handcrafted original, and many were 'donated' by individual supporters of the century-long cathedral-building project.

The cathedral hands out three flyers that guide you around its gargoyles and grotesques. Binoculars help. Should you feel the urge to adopt a beast, go to the cathedral's downstairs gift shop for miniature replicas of its critters, plus stuffed gargoyles (for your baby Goth), garden gargoyles (to eat the squirrels), blow-up life-size gargoyles, gargoyle jewelry, gargoyle lollipops ($4), and carve-your-own-gargoyle kits ($23).

RICHARD CUMMINS

Washington National Cathedral

and gardening, plus a delightful mishmash of souvenirs, icons, and toys.

Hours are 10 am to 4:30 pm Monday to Saturday, 12:30 to 4:30 pm Sunday. A donation is requested ($3/1 adults/kids). A self-guided tour pamphlet costs 25¢. Purple-caped volunteers lead good (but crowded) guided tours daily, but the best way to experience the cathedral is at a service – all are welcome (the program cues you on when to stand and other protocol). The main service, at 11 am Sunday, features fine choral signing.

Take Metro to Tenleytown station and hop on bus No 30, 32, 34, or 36 down Wisconsin Ave to the cathedral.

US Naval Observatory

At 3450 Massachusetts Ave NW, its entrance framed by a pair of stately white ship's anchors, the US Naval Observatory (☎ 762-1438) was created in the 1800s 'to determine the positions and motions of celestial objects, provide astronomical data, measure the Earth's rotation, and maintain the Master Clock for the US.' Modern DC's light pollution prevents it from doing important observational work these days, but its cesium-beam atomic clock is still the source of all standard time in the US. Free 1½-hour tours, at 8:30 pm each Monday (except holidays), let you peek through telescopes, yack with astronomers, and learn about the Master Clock. This popular tour doesn't accept reservations except for large groups, so arrive at 7:30 pm to snag a walk-in pass. At other times, the observatory's closed to the public.

On observatory grounds above Massachusetts Ave is the official **Vice President's Residence** (the Admiral's House). No tours are offered, so look at it from the sidewalk.

More Embassies

Along Massachusetts Ave near the observatory is the upper end of Embassy Row (see Dupont Circle & Kalorama, earlier, for sites on its lower stretches). Several embassies are worth a look, including the **Finnish Embassy** (☎ 298-5800), 3301 Massachusetts Ave NW, a beautiful postmodern green-glass oblong that's softened by covering vine trellises. It hosts occasional but excellent exhibits of Finnish photos and painting. Nearby, the imposing, Queen Anne–style **British Embassy** (☎ 588-7800), 3100 Massachusetts Ave NW, designed by Sir Edwin Lutyens, has award-winning gardens that host a fancy Queen's Birthday celebration each May.

Parks

A trio of small, elongated parks in upper northwest DC offer quiet, little-trafficked trails where you can bird-watch and stroll in peace.

Normanstone Park is a wooded ravine on Massachusetts Ave NW near the Observatory. In its midst is the **Kahlil Gibran Memorial Garden**, on the 3100 block of Massachusetts, which memorializes the arch-deity of soupy spiritual poetry. Its centerpieces are a moody bust of the Lebanese mystic and a star-shaped fountain surrounded by flowers, hedges, and limestone benches engraved with various Gibranisms: 'We live only to discover beauty. All else is a form of waiting.' It's a peaceful oasis.

From a trailhead just north of the garden, you can hop onto trails that link to both Rock Creek Park and **Glover Archbold Park**. Glover is a sinuous, winding park, extending from Van Ness St NW in the Tenleytown area down to the western border of Georgetown University. Its 180 tree-covered acres follow the course of little Foundry Branch Creek, along which a pretty nature trail runs. Another good place to access this trail is Reservoir Rd, which crosses the park just north of the university.

Farther west, skinny **Battery Kemble Park**, about a mile long but less than a quarter-mile wide, separates the wealthy Foxhall and Palisades neighborhoods of far northwestern DC. A rough trail winds through its woods. Managed by the National Park Service, the park preserves the site of a little two-gun battery that helped defend western DC against Confederate troops during the Civil War.

Kreeger Museum

In wealthy Foxhall, this exquisite museum (☎ 337-3050), 2401 Foxhall Rd NW, is housed in a coolly elegant Philip Johnson-designed building. Among DC's newest and most intimate museums, the Kreeger exhibits 19th- and 20th-century paintings and sculpture collected by David and Carmen Lloyd Kreeger, including works by Miró, Picasso, Monet, Kandinsky, and Henry Moore. Seminars, lectures, and musical performances round out its offerings.

It's open, by reservation only, for 1½-hour tours at 10:30 am and 1:30 pm Tuesday to Saturday. Call ☎ 338-3552 for reservations ($5 per person). It's closed in August, and no one under 12 may visit. No public transport serves the museum – take a cab, or catch Metrobus D2 to Reservoir and Foxhall Rds NW, then walk three blocks north on Foxhall Rd.

National Museum of Health & Medicine

Forensics junkies love this museum (☎ 782-2200), in Building 54 of the Walter Reed Army Medical Center, Alaska Ave NW and Fern St, which contains both straightforward scientific exhibits and freakish medical oddities. Visitors can see antique microscopes, some dating to the 16th century; old surgical instruments; and exhibits on renowned scientists and research initiatives. You can also see cannonball-shredded leg bones removed from Civil War soldiers, the bullet that killed Lincoln and fragments of his shattered skull, President Garfield's spinal column, a Peruvian mummy, photos of syphilitics, babies' skeletons from fetus to five-year-old, a preserved brain, a dwarf's skeleton, and lungs that have suffered various calamities from black lung to tuberculosis.

The museum was founded in 1862 to study Civil War battlefield medicine. It's attached to the Armed Forces Institute of Pathology, the largest US repository of human tissue samples, which is a treasure-house for medical researchers. The science writer Gina Kolata once called it the 'Library of Congress of the dead.'

All displays are tasteful and educational, but they may be too intense for little kids (who will clamor to see them anyway). It's open 10 am to 5:30 pm daily; free. To get here, take Metrobus 52 from the Takoma Metro station. Walking from the station takes 15 minutes.

Fort Stevens & Battleground National Cemetery

Hidden in far northern DC are a pair of sites that commemorate the only Civil War battle fought on the capital's soil. Fort Stevens, the northernmost of the defensive ramparts ringing the city (see Rock Creek Park, earlier), was attacked by Confederate General Jubal Early in a daring raid on July 11, 1864. A small but fierce battle raged until Early's men were forced back across the Potomac on July 12. Abraham Lincoln himself was drawn into the shooting: the president, observing the battle from Fort Stevens' parapet, popped his head up so many times to peek that Oliver Wendell Holmes Jr, then a Union captain, yelled: 'Get down, you damn fool, before you get shot!' The fort, at 13th and Quackenbos Sts NW, has been partially restored.

Forty-one Union men who died in the fort's defense were buried at tiny Battleground National Cemetery, 6625 Georgia Ave NW, a half-mile north of the fort, which was dedicated by Lincoln. You can wander around in daylight hours to see the markers and plaques honoring DC's defenders.

Activities

Biking

Washington is an ideal town for bike touring. There's lots of parkland (much of it along the water), few hills, and buckets of scenery.

Rock Creek Park's **Beach Drive**, between Military and Broad Branch Rds, closes to traffic all day weekends. Other good rides are on the **C&O Canal towpath**, which starts in Georgetown and stretches 184 miles northwest to Cumberland, Maryland.

There's also the 11-mile **Capital Crescent Trail**, running from Georgetown to northern Rock Creek Park, in Bethesda. For maps, call the Coalition for the Capital Crescent Trail (☎ 234-4874). The southern trailhead's under the Whitehurst Freeway and Key Bridge in Georgetown. Across the Potomac, the **Mount Vernon Trail** is a beautiful paved riverside path that's a favorite among local bikers. See Excursions for details.

City Bikes (Map 9; ☎ 265-1564), at 2501 Champlain St in Adams-Morgan, rents, sells, and repairs bikes. Mountain bikes and hybrids rent for $10/25 per hour/day. Look for the mural of cycling cows above the shop (there used to be a Ben & Jerry's next door). In Georgetown, Big Wheel Bikes (☎ 337-0254), 1034 33rd St NW, rents racing and mountain bikes at similar rates, and the Thompson Boat Center (see below) also rents bikes. Better Bikes Inc (☎ 293-2080) will deliver and pick up bikes all over DC for free. Rentals start at $25/hour.

JOHN NEUBAUER

'Bike the Sites' (☎ 966-8662) does guided bike tours of DC landmarks for $35; it provides 21-speed hybrids. It rents bikes for daily use, too.

Several good books describe local bike tours. Try *Short Bike Rides In & Around Washington, DC*, by Michael Leccese. Another good source is *ADC's Washington Area Bike Map*; find it at the Map Store (Map 3; ☎ 628-2608), 1636 I St NW. Serious bike fiends should check out the Washington Area Bicyclists' Association (☎ 628-22500, www.waba.org) for information on bike-advocacy and group rides. A favorite is BikeDC, an annual self-paced tour offering the thousands who participate a chance to traverse some of the city's major streets without cars. September 2000's 35-mile ride started and ended at (where else?) the White House.

Hiking & Running

Many trails used by bicyclists also provide fine hikes and jogs (see above). Rock Creek Park also has 15 miles of unpaved trails – see the Rock Creek Park after this chapter. It also has a 1½-mile exercise trail behind the Omni Shoreham Hotel (Ⓜ Woodley Park-Zoo), stopping at 18 exercise stations. Farther out are great hikes on both the Maryland and Virginia sides of Great Falls (see Excursions for more information).

If you want a downtown route, try the ever-popular gravel paths of the National Mall, the Tidal Basin loop, or the paved path running around the edge of Hains Point, in southwest DC.

The Potomac Appalachian Trail Club publishes *Hikes in the Washington Region*, also available at the Map Store (see above). The *Washington, DC Running Guide*, by Don Carter, outlines 38 great routes. The Sierra Club's DC chapter (☎ 547-2326) leads day hikes all over the capital region.

Boating

Boaters head to the Potomac River and the C&O Canal. Rent canoes (and bikes) at Thompson Boat Center (Map 7; ☎ 333-9543), 2900 Virginia Ave NW, on the Potomac north of the Kennedy Center. Open daily, it has canoes, rowboats, kayaks, rowing shells, rowing classes, and bikes. Rent similar equipment at Fletchers Boathouse (Map 11; ☎ 244-0461), upriver at 4940 Canal Rd NW.

Several companies at the southwestern waterfront offer dining and sightseeing cruises, including Spirit Cruises (Map 6; ☎ 554-8000), 6th and Water Sts SW, and Odyssey Cruises (Map 6; ☎ 488-6000), just north of Spirit. Prices range from $26 to $37.

Golf

DC has three public courses. The biggest is East Potomac Park Golf Course (Map 6; ☎ 554-7660), at Hains Point. This very busy place is a bit scrubby but has a marvelous river view. There are three courses: the par-72 18-hole Blue ($16.50/22.50 weekdays/weekends), nine-hole White, and 12-hole Red (both ($11/15). In northeast DC is Langston Golf Course (Map 4; ☎ 397-8638), 26th St NE and Benning Rd NE, which many consider DC's best public course. Its par-72 18 holes cost $15/19 weekdays/weekends. A third course is in Rock Creek Park; see that section.

Tennis

The city maintains over 50 free public courts; for information and a permit, call the DC Dept of Parks and Recreation (☎ 673-7671).

Team Sports

Looking to play soccer, ultimate, or softball? Call DC's main team-sports resource, the Washington Sport & Social Club (☎ 537-7353), which operates local sports leagues and can find you a team.

Rock Creek Park

Dropping a slice of wilderness into urban Washington, this national park begins at the Potomac's east bank near Georgetown and extends to and beyond the northern city boundaries. Narrow in its southern stretches, where it hews to the winding course of Rock Creek, it broadens into wide, peaceful parklands in upper northwest DC. Terrific trails extend along its entire length. Its boundaries enclose both Civil War forts and dense forest, recreational facilities and wildflower-strewn fields. Established in 1890, it's one of the country's finest urban parks, and as you walk in its midst you may forget you're in a city altogether.

For general park information, call ☎ 282-1063 or see www.nps.gov/rocr. The easiest way to reach the park by public transportation is to take Metro's Red Line to Cleveland Park or Woodley Park-Zoo station. The park's just a block east. Look for signs.

Things to See

Most interesting sites lie north of the National Zoological Park. You can walk to some from Metro, but others require a car for easy access.

A great first stop is the **Nature Center & Planetarium** (☎ 426-6829), off Military Rd in upper northwest DC. Besides informative exhibits on park flora, fauna, and history, it has two little nature trails and tons of information on the park, plus maps and field guides to the city. A fun 'touch table' is set up for little kids, and rangers lead kid-oriented nature walks featuring cool activities like poking around in the mud for salamanders. Pick up a monthly program schedule at the center, which is open 9 am to 5 pm daily from Memorial Day to Labor Day, and Wednesday to Sunday thereafter.

RICK GERHARTER

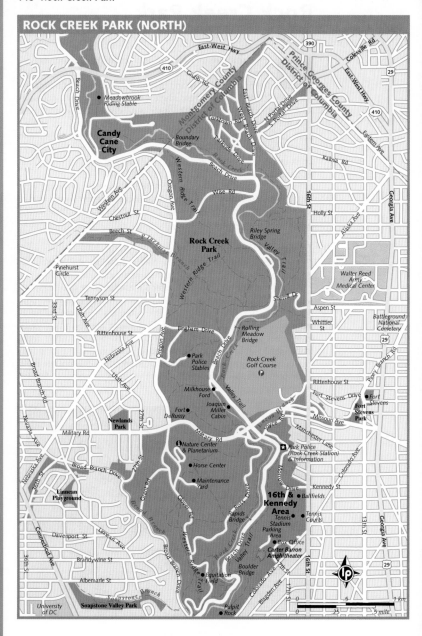

ROCK CREEK PARK (NORTH)

Meadowbrook Riding Stable

Candy Cane City

Boundary Bridge

Rock Creek Park

Riley Spring Bridge

Walter Reed Army Medical Center

Battleground National Cemetery

Rolling Meadow Bridge

Rock Creek Golf Course

Park Police Stables

Milkhouse Ford

Fort DeRussy

Joaquin Miller Cabin

Fort Stevens

Fort Stevens Park

Newlands Park

Nature Center & Planetarium

Horse Center

Maintenance Yard

Park Police (Rock Creek Station) & Information

Linnean Playground

16th & Kennedy Area

Ballfields

Tennis Courts

Rapids Bridge

Tennis Stadium Parking Area

Box Office

Carter Barron Amphitheater

Equitation Field

Boulder Bridge

University of DC

Soapstone Valley Park

Pulpit Rock

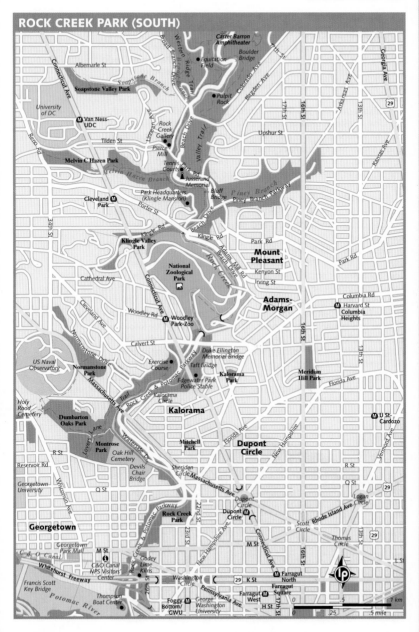

ROCK CREEK PARK (SOUTH)

A bit north of here, on the west side of Beach Drive, is the **Joaquin Miller Cabin**, a little log house that once sheltered the famed nature poet. Farther south, the park's western **Soapstone Valley Park** extension, off Connecticut Ave at Albemarle St NW, preserves quarries where the area's original Algonquin Indian residents dug soapstone for shaping their cookware.

Creekside on Tilden St is the 1820 **Pierce Mill** (☎ 426-6908). This small, beautiful fieldstone building was once a water-driven gristmill, and it's open to visitors noon to 5 pm Wednesday to Sunday. Next door, local artists display work at the **Rock Creek Gallery** (☎ 244-2482), 2401 Tilden St, in a 19th-century carriage house. The gallery holds poetry readings and art classes, sells handmade jewelry and crafts, and opens noon to 6 pm Thursday to Sunday.

If you visit in summer, get an events calendar at **Carter Barron Amphitheater** (☎ 426-6837), 16th and Kennedy Sts NW, a 4000-seat outdoor theater where concerts and plays – many free – are held on summer evenings.

The remains of **Civil War forts** are among the park's most fascinating sites. During the war, Washington was, essentially, a massive urban armory and supply house for the Union Army. Its position near the Confederate lines made it vulnerable to attack, so forts were hastily erected on the city's high points. By spring 1865, 68 forts and 93 batteries bristled on hilltops around DC. **Fort DeRussy**, in the park, is one of the best-preserved, with its moat and rammed-earth parapet still apparent. Reach it by following the trail from Military Rd and Oregon Ave NW. The remains of other forts – Battery Kemble near the Potomac, Fort Reno, Fort Stevens, and on to Fort Bunker Hill in northeast DC – are also administered by Rock Creek Park, and some earthworks remain visible. (See also Fort Stevens, in the Upper Northwest DC section of the Things to See & Do chapter.)

RICK GERHARTER

Left: Pierce Mill

RICK GERHARTER

Overlooking Rock Creek at 3545 Williamsburg Lane in Cleveland Park is the **Klingle Mansion**. Built in 1823 by Joshua Pierce, the 10-room Pennsylvania Dutch fieldstone house is now park headquarters, open 7:45 am to 4:15 pm weekdays only.

Activities

Watching Wildlife Rock Creek's a great place to observe native East Coast creatures: woodchucks, white-tail deer, beavers, raccoons, red foxes, flying squirrels, and a passel of birds from blue herons to owls to pileated woodpeckers. Rewarding spots include the park's meadows in the cool of early morning (the Nature Center can give you a pamphlet showing meadow locations).

Hiking & Biking Two main hiking trails run down the park. On the west side of Rock Creek, the 4 ½-mile Western Ridge Trail winds around through forest. On the east side, the 5 ½-mile Valley Trail runs closer to the creek. The trails are lightly trafficked; on weekdays you'll have them to yourself. Both are easy and clearly blazed. The Nature Center has free maps.

Extensive trail networks connect Rock Creek Park to other northwestern DC parks – Normanstone, Montrose, Dumbarton Oaks, Whitehaven, Glover Archbold, and Battery Kemble – so you can take a cross-city parkland ramble if you like. A good map, *Trails in the Rock Creek Park Area*, is published by the Potomac Appalachian Trail Club and sold in local shops ($5).

Bikers must stay on the paved 10-mile bike trail running the whole length of the park. It's a pretty, largely flat ride (you'll weave among packs of joggers on weekends) that hugs the creek. You can also bike Beach Drive on weekends, when it's closed to traffic.

Top right:
Klingle Mansion

RICK GERHARTER

Horseback Riding The Horse Center (☎ 362-0118) is near the Nature Center at 5100 Glover Rd NW. It offers guided trail rides ($25 per hour), pony rides for tots ($10), and lessons. Two park trails totalling about 12 miles are open to riders.

Golf The Rock Creek Golf Course (☎ 882-7332), 1600 Rittenhouse St NW, is an 18-hole course whose low hills offer a bit of challenge. It charges $15/19 weekdays/weekends; carts $10/17; club rental $6/9.

Tennis At 16th and Kennedy Sts NW are 25 courts, both hard- and soft-surface. You have to reserve 'em; call ☎ 722-5949. A small fee is charged in summer, but hard-surface courts are free in colder months.

Places to Stay

Tourism is Washington's bread and butter, so the city offers the complete range of accommodations, from dormitory-hostels to five-star historic hotels. Like any American city, it has all the predictable chains (Marriott, Hilton, Holiday Inn, etc), but it also boasts a wealth of small guesthouses, boutique hotels, and inexpensive inns, often in charming areas, that offer you an off-the-beaten-track way to meet locals and soak up neighborhood atmosphere.

Rates & Seasons

Most DC hotels, particularly upscale ones, have no set rates. Instead, rates vary week to week and even day to day, depending on season and availability. Here are some general rules to remember.

Rates on weekdays – when business and government travelers fill hotels – are generally higher than on weekends at accommodations within DC city limits. Prices drop, often dramatically, on weekends. (A note on the term 'weekend' – in hotelspeak it usually means Friday and Saturday nights, not Saturday and Sunday nights.) B&Bs and guesthouses, on the other hand, usually maintain constant rates throughout the week.

Although DC has no true 'low' seasons, rates are usually lowest in late summer (August) and early winter (January and February), when the weather is unpleasant. At these times, Congress is also out of session (meaning fewer government/business visitors), so you might find bargains at top-end hotels. On the flip side of the coin, hotels tend to raise prices around cherry-blossom time in late March or early April, the start of DC's busiest tourist season. In late spring and early summer, budget and mid-range hotels often fill with young people arriving for summer jobs or internships, so booking ahead during these times is a must.

Keep in mind that DC room prices can change faster than a senator's positions in re-election season. Occupancy, season, day of the week, the manager's whim – all affect rates. Also remember that many DC hotels offer special deals. If you're in town on government, military, or diplomatic business, you often can get lower rates. Discounts for families, auto-club members, seniors, NGO affiliation, veterans, etc, also may apply to you. Don't accept the first price a reservation agent quotes; always ask about discounts and special deals.

Unless otherwise noted, prices cited in this chapter are average high-season charges for a standard room, DC room tax (14.5%) not included. This chapter lists lodging in three categories: budget (hostels, guesthouses, and hotels with rates under $75), mid-range (under $125), and top end ($125 and up).

Lodging Districts

Hotel rates are generally highest in lodgings close to the Mall and drop as you move away from the city center. Wherever you choose to stay, proximity to a Metro station greatly increases your ability to get around town.

Capitol Hill and the downtown area primarily draw business travelers and convention trade and thus are expensive areas. They are, however, very convenient to major attractions and Metro. If you don't mind being farther from the Mall, stay in the upper northwest neighborhoods, where there are cheaper, smaller boutique hotels, inns, and B&Bs in vibrant nightlife districts like Dupont Circle and Adams-Morgan. These areas aren't all convenient to Metro, however.

Foggy Bottom and the White House area do not have much 'neighborhood' feeling, but they do have lovely, luxurious, often historic hotels (charging luxurious rates). Georgetown, too, has beautiful hotels, but it has no Metro station and is pricey.

If you want to save big on accommodations, stay in the suburbs, like Alexandria or Arlington. See the Excursions chapter for lodging options outside the District.

Reservation Services

Reservation services can often find you a better price than you can find on your own, so check out these services before you resign yourself to paying a hotel's pricey rack rate. Washington has numerous reservation services, and they sometimes compete with one another to offer the lowest rates.

They're particularly helpful for finding B&Bs. Although DC has about 100 B&Bs, only a few advertise or book rooms independently. Most rely on booking services instead, and the services keep their client lists as secret as the location of the Holy Grail. Citywide B&Bs are booked through the Bed & Breakfast League (☎ 363-7767) and Bed & Breakfast Accommodations (☎ 328-3510, www.bedandbreakfastdc.com).

Rental & Roommate Services

If you're in DC for a while and need a roof over your head, your first option is, of course, the *Post* or *City Paper* classifieds, but you also might try these services, which charge you weekly or monthly fees to use their listings:

Roommates Preferred (☎ 965-4004; ⓜ Woodley Park-Zoo), 3000 Connecticut Ave NW, Suite 136

Spectrum Apartment Search (☎ 800-480-3733, www.apartmentsearch.com); 7629 Old Georgetown Rd, Bethesda, Maryland (ⓜ Bethesda); 291 S Van Dorn St, Alexandria, Virginia (ⓜ Van Dorn St)

One-bedrooms in northwest neighborhoods start at about $800 a month. If you want to nail down a sublet before arriving in town, place a free ad specifying what you want (eg, 'studio near Dupont Circle, June to August') with *City Paper*'s online classifieds at www.washingtoncitypaper.com.

Businessfolk can check out the Corporate & Executive Living pages of the *Post*'s Monday Business section, which list (expensive) pied-à-terres.

For hotels, check Capitol Reservations (☎ 800-847-4832, www.capitolreservations.com), offering discounts on 100 DC hotels. Washington DC Accommodations (☎ 289-2220, 800-554-2220) provides a similar reservation service.

DOWNTOWN (MAP 3)
Hostels

Hostelling International – Washington, DC *(☎ 737-2333, 800-909-4776, www.hiayh.org, 1009 11th St NW;* ⓜ *Metro Center)*, at K St NW, is the main hostel of the worldwide HI-AYH organization, headquartered in DC. In a dull but safe area, it has 250 beds on men's and women's dorm floors, 11 private rooms, and 24-hour access. Linens are provided. Its basic but reasonably well-kept facilities include modern bathrooms and kitchen, dining and lounge rooms with TV, coin laundry, storage lockers, and Internet access. A small store sells guidebooks and travel supplies. The on-site travel center has maps, local-sights pamphlets, and transport information, and it acts as a travel agency (see details in the Getting There & Away chapter) This hostel is extremely busy and popular with American school groups (expect young teens). Reservations are a must March to October. Checkout is at 11 am. Rates are $20/23 members/nonmembers.

Hotels

Mid-Range The cheapest decent lodging near the Mall is ***Hotel Harrington*** *(☎ 628-8140, 800-424-8532, www.hotel-harrington.com;* ⓜ *Federal Triangle)*, at 11th and E Sts NW, with 260 rooms. This hotel is popular among tour and school groups and families, but the rooms' dun-colored wall-to-wall carpeting sort of sums up the place: unattractive but perfectly serviceable. All rooms have private baths and cable TV; three restaurants and laundry are on-site. Weekday singles and doubles cost $85 to $89. A room with two double/queen beds costs $95/99. Kids under 16 stay free with parents, but families can get the two-double-bed rooms for $85. Weekend rates go lower still.

A delightful mid-range option is family-run **Swiss Inn** (☎ 371-1816, 800-955-7947, 1204 Massachusetts Avenue, NW, www .theswissinn.com; Ⓜ Metro Center), a restored brownstone with just seven rooms. Some rooms have a queen bed, others a queen and a twin. All have a kitchenette, TV, phone, and private bath. Laundry's on-site, and small beasts – pets and children – are welcome. Rates start at $59 (winter) and go to $118 (summer), depending on room type. Look for the big Frederick Douglass mural on one exterior wall.

Sheraton's **Four Points Hotel** (☎ 289-7600, 888-481-7191, 1201 K St NW, www .fourpointswashingtondc.com; Ⓜ Metro Center), new in spring 2000, has 265 rooms and four suites with dataports, voicemail phones, and minibars. Bonuses include a rooftop heated pool, gym, business center, and underground parking. Thrifty Rent-A-Car is just across 12th St NW. Standard rooms (two double beds) cost $89/109 weekdays/weekends, but rates may rise once Four Points is no longer a newcomer to the DC hotel market.

Chinatown's a good choice if you want to be near the MCI Center. **Red Roof Inn** (☎ 289-5959, 800-733-7663, www.redroof .com, 500 H St NW; Ⓜ Gallery Place), on the main Chinatown drag, has 197 rooms. Coin laundry, an exercise room, and sauna are on-site. Kids stay free (there's in-room Nintendo), and little pets are OK. Recent renovations and the increasing toniness of the area have bumped rack rates up to $120 double weekdays, but ask about weekend discounts.

Top End Conjuring the spirit of the South, the **Morrison-Clark Inn** (☎ 898-1200, 800-332-7898, 1015 L St NW, www.morrisonclark .com; Ⓜ Mt Vernon Square/UDC) is listed in the National Register of Historic Places and often called one of DC's best hotels. Combining two 1864 Victorian residences, the boutique hotel has 54 rooms and suites furnished with fine antiques, lace, chintz, marble fireplaces, polished wood floors, and all modern conveniences. Outside are two

Convention Hotels

Washington's old convention center, between 9th, 11th, and H Sts NW and New York Ave, and its new convention center, being built just north of Mt Vernon Square, are surrounded by a gang of corporate-hotel biggies. Typical rates for weekday doubles are $150 to $250 at the following:

Grand Hyatt Washington (☎ 582-1234, 1000 H St NW; Ⓜ Metro Center)

Henley Park (☎ 638-5200, 926 Massachusetts Ave NW; Ⓜ Mt Vernon Square-UDC)

Marriott at Metro Center (☎ 737-2200, 775 12th St NW; Ⓜ Metro Center)

Washington DC Renaissance at Tech World (☎ 898-9000, 999 9th St NW; Ⓜ Mt Vernon Square-UDC)

shady verandahs; inside, the Morrison-Clark Restaurant serves highly praised Southern cuisine. Depending on the room and season, rates are $99 to $265; summer is the cheapest time.

Upscale chain hotels cluster on and near the K St business district. They're fairly interchangeable: all cater to business travelers with hefty per diems, and all offer the full range of business services. All are costly on weekdays, too, so you might consider them primarily for weekend visits.

Near Franklin Square, the new **Hilton Garden Inn** (☎ 783-7800, 800-445-8667, 815 14th St NW, www.hilton.com; Ⓜ McPherson Square) has microwaves, fridges, hair dryers, irons, dataports, two multiline phones, and cable TV in its 300 mass-produced rooms, plus a pool, gym, and 24-hour business center. You'll pony up $150 or more per double weekdays but as little as $95 weekends.

Nearby, **Crowne Plaza** (☎ 682-0111, 1001 14th St NW, crowneplazawashington@ meristar.com; Ⓜ McPherson Square) has 300 rooms and 17 suites with cable TV, dataport phones, hair dryers, and coffeemakers. There's a business center, 24-hour gym, sauna, and concierge and valet service. Off its lobby, the Franklin Exchange restaurant/ bar serves an American menu and has a pretty patio overlooking Franklin Square. Rates average around $150/180 single/ double weekdays, but check for frequent special offers.

With an excellent location close to the White House and Mall, *JW Marriott* (☎ 393-2000, 1331 Pennsylvania Ave NW, *marriotthotels.com;* Ⓜ *Federal Triangle*) is a great choice for convenience's sake. It's huge (15 floors, 772 rooms) and offers all the goodies you need: child-care services, concierge, full business center, rental-car desk, restaurants, gym, pool, and sauna. Rooms have voicemail phones with data-ports, cable TV, and minibars. You pay for all this, naturally: about $150/280 single or double weekends/weekdays.

Nearby, *Hotel Washington* (☎ 638-5900, 515 15th St NW, www.hotelwashington.com; Ⓜ *Federal Triangle*), circa 1918, is DC's oldest continuously operating hotel. Its 350 rooms start at $185/205 single/double; rates top out at $725. Rooms have every amenity

you expect for that price tag. Kids 14 and under stay free with parents; ask about special family-weekend discount packages. In the lobby is a friendly bar, piano lounge, and the Two Continents restaurant. On the roof, an open-air café is open in spring and summer for fine city views.

Round the corner is Washington's most history-laden hotel, the *Willard Inter-Continental Hotel* (☎ 628-9100, 1401 Pennsylvania Ave NW, washington.interconti.com; Ⓜ *Federal Triangle*). Here MLK wrote his 'I Have a Dream' speech, the term 'lobbyist' was coined (by President Grant to describe political wranglers trolling the lobby), and Lincoln, Coolidge, and Harding all stayed. Nathaniel Hawthorne observed that it could 'much more justly [be] called the center of Washington...than either the Capitol, the White House, or the State Department.' Today the luxuriously restored 1904 Beaux-Arts hotel – the third on this site – is still favored by power brokers, and its chandelier-hung hallways are still thick with lobbyists and corporate aristocrats buffing their loafers on the dense carpets. It

RICHARD CUMMINS

Willard Inter-Continental Hotel: the true center of power?

PLACES TO STAY

offers a gym, business center, concierge, airline and car-rental desks, upscale shops, the Willard Room restaurant, and the marvelous Round Robin Bar, which claims to be the birthplace of the mint julep. Rooms cost around $350 weekdays but can drop to $260 weekends. Kids under 17 stay free. Inquire about 'weekend saver' packages that go as low as $200.

WHITE HOUSE AREA (MAP 3)

The streets around the White House are home to luxury hotels catering to dignitaries and wealthy business travelers. There really are no bargains in this area, but if you're up for a splurge and love politician spotting, there's no finer place to do it.

North of the White House, the *Capital Hilton* (☎ 393-1000, 800-445-8667, 1001 16th St NW; ☻ *Farragut North*) is a corporate choice that manages to be both generic and very luxurious. All rooms have two phones, a dataport, cable TV, and minibar. On-site are a good gym, the Capital City Club, with personal trainers, masseurs, and a day spa; a business center; two restaurants; and multilingual staff. Kids stay free with parents. Rates – 'ever-shifting,' sigh the desk staff – hover around $130/290 weekends/weekdays in winter, about $10 more in spring and summer. Last-minute deals sometimes are as low as $115.

An ornate landmark on the political landscape, the *Hay-Adams Hotel* (☎ 638-6600, 800-853-6807, 1 Lafayette Square, www.hayadams.com; ☻ *McPherson Square*), opposite the White House, was named for two mansions that once stood on the site (owned by Secretary of State John Hay and historian Henry Adams). It has quietly beautiful rooms, palazzo-style public spaces, and a tasteful soupçon of Washington scandal: back in the '80s, Oliver North wooed contributors to his illegal contra funding scheme here. Interior rooms start at $220/325 weekends/weekdays; you'll pay about $50 more for a White House view. Special weekend packages start at $199.

If take-no-prisoners luxury is what you want, consider *St Regis Washington* (☎ 638-2626, 800-562-5661, 923 16th St NW, www.luxurycollection.com; ☻ *McPherson Square*). Strewn with Oriental rugs and antiques and frosted with gilt trim and velvet, its public spaces are breathtaking. The hotel's 200 rooms and suites have every provision, from dataports to marble baths, and there's a butler on each floor. Room No 1012 is infamous as the place where Monica Lewinsky spilled details of her shenanigans with President Clinton to Ken Starr's investigators. Weekend rates are $149 to $285; weekdays, $315 to $460.

FOGGY BOTTOM (MAP 3)

Like the White House area, Foggy Bottom – home to monolithic government office blocks, law firms, and the international development banks – caters to the business traveler. There are fewer ultra-luxurious places here, however. Instead, the district has heaps of all-suite hotels, generic and dull but very useful for working visitors. Here, too, on the banks of the Potomac, is the most infamous hotel in America: the Watergate.

Unless otherwise noted, Foggy Bottom is the closest Metro station to all hotels described in this section.

Hotels

Budget & Mid-Range A very plain, institutional-looking lodging, the *Allen Lee Hotel* (☎ 331-1224, 2224 F St NW, www.allenleehotel.com), south of the GWU campus, is a great deal if your expectations are modest. Staff are friendly and rooms are clean and have phones, TVs, and rather worn furnishings. Rates, including taxes, are $49/63 single/double with private bath, $52/39 with shared bath. Guests are young and international – it's a nice place to meet fellow students and travelers.

Hotel Lincoln Suites (☎ 223-4320, 800-424-2970, 1823 L St NW, www.lincolnhotels.com; ☻ *Farragut North*) is a serviceable, affordable all-suite hotel that's very convenient to the K St business area. Its 95 rooms have cable TV, two phones, a computer jack, and kitchenette with minifridge and microwave. Rates – $99 to $199 depending on season and availability – include continental breakfast on weekends, passes to a nearby gym, and bedtime cookies.

Top End The *George Washington University Inn* (☎ 337-6620, 800-426-4455, 824 New Hampshire Ave NW, www.gwuinn.com) is a newly renovated modern property with 95 fully equipped rooms in the heart of the university community. It's a good choice for those who want to be near the Kennedy Center and Georgetown. Downstairs is the yummy Japanese noodle house Zuki Moon (see Places to Eat). Spring and summer rates start around $140, but there's lots of seasonal variation.

South of GWU, with one entrance facing campus and the other facing the State Dept, *State Plaza Hotel* (☎ 861-8200, 800-424-2859, 2117 E St NW) is a workaday place full of government employees. It has 223 suites and efficiencies (dataports, cable TV, kitchens), a gym, coin laundry, and an OK restaurant, the Garden Café. Rates begin around $150. Another all-suite accommodation, *St James Suites* (☎ 457-0500, 950 24th St NW) is a peaceful, bland lodging that resembles an upscale condominium complex, with a modern brick facade and peach-beige decor. Each suite has a full kitchen and two phones. There's a small gym and outdoor pool. Rates start at $155/124 weekdays/weekends and include continental breakfast. Government and corporate travelers and AAA members can get discounts. *Doubletree Guest Suites*, at 2500 Pennsylvania Ave NW (☎ 333-8060) and 801 New Hampshire Ave NW (☎ 785-2000), is another suites-only choice, charging $159 weekdays.

Done up in funky where's-the-gondolier Venetian decor (shuttered doors, warm gold walls) and beloved by World Bank and State Dept types, the *Hotel Lombardy* (☎ 828-2600, 800-424-5486, 2019 I St NW, www.hotellombardy.com) has a multilingual staff and an international mood – you hear French and Spanish as often as English in its halls. On-site are the well-reviewed Café Lombardy and the decadent Venetian Room Lounge (with a fireplace, tasseled hassocks, and velvet banquettes). The 125

rooms, with equally entertaining decor (and kitchens), cost $159/179 single/double weekdays, $119/139 weekends.

One Washington Circle (☎ 872-1680, 800-424-9671, www.onewashingtoncirclehotel .com), at its eponymous address, is a sleek, modern all-suite hotel quite convenient to Metro and Georgetown. Nixon maintained offices here after the Watergate scandal totaled his presidency. In high season, standard suites cost about $139 to $239 (around $30 less in low season), including gym passes. The West End Café, which gets OK reviews for its modern American cooking, is attached.

Similar accommodations are offered at the all-suite *River Inn* (☎ 337-7600, 924 25th St NW, www.theriverinn.com), on a quiet residential block between I and K Sts NW (despite the name, it's *not* on the river). This generic-looking brick facility has 126 suites (with cable TV, phones, dataports, and full kitchens), a gym, laundry, and parking. Rates are $175 to $245 weekdays, $169 to $245 weekends.

One of many big business/luxury hotels clustered near Washington Circle, *Melrose Hotel* (☎ 955-6400, 2430 Pennsylvania Ave NW) offers weekday rooms for $199. The 14-story building has 400 rooms, a modern glass atrium, and elegant peach-and-green decor. Of course, you get valet parking, a fitness center, restaurant, and bar.

In the center of the futuristic Watergate complex is *Swissôtel Watergate* (☎ 965-2300, 2650 Virginia Ave NW, www.swissotel .com), where you can lodge in the company of political scandal (Nixon's operatives tried to bug Democratic National Committee headquarters here back in 1972). Its famed residents have included Bob Dole and Monica Lewinsky. The hotel itself is luxurious but, apart from its notoriety, remarkable. Bonuses include a gym, great Potomac views, and a fine location: just downriver from Georgetown. A whole self-enclosed village of swank (couture shops, the Aquarelle restaurant) is here, too. Standard rooms (most facing the river) cost $175 to $350, with most prices above $200.

CAPITOL HILL & SOUTHEAST DC (MAP 4)
Hostels

Young women visiting the city on long stays can consider ***Thompson-Markward Hall*** (☎ *546-3255, 235 2nd St NE;* Ⓜ *Union Station),* open to women 18 to 34 who are working or studying in Washington. (In summertime, 90% of its guests are Hill interns.) The minimum stay is two weeks; as of 2000, rooms cost $650 a month, which includes two meals a day plus Sunday brunch. That's good value, considering the average price of a sublet apartment in Washington. All rooms are small, furnished singles with phones, computer hookups, and shared bath. The mood is like that of an upscale dorm, with a spacious courtyard, sundeck, pretty dining room, and sitting areas. Coin laundry is available. Drawbacks: You can't drink, smoke, or bring male guests above lobby level. (Thompson-Markward's second name is 'The Young Woman's Christian Home,' but apart from these rules, you'd never know it.) If you start missing the Y-chromosome set, the Capitol Hill bar scene is just a couple blocks away.

B&Bs & Guesthouses

The most delightful B&B in town is the value-minded ***Hereford House*** (☎ *543-0102, 604 South Carolina Ave SE;* Ⓜ *Eastern Market),* an English-style place with four guest rooms. The cheerful owner, Ann Edwards, a British expat, has decorated the rooms in the styles of her homeland (there's a Welsh room, Scottish room, etc, with lots of frills and wildflowers). All share a bath. She offers a full breakfast of British treats, and her friendly hound, Trapper, co-hosts the place. Rates are super-reasonable for a B&B: just $54 single to $78 triple.

In a Federal-front rowhouse built in 1902, ***Maison Orleans Bed 'N Breakfast*** (☎ *544-3694, 414 5th St SE;* Ⓜ *Eastern Market)* has three guest rooms with private baths, TVs, and phones. The architecture, decor, and patio, with its fountains and fish pond, echo New Orleans' French Quarter, where owner Bill Rouchell grew up. The public living and dining rooms are decorated with family pieces from the '30s and '40s. Rates are $90 to $125 and include continental breakfast (that means sort of small).

Doolittle Guest House (☎ *546-6622, 506 E Capitol St, www.doolittlehouse.com;* Ⓜ *Eastern Market)* is a 1860s Victorian offering antiques-furnished rooms and hearty organic breakfasts. All rooms have private baths; one has a fireplace, too. An on-site library has a fax and computer. Rates start at $100. Nearby, in a pretty brick rowhouse, the ***B&B on A*** (☎ *544-2047, 630 A St NE;* Ⓜ *Eastern Market)* is convenient to the Capitol and offers one room for $115. Long-term stays are available.

The ***Bull Moose B&B*** (☎ *547-1050, 800-261-2768, 101 5th St NE;* Ⓜ *Eastern Market),* at A St NE, was named after the nickname for the Progressive Party, founded by Teddy Roosevelt in 1912. Formerly the Capitol Hill Guest House, this turreted red-brick 1892 Victorian has a lovely interior with nine newly redecorated guest rooms that

Stay on Capitol Hill for monumental views.

RICHARD CUMMINS

PLACES TO STAY

echo Teddy's times. Two rooms have private baths; the others share. Rates for its single, double, and triple rooms are $79 to $179.

Several years back, Jim and Mary Pellettieri left their day jobs to run **A Capitol Place** (☎ 543-1020, 134 12th St SE, www .bbinternet.com/capitol). A minimum three-night stay is required at this attractively furnished apartment that takes up the lower floor of a century-old Victorian rowhouse. It has a kitchen, living room, dining room, laundry, phone, answering machine, TV, and library of books and magazines. The kitchen is stocked with breakfast foods and (yay!) a big plate of brownies. Rates are $110/135/150/180 nightly for one/two/three/ four people. Disadvantages: It's nowhere near a Metro station (take Metrobus No 96 from Union Station) and is on the edge of a sketchy neighborhood. If you have no car, consider their associated property, **The White's House** (☎ 543-6377, 400 10th St SE), three blocks from Eastern Market Metro and $100 per night.

Hotels

South of the Capitol, **Capitol Hill Suites** (☎ 543-6000, 200 C St SE; ⓜ Capitol South) is a 152-room, all-suite property ideally located in the heart of Hill legislative action. It's heavily favored by congressional interns, so it's rife with type-A youth, especially in summer. All rooms (basic-looking but serviceable) have a kitchen or kitchenette. Desk staff are helpful and do copying and faxing for you. Laundry is on-site. Rates – $109 to $209, depending on the suite's size – include continental breakfast and passes to a nearby gym.

The mammoth **Hyatt Regency** (☎ 737-1234, 400 New Jersey Ave NW, www.hyatt .com; ⓜ Union Station) has 834 rooms with cable TV, computer hookups, and phones with voicemail. A business center, concierge, laundry, and gym are on-site, and staff help arrange babysitting. Standard-room rates are $125 single or double weekends but spike $100 or more weekdays. It too is very convenient to the Capitol.

Right across the street is **Holiday Inn on the Hill** (☎ 638-1616, 800-638-1116, 415 New Jersey Ave NW, www.basshotels.com; ⓜ Union Station), where the 343 standard-issue rooms have dataports, phones with voicemail, coffeemaker, and cable TV. There's a gym and rooftop pool. Rates are $129 to $189, depending on occupancy and day of the week. Government rates drop to $119.

Up the way is the **Washington Court** (☎ 628-2100, 800-321-3010, 525 New Jersey Ave NW; ⓜ Union Station), a 264-room corporate-and-convention-trade place where rates start at $150 but are often higher based on season, day of the week, and occupancy. Rooms have fridges, dataports, and voicemail phones. There's a gym. The lobby has a restaurant, bar, and – bonus – pool tables.

If you dislike corporate hotels, try the **Phoenix Park Hotel** (☎ 638-6900, 800-824-5419, 520 N Capitol St; ⓜ Union Station), which offers Irish hospitality and 141 rooms with computer hookups and phones, a small business center, gym, concierge, and laundry. Visiting Irish politicians like Gerry Adams have lodged at the Phoenix. Downstairs is the great Dubliner pub (see Entertainment), and the Powerscourt Irish restaurant is also here. Despite the hotel's size, the personable staff make it feel homey. Standard singles/doubles cost $189/209 weekdays, but rates can drop as low as $89 on weekends, depending on availability. Kids under 16 stay free.

The most chic Hill choice is the boutique **Hotel George** (☎ 347-4200, 15 E St NW, www.hotelgeorge.com; ⓜ Union Station). A few years ago the old Bellevue Hotel was done over into the George, and the public spaces now sparkle with steel, glass, coral, and contemporary art. The 139 rooms have all the niceties, including dataports, and there's a gym and steam rooms. Off the lobby is the stylish French bistro Bis (see Places to Eat). On weekdays, doubles start around $200, but ask about weekend specials.

UPPER NORTHEAST DC (MAP 5)
Hostels

Laid-back, super-friendly, and recommended by Lonely Planet readers, **India House Too** (☎ 291-1195, 300 Carroll St, *dchostel.com;* Ⓜ *Takoma)* is near the Maryland border in far northeast Washington. It's just 100 yards from the Metro in the bohemian, politically leftish neighborhood of Takoma Park (see more details on the area in the Excursions chapter). Set in a century-old Victorian, the hostel is frequented by crowds of British, Australian, Japanese, and German backpackers (the occasional Yank shows up, too). There's a backyard barbie and hammock, frequent impromptu parties, no curfew, a modern kitchen, lockers, laundry, dining room, and lounge with TV, all overseen by the affable Brit Angus Chapman and his partners. Its nine bedrooms have four or six bunks and shared baths; these go for $14 per night. There are private double rooms, too, with their own baths, for just $34 per night. Don't be frightened off by the hostel's distance from downtown: the Metro Red Line gets you to Capitol Hill in about 15 minutes, and this place is worth the short ride.

Motels

If you have a car and don't mind the lousy area, try the strip of cheap chain motels along New York Ave NE. Predictable offerings include *Super 8 Motel (☎ 543-7400, 501 New York Ave)*; *HoJo Inn (☎ 546-9200, 600 New York Ave)*, *Budget Motor Inn (☎ 529-3900, 1615 New York Ave)*; and *Days Inn (☎ 832-5800, 2700 New York Ave)*. At all these choices, singles/doubles begin around $50/60, and rooms have basic comforts like phones and TVs. During slow seasons (especially winter), the motels sometimes wage price wars – if you drive along New York Ave, you may see posted prices as low as $40.

SOUTHWEST DC (MAP 6)

Best Western Skyline Inn (☎ 488-7500, 800-458-7500, 10 I St SW, www.bestwestern.com; Ⓜ *Navy Yard)* is a basic, reasonably priced option for this area. A large concrete-and-glass establishment with 203 rooms, it's five blocks south of the Capitol near the intersection of I-395 and S Capitol St. Don't expect character or charm, but all rooms do have AC and a TV, and there's a pool out-

doors. Rates start at $79 single or double in winter, $109 in other seasons. Kids under 16 stay free with parents; military/government employees get discounts.

Booked through Bed & Breakfast Accommodations (☎ 328-3510), *Waterfront Row (*Ⓜ *Waterfront)* is a townhouse in the Tiber Island residential complex, a block from the waterfront. This four-story, 32-year-old townhouse is chockablock with antiques, French, Asian, and contemporary furniture, and art. The one guest room here, on the 2nd floor, has a private bath, cable TV, queen-size bed, and balcony. On the same floor is a music room that can hold one more guest. March to July and September to November, the rate is $110; the rest of the year, it's $90.

The bland, nine-story *Holiday Inn Capitol (☎ 479-4000, 550 C St SW, www .basshotels.com;* Ⓜ *Federal Center SW)* is just a block south of the National Air & Space Museum. Its 528 rooms have the chain's usual amenities (TV, two-line phone, modem, ironing board, hair dryer, coffeemaker), and there's a gym, bar, restaurant, rooftop pool, and underground parking. Rates start at $119/129 single/double. Government/military visitors receive modest discounts.

Channel Inn (☎ 800-368-5668, 650 Water St SW, www.channelinn.com; Ⓜ *Waterfront)* is a modern hotel right on the Washington Channel. Many of its spacious rooms have balconies facing the water, which is especially nice at sunset. There's a pool and restaurant; close at hand are lively marinas, tour-boat operators, and giant seafood restaurants drawing tour-bus crowds (see Places to Eat). Rooms start at $118/125 weekends/weekdays.

You may prefer top-end *Loews L'Enfant Plaza (☎ 484-1000, 480 L'Enfant Plaza SW, www.loewshotels.com)*, a big convention and business-traveler hotel two long blocks south of the Mall, sits atop the L'Enfant Plaza Metro station. It has a gym, year-round pool, business center, and, off the lobby, the American Grill restaurant and Old Dominion Brewing Company. Pet and child care are arranged via outside

PLACES TO STAY

agencies. Rates are $189 (standard) to $309 (deluxe), but seasonal specials run between $129 and $139. If you can afford it, this is a good hotel to stay in with children (see the Washington, DC for Kids section).

GEORGETOWN (MAP 7)

Georgetown is a tourist mecca with beaucoup bars and restaurants, but it has few hotels. In addition to the places listed below, consider those in the western part of Foggy Bottom, just across Rock Creek Park from Georgetown. Note that there's no Metro station; the closest one is at Foggy Bottom, several blocks southeast along Pennsylvania Ave.

If you don't mind being 10 blocks north of the main M St NW entertainment and shopping strip, consider *Holiday Inn Georgetown* (☎ 338-4600, 2101 Wisconsin Ave NW, www.basshotels.com) abutting lovely Dumbarton Oaks Park. It has its own jogging trail and an outdoor pool, and its 296 rooms have all the chain's usual amenities, including dataports. Doubles cost $140 and up.

If Georgetown University is your destination, try the Marriott-operated *Georgetown University Conference Center* (☎ 687-3200, 3800 Reservoir Rd), on the campus' northern edge. It has 146 rooms (with dataports and cable TV), the upscale Faculty Club for dining, and nearby walking trails and full gym facilities. Singles and doubles start at $109/199 weekends/weekdays.

An attractive boutique hotel popular among European visitors, *Hotel Monticello* (☎ 337-0900, 1075 Thomas Jefferson St NW) is just off M St near the C&O Canal. It has 47 suites, each with a kitchen, brass-and-crystal chandeliers, colonial-reproduction furniture, and flower arrangements. Usual rates are $209/219 single/double, but occasional specials dip to $129/139. With your room, you get a continental breakfast, and there's free parking (a real find in Georgetown). Another all-suite option, this one rather soulless, is *Georgetown Suites* (☎ 298-7800, 1111 30th St NW, www.georgetownsuites.com), a modern facility with studio, one-, and two-bedroom accommo-

dations, all with kitchen. Weekday doubles cost $175, but ask about weekend discounts. It's also convenient to M St.

The very blue-blooded *Georgetown Inn* (☎ 333-8900, 800-424-2979, 1310 Wisconsin

---

Time Out: DC Day Spas

Every now and then, even the most determinedly budget-minded traveler gets a little down. Hair gets frizzy, feet get sore, minds grow weary, and nothing but a little pricey self-indulgence can fix matters. Here's a list of good day spas at which to spoil yourself:

Andre Chreky Salon (Map 3; ☎ 293-9393), 1604 K St NW, is a sleek business-district spa fixing up skin, hair and nails. It has a coffee bar to keep you awake while you're fussed over.

Aveda Georgetown (Map 7; ☎ 965-1325), 1325 Wisconsin Ave NW, opened in spring 2000 and does nice herbal things to skin, body, and hair.

EFX/Blue Mercury (Map 7; ☎ 965-1300), 3059 M St NW, Georgetown, is a small spa drawing a hip young clientele. It has facials, massages, friendly, low-key staff, and better-than-average piped-in music.

Four Seasons Fitness Club/Spa (Map 7; ☎ 944-2022), 2800 Pennsylvania Ave NW, Georgetown, is part of the luxurious Four Seasons Hotel. You can't use the gym itself unless you stay overnight, but exercise classes and spa treatments are available to nonguests – facials, two-masseuse massages, you name it, it's all costly.

Jolie (☎ 301-986-9293), 7200 Wisconsin Ave, Bethesda, is one of the area's better-known spas. It's pretty affordable, despite its expensively frilly decor, and offers all the services: massage, vitamin facial wraps, pedicures, etc.

Tara Salon (Map 7; ☎ 333-8099), 2715 M St NW, Georgetown, offers all sorts of skin and hair stuff, from basic leg waxes ($60) to massage ($65/hour) and electrolysis ($65/hour).

Ave NW), two blocks north of M St, is a gorgeous property favored by Georgetown University alumni and parents on college weekends. The inn spreads 95 rooms through a collection of restored 18th-century townhouses, and its stately decor (four-poster beds, furniture with feet on it) is matched by stately service. Rates range from $175 to $255 depending on season and availability.

In the midst of the M St scene is the red-brick *Latham Hotel (☎ 726-5000, 800-424-2979, 3000 M St NW)*, a boutique hotel with 142 rooms (including two-story 'carriage house' suites) for $150 to $350 single or double. The hotel is anchored by one of DC's finest restaurants, Citronelle, and there's a very pleasant rooftop sundeck and pool.

Topping most 'best hotels in Washington' lists is the ultra-luxurious *Four Seasons Hotel (☎ 342-0444, 2800 Pennsylvania Ave NW, www.fourseasons.com)*, perched atop Rock Creek Park's south end. This Five Diamond property looks boxy and plain on the outside (it has none of the architectural charms of, say, the Willard). But inside, the 260 spacious rooms and suites are strewn with antiques; a full-service gym and day spa tones and pampers the guests; and the staff are extraordinarily warm and attentive. Kids' activities and babysitting are provided. Rack rates begin at $350, but packages and special weekend rates are often available.

DUPONT CIRCLE & KALORAMA (MAP 8)

Dupont is a great place to stay. Many of its lodgings, from cheapola hostels to costly B&Bs, are funky and eclectic, and there are a wealth of small inns and boutique hotels here. Yet there are also upscale corporate chains for those who want 'em. Vibrant dining and nightlife are right outside your front door, and if you tire of them, the Red Line carries you downtown in just a few minutes.

Unless otherwise noted, Dupont Circle is the closest Metro station to all accommodations listed here.

Hostels

Davis House (☎ 232-3196, 1822 R St NW), a rowhouse on a quiet residential block, is an 11-bed hostel operated by the American Friends Service Committee (the Quakers). It's open to international visitors, AFSC staff, and people 'working on peace and justice projects' (if you work or volunteer for an NGO, this means you). Shared/private rooms cost $35/45; all rooms share a bath, and there's no alcohol, smoking, or kitchen on-site.

A cheerful, vibrantly multicultural place is just across the street: the *International Student House (☎ 387-6445, 1825 R St NW, www.ishdc.org)*. It offers 100 guests (mostly interns and students) an 'in-depth experience in international living.' Americans as well as international visitors are welcome. You must apply for residency and stay a minimum of three months in summer, four months at other times. Rates include 13 meals weekly and start at $660 a month for shared rooms with phones (higher for single rooms, private baths, parking, etc). There are comfortable common areas (such as a library and piano room) with Tudor accents, plus a walled courtyard.

In an 1888 Victorian townhouse, *Simpkins Bed & Breakfast & Hostel (☎ 387-1328, 1601 19th St NW)*, a block from Dupont Circle at Q St NW, is a small place favored by bohemian travelers and NGO professionals on a budget. The six guest rooms share a bath. Private rooms cost $60/80 single/double. If you're willing to share a room (two people), you pay $28. Bring along a passport (US or otherwise), student card, or public-interest group professional card to get these rates; they're doubled otherwise.

Shalom House (☎ 328-3510 for reservations, 234-0010 for the house, 1902 R St NW) is a pretty rowhouse where host Paul Shalom Rhodes offers six attractively decorated rooms for monthly or longer rental. The three larger rooms have private baths; others share. Common spaces include a kitchen, dining room, deck, and office suite with fax and Internet-linked computer. Two spaniels wander around. Monthly rates start at $1000 depending on the room, including breakfast and Friday interfaith Sabbath dinner. It's a friendly, quiet, nonsmoking place.

B&Bs & Guesthouses

The Inn at Dupont Circle (☎ 467-6777, 888-467-8486, 1312 19th St NW) is a 19th-century Victorian once owned by astrologist-to-the-stars Jeanne Dixon. Rooms have phones, cable TV, and fireplaces, and the inn's assets include a solarium, fax and copy machines, and laundry facilities. Breakfasts are continental. With shared bath, single or doubles cost $65 to $90; with private bath, $120 to $135. On weekends, you must book a two-night stay.

The most gay- and lesbian-friendly option in DC is *The Brenton* (☎ 332-5550, 800-673-9042, 1708 16th St NW), a century-old Victorian rowhouse just north of R St. Manager Ed Eccard has nine rooms decorated with antiques. Most rooms share a bath, and there's a free continental breakfast and a daily drinks hour. Rates are $79 to $99.

Swann House (☎ 265-4414, 1808 New Hampshire Ave NW, www.swannhouse.com), an 1883 Romanesque brick mansion with a deep porch, offers nine rooms with private baths, cable TV/VCR, and dataport phones; some have fireplaces or Jacuzzis, too. There's a sunroom, outdoor pool, and garden. With the rates of $125 to $275, you get a continental breakfast, afternoon snacks, and evening cordials.

The equally upscale *Dupont at the Circle* (☎ 332-5251, 888-412-0100, 1604 19th St NW, www.dupontatthecircle.com), a stately brick Victorian rowhouse, is a block north of the circle. Its seven fully equipped guest rooms and suite are furnished with antiques and have private baths with clawfoot or Jacuzzi tubs. Breakfasts are modest affairs: muffins, granola, fruit. Rates are $140 to $250, depending on the room. The house is smoke-free.

It doesn't advertise. It doesn't even have a sign. But *The Mansion on O Street* (☎ 496-2000, 2020 O St NW, users.erols.com/mansion) has quite a reputation anyway. It's just about

the most flamboyant, original B&B around. Housed in a 100-room 1892 mansion (a remnant of the days when Dupont was a millionaires' neighborhood), it's part inn, part gallery/performance/party space, and part private club that's hosted Hollywood celebrities and Chelsea Clinton's sweet-sixteen party. Its owner, grande dame HH Leonards, has done the place up like a wedding at Castle Dracula: swags of velvet drapery, ornate chandeliers and lampshades, candelabra, concealed doorways, etc. No two rooms, from the Russian Tea Room to the Log Cabin, are alike, and everything from the bedstead to the pictures can be purchased if you want. This fairyland for grownups costs $125 to $250 for rooms with shared bath, $160 to $400 with private bath.

Taft Bridge Inn (☎ 387-2007, 2007 Wyoming Ave NW), near Adams-Morgan, is named for the bridge that leaps over Rock Creek Park just to the north. In a beautiful 19th-century Georgian mansion, the inn has a paneled drawing room, comely antiques, six fireplaces, and a garden. Rates for its 13 guest rooms, including continental breakfast, are $59 to $75 with shared bath, $110 to $120 private bath, for singles; add $15 for double occupancy. Parking and laundry are on the premises, and it's an easy walk to either 18th St or Dupont Circle from here.

An atmospheric choice is the *1836 California* (☎ 462-6502, 1836 California St NW), an elegant, beautifully kept Victorian west of 18th St. There are six antiques-furnished rooms with TVs and phones. Four share baths (and cost $70). The two top-floor suites have privates baths and separate sitting rooms ($100 per person). A generous continental breakfast is served.

Hotels

Budget & Mid-Range The *Braxton Hotel* (☎ 232-7800, 1440 Rhode Island Ave NW; Ⓜ McPherson Square), between downtown and Dupont Circle proper, is a somewhat rough-around-the-edges 62-room joint offering funky furnishings, free continental breakfast, and good rates: singles/doubles cost $50/60. Fourteen rooms are done up in 'themes' (antiques, Victorian, etc). The neighborhood's not great, however; take a cab back to the hotel at night rather than walking.

About 900 varieties of beer are served at Brickskellar, a chummy beer cellar near Rock Creek Park. But you can sleep as well as imbibe here: the ***Brickskellar Inn*** (☎ *293-1885, 1523 22nd St NW*) is upstairs. All its clean, basic rooms share a bath, but most have a sink and/or TV; singles/doubles start at $54/73.

The ***Tabard Inn*** (☎ *785-1277, 1739 N St NW, www.tabardinn.com*), set in a trio of Victorian-era rowhouses and named for the inn in *Canterbury Tales*, is a delight: a historic hotel that actually feels historic rather than kitschy. Its 40 rooms are furnished with vintage quirks like iron bedsteads, overstuffed flowery sofas, and wingbacked armchairs. Downstairs, its parlor, beautiful courtyard restaurant (see Places to Eat), and bar are low-ceilinged, filled with funky old furniture, and highly conducive to curling up with a vintage port and the Sunday *Post*. The Wife of Bath never had it so good. Rooms

with shared bathroom cost $67 to $95; with private bathroom, $99 to $170.

Embassy Inn (☎ *234-7800, 800-423-9111, 1627 16th St NW*), a couple blocks east of Dupont Circle, is a 38-room boutique hotel with a friendly, cozy mood. You get a small continental breakfast and evening sherry included in the rates of $79 to $110 double; rooms are pleasantly furnished and have cable TV, phones, and private baths. Up 16th St is another, similar hotel: ***Windsor Inn*** (☎ *667-0300, 800-423-9111, 1842 16th St NW*). Its small, tastefully decorated 36 rooms have private baths, cable TV, and phones, and guests get continental breakfast and evening snacks and sherries. Spring rates are $89 to $99 single, $89 to $129 double. In summertime, you can find great bargains, like weekend doubles for about $70.

Set near Rock Creek Park in sleepy Kalorama, ***Windsor Park Hotel*** (☎ *483-7700, 800-247-3064, 2116 Kalorama Rd NW, www.windsorparkhotel.com*) advertises itself as a B&B, but it's a boutique hotel serving continental breakfast. Rooms have private

RICK GERHARTER

PLACES TO STAY

baths, little fridges, color TVs, phones, and frilly Queen Anne knockoff furniture. Rates are \$108/120 single/double, but in July and August you can get a room for just \$88.

Also in Kalorama, **_Normandy Inn_** (☎ 483-1350, *2118 Wyoming Ave NW*) is a pricey but generic boutique hotel that appeals to visiting diplomatic folks. Its 75 rooms have cable TV, phones, and minifridges. You get coffee, cookies, and breakfast in the lounge, and there are wine-and-cheese receptions on some evening. The hotel has a small patio. Rooms cost \$139/149 single/double.

Top End A large chain hotel, the **_Radisson Barceló Hotel Washington_** (☎ 293-3100, *800-333-3333, 2121 P St NW*) has 300 big, well-appointed rooms with anonymously upscale furnishings, three phones, cable TV, and dataports. There's a nice courtyard pool, gym, and business center, and the Spanish-Latin fusion restaurant Gabriel is here, too. Singles and doubles begin around \$130, but you can score the occasional \$99 rate.

In a more removed, residential area of Dupont, **_Carlyle Suites_** (☎ 234-3200, *1731 New Hampshire Ave NW*) has 170 modern suites with full kitchens, TVs, phones, brightly colored furnishings, and Art Deco touches. Rates are usually between \$129 and \$139, but sometimes you can find rates under \$100. Kids under 18 stay free.

Governor's House (☎ 296-2100, *1615 Rhode Island Ave NW*), southeast of the circle, is another boutique hotel, but it's too big to feel homey. Its 150 recently renovated rooms (some with kitchenettes) have business-traveler basics like two phones and computer hookups; also in the hotel are a modest gym, outdoor pool, and restaurant. You can use extensive workout facilities at the nearby YMCA for free, too. Rates are usually about \$150 single or double, but weekend summer packages drop to \$120.

Amid the stately mansions of Embassy Row, the **_Hilton Embassy Row_** (☎ 265-1600, *2015 Massachusetts Ave, www.hilton.com*), near the Indian and Indonesian embassies, is a luxurious yet reasonably priced choice

favored by diplomatic visitors. Although it's big (193 rooms, 11 floors), it blends modestly into its elegant surroundings. Its rooms have niceties like two phones (one in the bathroom), and there's a rooftop pool, outdoor bar, and underground parking (although Metro is nearby). Staff speak six languages. Weekend singles/doubles start at \$145/165; weekdays, costs rise to \$175/195. Seasonal specials can go down to \$116. Round the circle and up Connecticut is the **_Washington Hilton & Towers_** (☎ 483-3000, *1919 Connecticut Ave NW*), a '60s-modern semicircular rampart with similar rates. It's best known as the place where John Hinckley tried (and failed) to kill Ronald Reagan.

Washington Courtyard by Marriott (☎ 332-9300, *1900 Connecticut Ave NW*), at Leroy Place, is another polished corporate option. Its 147 rooms offer you all the standard features of the Courtyard chain, including an outdoor pool, small exercise room, and parking. The standard-room rack rate is \$175/190 single/double.

J Edgar Hoover dined here; Nixon resided here; and there are rumors that Kennedy sampled the charms of the fairer sex here. The **_Renaissance Mayflower Hotel_** (☎ 347-3000, *1127 Connecticut Ave NW, www.renaissancehotels.com;* ❶ *Farragut North*) has been around since 1924, and although it's not the exclusive enclave it once was, it's still pretty darn regal, with lots of frills and marble and a beautiful grand ballroom. Rooms sport all the comforts, and a business center, babysitting, concierge, and currency exchange are available. High tea in the lounge-ish hotel restaurant is great. Rates begin around \$150 single or double on winter weekends; in summer you can expect to pay about \$100 more.

On Embassy Row is the **_Westin Fairfax_** (☎ 293-2100, *888-625-5144, 2100 Massachusetts Ave NW, www.westin.com*), an appropriately international-looking hotel with its flag-draped, majestically columned entrance. The hotel's interior decor retains suave touches of the 1920s, when the hotel was built, and the 200 rooms have both old-fashioned elements (down pillows, overstuffed furniture) and modern ones (dataports, cable TV, honor bars). On the main floor is the preppie Jockey Club, populated by embassy staff after work for dinner and drinks. The Westin's pricey – as much as $300 single or double – but you can usually wrangle a discount.

The quiet, elegant *Jefferson Hotel* (☎ 347-2200, 800-555-8000, 1200 16th St NW, www.camberleyhotels.com; Ⓜ *Farragut North*), at M St across from the Russian embassy, is a two-winged 1923 mansion with an ornate *porte-cochère*, Beaux-Arts architecture, and a luxurious interior full of crystal and velvet. Favored by diplomatic visitors, its 100 antique-furnished rooms have dual-line speakerphones, CD players, VCRs, computer hookups, faxes, and black-marble baths. Despite all the glitz, the staff are unstuffy and friendly. Rates are $249 January through March and mid-June through mid-September, $319 the rest of the year. Packages drop as low as $199, and government visitors get discounts.

You gotta feel a little sorry for the *Wyndham Washington* (☎ 429-1700, 1400 M St NW, www.wyndham.com; ⓂMcPherson Square), near Thomas Circle: in its former incarnation as the Vista Hotel, it's where the FBI busted former Mayor Marion Barry for smoking crack with an ex-girlfriend. It's a perfectly decent business hotel despite that stigma, with high-speed Internet access in its 12 floors of generic rooms. Standard weekday rack rates start around $220, but weekend and seasonal specials are nearly always available.

A nice luxury choice in the West End area, between Dupont Circle and Foggy Bottom, is the big, pretty *Washington Monarch Hotel* (☎ 429-2400, 877-222-2266, 2401 M St NW, www.washingtonmonarch .com; ⓂFoggy Bottom). It has 415 spacious rooms, an atrium lobby overlooking a flowery courtyard, the upscale Bistro restaurant, and a full health club with a lap pool and ball courts. Every room has three phones and a fridge in addition to the usual comforts. Weekend/weekday rack rates are $259/309 double, but special offers sometimes dip to $199, depending on availability.

Just across 24th St is the *Park Hyatt* (☎ 789-1234, 800-233-1234, 1201 24th St NW; Ⓜ *Foggy Bottom*), a massive, mint-and-beige-decorated hotel with lots of quiet lounge and meeting spaces. Currency exchange, the praised Melrose restaurant, and a full gym are on-site. Its rooms – so crisply fresh that they smell like new cars – have every luxury (even TVs in the bathrooms) and cost a whopping $340 single or double weeknights but drop to $199 weekends.

Ritz-Carlton (☎ 800-241-3333) was due to open a new luxury hotel at 2200 M St NW in late 2000, with 300 rooms and all amenities typical of this worldwide chain, plus shops, restaurants, and a big gym.

ADAMS-MORGAN (MAP 9)

Like Dupont Circle, Adams-Morgan is a good lodging district for those who want bars, nightclubs, and great ethnic dining close at hand. It doesn't have as many options as Dupont, but its hotels and guesthouses are a charming, homey lot that offer good value for your money. The nearest Metro station is Woodley Park-Zoo, a 10-minute walk away.

Hostels

Young travelers who want to be right in the midst of 18th St's swarming entertainment strip choose *Washington International Backpackers* (☎ 667-7681, 800-567-4150, 2451 18th St NW). Its no-frills dorm lodging, in a worn walk-up building, includes five little bedrooms (six to eight beds per room, triple bunks, linens provided), three decent baths, a common room with TV, beat-up kitchen facilities, cheap bike rentals, lockers, and a small breakfast. Limited parking is available, and there's no curfew: you just get a key and come and go as you please. The rate is $16 per night – pretty unbeatable. Free pickup from train or bus station is available by advance request.

B&Bs & Guesthouses

The owners of the welcoming *Adams Inn* (☎ 745-3600, 1744 Lanier Place NW) converted two adjacent townhouses and a carriage house on a shady residential street into a homey guesthouse. Common areas include a nice porch, garden, patio, and living room. The 25 walk-up rooms are modestly furnished with old Asian rugs. Some rooms have private baths; others share. Singles cost $45 to $60, doubles $55 to $70, and guests get continental breakfast. Rooms lack phones, but the house has payphones and a coin laundry. It's just a block north of Columbia Rd.

Among Washington's first B&Bs was *Kalorama Guest House* (☎ 667-6369, 1854 Mintwood Place NW), a Victorian townhouse a couple blocks west of 18th St. It has an open, friendly mood, 31 peaceful, pretty rooms, and a devoted band of return guests, and you get continental breakfast and afternoon sherry in the parlor. Prices are $45 to $70 single and $50 to $75 double with shared bath; rooms with private baths cost $65 to $95 single, $70 to $100 double. Weekly rates are cheaper. The house is non-smoking.

SHAW & THE NEW U DISTRICT (MAP 10)

Shaw is an up-and-coming entertainment district but hasn't yet developed much of a hotel scene. There are, however, a few real bargains on Shaw's fringes.

McMillan House (☎ 986-8989, 800-240-9355, 2417 1st St NW), east of Howard University, is a 10-room B&B set in a nicely renovated early-20th-century rowhouse. Host Albert Ceccone speaks English, Spanish, and Italian. It's a calm, sunny place with value-minded rates ($60/70 single/double), but it's several blocks from the nearest Metro station. South of Logan Circle, *Center City Hotel* (☎ 682-5300, 1201 13th St NW; Ⓜ McPherson Square) offers 100 well-maintained but uninspiring rooms. You get a free continental breakfast with rates starting at $89/99 single/double.

Washington Plaza (☎ 842-1300, 10 Thomas Circle; Ⓜ McPherson Square), a big, bland place at 14th St NW, has a pool, restaurant, and gym on-site and cable TV in its 340 rooms. Rates range from $85 (weekends) to $145 (weekdays), depending on room and availability.

The *Holiday Inn Downtown* (☎ 737-1200, 1155 14th St NW, www.basshotels .com; Ⓜ McPherson Square) has 212 recently renovated rooms for $159/189 weekends/weekdays.

UPPER NORTHWEST DC (MAP 11)
B&Bs & Guesthouses

Across Rock Creek Park from Adams-Morgan, the compact Woodley Park neighborhood is home to several attractive accommodations that are convenient to the Woodley Park-Zoo Metro station, the National Zoo, and many places to eat and drink.

The old-fashioned *Connecticut-Woodley Guest House* (☎ 667-0218, 2647 Woodley Rd NW; Ⓜ Woodley Park-Zoo) is a big 1920s-era home on an upscale residential street. With flowery wallpaper, chenille spreads, and a low-key mood, it feels kinda like Grandma's house. A nice advantage is its proximity to the Omni Shoreham hotel's wide green lawn. Some rooms share baths, but all have their own sinks and toilets. In fall 2000, the owners did a complete renovation and overhaul of the place. Rates were in flux at press time, but the owners expected to keep them under $100. From the Woodley Park/National Zoo Metro station exit, turn around, walk to Woodley Rd and turn left; it's near the corner.

The *Kalorama Guest House at Woodley Park* (☎ 328-0860, 2700 Cathedral Ave NW; Ⓜ Woodley Park-Zoo) is a sister to the Kalorama Guest House in Adams-Morgan (see that description, earlier). It's a cozy 1910 Victorian rowhouse with 19 antiques-furnished rooms for $45 to $110 (higher prices apply to the 12 rooms with private bath). In winter you get free sherry, in summer free lemonade; continental breakfast is always served.

North of Adams-Morgan in a peaceful residential area, *International Guest House* (☎ 726-5808, 1441 Kennedy St NW) offers five neat, clean guest rooms that can accommodate a total of 12 people. Singles/doubles cost $25/50, and you can add a third person for $25. Rates include breakfast and afternoon tea, and there's a common room, backyard, and limited parking. To get there, take Metrobus S2 or S4 up 16th St NW from the White House. Note the early curfew: the house closes 11 pm to 7 am daily and 10 am to 2 pm Sunday. No drinking or smoking.

Hotels

With the air of a drowsy country resort, the manorial ***Omni Shoreham*** (*☎ 234-0700, 2500 Calvert St NW, www.omnihotels.com; Ⓜ Woodley Park-Zoo*) borders Rock Creek Park and is surrounded by 11 acres of mani-cured lawns. Yet Metro, restaurants, and shopping are all within walking distance. The 836-room hotel's timeless design dates from 1929, and the building has hosted both pres-idential inaugural balls and celebrities like Marilyn Monroe throughout its career. Inside, it's lush with antiques, velvet drapery, and greenery. It offers restaurants, a spa and gym, jogging trails, and outdoor pool, and rooms have all comforts. Rack rates start near $300, but occasional weekend deals can dip to $143.

Places to Eat

For many years, DC got a bad culinary rap. Until the 1970s, upscale dining mostly consisted of classic French or Continental cuisine, and many Washingtonians hadn't yet discovered the joys of international cuisine or bothered to sample the city's interesting Southern and soul-food restaurants. But in the 1980s and '90s, chefs from New York and other culinary capitals began to notice DC and open new, adventurous restaurants here. Meanwhile, the city's vibrant Vietnamese, Salvadoran, East African, Caribbean, and Middle Eastern communities began exciting restaurants of their own. Today, DC is one of the most interesting cities in the country for dining – indeed, it has a stunning variety of restaurants, given its small size.

Food is pretty expensive in DC, and travelers can expect to spend a fair amount of their budgets on it. Decent pasta dinners usually cost at least $8 to $10, and deli lunches, with fruit and a soda, can easily cost the same. That said, however, plenty of ethnic eateries offer hearty, low-priced meals, many of them vegetarian. To keep costs down, visit DC's top-end restaurants – most of them clustered near the White House and the National Mall – at lunchtime, when you can assemble a meal from low-cost appetizers. (At restaurants popular among politicos, you'll also see lots of $9.95 specials, a result of congressional ethics laws that place a $10 limit on lobbyists' 'gift meals.') Travel to Adams-Morgan, Dupont Circle, or the upper reaches of the city to find inexpensive dinners.

Most restaurants are open for lunch and dinner daily, but there are some exceptions. Restaurants around the White House and in Foggy Bottom may close on weekends, as they depend mostly on weekday business-lunch trade. Restaurants throughout the city may close on Sunday or Monday; also, some do not serve lunch on weekends. In this chapter, assume that all restaurants are open for lunch and dinner daily unless otherwise noted.

NATIONAL MALL (MAP 3)

The cheapest, easiest Mall lunch options are the streetside *food carts*, selling cheap hot dogs, pretzels, and ice creams that you can eat on the grass or in the Smithsonian's pretty gardens (try the Enid A Haupt Memorial Garden behind the Castle).

Most big Mall museums have a cafeteria, coffee bar, or full-service restaurant, and sometimes all three (call ☎ 357-2700 for details). They're convenient, but their food is rather expensive and often bland. A basic lunch (hamburger, fries, soda) can edge up toward $10. Generally, museum food service is open during lunchtime hours daily. The Smithsonian Metro station is close to all sites in the National Mall.

Among the better choices are three spots at the National Gallery of Art: the plant-filled *Garden Café* (serving American cuisine and thematic dishes related to current exhibitions), in the West Building; the underground *Cascade Café* (pizzas, cookies, burgers, deli stuff), where you can watch an IM Pei–designed waterfall tumble downward; and the *Coffee Bar*, overlooking the Mall from the airy East Building.

The National Museum of American History's *Ice Cream Parlor* features Victorian-era decor, thick milkshakes, hot-fudge sundaes, and the mountainous Star-Spangled Banner Split. The summer-only *Full Circle Café*, on the Hirshhorn Museum's plaza, serves sandwiches, salads, and pizzas. The Castle contains the clubby, lovely *Commons Restaurant (☎ 357-2957)*, which is mostly for museum members but opens for public weekend brunch ($22). Other Smithsonian museums – including Natural History and Air and Space – have cafeterias, too, but their food isn't a good value.

DOWNTOWN (MAP 3)

With the boom years of the 1990s, the neighborhoods north of the Mall transformed themselves. Once this area was a ghost town after dark, but now you can find flourishing restaurant districts in Chinatown, along 7th and 8th Sts NW, and close to the White House, offering meals that range from hamburgers-and-fries to tapas to eclectic American fusion cuisine.

Budget & Mid-Range

Dozens of inexpensive takeout delis and cafés throughout downtown feed hungry worker bees (*Au Bon Pain*, *China Cafe*, etc). They're generally closed evenings and weekends, however. One standout is *Dean & DeLuca (1299 Pennsylvania Ave NW;*  *Federal Triangle)*, selling salads and sandwiches on great breads ($5 to $8). Also consider the downtown food courts (see the boxed text 'Food Courts'), especially the one at the *Old Post Office Pavilion*, just off Pennsylvania Ave.

Among DC's first racially integrated restaurants, *Reeves Restaurant & Bakery* (☎ 628-6350, 1306 G St NW; ⓂMetro Center) is a touch of old Washington and a down-home alternative to bland deli chains. Stop in for home-baked yellow cake or chocolate pie ($2), rotisserie chicken ($6.50), and juicy burgers ($4.50); the motherly waitresses fuss over you and call you 'honey.' Open 7 am to 6 pm daily except Sunday.

Teaism (☎ 638-6010, 400 8th St NW; ⓂArchives) is a Japanese teahouse with three DC locales. Its focus is, of course, tea (cold and hot drinks and loose-leaf teas), but it serves excellent breakfasts and lunches; shrimp *ochazuke* (rice soup) costs $6.40, generous bento boxes $7.75. Nearby, *Footnotes* (☎ 638-4882, 418 7th St NW; ⓂArchives) is the café inside Olsson's Books and Records; cappuccino ($2), muffins, croissants, scones, and sandwiches are available.

At *Jaleo (☎ 628-7949, 480 7th St NW; ⓂArchives)*, a lively, pretty tapas restaurant decorated with Spanish pottery and centered around a big semicircular bar, you can assemble a cheap meal (under $10) from 40 tapas. Favorites include the *patatas bravas* (fried potatoes with peppery tomato sauce; $3.25) and sautéed spinach ($4);

with a bottle of Rioja, who could ask for more? You *really* need dinner reservations, as Jaleo is very popular. Another good option for tapas is *El Catalan (☎ 628-2299, 1319 F St NW;* Ⓜ *Metro Center)*, with choices for $6.50 to $8.50; closed Sunday.

Jaleo's sister restaurant, *Austin Grill* (☎ 393-3776, 750 E St NW; Ⓜ Archives) is a city favorite that dishes up standards (burritos, quesadillas) and its own creations (chile rellenos with portobellos, catfish in orange-tequila sauce) for $7 to $15. Another Austin Grill is at 2404 Wisconsin Ave NW.

The cozy dive *Stoney's (☎ 347-9163, 1307 L St NW;* Ⓜ *McPherson Square)* draws neighborhood regulars and Secret Service agents from their neighboring headquarters to chow down on basic 'dude burgers,' chili, and Philly cheesesteaks ($5 to $9). *Mayur's Kabab House (1108 K St NW;* Ⓜ *Metro Center)*, near the DC youth hostel, is in a funny half-timbered faux-German house and provides value-minded fare like all-you-can-eat lunch ($5) and charcoal-grilled chicken kabobs ($6). Closed Sunday.

Near the National Museum of Women in the Arts, *Café Mozart (☎ 347-5732, 1331 H St NW;* Ⓜ *McPherson Square)* is a German deli offering takeout and eat-in: hearty eats like Westphalian ham sandwiches ($6), bratwurst plates ($7) and venison goulash ($10) are served 8 am to 4 pm daily except Sunday.

Those in search of impressive Cuban cooking go to **Havana Breeze** (☎ 789-1470, 1401 K St NW; ❶ McPherson Square). A picante de pollo (chicken in tangy Caribbean sauce) platter costs $6.60; a classic ropa vieja sandwich is $4.75. A DJ plays Latin dance music upstairs on Friday nights. Closed weekends.

The little self-service cafeteria **3rd & Eats** (☎ 347-8790, 500 3rd St NW; ❶ Judiciary Square), staffed by homeless folks and people training to enter the workforce, serves very good, very cheap deli and soul food (biscuits, red beans and rice, chicken salad, ham hocks). The menu changes almost daily; open 7 am to 3 pm weekdays only.

Chinatown You'll find a clutch of tempting restaurants – not all Chinese – near the MCI Center in DC's microscopic Chinatown. All are easily reached from the Gallery Place Metro station.

Upstairs at **Tony Cheng's Seafood Restaurant** (☎ 371-8669, 619 H St NW), a favorite Chinatown eatery, the Cantonese and Hong Kong specialties (Dungeness crab, 'Shrimp Double Flavor,' garlic grouper) average $10 to $15. Your dinner swims about, blithely unaware of its fate, in decorative tanks. Downstairs is Cheng's build-your-own Mongolian barbecue restaurant.

Burma Restaurant (☎ 638-1280, 740 6th St NW), upstairs, is a plain-looking place that concocts great, spicy entrées, from papaya salads to seafood noodles ($6 to $8), plus specialties like whole roast duck ($22). No lunch weekends.

In a rowhouse where the Lincoln-assassination conspirators once met, **Go-Los** (☎ 347-4656, 604 H St NW) offers decent Hunan and Szechuan specialties and veggie choices ($9 to $20). **China Doll Gourmet** (☎ 289-4755, 627 H St NW) serves dim sum (about $9) 11 am to 3 pm daily, plus Cantonese, Szechuan, and Thai entrées and, curiously, French pastry.

A lonesome cowpoke on the Chinatown scene, **Capital Q** (☎ 347-8396, 707 H St NW) is a little Texan joint with Lyle Lovett and Stevie Ray Vaughan blasting on the sound system and eight kinds of barbecue meats cooking behind the counter. Brisket and

Food Courts

Although 'food courts' have a bad name in the US (they're associated with the chain-restaurant junk food found in shopping malls), DC's best food courts are attractive, lively places where you can find a variety of inexpensive food to eat quickly. They're particularly handy if you have kids in tow. You can commonly find vegetarian Indian curries, sushi, burritos, Chinese stir-fry, and fruit smoothies alongside the traditional American burgers-and-fried-stuff choices.

Undoubtedly the most popular food court is on Capitol Hill at **Union Station** (Map 4). This magnificently restored Beaux-Arts railway station's main floor features many self-contained and rather pricey restaurants, but the bargain-diner's paradise awaits you on the lower level: galleries of tables and more than two dozen fast-food vendors serving a variety of American and ethnic cuisine, from pizza to Cajun. It jumps at lunchtime with young Hill staffers and tourists, and people leap upon empty tables like hungry lions.

Downtown are a number of popular food courts. The best is in the **Old Post Office Pavilion** (Map 3), Pennsylvania Ave at 12th St, and another's just across the way inside the **Ronald Reagan Building**. Both are easily accessed from the Federal Triangle Metro station. A third – the least interesting of the lot – is in the **Shops at National Place** (Map 3), in the Press Club Building at 14th and F Sts NW. South of the Mall, the Metro stop at **L'Enfant Plaza** (Map 6) connects directly with subterranean delis, cafés, markets, and shops.

Georgetown Park mall (Map 7), at Wisconsin and M Sts NW, contains another good food court, with a small seating area enlivened by white-tile floors and pretty fountains pulled-chicken sandwiches ($5), sausage platters ($8.50), 'Chinese cowboy' plates (meat over rice; $6), and lots of Lone Star beer float you away to the range. Closed Sunday.

Top End

Sniff, sniff: is that raw steak you smell, or raw power? At **Capital Grille** (☎ 737-6200, 601 Pennsylvania Ave NW; Ⓜ Archives), congressional committee heads puff stogies and quaff gin at the bar, cabinet secretaries' limousines purr outside, and lobbyists seduce willing prey over buttery beef at linen-covered tables. There's a stock ticker in the bar, stuffed buffalo heads on the walls, and a windowed meat locker and private wine cabinets at the entrance. If the maitre d' deigns to seat you (we waited 40 minutes past our reservation time), you can tuck into dry-aged 24oz porterhouses ($30), veal chops ($28), 5lb lobsters, and other red-blooded fare that isn't half as interesting as the clientele. No lunch on weekends.

Steak's also the word at **District Chop House** (☎ 347-3434, 509 7th St NW; Ⓜ Archives), but the mood is less type A (and way more fun). Entrées (New York strip, plank salmon) run $16 to $27. With an in-house brewery and cigar humidor, pool tables, Sinatra on the stereo, and an elegant, pillared setting, it's a popular late-night spot. No lunch on weekends.

Innovative pan-Latin cooking – chicken-polenta canapés, Veracruz-style seafood, portobello steak huitlacoche – makes **Café Atlántico** (☎ 393-0812, 405 8th St; Ⓜ Archives) one of downtown's most popular places. Capirinhas, mojitos, and pisco sours wash it all down. Entrées run $13 to $17. On Saturday, try fabulous 'Latin dim sum' – 25 mini-courses for $20. No lunch Sunday.

An inventive American menu is featured at **The Mark** (☎ 783-3133, 401 7th St NW; Ⓜ Archives), favored by local gallery denizens and agents from the nearby FBI. Its corner dining room serves dishes like gin-cured gravlax ($8.50) and seared dry Maine scallops ($19). Closed Sunday.

Coco Loco (☎ 289-2626, 810 7th St NW; Ⓜ Gallery Place), in Chinatown, offers a full tapas menu and an all-you-can-eat churrasqueria ($30) that delights committed carnivores, and it becomes a Latin dance club after dinner Thursday to Saturday – all of which makes it manically crowded. Closed Sunday; no lunch Saturday.

On warm days, lunch at **Les Halles** (☎ 347-6848, 1201 Pennsylvania Ave NW; Ⓜ Federal Triangle) is an appealing choice – its expansive streetside plaza is filled with umbrella-shaded tables where brasserie classics like escargots ($7), boudin aux pommes ($15), and steak and frites ($22) are served.

M&S Grill (☎ 347-1500, 600 13th St NW; Ⓜ Metro Center) is a gorgeous dark-wood saloon that attracts after-work drinkers ($2 appetizers 3 to 6 pm weekdays) and diners for comfort food like short ribs and whiskey-cured salmon. Most entrées cost $10 to $20. No lunch on weekends.

The vaunted decor at **Red Sage** (☎ 638-4444, 605 14th St NW; Ⓜ Metro Center) looks like Fred Flintstone cross-bred with Georgia O'Keeffe: cave-like, rose-stuccoed, subterranean rooms roofed with wood beams and decorated with Southwestern sculptures and fancy ironwork. Bill Clinton favored chef Morou Ouattara's Southwestern-inflected American cuisine: red-chile pecan-crusted chicken ($19), grilled diver scallops with saffron ($12), acorn squash risotto ($22), and smoked antelope, bison, and ostrich. It's all extraordinarily tasty and served in those little 'food towers' that you have to smoosh with a fork before eating. No lunch on weekends. At street level are the less-expensive **Border Café** and a weekdays-only sandwich shop, the **Red Sage Market**.

On the K St corridor, you'll find a star of the culinary firmament, **DC Coast** (☎ 216-5988, 1401 K St NW; Ⓜ McPherson Square), which does serious lawyer-and-lobbyist-lunch trade in a sleek, Beaux Arts–inspired atmosphere and wins critical raves for its seafood-heavy menu. Appetizers start around $9; entrées like pan-seared Scottish salmon cost $15 and up. Closed Sunday; no lunch Saturday.

An older DC institution, **Occidental Grill** (☎ 783-1475, 1475 Pennsylvania Ave

NW; **M** *Metro Center*) is practically wallpapered with mug shots of congressmen and other political celebs who have dined here throughout the years. Although the Occidental isn't the nerve center it once was, plenty of bigwigs still roll up their pinstripes to dive into hamburgers, chops, and steaks (about $10 to $20).

For a sleeker meal, go to the nearby *Willard Room* (☎ 628-9100, *1401 Pennsylvania Ave NW*; **M** *Metro Center*), in the Willard Inter-Continental Hotel, with gilt-trimmed ceilings, heavy chandeliers, carpets thick enough to drown in, and French entrées like poached lobster that cost $18 and up (way up). Closed Sunday; no lunch Saturday.

Old Ebbitt Grill (☎ 347-4801, *675 15th St NW*; **M** *Metro Center*) has been around since 1846, serving local favorites like Maryland rockfish, crabcakes, steak, and burgers, along with grilled chicken salad and pasta plates (entrées $8 to $16).

Washington's first two-Michelin-star chef, Gerard Pangaud, runs diminutive *Gerard's Place* (☎ 737-4445, *915 15th St NW*; **M** *McPherson Square*). A quietly elegant red-walled room with high-backed chairs and heavy linens, Gerard's Place has the ambience of a wealthy French provincial dining room and extraordinary food: appetizers like cassolette of sweetbreads ($12), entrées like duck confit and Pangaud's signature poached lobster with Sauternes ($17 to $40), and desserts like red-wine-poached pear tart ($10). Tasting menus cost $58 (vegetarian) and $72 (carnivore). Closed Sunday.

Across the square, *Georgia Brown's* (☎ 393-4499, *950 15th St NW*; **M** *McPherson Square*) offers high-style Southern cuisine and hospitality and is particularly popular among DC's black elite. There's a live R&B brunch Sunday ($22) – try the wonderful crab-hash Benedict.

On an ugly block near the Convention Center is a minimalist gem called *Rupperts* (☎ 783-0699, *1017 7th St NW*; **M** *Mt Vernon Square-UDC*). Its limited menu of New American cuisine shifts seasonally: you might dine on venison and root vegetables

The Presidential Nosh

Perhaps it's something about the job, but US presidents seem to have a predilection for odd or even downright unsavory food and drink. Here's a sampler of past White House treats:

Liver with bacon, kidney stew – Theodore Roosevelt

Cottage cheese dressed with ketchup – Richard Nixon

Jelly Bellies – Ronald Reagan

Hominy grits – Ulysses S Grant

Creamed chipped beef – Franklin Roosevelt

Fresca – Lyndon Johnson (who had a tap for it installed in the White House)

Fried pork rinds – George Bush *père* (who ate them as a 'common man' political tactic)

Booze – Franklin Pierce (who died of cirrhosis)

Anything at all – William Taft (who weighed 330lbs)

in fall, sparkling-fresh seafood and berries in summer. Dinner runs about $30 per person. Dinner Tuesday to Saturday, plus lunch Thursday.

WHITE HOUSE AREA (MAP 3)

This is the stomping ground of lobbyists and executive-branch power brokers, as the area's plethora of expensive restaurants attests. Budget-minded visitors might choose to lunch here but head north to Dupont Circle or Adams-Morgan for dinner.

Budget & Mid-Range

The polished bakery/sandwich shop *Bread Line* (☎ 822-8900, *1751 Pennsylvania Ave NW*; **M** *Farragut West*) is run by chef Mark Furstenberg, whose ways with dough produce astonishingly good sandwiches (under $8) and sweet treats – try the peach tarts or 'Oreos' (big mascarpone-filled chocolate cookies). Open 7 am to 5 pm weekdays only.

Just off Lafayette Square near the White House is a **Teaism** teahouse (☎ 835-2233, *800 Connecticut Ave NW;* Ⓜ *Farragut West)*, with its entrance on H St, which offers simple noodle or bento-box lunches ($7.75). Open for breakfast and lunch weekdays only.

Top End

Boston-based chef Todd English operates **Olives** (☎ 452-1866, *1600 K St NW;* Ⓜ *Farragut North)*, just north of the White House. This popular debutante on the DC scene serves excellent Italian-influenced fare in a sunny two-floor place: veal agnolotti *alla nonna* ($16.50), sirloin on Tuscan bruschetta ($25.50), venison and squash gnocchi ($27). Sitting at the kitchenside bar is the best choice – you can watch the sous-chefs chop and stir, and then order what looks best. No lunch Saturday; closed Sunday.

McCormick & Schmick's (☎ 861-2233, *1652 K St NW;* Ⓜ *McPherson Square)* is a seafood restaurant with a Pacific Northwest–influenced menu. With dark wood all around and panels of stained glass atop the banquettes, it's an attractive setting for business meals. Entrées (grilled salmon, Dungeness crab) cost $12 to $24. No lunch on weekends.

A formal choice is the Hay-Adams Hotel's **Lafayette Room** (☎ 638-6600, *800 16th St NW;* Ⓜ *McPherson Square)*, a chandeliered, velvet-draped salon with White House views and hushed tables full of Very Important Politicians. Its American-international fusion cuisine gets so-so reviews, however. Entrées cost $20 to $27.

The Oval Room (☎ 463-8700, *800 Connecticut Ave NW;* Ⓜ *Farragut West)* is a very sleek place beloved of politicians and media folk, but its formality is lightened by the amusing mural of famous Washingtonians along one wall. The menu is modern American and uniformly fine, but seafood shines in unusual combinations like salmon with clams. Most entrées cost $15 to $25. Closed Sunday.

One of the best top-end bargains going, **Equinox** (☎ 331-1818, *818 Connecticut Ave NW;* Ⓜ *Farragut West)* charges less than $20 for most entrées, $50 for a six-course dinner of straightforward but excellent New American cuisine like grilled quail, mango crab-cakes, or lamb with morels. Sit on the patio if it's sunny. No lunch Saturday; closed Sunday.

Spanish and Basque dishes lure the international-banking and diplomatic sets to **Taberna del Alabardero** (☎ 429-2200, *1776 I St NW;* Ⓜ *Farragut West)*, an offshoot of a noted Madrid restaurant. With its flowery decor and saffron-colored walls, it's as appealing as the food: tapas ($4.25 to $8.75), seafood, and paella ($22). No lunch Saturday; closed Sunday.

FOGGY BOTTOM (MAP 3)

Although Foggy Bottom is anchored by a university – George Washington University – it isn't overrun with bargain options, which forces many GWU students to head to Dupont Circle or Georgetown for their food and grog. Instead, lots of glossy expense-account restaurants fill Foggy

RICK GERHARTER

PLACES TO EAT

Bottom, many run by celebrity chefs and dependent on the government agencies and law firms based in the neighborhood.

Budget & Mid-Range

Plain as a bucket, with prices to match, **Sholl's Colonial Cafeteria** (☎ 296-3065, 1990 K St NW; ⓜ Farragut West) is a DC institution beloved by the wealthy and the down-and-out, the tourists and the locals alike. Dive into Southern comfort food – biscuits, spoonbread, mashed potatoes (85¢), chopped steak ($2), pork chops ($3.25), and Famous Rhubarb Pie ($1.65) – while you read the little homilies scattered around ('The family that prays together stays together'). Rising rents have almost sounded Sholl's death knell on occasion, but it's 72 years old and still kicking. Cash only. Open 7 am to 10:30 am, 11 am to 2:30 pm, and 4 to 8 pm Monday to Saturday, 8 am to 2:30 pm Sunday.

Tequilla Grill (☎ 833-3640, 1990 K St NW; ⓜ Farragut West), tucked in a basement, resembles a set for a Jimmy Buffett south-of-the-border song, and the Parrothead himself is on the sound system frequently. It's a college hangout that draws crowds for standard Mexican dishes (burritos around $7) and drinks specials; a bucket of six 7oz beers goes for $5.

Kaz Sushi Bistro (☎ 530-5500, 1915 I St NW; ⓜ Farragut West), headed by chef Kaz Okochi, who used to be at Sushi-Ko, serves up inventive, very fresh, reasonably priced sushi, including rolls like crunchy eel ($4.25). The omasake ($21) is the best choice: you put yourself in the chef's hands and he serves you his favorites. The short ribs ($15) are juicy and sweet. No lunch Saturday; closed Sunday.

Aroma (☎ 833-4700, 1919 I St NW; ⓜ Farragut West) serves decent Indian chow at very reasonable prices. Beef and lamb curries cost about $10, but veggie entrées cost around $8. Spring for the sweet, perfectly charred tandoori chicken if you can.

Nearby, Chilean recipes are prepared at **Chalán** (☎ 293-2765, 1924 I St NW). Dark corners, candlelight, and limited seating in the basement room create a great out-of-

the-way spot for a tryst. You can get ceviche for $8.

GWU students have descended on **Lindy's Bon Appétit** (☎ 452-0055, 2040 I St NW; ⓜ Foggy Bottom) for decades to get 22 choices of takeout burgers ($3 apiece). In warm weather, you can grab a café table out front; in cooler weather, head upstairs to the **Red Lion** bar.

For inexpensive Middle Eastern takeout, visit **Mehran** (☎ 342-0056, 2138 Pennsylvania Ave NW; ⓜ Foggy Bottom) – you can smell the curry simmering from a half-block away. The daily curry specials cost less than $6.

A favorite for Asian dinners before Kennedy Center shows, **Zuki Moon** (☎ 333-3312, 824 New Hampshire Ave; ⓜ Foggy Bottom), in the George Washington University Inn, serves Japanese-inflected soba and udon soups, plus grilled, healthful fish entrées like wasabi tuna. Entrées start under $10; no lunch on weekends.

Top End

Many costly restaurants, most of them business-meal-oriented, line K St NW. **Le Tarbouche** (☎ 331-5551, 1801 K St; ⓜ Farragut West), with its lovely decor of saffron-colored walls accented by ultramarine glassware, serves Lebanese-French cuisine. Mezze (tapas-like appetizers) cost $5 to $11, entrées $17 to $29 (try falafel-crusted sea bass). The name 'Tarbouche' means 'fez,' if you're curious. A dance party starts here late on Saturday nights, with world-beat Latin and Middle Eastern music. No lunch Saturday; closed Sunday.

Teatro Goldoni (☎ 955-9494, 1909 K St; ⓜ Farragut West) serves Venetian cuisine in a wonderful little room done up in blue-green-and-gold harlequin motley. Entrées (lobster risotto, shrimp agnolotti) cost $19 to $25, but the best thing here is the vodka selection: 35 at last count, including melon, chocolate, and berry flavors. No lunch Saturday; closed Sunday.

Legal Sea Foods (☎ 496-1111, 2020 K St; ⓜ Farragut West) is an offshoot of the famed Boston restaurant. The restaurant has a hearty masculine mood and serves big platters of things like baked stuffed shrimp,

'New England clambake,' and grilled swordfish, plus fine chowders. Entrées cost $12 to $19. No lunch on weekends.

Kinkeads (☎ 296-7700, 2000 Pennsylvania Ave NW; Ⓜ Foggy Bottom) is the creation of acclaimed chef Robert Kinkead, who specializes in imaginative seafood recipes like coconut-peanut snapper, monkfish with potato gratin, and fish tamales ($13 to $40). The raw bar is great: a half-dozen oysters and a stiff whiskey here are the antidote to your midwinter blues. There's a tavern downstairs and a formal dining room upstairs.

Aquarelle (☎ 298-4455, 2650 Virginia Ave NW; Ⓜ Foggy Bottom), in the Watergate, serves swanky French bistro fare (entrées $18 to $30), and its windowside tables offer phenomenal views of the Potomac. Just south of the Watergate, the Kennedy Center's **Roof Terrace Restaurant** (☎ 416-8555) is the perfect pre-theater choice, and it has a good Sunday brunch ($27). At dinner,

sample excellent seafood and ribs, then recover on the outdoor terrace high above the river. Entrées cost about $25. Dinner Tuesday to Saturday and brunch Sunday.

CAPITOL HILL & SOUTHEAST DC (MAP 4)
The Hill offers a wonderfully mixed bag of dining options. You've got old-boy, cigars-and-gin steakhouses where senators conspire; free-chips-and-cheap-booze eateries where their underpaid staffers drown their sorrows and perform their mating dances; and the friendliest open-air farmers' market in town. Restaurants are clustered around Union Station and Massachusetts Ave NE; along Pennsylvania Ave SE; and around Eastern Market, southeast of the Capitol.

Budget & Mid-Range
You could dine pretty happily on the Hill without ever leaving Union Station. Nearly a dozen restaurants sit within its grand

---

The Public Trough: Eating at the Capitol

With a few exceptions, food at Smithsonian cafeterias is both overpriced and crappy. So what to do when your tummy rumbles in the midst of your museum tour?

Head up to the Capitol, where several good restaurants and cafeterias are open to the public but surprisingly little-known. The food's tasty and quite cheap (yer tax dollars at work, folks), and sometimes you can spot a famous pair of legislative jowls chowing down at the next table. Here are some choices (note that most open weekdays only):

Capitol The **Senate Dining Room** is the best place to spot powerbrokers. Request permission to visit it from your senator's office. Entrées cost $4 to $14; open to the public 1 to 3 pm. On the House side, the **Bennett Dining Room** feeds representatives. **The Refectory**, on the 1st floor of the Senate side, is a cafeteria-style spot serving sandwiches, soups, salads, etc; no special permission is needed.

Longworth House Office Building The **Longworth Food Court** offers fast food from pizza to seafood to Chinese.

Rayburn House Office Building Here you'll find **Special Orders Deli**, **Rayburn Pizza Plus**, and the **Rayburn Cafeteria**.

Dirksen Senate Office Building The **North Servery** offers cafeteria-style choices.

For absolutely free eats, jump onto the Hill-rat reception circuit. Dress nicely, wander into the House or Senate office buildings around quitting time, and look for rooms full of young staffers munching free offerings from trade groups like the US Pork Producers Council. Walk in, act natural, eat, and flee before anyone tries to schmooze you.

marble confines, and its Metro station makes access a snap. Its downstairs **food court** (see the boxed text) offers cheap eats that tour the globe from India to the southern US; it's open daily. The station has standard-issue fast-food chains, too (Pizzeria Uno, McDonald's), but why bother with them?

Just inside the station's front doors, **Thunder Grill** (☎ 898-0051) dishes up decent Tex-Mex chow: quesadillas, burritos, enchiladas, and nachos in meat, seafood, and veggie varieties, all under $15. A big bar and strong margaritas make it a popular after-work stop, and the amusing decor (check out the phallic chile-pepper lamps dangling from the ceiling) makes it a cheerful place.

On the station's west end is **America** (☎ 682-9555), with seating at the bar, on a narrow mezzanine, or at tables in the main station hall. Uniformly tasty dishes such as Mississippi fried catfish and Boston cream pie (around $10 each) are listed on a map-shaped menu with selections organized by regions; there are a few bloopers, like the 'Nebraska Reuben' – say what? The scene here is Hill-rat on weekdays, touristy on weekends. On the station's upper floor, **East Street Café** (☎ 371-6787) serves big portions of pan-Asian fare (Filipino *pancit bihon* and Thai curries, most about $10).

Nearby, the Massachusetts Ave NE bar-and-restaurant strip features both upscale options and burgers-and-beer joints. For takeout lunches, try **Neil's Deli** (☎ 546-6969, 208 Massachusetts Ave; Ⓜ Union Station), with thick turkey sandwiches for $5. Right-wing pizza fans can check out **Armand's Chicago Pizzeria** (☎ 547-6600, 226 Massachusetts Ave; Ⓜ Union Station), next to the conservative Heritage Foundation think-tank, with build-your-own 'zas and a lunch buffet. Prices start at $7.

For Tex-Mex, you have two options. At lunchtime and most nights, Capitol staffers pack the booths and outside plaza and cluster around the bar of dark, smoky **Red River Grill** (☎ 546-7200, 201 Massachusetts Ave; Ⓜ Union Station). Primarily a drinkin' spot, it also has rather overpriced entrées

($10 burritos!). Stick with the basic chili ($5) or nachos ($9). **La Loma** (☎ 548-2550, 316 Massachusetts; Ⓜ Union Station) offers outdoor plaza seating, big combination platters ($10), and entrées like ceviche, burritos, and enchiladas for $7 to $13.

The Hill's best outdoor patio is at **White Tiger** (☎ 546-5900, 301 Massachusetts; Ⓜ Union Station): a big fenced deck shaded by light-festooned trees. Here upscale Indian classics like chicken *tikka* start around $12; plentiful vegetarian choices are available, and a full multicourse feast costs $19.

Lots of Hill staffers and tourists flock to three pubs with decent menus. **Capitol City Brewing Company** (☎ 842-2337; Ⓜ Union Station), in the Post Office building across 1st St NE from Union Station, accompanies its microbrews with American bar food like jalapeño poppers ($4), burgers ($7) and platters of chicken, ribs, and crabcakes. The food's bland but served in copious portions.

An Irish pub menu is featured at **Dubliner** (☎ 737-3773, 520 N Capitol St; Ⓜ Union Station), where Guinness pints go nicely with fish-and-chips or shepherd's pie ($10 to $15). At neighboring **Kelly's Irish Times** (☎ 543-5433, 14 F St NW; Ⓜ Union Station), you'll find all the corned beef and cabbage ($10) or Irish stew ($8) you can eat.

The wonderful **Eastern Market** (and nearby Eastern Market Metro), at 7th and C Sts SE, anchors another mini restaurant district. The Eastern Market hosts the city's most vibrant farmers' market on Saturday and Sunday, when you can shop for produce and ready-made foods, plus crafts, flowers, and jewelry. The South Hall (closed Monday) has lots of food counters and **Market Lunch**, the best little seafood stop in town. Order a divine crab-cake sandwich ($6) or fried-oyster sandwich ($7) with slaw from the old dames at the counter, then eat it at indoor tables or outside in the sun.

During the weekend farmers' market, the ebullient owner of **Misha's Deli** (☎ 547-5858, 210 7th St SE; Ⓜ Eastern Market) stands outside and offers folks tastes of Russian delicacies. Inside, treats like mushroom caviar ($6/lb), Ukrainian bread ($5.50),

Chitterlings, just one of the delicacies available at the Eastern Market

'Trotsky' (chicken schnitzel) sandwiches, and stuffed cabbage are served; open daily.

Long, drowsy outdoor lunches are the thing to do on summer weekends at **Tunnicliff's Tavern** (☎ 546-3663, 222 7th St SE; Ⓜ *Eastern Market*), which serves Cajun dishes like catfish paella ($14.50).

A nearby breakfast option is **Bread & Chocolate** (☎ 547-2875, 666 Pennsylvania Ave SE; Ⓜ *Eastern Market*), where steaming espressos ($1.50) go nicely with muffins, pastries, and sandwiches (about $4). A fabulous stop is **Jimmy T's** (☎ 546-3646, 501 E Capitol St; Ⓜ *Eastern Market*), five blocks east of the Capitol, a tiny corner diner jammed on weekends with coffee-swilling, *Post*-reading locals at the little counter and in the scuffed-up booths. Breakfast is served all day (waffles $4) alongside short-order sandwiches and burgers. Open till 3 pm daily except Monday.

Northeast of Capitol Hill proper, **French's Fine Southern Cuisine** (☎ 396-0991, 1365 H St NE) is a good stop for cheap breakfasts (50¢ to $8) and lunches ($3.25 to $10) of Southern chicken, meatloaf, and tastier-than-it-sounds 'road beef.'

A long line of bars and restaurants marches down Pennsylvania Ave SE from the Capitol, all popular among young Hill staff and neighborhood professionals.

Awesome little **Sherrill's Restaurant & Bakery** (☎ 544-2480, 233 Pennsylvania Ave; Ⓜ *Capitol South*) is a time-warp diner with ancient waitresses, faded duck-huntin' murals, dusty pastry cases, and cheap-as-dirt burgers and sandwiches (most under $5).

Thai Roma (☎ 544-2338, 313 Pennsylvania Ave; Ⓜ *Capitol South*) features the oddest fusion around – Italian and Thai – but its pastas blend surprisingly well with chili-and-coconut curry sauces. Pad Thai and spicy raviolis are two standouts. Entrées cost about $10. If Mexican is on your mind, visit **La Lomita Dos** (☎ 544-0616, 308 Pennsylvania Ave) for inexpensive, big platters and industrial-strength margaritas. There's another **La Lomita** at 1300 Pennsylvania.

South of the Cannon House Office Building are two major Hill-rat hangs. Alcohol figures prominently on the menu of both. At **Bullfeathers** (☎ 543-5005, 410 1st St SE; Ⓜ *Capitol South*), the cuisine is straight-up

RICK GERHARTER

American food: burgers, pasta, steak, and chicken dishes, most about $10. *Tortilla Coast* (☎ 546-6768, 400 1st St SE; ⓜ Capitol South) features Tex-Mex cuisine like chicken flautas and steak fajitas ($8 to $12), pitchers of frozen margaritas, and a glass-enclosed porch for espying approaching political opponents. Closed Sunday.

The *Library of Congress cafeteria* (☎ 707-5000; ⓜ Capitol South), on the 6th floor of the Madison Building, Independence Ave and 1st St SE, is open to the public for breakfast and lunch weekdays. It's a great value, with catered food from a variety of DC restaurants, and overlooks the Anacostia River.

Banana Café & Piano Bar (☎ 543-5906, 500 8th St SE; ⓜ Eastern Market) is a delightful Cuban/Puerto Rican joint painted in happy tropical colors, with *Buena Vista Social Club* on an (apparently) constant tape loop, inexpensive *ropa vieja* (stewed beef), and some of the tastiest carnitas in DC.

Top End
At Union Station's east end, in the majestic former Presidential Reception Room, is *B Smith's* (☎ 289-6188). Run by former model Barbara Smith, whose unclouded complexion once graced Oil of Olay ads, it dishes out dressed-up down-home cuisine, including Swamp Thing (mixed seafood with greens; $19), catfish fingers with caramelized-onion tartar sauce ($7), and an excellent – albeit pricey – Sunday brunch.

In the elegant rowhouses along nearby Massachusetts Ave NE are many fine-dining options. Because of limits on lobbyists' gifts, many feature inexpensive lunch specials, so even budget travelers can consider them.

The rich and powerful favor *La Brasserie* (☎ 546-9154, 239 Massachusetts Ave; ⓜ Union Station), with a pleasant patio; try butternut squash soup ($6), homemade goat-cheese-and-leek tarts ($13.50), or filet mignon *bearnaise* ($26). Open for all three meals weekdays, dinner only weekends, plus Sunday brunch.

Frilly, romantic, and loaded with chintz and cushions, *2 Quail* (☎ 543-8030, 320 Massachusetts Ave; ⓜ Union Station) is an ideal date restaurant. Its very good Continental cuisine – pan-roasted Muscovy duck, seafood penne in macadamia-cream sauce, and the signature quail – costs $10 to $20 per entrée, but prix-fixe lunch costs just $9.95.

Cafe Berlin (☎ 543-7656, 322 Massachusetts Ave NE; ⓜ Union Station) is among DC's few German restaurants. Classics like Wiener schnitzel ($17) and marinated *heringstrip* ($6.50) share the menu with highly un-Prussian entrées like grilled mahi-mahi ($16). Closed Sunday.

La Colline (☎ 737-0400, 400 N Capitol St; ⓜ Union Station) is the elegant, highly praised brasserie on the 1st floor of the big, bland C-Span Building. Its menu changes often but frequently features sinfully rich

Farmers' Markets

In addition to Eastern Market (the granddaddy of DC open-air markets), numerous local farmers' markets offer yummy eats. They're great places to find fresh produce, meats, seafood, flowers, locally made baked goods, jewelry, crafts, and even clothing – and to experience the flavors and moods of DC's neighborhoods. Try the following:

Adams-Morgan Market – Columbia Rd and 18th St NW (Crestar Bank plaza); summers beginning June 10; 8 am to 1 pm Saturday

DC Farmers' Market – 1309 5th St NE; year-round; 7 am to 5:30 pm Tuesday to Thursday, 7 am to 6:30 pm Friday and Saturday, 7 am to 2 pm Sunday

DC Open-Air Farmers' Market – RFK Stadium parking lot, Oklahoma Ave and Benning Rd NE; year-round; 7 am to 5 pm Thursday and Saturday (open Tuesday, too, June through September)

foie gras; other specials include bouilla-baisse and shrimp creole. Entrées cost around $20. Closed Sunday. Nearby is a young rival for the best-French-on-the-Hill crown: **Bis** (☎ 661-2700, 15 E St NW; Ⓜ Union Station), which DC's beautiful people discovered as soon as it opened in 1998. Inside the chic Hotel George, it features top-notch bistro classics like duck terrine, veal stew, and calamari *basquaise* for $17 to $23.

The best place to spot your senator off-duty and glass-in-hand is **The Monocle** (☎ 546-4488, 107 D St NE; Ⓜ Union Station). With the decor and mood of a powerful men's club, it often hosts political fundraising dinners and has walls festooned with politicians' quotes ('If you want a friend in Washington, get a dog') to aid digestion. Yet its food – surf-and-turf American classics like salmon and rib eye steak – is less interesting than its people-watching. Entrées cost about $20; open weekdays only.

Regal **Barolo** (☎ 547-5011, 223 Pennsylvania Ave SE; Ⓜ Capitol South) was created by Roberto Donna, the New York restaurateur widely credited with helping to invent DC's Italian-cuisine scene in the 1980s. Northern Italy is the focus here, with a number of game entrées that cost $17 to $25. The funky decor features weaponry on the walls and amusingly oversized chairs – it's like being a toddler in the king's throne room. Closed Sunday.

UPPER NORTHEAST DC (MAP 5)
Colonel Brooks' Tavern (☎ 529-4002, 901 Monroe St NE; Ⓜ Brookland) is a two-floor restaurant/jazz club serving pub grub and Southern treats: fried catfish ($7), pulled-pork sandwiches ($7), and the like. The Federal Jazz Commission plays Tuesday night – a gig that's been going 20 years now.

Next door at **Island Jim's Crab Shack & Tiki Bar** (☎ 529-4002), romp in a palm-tree–shaded sandpit or sip umbrella drinks and nosh seafood on an outdoor deck. A bucket of mussels is $9, softshell crabs $17. There are Caribbean treats, too, like jerk chicken and spicy seafood soup. Closed Sunday and Monday.

Discerning gourmands go to **Ella's Barbeque** (☎ 635-3991, 1233 Brentwood Rd NE; Ⓜ Rhode Island Ave) for North Carolina-style chopped barbecue, sliced beef, and short ribs ($7 to $8) and soul-food classics like bonefish, pigs' feet, and chitterlings ($5.50 to $8.50), all served cafeteria-style.

SOUTHWEST DC (MAP 6)
For seafood meals on the water, head south of the Mall to Maine Ave and the walkway along the Washington Channel. The Waterfront Metro station is close at hand.

At the delightful waterside **seafood market**, just south of the I-395 bridge, barges and stalls sell fresh seafood; with all the tentacles, smells, and flying shells, it's a sensory spectacle even if you're not hungry. Prepared foods – such as softshell-crab sandwiches (in season; $3 to $5), fish-and-fries platters ($5 to $6), great crab-cakes ($5) – are offered, too. Alas, there are no tables, so take your meal south along the channelside walkway to sit on benches.

Lined up south of the market are industrial-size seafood restaurants cranking out blue crabs and fried shrimp for the masses. **Hogate's** (☎ 484-6300, 800 Water St SW) is gargantuan – more than 1100 people can eat here at once – and caters to the tour-bus crowd. Famous for free rum buns, it offers both good grilled offerings, like wood-grilled salmon, and standard fried-stuff platters. Entrées cost in the $20s. **Phillips Flagship** (☎ 488-8515, 900 Water St) trumps its neighbor: it can seat 1400. The seafood buffet ($20) is the reason to come; it's loaded with spicy crabs, shrimp, fish, and afterthoughts like salad and dessert.

At **Zanzibar** (☎ 554-9100, 700 Water St SW), try creative Caribbean- and African-inspired seafood, like rock lobster *foo-foo* ($23), amid brightly colorful decor. Later in the evening, this place heats up as a nightclub patronized by elegantly togged African American couples. Closed Monday.

The waterfront's best restaurant, **Le Rivage** (☎ 488-8111, 1000 Water St SW), near the channel's northern end, is popular for romantic suppers before shows at nearby Arena Stage. It's a lovely place, with

RICK GERHARTER

The farmers' market in Adams-Morgan

candlelight and picture-window sunset views. Entrées ($15 to $20) focus on French-style seafood. The pre-theater menu is $18. Dinner only on weekends.

GEORGETOWN (MAP 7)

Some visitors find Georgetown, with its expensively restored Federal townhouses and student crowds, just too dang quaint and preppy. But hungry visitors will welcome the wall-to-wall eateries (over a hundred of them) lining M St NW and Wisconsin Ave, serving everything from pub grub to Vietnamese *pho*. As an added bonus, many places stay open until 1 or 2 am, especially on weekends, because this is a hopping bar district. Foggy Bottom is the closest Metro station, but it's several blocks southeast along Pennsylvania Ave.

Budget & Mid-Range

You'll find the cheapest options at the *Georgetown Park food court*, on the lower level of the mall at M St and Wisconsin Ave. Other inexpensive choices for hearty American chow – burgers, chicken, and sandwiches – are the pubs throughout the area. Try *Mr Smith's* or *Clyde's* (see the Entertainment chapter for details).

Near the east end of the M St drag, *Zed's Ethiopian Cuisine* (☎ 333-4710, 2801 M St) is comparable to Adams-Morgan's Ethiopian restaurants (that means good). Most of its veggie and meat choices are under $12. Among DC's oldest Mexican restaurants, *Enriquetas* (☎ 338-7772, 2811 M St) has a loyal clientele who keep the cooks busy making their beloved enchiladas (under $9).

Two good, basically interchangeable Vietnamese restaurants are up the street. *Saigon Inn* (☎ 337-5588, 2928 M St) has delicious meat and seafood dishes, most under $12; the slightly more touristy *Vietnam Georgetown* (☎ 337-4536, 2934 M St) offers a weekday lunch buffet for just $5.25.

Cafe La Ruche (☎ 965-2684, 1039 31st St), set away from crowds near the canal, features a sunny dining room full of colorfully tiled tables and a garden. French entrées like *moules* (mussels) and *saucisses* (small sausages) start at about $10.

The irresistibly named ***Moby Dick House of Kabob*** (☎ 333-4400, 1070 31st St NW) offers a Persian menu. Clay-oven pita bread and delicious beef and chicken, much of it spiced with sumac, are warm and welcome on a rainy winter's eve. A kabob flatbread roll costs $5.25.

Old Glory All American Barbecue (☎ 337-3406, 3139 M St) is a dressed-up Southern rib shack with a rowdy bar, where the meats sizzle over hickory or oak fires and six different sauces are yours for the choosing. A full rack of baby-back ribs costs $18, a half-rack $13, but the pork-shoulder sandwich is $9, the chicken wings just $6. House-cured ham smoked over corncobs is a divine house specialty.

The gourmet ***Dean & DeLuca Market*** (☎ 342-2500, 3276 M St) has a beautiful glassed-in café selling sandwiches, snacks, pastries, and coffee. It's a bit steep ($5 or more for a latte and croissant), but the pretty setting and top-notch food are worth a wee splurge.

Another of DC's fabulous Middle Eastern restaurants, ***Fettoosh*** (☎ 342-1199, 3277 M St) has a menu of little appetizers called *mezze* ($2.75 to $3.75) that make a great meal. We dined happily on *foul madamas* (favas with lemon and garlic) and *fettoosh* salad (toasted bread with chopped veggies). Entrées like *kibbi bi-leben* (yogurt-sauced beef with onions and pine nuts) cost around $10.

Appas (☎ 625-6685, 3291 M St), among Georgetown's best budget-meal bets, is a hole-in-the-wall takeout with a few tables and a cook specializing in Peruvian charcoal-grilled chicken. A leg and thigh cost about $2.50, a breast and wings just pennies more. ***Aditi*** (☎ 625-6825, 3299 M St) offers tangy Indian food and made-to-order breads (try onion-stuffed *kulcha*). Hot means *hot* here, so specify mild if you're sensitive. A sampler 'feast' dinner costs $14.

For upscale Italian fare, go to ***Paolo's*** (☎ 333-7353, 1303 Wisconsin Ave), a bistro famous for its wine collection. Brick-oven

baking, an outdoor patio, and big streetside windows draw in both Georgetown yupsters and the international set. Pizzas, grilled meats, and pastas cost $8 to $18.

Away from the tourist crowds, ***Peacock Cafe*** (☎ 625-2740, 3203 Prospect St NW) has sunny outdoor tables and a laid-back mood that encourages people to linger, read, and yack for hours. Basic American breakfasts, lunches, and dinners cost about $8 to $12.

Neighboring ***Bangkok Bistro*** (☎ 337-2424, 3251 Prospect St NW) is a beautifully decorated place with iridescent tabletops and gold-and-green walls. Prices are a little steeper than usual for Thai, but not excessive. Pad Thai is $10, *tom yam gong* (spicy shrimp soup) $4. Try the rockfish in banana leaves, too.

Top End

The Washington Harbour condominium and retail complex at 3000 K St shelters several upscale restaurants that offer, in warm weather, deck seating and wonderful river views. All lure professionals and wealthy students, and in both groups, spooning couples. Try ***Sequoia*** (☎ 944-4200) for new American cuisine (entrées about $20). ***Tony & Joe's*** (☎ 944-4545) is a premiere people-watching venue, packed Friday through Sunday nights. Seafood entrées like crab legs and shrimp run about $22.

Inside the Latham Hotel, you'll find one of DC's most acclaimed restaurants: ***Citronelle*** (☎ 625-2150, 3000 M St NW). Amazing dishes here include the *osso buco*, truffle-and-celery-root tart, and eggplant terrine. Chef Michel Richard – considered among the country's best – began his career as a pastry chef, so desserts are no afterthought: try the 'chocolate bar' with hazelnut sauce. Dinner with wine for two runs well over $200; the chef's tasting table costs about $175 per person. No lunch on weekends.

La Chaumière (☎ 338-1784, 2813 M St), with its big central fireplace, has a French country inn flavor. It began life as a *charcuterie* and now serves classic dishes such as sole meunière as well as more adventurous things like Algerian couscous and sea bass in walnut crust. Entrées top out at $18. Closed Sunday; no lunch Saturday.

Tahoga (☎ 338-5380, 2815 M St) features contemporary American regional cuisine on its seasonally changing menu. Offerings – most around $20 – have included pheasant chowder, venison, and crayfish croquettes. No lunch on weekends.

The pretty new girl on the Georgetown scene is *Neyla* (☎ 333-6353, 3206 N St), a sleek Mediterranean-Lebanese joint. It offers the traditional meze but dresses them up: hummus, for example, has pomegranate in it. Mezze cost about $7, entrées $20. Open Tuesday to Saturday for dinner only.

A trio of Wisconsin Ave bistros serve classic French dishes that are worth a small splurge. At *Aux Fruits de Mer* (☎ 333-2333) and *Au Pied du Cochon* (☎ 337-6400), both at 1335 Wisconsin Ave, seafood starts at $14, land food at $12. Thirteen beers are on tap, and people crowd in late at night after leaving local bars to dive into crispy *frites* and eggs Benedict. Au Pied de Cochon stays open 24 hours. *Bistrot Lepic* (☎ 333-0111, 1736 Wisconsin Ave) offers hearty favorites like Basque chicken stew, pigs' feet, and braised veal, plus newer concoctions like potato-crusted salmon. Closed Monday.

Dining at *1789* (☎ 965-1789, 1226 36th St), in a beautiful Federal rowhouse, is like attending an upscale Pilgrims' feast. Chef Ris Lacoste's modern American menu highlights the mid-Atlantic's seasonal produce and game in dishes such as rabbit and sweetbreads, mussel-and-clam stew, and softshell crabs with corn pudding. Entrées cost $19 to $30. Open for dinner only daily.

DUPONT CIRCLE & KALORAMA (MAP 8)

Dining in Dupont Circle offers an abundance of choices: inexpensive sushi, Greek, Chinese, and American; mid-range seafood and Asian cuisine; or upscale Mediterranean and Italian. Restaurants line Connecticut Ave NW and the other streets flaring from the circle itself. Unless otherwise noted, Dupont Circle Metro station is convenient to all the places described in this section.

Budget & Mid-Range

Attached to the independent bookstore Kramerbooks, *Afterwords Café* (☎ 387-1462, 1517 Connecticut Ave) changes its moods throughout the day: in the morning, people schmooze over lazy cups of coffee and muffins; in the afternoon and early evening, readers peruse daily over newspapers and new-bought novels; at night, it's a bar scene with live music. The basic café menu is pretty overpriced for what you get, but it's a peerless see-and-be-seen place.

Zorba's Cafe (☎ 387-8555, 1612 20th St NW) is beloved for its cheap, generous portions of Greek food and its small patio. Chicken souvlaki costs $5.50; excellent *tzatzíki* (yogurt dip with cucumber and garlic) is $4.

Firehook Bakery (☎ 588-9296, 1909 Q St NW), a nice neighborhood joint with a windowside counter from which you can scope passersby, offers big-as-your-head cookies and good lunchtime sandwiches (on diverse breads from levain to spelt) and salads; tabbouleh costs $6/lb.

Across the street, *Raku* (☎ 265-7258, 1900 Q St) enjoys a great corner location with wraparound windows for people-watching and offers a menu of 'pan-Asian tapas' (tuna napoleons, ginger mussels) and sushi. It's moderately priced – tapas $3.25 to $8, maki about $5 – and has a funky drinks menu, too. Try the green-tea martini, watermelon margarita, or plum wine-sake mix.

La Tomate (☎ 667-5505, 1701 Connecticut Ave) offers pasta plates and Italian dishes (entrées $9 to $12) in a bright and airy downstairs bar or upstairs on its deck. *Thai Chef* (☎ 234-5698, 1712 Connecticut Ave) features a lengthy menu of soups, curries, salads, and noodles, most under $10. Nearby, *Timberlakes* (☎ 483-2265, 1726 Connecticut Ave) is popular for its burgers (around $7) and fish and chips ($8) made with farm-grown catfish.

Consistently named among DC's favorite Chinese restaurants, *City Lights of China* (☎ 265-6688, 1731 Connecticut Ave) has wonderful dumplings, Hunan chicken, and other favorites for $9 to $20. *Teaism* (☎ 667-3827, 2009 R St NW), an organic Japanese teahouse, offers more than 30 varieties of tea, including oolong, green, tisanes, and Darjeeling. Bento boxes cost $7.75, and you can eat them in the sun in front of this small, pretty townhouse.

On the Dupont Circle stretch of 18th St NW, *Lauriol Plaza* (☎ 387-0035, 1835 18th St) graciously serves sophisticated Tex-Mex and Spanish cuisine, featuring knock-you-down margaritas. It's a crowded, happy place, popular with after-work diners. Entrées cost $9 to $17. You'll find Malaysian and Singaporean dishes like *nasi goreng* ($9) and satay ($7) with peanut sauce at *Straits of Malaya* (☎ 483-1483, 1836 18th St).

On the circle's south side is a *Xando Coffee and Bar* (☎ 296-9341, 1350 Connecticut Ave), with windows on both sides, big armchairs for flopping in, and relaxed tables full of folks reading and chatting. There's a wide range of espressos and teas, plus sandwiches, panini, and wraps for about $6. Another Xando is on Connecticut Ave north of the circle.

Nearby, *Sticks & Bowls* (☎ 296-4001, 1300 Connecticut Ave) serves simple Asian noodle and rice dishes, topped by your choice of veggies and meats (sausage, shrimp, etc), for about $5; closed weekends.

Across the street, *Luna Grill & Diner* (☎ 835-2280, 1301 Connecticut Ave) is a cheery storefront operation with sun-and-moon decor, a parquet floor, and secluded booths. Luna does diner cuisine like grilled-cheese sandwiches, sweet-potato fries, and comfortingly creamy mashed potatoes, most under $10. East of the circle, *Café Luna* (☎ 387-4005, 1633 P St NW) features inexpensive Italian fare like mozzarella-and-tomato sandwiches and garlic penne for about $6.

At *Bertucci's Brick Oven Pizzeria* (☎ 463-7733, 1218 Connecticut Ave), you could pay $13 for a pizza. But the soup and salad in this popular chain costs only about $5, and there's an endless supply of hot, freshly baked rolls.

A great little takeout place with one glass table, *Julia's Empanadas* (☎ 861-8828, 1221 Connecticut Ave NW) serves up its namesake food in big portions – buy a large *chilena* empanada (about $3.50) and eat it while you sightsee.

Down in the 'West End' area of Dupont, *Lulu's New Orleans Cafe* (☎ 861-5858, 1217 22nd St NW; ⓜ Foggy Bottom) makes a good turtle soup ($3.25), catfish-and-oyster po'boys ($8), and decent jambalaya ($8.25).

A fine lunch stop, the popular pan-Asian *Oodles Noodles* (☎ 293-3138, 1120 19th St NW; ⓜ Farragut North), ventures far beyond chow mein and pad Thai to spicy Singapore rice noodles and variations on ramen, udon, and stir-fry that demonstrate just why Marco Polo supposedly brought pasta from Asia back to Italy. Most dishes cost around $8. No lunch Saturday; closed Sunday.

Meiwah (☎ 833-2888, 1200 New Hampshire Ave NW; ⓜ Foggy Bottom) is a new Chinese place opened by Larry La, former owner of City Lights of China. It's a big, elegantly designed venue for top-notch mid-range dishes like pan-fried jumbo shrimp and yummy sautéed spinach. A full dinner costs about $20.

Several good restaurants are found on the far northeastern border of Dupont Circle, between the Adams-Morgan and Shaw districts. The Salvadoran-Mexican restaurant *El Tamarindo* (☎ 328-3660, 1785 Florida Ave NW; ⓜ Woodley Park-Zoo) serves its goodies 24 hours a day in a homey checkered-tablecloth setting. Enchiladas, tacos, and flautas fall in the $8 range. Its Salvadoran *pupusas* (cheese-filled treats) are very good – one of these, with a ceviche and a Mexican beer, is the ideal summer-day lunch. In the same area, a good no-frills choice for Ethiopian fare is *Addis Ababa* (☎ 232-6092, 2106 18th St NW; ⓜ Woodley Park-Zoo).

Down U St NW from Adams-Morgan is *Julio's* (☎ 483-8500, 1604 U St; ⓜ U St-Cardozo), a pizza joint whose rooftop deck offers fabulous street views. Come on Sunday for a $15 all-you-can-eat brunch (eggs, ham, hash, waffles – and, yes, pizza). Farther east, *U-topia* (☎ 483-7669, 1418 U St; ⓜ U St-Cardozo), a restaurant, bar, jazz joint, and gallery with a hip clientele, boasts an adventurous multicultural menu that includes

RICK GERHARTER

Restaurant Nora

PLACES TO EAT

jambalaya but also Middle East couscous and 'U-Street Shrimp-and-Rice' (around $10). No lunch Saturday.

Top End

Restaurant Nora (☎ 462-5143, 2132 Florida Ave NW) is fronted by an herb garden and decorated with elegantly rustic furnishings and dried flowers. Its New American cuisine, all of it certified organic, is beloved by a devoted band of regular diners, who tuck into starters of calamari *escabèche* and entrées of coriander lamb and pan-seared scallops with saffron risotto. The cuisine can be uneven: some dishes are exquisite, others dull, but they're always interesting. Entrées cost $24 to $30. Open Monday to Saturday for dinner only.

Set in three beautiful 18th-century rowhouses, the *Tabard Inn* (☎ 331-8528, 1739 N St NW) is a delightful oasis: inside is a warm, dark bar; outside is a sun-dappled, walled garden filled with tables and decorated with cast-iron sculptures. Eclectic entrées – fish

stew, pastas, chops – cost about $20. Come here for weekend brunch and dive into beignets with vanilla whipped cream or chocolate-almond pancakes, or show up on a cold, rainy night for a fireside toddy in the lounge. Life is sweet.

You'll find another storybook setting – but less interesting food – across the street at *Iron Gate* (☎ 737-1370, 1734 N St NW), which serves high-end romantic dishes like lamb chops with ruffly paper garters (about $20). Closed Sunday.

Classic southeastern American seafood is on the table at *Johnny's Half Shell* (☎ 296-2021, 2002 P St NW): Maryland crabcakes, fried oysters, barbecued shrimp, plus carnivores' favorites like Eastern Shore chicken stew, all of it delightful. Entrées cost $7 to $18. Closed Sunday. *Pesce* (☎ 466-3474, 2016 P St NW) is, as the name says, a fish restaurant. Things with fins are the seabeasts to order in this crowded little café – bluefish, salmon, grouper, all perfectly fresh and simply prepared – but shellfish are on the menu, too. Entrées start at about $12. No lunch Sunday.

Obelisk (☎ 872-1180, 2029 P St NW) serves exquisite, plainly presented Italian cuisine such as veal with mushrooms. The prix-fixe menu ($40) offers only a handful of choices, but everything is perfectly prepared. Open for dinner only, Monday to Saturday.

I Ricchi (☎ 835-0459, 1220 19th St NW) serves Tuscan cuisine (in other words, a lot of grilled meats). Rabbit and grilled sausage are two dishes to try, but there are lots of grilled seafood dishes on the menu, too (although these aren't quite as pleasing). The pappardelle with rabbit sauce is great. Entrées run $15 to $28. Closed Sunday; no lunch Saturday.

The Palm (☎ 293-9091, 1225 19th St NW), a media and political celebrity magnet (Larry King likes to hang out here), is great fun for people-watching. It's another of DC's power-center steakhouses, where everyone's lunch seems to consist of sirloin, straight-gin martinis, and cigar smoke. Entrées start around $13 and top out at $30. No lunch weekends.

In southern Dupont, near the K St NW corridor, are many top-end restaurants that appeal to business diners. The New York–based steakhouse **Smith & Wollensky** (☎ 466-1100, 1112 19th St NW; Ⓜ Farragut West) is a chummy place, more laid-back than most of its DC brethren. The meat is nicely aged and *big* – you can get a 44oz porterhouse here. Good thing the tables are sturdy. Entrées are $19 to $39. Nearby is the slightly less-expensive steakhouse **Sam & Harry's** (☎ 296-4333, 1200 19th St NW; Ⓜ Dupont Circle). Closed Sunday; no lunch Saturday.

Galileo (☎ 293-7191, 1110 21st St NW; Ⓜ Foggy Bottom) is owned by DC's Italian-cuisine wonder kid, Roberto Donna. Wonderful pastas, risottos, and grilled meats – the lamb is especially heavenly – run $12 to $30. No lunch on weekends.

Asia Nora (☎ 797-4860, 2213 M St NW; Ⓜ Foggy Bottom) is the younger sister of Restaurant Nora. In this beautiful setting, with dark-green walls and handmade furnishings, seasonal seafood is given an Asian twist. Local critics say the chefs haven't worked the kinks out of their pricey organic menu, but we enjoyed our grilled sea bass. Entrées start at $18. Open Monday to Saturday for dinner only.

ADAMS-MORGAN (MAP 9)

Adams-Morgan is Washington's international smorgasbord. Here you can dine on *mee goreng*, shish kabobs, *yebeg alecka*, calzones, jerk chicken, ceviche, *pupusas*, and, of course, Happy Meals. An incredibly dense concentration of inexpensive eateries – many doubling as bars – keeps Adams-Morgan streets crowded all week with young, adventurous diners. One drawback: there's no Metro station here. Use the Woodley Park-Zoo station and walk the few blocks east to the district, because street parking is limited.

Budget & Mid-Range

To many folks, Adams-Morgan means just one thing: Ethiopian food. You can eat it at several restaurants here, but the leading place is **Meskerem** (☎ 462-4100, 2434 18th St NW), named for the first month of the Ethiopian calendar. With traditional woven-straw basket-tables and camel-leather hassocks upstairs and two floors of ordinary tables below, it serves beef, poultry, lamb, seafood, and vegetarian dishes on *tef*, or whole-wheat *injera* (pancake-like bread). The generous vegetarian *mesob* (mixed platter) is a bargain at $8.50 per person; also good is *tibbs* (lamb stew with onion, green chile, and seasoned butter; $11). Across the street, **Red Sea** (☎ 483-5000, 2463 18th St) offers a similar menu and similar prices in less polished surroundings.

If Ethiopian doesn't tickle your fancy, you still have dozens of choices.

When Washingtonians want Southwestern food, they dine at **Roxanne** and the upstairs **Peyote Grill** (☎ 462-8330, 2319 18th St), which features a great rooftop deck, veggie black-bean chili ($5) and Corona-beer-battered shrimp ($8).

New Orleans (☎ 234-0420, 2412 18th St), lookin' like a genuine bayou crab shack, is Adams-Morgan's extremely popular Cajun restaurant. Crowds gather early here on weekends, so you may have to queue up. Prices are very reasonable: shrimp gumbo costs about $6, chicken jambalaya $10. For a taste of the Caribbean, head to **Mobay** (☎ 745-1002, 2437 18th St), a happy place with indoor and outdoor café tables, a young crowd, and plenty of Peter Tosh on the stereo. Try 'Chicken Rundown' (coconut chicken) for $10.

West, not East, Africa is the focus of **Bukom Café** (☎ 265-4600, 2442 18th St).

Dinner on a Pancake

DC is among the world's best places – outside East Africa – to sample Ethiopian and Eritrean cuisine. Beginning in the early 1980s, East African immigrants began opening DC restaurants that showcased their spicy, inexpensive, fun-to-eat cuisine, and they won an instant place in the hearts of hungry Washingtonians.

RICK GERHARTER

Adams-Morgan is the usual place for newcomers to start – it has numerous East African restaurants, and waitstaff are happy to show newbies what to order and how to eat. An Ethiopian meal consists of *injera* (spongy, pancake-like bread rounds made with *tef*, or buckwheat flour) and *wat* (a mélange of simmered vegetables or meat in sauce). Wat has two varieties: red, fiery *kay wat* and milder, yellowish *alicha wat*. It can include meat, like savory *doro wat* (chicken stew, often with a hard-boiled egg sitting in its center) and *sega wat* (lamb stew). Ethiopian cuisine is also beloved by vegetarians, who dig into vegetable *alicha*, *yemiser wat* (spicy lentil stew), and *fitfit* (tomato-and-chile salad).

A traditional meal is served to diners seated on low divans or hassocks. A cloth-covered wicker table *(mesab)* is placed among them. On top of the table is a large platter blanketed by a single round of injera; upon the injera are scoops of wat. To the side rests a platter heaped with folded injera. Diners take up an injera, tear off a piece with their fingers, and use it to fold a bit of wat into their mouths. (Waitstaff sometimes proffer a copper basin in which to wash your hands before the meal, plus Wetnaps to wipe down afterward.) Once the wat is gone, the bottom injera itself is eaten – there's something very satisfying about eating your 'tablecloth'! It all goes down well with *tej* (gentle, honey-sweetened white wine) or lager.

This dinner isn't intended to be the typical American gobble-and-dash – it's a leisurely affair that's as much about conversation as about food. East African diners in DC restaurants generally linger over their food, interspersing bites with long chats with their friends and families.

Should you fall in love with the cuisine, as most diners do, you can buy ingredients and recipe books to make your own at several groceries (see the Shopping chapter). Which DC restaurant offers the best East African cuisine? That's a matter of rollicking debate. On 18th St NW are two perennial favorites: Meskerem (see the Adams-Morgan section of this chapter), which is wall-to-wall with diners most nights and offers traditional mesabs upstairs, and Addis Ababa, a plainly decorated joint drawing more East African customers (see the Dupont Circle section).

Fish, meat, and vegetarian dishes from Ghana and the Côte d'Ivoire cost about $10. The decor is cheerful, with lots of West African textiles and masks, and the place becomes a popular dance club at night. Opens at 4 pm Thursday to Sunday only.

Rumba (☎ 588-5501, 2443 18th St) is a little Cuban cigar bar/bistro decorated with Latin-American artwork and religious *santos* figurines. Che Guevara's picture hangs behind the bar. Here you eat grilled meats, *yuca frita* (fried yucca root), and other dishes ($8 to $14) while Celia Cruz and other salsa stars dominate the sound system. Opens at 5:30 pm daily.

The French bistro *La Fourchette* (☎ 332-3077, 2429 18th St) makes a great bouilla-baisse, along with other moderately priced classics like escargots and pâtés. No lunch weekends.

Another restaurant strip is round the corner on Columbia Rd NW. *Perry's* (☎ 234-6218, 1811 Columbia Rd) is a sushi restaurant/bar greatly beloved for its rooftop deck and Sunday drag-queen brunch (see the Entertainment chapter). It can be hard to spot because there's no real sign – the doorway canopy uses rebus symbols (like a pear) to spell out the name. Just look for the deck.

Rocky's Café (☎ 387-2580, 1817 Columbia Rd) serves fine Southern and Creole dishes at moderate prices: jerk chicken wings ($6), catfish and sweet-potato fries ($14), and the like. Open for dinner weekdays, plus Saturday brunch. *Astor* (☎ 745-7495, 1829 Columbia Rd) is a great sandwich stop, particularly for its 10 veggie platters (like the falafel with pita bread, hummus and Egyptian salad for $6).

Near Rock Creek Park, *Mama Ayesha's* (☎ 232-5431, 1967 Calvert St NW) is a Middle Eastern joint that's been here since the 1950s and has hardly changed a thing. Standbys like baba ghanoush and lamb kabobs cost $9 to $13.

Mount Pleasant Just north of Adams-Morgan, this district offers ultra-cheap snacks, particularly Salvadoran pupusas, which usually cost no more than a couple of dollars and often are accompanied by cold marinated-cabbage salad. Try *Pupuseria San Miguel (3110 Mt Pleasant St)*, downstairs, for takeout, or *Don Juan's*, at the southwest corner of Mt Pleasant and Lamont Sts.

For dessert, stop by *Heller's Bakery (3221 Mt Pleasant St)*, a neighborhood fixture with pleasant window seating where you can enjoy a rich frosted brownie or Russian tea cookie (both $1).

Top End

Felix (☎ 483-3549, 2406 18th St) is an elegant steel-and-glass nightclub that serves upscale meals before 10 pm Thursday to Sunday. Try sautéed shrimp with angel-hair pasta, asparagus tips and tomato-basil sauce ($18), duck confit, or, on Friday and Sunday, Jewish specialties like brisket and matzoh-ball soup. Most dishes are under $20.

Our neighborhood favorite is *Belmont Kitchen* (☎ 667-1200, 2400 18th St), at the corner of Belmont Rd, an intimate bistro with a fat red tomato logo. Popular for its outdoor fenced patio, it has a short but wonderful menu of American and Mediterranean dishes. The sautéed shrimpcakes ($16) are amazingly fresh and savory. Entrées run between $12 and $18.

For Italian, try *I Matti* (☎ 462-8844, 2436 18th St), a bright, airy spot on this fashionably dark street, with red-tile floors, blond-wood tables, and big picture windows for good people-watching. A locally renowned chef invents pasta plates and modern Italian fare garnished with fried radicchio or fava beans ($13 and up). Open for dinner only; closed Sunday.

Cashion's Eat Place (☎ 797-1819, 1819 Columbia Rd) is a casual bistro where the new American entrées cost $17 to $20. Mediterranean-influenced dishes, such as ravioli and *fritto misto*, are great. Open for dinner Tuesday to Sunday, plus Sunday brunch.

SHAW & THE NEW U DISTRICT (MAP 10)

There's an intriguing mix of soul-food landmarks and avant-garde cafés within walking distance of the U St Metro, all suitable for cost-conscious diners.

Back in 1958, **Ben's Chili Bowl** (☎ 667-0909, 1213 U St) appeared on the Shaw scene, and it's been a neighborhood shrine ever since. DC-government bigwigs, Howard University professors, and schoolkids all come for chili dogs ('Our chili will make a hot dog bark!') and conversation at the no-frills Formica counters. Everyone from Red Foxx to Duke Ellington to Bill Cosby has eaten at Ben's. The 'dogs start at around $2, chili around $4. Open till 4 am Friday and Saturday.

Across the street, Marley lives on at **Kaffa House** (☎ 462-1212, 1212 U St), a collective named for the Ethiopian region where the coffee bean was first discovered, according to the owners. Spicy Jamaican cuisine (under $10), veggie soups, coffees, and muffins, plus live reggae, open-mike nights, and drink specials, attract a politically aware young crowd. Open at 4 pm daily.

A fixture of black Washington life, the **Florida Avenue Grill** (☎ 265-1586, 1100 Florida Ave NW) has been around for almost 60 years. Its walls are lined with signed photos of singers, actors, and politicos who have enjoyed its soul food, including the down-home grits, meatloaf, and barbecued ribs ($6 to $9). Closed Sunday and Monday.

Inexpensive Jamaican's the thing at **Negril** (☎ 332-3737, 2301 Georgia Ave NW), with no-fuss counter service and goat curry, flaming jerk chicken, and spicy patties. No alcohol; closed Sunday.

UPPER NORTHWEST DC (MAP 11)
Woodley Park

Connecticut Ave NW near the Woodley Park-Zoo Metro is lined with inexpensive ethnic restaurants, mostly frequented by neighborhood residents and families wandering to the National Zoo.

Lebanese Taverna (☎ 265-8681, 2641 Connecticut Ave) ranks among our favorite DC restaurants. Make a whole meal out of mezze like moussaka, grape leaves, kibbeh (beef-stuffed pasta), and foole m'damas (fava-bean dip), which please both vegetarians and meat-eaters and cost $4.25 to $5.75 apiece. An outdoor patio makes this a fine summertime choice. Neighboring **Acapulco** (☎ 986-0131, 2623 Connecticut), for Mexican cuisine, and **Tono** (☎ 332-7300, 2605 Connecticut), for Japanese, are also moderately priced and have outdoor seating.

For Thai, consider **Jandara** (☎ 387-8876, 2606 Connecticut Ave), which serves good soups like poh tack (hot-and-sour seafood with lemongrass) for under $5 and noodle dishes for under $10. **Rajaji** (☎ 265-7344, 2603 Connecticut Ave) offers Indian curry dishes (about $9) and has abundant outdoor seating.

New Heights (☎ 234-4110, 2317 Calvert St NW), overlooking Rock Creek Park, is an airy 2nd-floor restaurant focusing on New American dishes such as buttermilk-fried oysters and venison with celery root and cabbage ($17 to $26). Try the signature appetizer, amazing black-bean pâté. Dinner only, all week, plus Sunday brunch.

Cleveland Park

This district has two restaurant enclaves, one on Connecticut Ave NW (convenient to Cleveland Park Metro), the other west on Wisconsin Ave NW (accessible via Metrobus Nos 30, 32, 34, or 36).

For inexpensive Indonesia and Thai treats, stop at **Ivy's Place** (☎ 363-7802, 3520 Connecticut Ave), a spot with a small streetside patio. Drunken noodles with chicken ($10) and mini-lumpia (eggrolls; $3.25) are good choices. Rijstoffel (an Indonesian-Dutch curry feast) is available by special order. Dinner only Monday to Thursday; lunch and dinner Friday to Sunday.

Costly **Yanÿu** (☎ 686-6968, 3435 Connecticut Ave), decorated with beautiful murals and Japanese fabrics, serves pan-Asian fare that sometimes misses the mark and sometimes hits the bull's-eye (try the soup-filled Shanghai dumplings and the juicy 'Big Duck'). Dinner only daily.

Italian Ligurian cuisine is featured at neighborhood fave **Vigorelli** (☎ 244-6437, 3421 Connecticut Ave), where grilled meats take center stage on a frequently shifting menu. On its roof is a grill, L'Arenella, where everything is prepared on an open hearth: lamb chops, trout, even bread. Entrées cost $16 to $20. No lunch Sunday. Comparable in price, ***Ardeo's*** *(☎ 244-6750, 3311 Connecticut Ave)* offers modern American cooking.

On Cleveland Park's Wisconsin Ave restaurant row, you'll find perennial favorite ***Cactus Cantina*** *(☎ 686-7222, 3300 Wisconsin Ave)*, a bright, airy setting for top-notch Mexican treats like mesquite-grilled quail and juicy tamales. Dishes cost $8 to $15. For fine carryout Texas barbecue, there's ***Rocklands Barbecue*** *(☎ 333-2558, 2418 Wisconsin Ave)*. Order chopped pork or Texas ribs, and don't forget a side of greens. Dishes run $5 to $15.

Sushi-Ko *(☎ 333-4187, 2309 Wisconsin Ave)* was DC's first sushi bar and is still beloved for impeccably fresh fish. The kitchen serves the basics (tuna belly, Cali-fornia roll) and the exotic (raw-trout napoleons). Dinner for two costs about $50. Open daily; lunch Tuesday to Friday only.

Tenleytown

The ***Dancing Crab*** *(☎ 244-1882, 4611 Wisconsin Ave NW; ⓜ Tenleytown-AU)* is a DC institution. A dozen blue crabs are spilled onto paper-covered tables; you, in paper bib with mallet in hand, hammer and pick away for hours, covering yourself with Old Bay seasoning and happiness. Prices vary seasonally. No lunch Sunday.

Neighboring ***La Vida Loca*** *(☎ 537-3200, 4615 Wisconsin Ave; ⓜ Tenleytown-AU)* features not Ricky Martin but carnivore-friendly Brazilian cuisine. Entrées start around $14 and include seafood *moqueca* and sea-salt–crusted rump roast; start with a strong *caipirinha*. Open for dinner only daily except Monday.

PLACES TO EAT

Entertainment

For a relatively small city, DC has a staggering number of bars and clubs. After a few nights out, in fact, you may be convinced that the levers of government are lubricated not by tax dollars but by alcohol. There's a scene for everyone, from buttoned-down professionals to go-go boys, from punks to Euro-hipsters. There's also a thriving fine-arts scene, anchored by the landmark Kennedy Center.

The best place to find out what's happening is the free weekly *Washington City Paper*, issued Thursday and available in street corner boxes and in heaps at the entrances of stores and clubs. *The Bar Stool*, another free tabloid, has great bar profiles written by staff who really know their booze. Issued about every three weeks, it includes events and drinks-specials information, plus editorials on such burning topics as whether Britney Spears should be permitted to cover '(I Can't Get No) Satisfaction.'

More mainstream resources are the Weekend tabloid in the Friday *Post* and the *Post*'s daily Style section and Sunday Show section. The free *Washington Blade,* available at stores and clubs, gives the scoop on gay and lesbian happenings. For advance planning, request the calendar of major cultural events from the Washington, DC Convention and Visitors Association (Map 3; ☎ 789-7000), 1212 New York Ave NW, 6th floor, Washington, DC 20005-3992.

The drinking age in DC – as in the rest of the US – is 21. Many clubs and bars don't let anyone under that age through the door. Some 'over-18' clubs let you enter to dance or see shows but don't give you the hand-stamp that lets you buy alcohol. Bring a photo ID to prove your age: a driver's license is the usual.

See the Excursions chapter for important suburban clubs and performance venues.

Tickets

There's one discount-ticket outlet in DC: Ticketplace (☎ 842-5387), 1100 Pennsylvania Ave NW, in the Old Post Office Pavilion (Map 3; Ⓜ Federal Triangle), which sells day-of-performance tickets to citywide concerts and shows for half price plus 10%. Available tickets are listed on a board hanging in the office. It's open 11 am to 6 pm Tuesday to Saturday, closed Sunday and Monday (tickets for Sunday and Monday shows are sold Saturday). Full-price advance sales are also available. Also check with theaters and concert venues directly on performance day to see if tickets are available for less than face value.

Ticketmaster (☎ 432-7328) has information on and sells (full-price) tickets to citywide events. Its outlets include Tower Records, 2000 Pennsylvania Ave NW.

Free or Cheap Events

It's unnecessary to pay anything to entertain yourself in DC. The Smithsonian, which is free all day long, also sponsors numerous evening lectures, films, concerts, and unusual performances from puppet shows to bluegrass jams, many of them free. Check out the *Post*'s Weekend section, call Dial-a-Museum (☎ 357-2020) for recorded listings, or pick up calendars at museum desks. DC's smaller museums, the Library of Congress, and local churches also host a cornucopia of free or low-cost events.

Free plays and jazz and classical-music concerts are held outdoors in Rock Creek Park's 4200-seat Carter Barron Amphitheater (Map 11) on summer weekends; it's near 16th and Colorado Sts NW. Call Dial-a-Park (☎ 619-7275) for a performance schedule.

The cheapest entertainment of all is checking out memorials by night. Most major ones are beautifully illuminated in the evening, so you can avoid crowds and conserve your daytimes for museums by covering such sights as the Lincoln Memorial, Jefferson Memorial, and Washington Monument at night (at the latter, the elevator to the top runs until midnight from April through September).

BARS, DANCE CLUBS & LIVE MUSIC

Great bars and clubs are scattered all over town, but the densest concentrations are in Adams-Morgan (mostly 18th St NW between Florida Ave and Columbia Rd) and Georgetown (M St NW between 29th and 33rd Sts NW). Clustered around Dupont Circle is another thriving bar district, catering especially to gays and lesbians. Many bars also offer eats, live music or DJs, and dancing. Happy hour is practically a city mandate – the plethora of students and modestly paid young government workers means that between 5 and 8 pm on any given weeknight, you can snap up ultra-cheap booze and low-cost or free snacks at dozens of bars.

Although the capital has plenty of classical music, DC's music scene really thrives in bars and clubs. Washingtonians have long had a love affair with jazz and blues, but in this most international of American cities, you'll also find abundant places to groove to reggae, salsa, African beats, and world-music fusion.

Note: Most DC bars and clubs are open till 2 am Sunday to Thursday, 3 am Friday and Saturday. Unless otherwise noted, all establishments in this chapter keep these hours.

Downtown (Map 3)

Because this area was all but deserted after dark until the MCI Center opened in the late '90s, rents were cheap, and dance clubs started popping up in defunct retail spaces. Now that the Center draws crowds to sporting events, the city is dumping money into neighborhood development, and downtown is becoming DC's newest entertainment district.

Bars A lot of downtown's bar scene happens in its upscale restaurants (see Places to Eat for details). Many lobbyists' and lawyers' lunchtime playgrounds – *DC Coast, Capital Grille, McCormick & Schmick's, Old Ebbitt Grill* – do hefty after-work bar business, too. Folks are more likely to tuck into steak and gin than salads

and sparkly water, but the clientele and type-A ambience remain the same.

Two downtown bars offer elegant settings in which to imbibe. ***701 Pennsylvania Avenue Bar & Restaurant*** (☎ 393-0701; ⓜ *Archives*), a 'caviar and champagne lounge,' has arabesque banquettes in its quietly lush room, plus DC's best vodka bar in back. Open till 1 am nightly. ***Butlers Cigar Bar*** (☎ 637-4765, 1000 H St NW; ⓜ *Metro Center*), in the Grand Hyatt, has large, costly martinis, live jazz on Thursday, a prosperous yuppie crowd, an impressive humidor, and marble tables. Open till 1 am Monday to Saturday.

Perhaps serene luxury's not for you. Try ***ESPN Sports Bar*** (☎ 783-3776, 555 12th St NW; ⓜ *Metro Center*), a three-floor, 200-TV emporium featuring a massive screening room with speakers in its chairs and a 16-foot TV that looks like a war-room missile monitor; the crowded Sports Grill; and the Sports Arena, packed with video and table games. Lots of tourists visit. A better sports bar, if only because it gives you free popcorn, is back inside the Grand Hyatt: ***Grand Slam*** (☎ 637-4736; ⓜ *Metro Center*), which also has lots of TVs but isn't so crowded. Both are open daily.

Fadó (☎ 789-0066, 808 7th St NW; ⓜ *Gallery Place*), a stylish Irish pub, sticks out in Chinatown like James Joyce in Shanghai. The owners dropped a bundle here before opening in 1998, decorating every room in unique Celtic styles – country library, medieval castle, etc – but the lovely results feel more like a movie set than a true pub. Nevertheless, it packs in the thirsty, especially after games at the nearby MCI Center. It screams on St Patrick's Day – don't even try. Open till 2:30 am nightly.

John Harvard's Brew House (☎ 783-2739, 1299 Pennsylvania Ave NW; ⓜ *Federal Triangle*) is just south of the Warner Theatre entrance. Stained-glass pics of JFK and Teddy Roosevelt crowned as saints greet you at the entrance; downstairs, the low-ceilinged room draws a mixture of tourist families (burgers and sodas can be had for kiddies), sports fans (TVs behind the bar), and the pre-theater crowd. It's a cheerful place conveniently close to the Mall – stop for a cooling homebrew in summer or Irish coffee in winter. Open till 11 pm nightly (midnight Friday and Saturday).

In the hot, miasmic swamp that is midsummer DC, take refuge at **Round Robin Bar** (☎ 628-9100, 1401 Pennsylvania Ave NW; ⓜ Federal Triangle), inside the Willard Inter-Continental Hotel, where sweet liquid solace awaits: the best mint juleps in town. Some claim that the original julep recipe was first recorded on this site, before the hotel was built – Sen Henry Clay supposedly wrote it down for a journalist.

My Brother's Place (☎ 347-1350, 237 2nd St NW; ⓜ Judiciary Square), at Constitution Ave, is primarily an after-work spot, with a primarily male clientele, $10 all-you-can-drink Saturdays, and pitchers of Guinness or Bass for $8 on Friday. It's hard to find, tucked in an alley next to the mammoth Dept of Labor, and that ensures a non-touristy mood. Open till 2 am Wednesday to Saturday.

Dance Clubs Downtown clubs are huge multiplexes housing several miniclubs under a single roof, to please all sorts of patrons. Their dance parties change constantly, so call ahead to learn what's on.

The Spot (☎ 262-0321, 919 E St NW; ⓜ Gallery Place) is downtown's leading dance palace, a 10-bar, five-club emporium. Latin, retro, trance, reggae: it's all spinning here, and you can find everyone from lawyers to graffiti artists to dance with. It even has a breakfast café for those who just can't leave, or get lost finding the door. It's closed Tuesday, open till the wee hours, and charges about $10 cover (women enter free till midnight).

Club Element (☎ 347-7100, 714 6th St NW; ⓜ Gallery Place), in Chinatown, is an upscale club with elegant neo-brutalist decor – lots of iron and bare cement – and a rotating menu of theme nights, from Sunday's 'Sin' (fetish and S&M) to Thursday's world music. The crowd is extremely mixed – plenty of straights and gays and all colors of skin, most of it young, pretty, and in a tank top. The cover is $10 but climbs to $15 after midnight Saturday. Open till 4 am Thursday to Sunday.

DC Live (☎ 347-7200, 932 F St NW; ⓜ Gallery Place) is yet another dance factory, this one with four floors of reggae, hip-hop, and rap in an old department store. Thursday is 'Earth,' when each floor plays a different continent's music. It's difficult to meet people in this huge club, but if you do, you can cuddle your new friend in nice little rooms off the main dance floors, with pool tables and armchairs. The cover charge is $10; open to 3 am nightly (4 am Friday and Saturday).

Zei (☎ 842-2445, 1415 Zei Alley; ⓜ McPherson Square), on an alley between 14th and 15th Sts NW, is a Euro-chic world-beat club that draws an international crowd, including diplomatic kiddies, and has a megalithic video and sound system. The staff are snotty – hoi polloi are barred from the pretentious top-floor 'Privee' club – but it's amusing to don your strapless dress and play poseur here. The cover is $10; open 10 pm to 2 am Thursday to Saturday only.

The Brazilian *churrasqueria* **Coco Loco** (☎ 289-2626, 810 7th St NW; ⓜ Gallery Place), in Chinatown, does a quick change into a hot club where salsa and merengue pound after 11 pm Thursday, Friday, and Saturday. The scene is high-fashion and multiethnic, and cruising 30-somethings pack the floor. Many locals consider this place among DC's top Latin clubs. The cover's $10 for men but only $5 for women.

If you can't get enough of *Gilligan's Island* or *The Brady Bunch*, head for **Polly Esther's** (☎ 737-1970, 605 12th St NW; ⓜ Metro Center), a dance club that recreates the last three decades: '70s-era disco, '80s bubble-gum pop (called 'Culture Club') or '90s Top 40, all on different dance floors. The nostalgia is a little thick – does the world really need a drink called The Exorcist? – but it's fun. The crowd here is totally mixed, and sometimes you get waves of folks in town on conventions. Expect an $8 to $10 cover. Open till 4 am weekends.

One of the moment's hottest clubs is **Platinum** (☎ 393-3555, 915 F St NW; ⓜ Metro

Center), a three-floor operation housed in a grand former bank where dressy pretty people dance to the usual mélange of world and electronic music. On 'Millennium Fridays,' trance, house, and progressive play on the main floor and Latin and hip-hop rule the basement lounge. Be warned: sitting at a table requires a reservation and the purchase of an expensive bottle of liquor. The cover charge is $10; the club's open till 3 am Thursday to Sunday.

Live Music At *BET on Jazz* (☎ 393-0975, 730 11th St NW; Ⓜ Metro Center), a sleek supper club owned by Black Entertainment Television, the leather banquettes are full of folks in slinky clothes (no T-shirts or sneakers allowed), mostly over-30 black professionals. Wednesday to Saturday, the calendar's loaded with 'smooth jazz' musicians, with some New Orleans performers, too. Cover prices vary with the performer.

White House Area & Foggy Bottom (Map 3)

Nightclubs and bars in these areas – which are a bit dead once the workday's done – depend heavily on GWU students and thirsty bureaucrats for their trade.

Bars Puns on 'Foggy Bottom' run rampant among bar names. First, there's *Foggy Dogg* (☎ 463-3025, 2519 Pennsylvania Ave NW; Ⓜ Foggy Bottom), a cozy wood-floored bar next to One Step Down jazz club (both are in old brick rowhouses). The Dogg's beloved by preppy students and recent grads, and its bartenders are friendly as they come. Downstairs a small restaurant serves pub fare, but upstairs is where serious drinking happens. Try the quintessential college libation, 'Stoli Doli' (vodka with pineapple), or the eponymous house brew, a nicely hoppy pilsner. Nearby, *Froggy Bottom Pub* (☎ 338-3000, 2141 Pennsylvania Ave NW; Ⓜ Foggy Bottom) is another popular GWU hangout. The big attractions here are grub-and-pub specials, like Saturday's $10 all-you-can-eat-and-drink. Happy-hour specials run 5 pm to midnight. Friday has a free buffet. Closed Sunday.

Despite its screaming-red façade, *Mackey's Public House* (☎ 331-7667, 1823 L St NW; Ⓜ Farragut North) is a calm bar conjuring the mood of an Irish country pub, with its fireplace and easy chairs to flop in while sipping pints of Guinness, Harp, or Caffrey (all on tap). It's a grown-up place where the music and lights are kept low, and it serves corned-beef-and-cabbage Irish favorites. Closed Sunday.

For sports, folks head to *Tequilla Grill* (☎ 833-3640, 1990 K St NW; Ⓜ Farragut West). Mexican food and $1.50-a-beer happy-hour specials attract students. DJs offer dance music Thursday through Saturday, and, in fall and winter, Sundays are all football, all day, on a 4-foot TV.

Red Lion is the pub above the ever-popular Lindy's Bon Appétit (see Places to Eat). Both despondent and euphoric students wander in nightly for $1.50 shooters and hang out to watch TV and talk school with their buds.

The Bottom Line (☎ 298-8488, 1716 I St NW; Ⓜ Farragut West) is a downstairs bar, long and narrow as a bowling alley, that draws prosperous after-work patrons. It's more grown-up than most pubs in Foggy Bottom, and not a few folks seem to be having business-related tête-à-têtes when they're not chatting with the folksy barkeeps.

Those in search of fine martinis visit *Ozio* (☎ 822-6000, 1835 K St NW; Ⓜ Farragut West), a dressed-up bar with an impressive cigar selection, a menu of beef and tapas, and a heavily international scene. Put on your best dress or Armani suit beforehand, and the bouncers will be nicer. Martinis are a reach at around $8, but they're darn tasty. You can dance on weekends to Latin and '80s pop. Closed Sunday.

Dance Clubs A salsa and Latin-dance club for the under-30 set, *Bravo Bravo* (☎ 223-5330, 1001 Connecticut Ave NW; Ⓜ Farragut North) is an enormous basement club where the mood is flirty, the dancers are polished, and both men and women wear their best. The place gets going after midnight. It admits people 18 to 20 but charges them $10. People over 21 pay $5.

ENTERTAINMENT

Live Music *One Step Down* (☎ *955-7141, 2517 Pennsylvania Ave NW;* Ⓜ *Foggy Bottom*) has been around 35 years, which makes it the US's second-oldest jazz club. This dark, smoky place (squint and you're in the Village) books premier out-of-town talent on weekends, local artists weekdays. Blues pops up on the calendar sometimes. Patrons are generally professional folks in their 20s and 30s. Weekdays the cover is $5, weekends $12 to $20. All shows start at around 9 pm.

Capitol Hill & Southeast DC (Map 4)

Hill bars are all about gossip: political, social, romantic. To your left, two junior House aides pretend they've got all-access passes to the back rooms of government; to your right, two gay lawyers analyze their latest candidates for the office of Mr Right; in the back, a lobbyist dangles choice tidbits of information before a pliant bureaucrat. Nonetheless, most bars are a nice political mix where lefties and righties set aside partisanship in favor of beer.

Bars On the Senate side of the world, look for *Red River Grill* (☎ *546-7200, 201 Massachusetts Ave NE;* Ⓜ *Union Station*), a smoky Tex-Mex place packed with students and young Hill rats, most in high mating mode. The drinks are cheap and the food greasily satisfying. Word has it that its outdoor deck was the place Monica Lewinsky first hinted to friends about some guy named Bill. Open till 1 am nightly (2:30 am Saturday).

A pair of fine Irish pubs are nearby, west of Union Station. Both are open till the wee hours nightly. *Dubliner* (☎ *737-3773, 520 N Capitol St*) is a big, upscale, Guinness-dark pub that draws folks in their 40s. There's live Celtic music or folk nightly, and the big outdoor patio is jammed in summer. Pints cost about $4. It serves its own toothsome brew, Aulde Dubliner, plus the usual Eire beers. A younger crowd goes round the corner to *Kelly's Irish Times* (☎ *543-5433, 14 F St NW*) – motto: 'Give me your tired, your hungry, your befuddled masses' – whose long bar and booths are filled with fans of the on-tap Guinness and live music offered Wednesday to Saturday. More than

Raise a pint at the Dubliner.

a few Hill staffers say that Kelly's was the first DC bar that served them.

For a more Yankee experience, **Capitol City Brewing Company** (☎ 842-2337) is also nearby, in the Post Office building across from Union Station. It's pretty – down the center of its light-flooded, lofty-ceilinged room marches a platoon of tall copper brew vats – but hasn't much character, with its mix of after-work drinkers and tourists. But eight serviceable brews, including eat-with-a-spoon Blackout Stout and tasty Prohibition Porter, make it OK for an early-evening drink. Pints run about $4. Open till 11 pm nightly (midnight Friday and Saturday).

You'll also find popular pubs on the House side of Capitol Hill, along Pennsylvania Ave between 2nd and 5th Sts SE. Access them via Eastern Market or Capitol South Metros. For a cigar and game of pool in elegant surrounds, **Capitol Lounge** (☎ 547-2098, 229–31 Pennsylvania Ave SE) is the place. Downstairs the cigar bar pours martinis; upstairs the brick-walled bar is packed with suits after work. A dozen TVs show sports, and there are three pool tables. One recent visit turned up drunken Library of Congress staffers engaged in a fierce tourney – good to see that librarians get loose, too.

PoliTiki (☎ 546-1001, 319 Pennsylvania Ave SE), gussied up in Bali Hai's finest – tiki torches, wooden Easter Island guys, palm fronds – is popular with young Hillies for its ironically retro decor, downstairs tiki bar and pool tables, upstairs swing-dancing scene, and cheap drinks. It pours Singapore slings, zombies, mai tais, fearsome four-person flaming bowls, and lots of ordinary beer. Tuesday is free-eats day: with a drink, you get a buffet featuring roasted pork.

Hawk & Dove (☎ 543-3300, 329 Pennsylvania Ave SE), where dusty hunting trophies decorate the walls, has been an institution since the late '60s. If Congress is in session, you might see younger representatives here. You'll certainly see their staffs. Come with the crowds on Friday, when 20oz Bud drafts are $2.50 and tacos are free. It's a good pickup scene if you're under 30. Shoot a game of pool downstairs. Monday is

'Intern Night' (no jokes, please): $1 pints, if you're old enough to drink 'em.

The Hawk has the reputation of being a Republican hang; more Democrats go next door to beloved **Tune Inn** (☎ 543-2725, 331½ Pennsylvania Ave SE), which once won an award for being DC's best dive. In this dark, narrow room (also decorated with stuffed beasties), the patrons are young (lots of interns) and the mood boisterous – shots of Jagermeister are on offer. Burgers and fried Southern munchables are available, and drinks are cheap.

Conrad's Pub (☎ 544-2338, 313 Pennsylvania Ave SE), adjoining Thai Roma restaurant, is an English-style pub right down to its dartboard. Small and crowded, it's a good place to just drink and watch the back-of-bar TV. It's not a pickup or schmooze scene – it's a comfortable local, with an older, primarily male crowd. Open till 1 am nightly. Another relaxed local is **The Little Pub** (☎ 543-5526, 655 Pennsylvania Ave SE), a tiny hole-in-the-wall: the front room has a bar and a TV, and stashed in the wee back room are two pool tables and dartboards.

Two classic gossip pits lie a few blocks farther west. The bar/Tex-Mex joint **Tortilla Coast** (☎ 546-6768, 400 1st St SE) is where, after hard labor in the legislative mines, staff decompress with a choice of 20 tequilas and industrial-strength margaritas. By the streetside booths, plate-glass windows open in fair weather for first-class people watching. Open till midnight daily. Its neighbor, beer-sodden **Bullfeathers** (☎ 543-5005, 410 1st St SE) is decorated in early-20th-century Americana, named after Teddy Roosevelt's folksy epithet for political bullshit, and full of 30-something staffers slinging exactly that. A basic pub menu helps you balance your booze. Open till 2 am daily.

Dance Clubs & Live Music

The Nation (☎ 554-1500, 1015 Half St SE; Ⓜ Navy Yard) is DC's largest dance and live-music club: six bars are scattered over several levels, and the monster outdoor deck has an unparalleled view of the Capitol. Shows happen on weekdays, dance parties on weekends. The music they play is all over

Going to a Go-Go

No, it doesn't involve girls dancing in cages. Go-go is a unique brand of percussion-driven dance music with both its funky boots planted squarely in DC's black neighborhoods, and although it's been around almost three decades, you can hear it only in the District and its suburbs. The go-go scene hit its peak in the mid-80s and never gained a national following, but fame and recorded tracks aren't really the point with go-go, whose essence is the live jam and the dance party. Going to a DC go-go show remains a hell of a good time.

African-derived rhythms, loud brass and bass drums, and audience call-and-response ('Are you ready to go? *Hell, no!*') keep the floor moving at go-go shows. The musicians trace their influences back to the pre-1970s de facto segregation of DC. White clubs wouldn't admit black patrons, so they flocked to neighborhood dance halls and black-run venues like the Howard Theatre and Northeast Gardens, which gave rise to a vibrant new soul music played by bands such as the Young Senators and Black Heat. Go-go's daddies, Chuck Brown and the Soul Searchers, emerged from this club culture. In the mid-70s, Brown mixed disco's nonstop format with funk, syncopated African and Latin rhythms, and call-and-response, and the infectiously danceable result spawned other great go-go bands, such as Rare Essence, Trouble Funk, and Experience Unlimited.

Shootings at a few shows in the late '80s gave the whole scene a bad (and rather unfair) rep for violence, as did the 1985 film *Good to Go*, which used a go-go soundtrack for its story of rape and murder. The rise of hip-hop soon overshadowed go-go. But the music plays on, and numerous bands still work regularly in DC, many straddling the hip-hop and go-go genres. Some of the scene has migrated into the suburbs, especially Maryland's Prince Georges County. Find show listings at http://members.tripod.com/~kid_mysfit/gogo.html, or in *City Paper*'s Go-Go section in the CityList. Look for shows by Rare Essence, DJ Kool, the Backyard Band, and Northeast Groovers.

the map – house, funk, electronica – and on Friday is 'Sting,' a gargantuan techno party. Saturday's wee hours attract a gay dance scene. If you're 19 or over, you're welcome for shows. Cover varies with the night.

Upper Northeast DC (Map 5)

Nightlife up here tends to be a locals-only scene, but some places are worth checking out. ***Kelly's Ellis Island*** (☎ 832-6117, *3908 12th St NE;* Ⓜ *Brookland*), sister to Kelly's Irish Times on Capitol Hill, keeps the students of neighboring Catholic University well lubricated and cheerful with pints of Guinness and Harp. And with Jesus, Mary, and assorted saints on its walls, it maintains the appropriately devout mood. A friendly dance club, mostly drawing middle-aged black couples, is ***Eclipse*** (☎ 526-3533, *2820 Bladensburg Rd NE*), where DJs typically spin Motown and soul. The cover runs around $5. Closed Sunday.

Southwest DC (Map 6)

Bars A cozy bureaucrats' bar (if that's not an oxymoron), ***Market Inn*** (☎ 554-2100; Ⓜ *Federal Center SW*), at 2nd and E Sts SW, is lined floor to ceiling with photos and drawings of nude ladies, from famous old paintings to '50s pinups. It has a piano bar, which gets crowded on weekends, and serves a menu of moderately priced seafood entrées. Open till 11 pm daily (midnight Friday and Saturday).

Dance Clubs & Live Music *Zanzibar* (☎ 554-9100, *700 Water St SW;* Ⓜ *Waterfront*) is an elegant waterfront dance club that draws primarily a well-dressed black clientele. Live bands play downstairs, and DJs spin techno, zouk, Caribbean, and worldbeat. Relax in chairs set before each window for optimal sunset watching. Tasty Caribbean is on the menu. The cover charge is $10; open till 3 am weekends.

Georgetown (Map 7)

With dozens of watering holes along its narrow streets, Georgetown floats on a happy sea of alcohol and youthful hormones. Its bars have a preppy reputation, catering mostly to white students and professionals who live in the neighborhood (and suburbanites who wish they did). The parking situation is dreadful, so take Metro to Foggy Bottom and walk up Pennsylvania Ave NW to Georgetown.

Bars *The Tombs* (☎ *337-6668*), under 1789 restaurant (see Places to Eat), is close to the Georgetown campus and – appropriately, given its name – the *Exorcist* steps. The preppier side of the student body hangs out here, just as Clinton did during his Gtown days, and it's a decent place to talk. People even study at the tables sometimes. Pitchers are always $6, and there's live music (serviceable rock) Sunday and Tuesday nights. Georgetown crew memorabilia hangs about, should you need to smack anyone with a paddle.

Garrett's (☎ *333-1033, 3003 M St NW*) is an English-style pub with a teeny downstairs bar, roomier 2nd floor, and outdoor patio. Its bar is copper-topped, its floors wooden, and its mood welcoming. Bottled domestic beer costs about $1.50 during happy hour, and in summertime the patio's a low-key meat market for well-educated recent graduates.

Mr Smith's (☎ *333-3104, 3104 M St NW*) is a comfortable old restaurant/bar that draws graybeards of 30 as well as students. The crowded front bar (you'll rub bodies with at least two strangers while drinking) hides a more spacious rear seating area with a fireplace and open patio. The menu includes crunchy fish-and-chips and baked Brie, and during happy hour (4 to 7 pm) some drafts cost just $1. Rock bands play 11 pm to 2 am Thursday to Saturday.

Clyde's (☎ *333-9180, 3236 M St NW*), a true Georgetown warhorse, has been around for almost 40 years. A lot of Georgetown students got plotzed for the first time here, back in the days when 18-year-olds could drink. Clyde's has gotten more upscale in recent years, and now as many yuppies as kids are found in this lovely saloon. The pretty 'Railroad Bar,' salvaged from a Baltimore station, is the nicest place to drink (it's in back). The kitchen serves typical pub fare and stays open till midnight weekends.

J Paul's Tavern (☎ *333-3450, 3218 M St NW*) is that big raw bar you espy through the front windows of Georgetown Park mall. A fancy old-school oyster house with a giant front bar and lots of dark wood and brass, it washes its bivalves down with single-malt Scotch (two dozen varieties) and its own Amber Ale. Lots of tourists visit. Open till 1:30 am daily (2:30 am Friday and Saturday).

DC's über sports bar is *Champions* (☎ *965-4005, 1206 Wisconsin Ave NW*). Decorated with signed baseballs, photos of famed touchdowns, and other memorabilia, it's a notch above the average sports den, and its many TVs draw standing-room-only crowds on big game days. (They're tuned to various matches, so you don't need to argue with the barkeep.) The young patrons resemble a J Crew catalog shoot and are attired in university sweatshirts. Open till 2 am daily (3 am Thursday to Sunday).

While we're on the topic of memorabilia, there's *Music City Roadhouse* (☎ *337-4444*), on 30th St NW at the canal, a smoker-friendly country-and-western restaurant/saloon in a former foundry. Its walls are papered with old album covers, misty Patsy Cline pics, and kitschy trophies like Tanya Tucker's jeans. On Sunday, there's gospel brunch; all week long, 'Cheap Bastard' specials let you drink for about $2.50. There is a truly evil lemonade here – God knows what's in it, but try not to fall in the canal on your way out the door. Open till 2 am nightly except Monday.

Dance Clubs For a cinematic college-bar experience (it was in the 1985 film *St Elmo's Fire*), visit *Third Edition* (☎ *333-3700, 1218 Wisconsin Ave NW*), serious junior breeder territory where the pick-up lines are more important than the music. Upstairs, the DJs crank out lively dance mixes from hip-hop for the tiki bar on the back patio. Nearly everyone who graduates from Georgetown has some story about this place, be it a tragedy or comedy. The cover is $5. **Rhino Bar & Pump House** (☎ 333-3150, 3295 M St NW), named for – among other things – the wooden rhino on the bar back, used to be Winston's, a skeevy dance-and-grope palace. Rhino's sanitized the premises a bit, but the college-age crowd still checks its inhibitions at the door. DJs play dance music (pop, usually) Thursday to Saturday. No cover.

Live Music Georgetown has a pearl in its midst: the city's preeminent jazz and blues club, **Blues Alley** (☎ 337-4141, 1073 Rear Wisconsin Ave). A modest brick building in an alley off Wisconsin houses this elegant, candlelit supper club, which has attracted such artists as Ahmad Jamal and the late Dizzy Gillespie. Current performers include Nancy Wilson, Danilo Pérez, and various Marsalises. The cover charge is steep ($13 to $40), as are the drinks and Creole specialties. The racially mixed crowd is largely professional. Open till 12:30 am daily.

The Saloun (☎ 965-4900, 3239 M St NW) is the place for a more casual, cheaper musical evening, so patrons here are younger and less polished. Blues play Saturday and all other nights it's jazz (mostly local rather than headliner acts). It offers 18 beers ($5 to $7 per pint) and a Cajun menu. The cover is $3 weekends, $2 weekdays; closed Monday. Another cheap-blues alternative is **Old Glory All American Barbecue** (☎ 337-3406, 3139 M St NW), with a $2 cover.

Dupont Circle & Kalorama (Map 8)

The streets around Dupont have a well-earned reputation for great gay and lesbian bars (especially along 17th St NW), but there's hardly a Berlin Wall between the gay and straight scenes. Both are welcome in each other's places. Whatever their persuasion, barhoppers here tend to be 30ish, professional, lefty, and casual. Rounding out Dupont's numerous bars are cafés, coffeehouses, and a handful of chi-chi dance clubs. Unless otherwise noted, Dupont Circle

Metro station is reasonably near all the places listed here.

Bars **Brickskellar** (☎ 293-1885, 1523 22nd St NW) is an underground beer paradise with 900 varieties, listed on a menu heavy enough to cause problems after the fifth pint or so. Shandies, stouts, darks, lights, lagers, and creams – it claims the world's largest selection. Its subterranean red-brick warren is usually choked with college-age folks arrayed around big circular tables. Most bottles cost around $4, but true exotics can cost up to $15.

Childe Harold (☎ 483-6700, 1610 20th St NW) is another clubby pub below street level – it appeals to the working gentry, who show up in coats and ties to tell horror stories about bosses and clients. There's patio seating in the summer, so you can watch the Connecticut Ave parade go by. Domestic beer runs about $2 during happy hour. Both bars draw mostly straights.

Or try DC's cheapest bar that doesn't involve brown paper bags, **Common Share** (☎ 588-7180, 2003 18th St NW). A place that commendably considers the buzz a basic human right, it sells every beer (even nice ones like Guinness) and mixed drink for just $2. Beaten-up curbside freebies furnish the place. But at these prices, who complains? Closed Sunday; cash only.

The Big Hunt (☎ 785-2333, 1345 Connecticut Ave NW) – yes, that name gets played for all the puns it's worth – advertises itself as the 'happy hunting ground for humans in pursuit of a mate, food, and drink.' But it's not really all that cruisy. Most patrons – yuppies, GWU students, and government staffers – focus on the 27 on-tap beers and bar-eats deals (25¢ chicken wings!), amid decor gently described as cheesy Hemingway: animal-print upholstery, mosquito nets, etc. Coin-operated pool tables are on the 2nd floor. Similar in spirit (but lacking leopard spots) is **Sign of the Whale** (☎ 785-1110, 1825 M St), a cozy, Brit-style pub with a fireplace, high ceilings, and, upstairs, a dance floor where DJs play rock mixes Tuesday to Saturday.

(continued on page 207)

Out on the Town in Gay & Lesbian DC

by David Zingarelli

Washington, DC, offers an increasingly progressive gay nightlife scene despite the community's long-standing reputation for buttoned-downed conservatism. That said, you're likely to see more collared shirts than T-shirts and a rowdiness factor to match. As with most big-city club scenes, DC's gay nightspots come and go at a bewildering rate – check out the local papers. You can pick up free flyers and publications at Lambda Rising (☎ 462-6969), 1625 Connecticut Ave NW, a landmark lesbigay bookstore in the heart of Dupont Circle, the city's gayest neighborhood. (For information on gay publications with entertainment listings, see Gay & Lesbian Travelers in the Facts for the Visitor chapter.)

Unless otherwise noted, all of the following bars and clubs are open nightly till 2 am Sunday to Thursday, 3 am Friday and Saturday. Cover charges apply only where indicated.

Dupont Circle (Map 8)

Ground zero for Washington's gay scene, Dupont Circle offers the bulk of the city's nightlife options, clustered on trendy 17th St NW, roughly between P and R Sts NW; and on P St NW, west of the circle itself. The following venues are within easy walking distance of the Dupont Circle Metro stop.

Head for the weekday happy hour at *JR's* (☎ *328-0090, 1519 17th St NW)* and you might think you've stepped into a living Banana Republic ad: chinos and button-downs are *de rigueur* at this popular local hangout frequented by the 20- and 30-something, work-hard and play-hard set. Some DC residents claim that the crowd at JR's epitomizes the conservative nature of the capital's gay scene, but even if you love to hate it, as many do, JR's is *the* happy-hour spot in town and is packed more often than not.

Just up the street is *Club Chaos* (☎ *232-4141, 1603 17th St NW)*, a steamy basement space with an adjoining restaurant. Thursday's Latin night packs in the boys and draws a fair number of women for dancing to salsa and merengue; Saturday nights are also popular. Early evenings

RICK GERHARTER

RICK GERHARTER

midweek, live comedy and drag shows attract a more mature crowd.

Mr P's (☎ 293-1064, 2147 P St NW) and its upstairs annex, **The Loft**, tend to appeal to an older crowd. This place has seen better days, but it gets high marks from locals for its low-attitude, friendly atmosphere and drag shows.

The Fireplace (☎ 293-1293, 2161 P St NW) may look a bit run down, but the character of this snug neighborhood watering hole more than makes up for its rough edges. The downstairs video bar tends to be more racially mixed, while the upstairs crowd is predominantly black, young, and cruisy. Friday and Sunday nights are big draws here; the guys pack the upstairs bar by 9 pm for DJ-spun disco sounds and upbeat, gospel-inspired house.

Tucked in an alley just off P St, the testosterone-heavy **Omega DC** (☎ 223-4917, 2122 P St NW) gets busy by midnight on weekends and attracts an interesting mix of ages and races. The neon-lit downstairs video bar has an '80s feel to it, while the upstairs bar is darker and cruisier, with loud dance music and a dark alcove where porn videos set the mood.

Crown jewel of the P St scene is **Badlands** (☎ 296-0505, 1415 22nd St NW), the neighborhood's longest-running dance club. Best on Friday, Badlands brings out the college kids and buff boys in droves. Don't come here to cruise, though – everybody is far too busy getting his groove on to be bothered. This is a popular spot for the 18-and-up crowd (Tuesday and Thursday) and for after-hours dancing on Friday and Saturday. Closed Monday and Wednesday; cover $4 ($8 after 10 pm).

Lizard Lounge (☎ 331-4422, 1520 14th St NW) is a colorful, candlelit space complete with cushy lounge area and fireplace; its techno and hi-energy sound appeals to a younger, mostly white, crowd. Open Sunday only, it's far from Metro; take a cab. Just a stone's throw away, *Diversité* (☎ 234-5740, 1526 14th St NW) pulls in a trendy 20-something crowd for its gay Sunday-night dance party. With DJ-spun contemporary house and soul, Diversité caters to a mostly black crowd, though patrons of both clubs wander back and forth between these neighboring venues; there's a $5 cover.

Downtown (Map 3)

The renowned daddy of Washington leather establishments, the *DC Eagle* (☎ 347-6025, 639 New York Ave NW; Ⓜ Gallery Place) is the city's cruisiest bar. Skip the cavernous lower level and head upstairs, where things get a

Top left: A sunny day at Dupont Circle

little hotter – literally – as patrons crowd around the bar beneath a menacing array of machinery suspended from the ceiling. This is a relatively tame crowd as leather scenes go: there's nothing like having a bear of a guy, decked out in chaps and chains, call you 'sweetie.'

White House Area & Foggy Bottom (Map 3)

Ask local women about lesbian nightlife in DC and you'll get a lot of snickers; nevertheless, the city has a few interesting options for women. Aside from the dyke bars described below, a few gay clubs that generally cater to men also host weekly

RICK GERHARTER

women's nights. See Gay & Lesbian Travelers in the Facts for the Visitor chapter for other women's events and meeting places.

A hip girl crowd throngs to **Hung Jury** (☎ 785-8181, 1819 H St NW; Ⓜ Farragut West) to shoot pool in the spacious lounge area or groove to an eclectic mix of tunes on the dance floor. Older dykes have playfully dubbed this club 'lesbian day care' because of its reputation for attracting a younger crowd. Open Friday and Saturday only; $10 cover.

Capitol Hill (Map 4)

Take a cab or take your chances getting to the following establishments on foot; you'll find most of them are within walking distance of the Eastern Market Metro station.

Conveniently located next to Red River Western Wear, **Remington's** (☎ 543-3113, 639 Pennsylvania Ave SE) draws DC's country & western aficionados for tall drinks and two-stepping. Boots and bolo ties blend with T-shirts and jeans at this mostly male watering hole decked out with the requisite antlers and wagon wheels. Grab your partner and hit the

THE HOT SPOT

Top right: A different kind of memorial: the AIDS Memorial Quilt

RICK GERHARTER

dance floor or shoot a round of pool or pinball in the upstairs video bar. Can't dance? Show up for the twice-weekly lessons ($5; call ahead for schedule); $4 cover.

The **Banana Café & Piano Bar** (☎ 543-5906, 500 8th St SE) is an elegant venue nestled above its namesake restaurant (enter through the side door on E St). This cozy, warmly lit gathering spot has a distinctly Caribbean flair, drawing an older gay and straight mix for its nightly offerings of live jazz. Lounge in an oversize wicker chair, sip a martini beneath the palm fronds and take in the show, or order up a late-night snack from the restaurant's tapas menu.

Just across the street, **Phase 1** (☎ 544-6831, 525 8th St SE) rocks on weekends, when the tiny dance floor is packed with a fun-loving female crowd of all ages grooving to a mix of upbeat dance tunes, with breaks for slow dancing to the likes of Marvin Gaye's 'Let's Get It On.' Head here for a round of pool or to catch a Redskins game on the big-screen TV. Male patrons may get a few curious looks, but all in all this is a fun place to hang with the locals. Open Thursday to Sunday; $5 cover on Friday and Saturday.

THE HOT SPOT

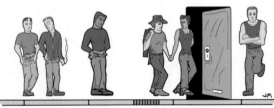

Southeast DC (Map 4)

Although the following venues are near the Navy Yard Metro station, after dark it's safer to reach them by cab.

Among DC's better-known gay African American clubs is the **Bachelor's Mill** (☎ 544-1931, 1104 8th St SE), where notoriously potent drinks and mixed house sounds draw men of all ages for dancing and the occasional talent and drag show. The Mill's best nights are Thursday and Saturday; $5 cover.

On Saturday, *The Nation* (aka 'Velvet Nation'; ☎ 554-1500, 1015 Half St SE) features a late-night gay dance party and now ranks as the hottest gay venue in town, having taken the tiara from the once-glorious Tracks (now closed). On the immense dance floor, the pumped-up and shirtless pulse in unison to the sounds of hard house, hi-energy and trance under a suspended disco ball the size of a small planet. This swanky affair attracts everyone from circuit boys and drag queens to hip dykes, club kids, and cruisers. Velvet Nation doesn't really start kicking until around 12:30 am on Saturday, and dancing goes on till 5 am. Doors open at 10 pm; $8 cover ($12 after 11 pm).

The popular male 'strip' clubs in DC – one of the few places in the US where full nudity is legal – leave little to the imagination. The male dancers make a big impression at **Wet** (☎ 488-1200, 52 L St SE), where they lather up in an open shower before cavorting on top of the bar. (Don't try the handstand-in-the-shower thing at home.) This place packs in a lively crowd on weekends and during the popular Tuesday-night 'Hot Chocolate,' when a cast of male African American dancers strut their stuff. The $7 cover ($3 before 9 pm) seems a little steep for this uninspired spot with concrete floors, but let's face it – nobody comes here for the décor.

Bar-hoppers wander freely between the adjoining **Ziegfeld's** and **Secrets** (☎ 554-5141, 1345 Half St SE), a bizarre cabaret–strip club combo. Ziegfeld's is best known for its classy drag shows, and these divas mean business – don't even think about being stingy with your dollar bills. The cabaret is a popular gathering spot for members of DC's transgender community, especially on Saturday. Other transgender favorites include Perry's, for its Sunday drag brunch (see the Adams-Morgan section of the

THE HOT SPOT

A Vocal Favorite

Had enough of the bars? For a fun alternative, check out the award-winning *Gay Men's Chorus of Washington, DC* (GMCW; ☎ 338-7464, 2801 M St NW). The chorus performs three seasonal concerts per year and appears at a variety of community events taking place at venues all over the city; you can call, or visit the GMCW Web site (www.gmcw.org) for schedule and ticket information.

Entertainment chapter), and Mr P's, for its live entertainment, particularly on Sunday (see Dupont Circle, above).

Next door at Secrets, go-go boys play on a variation of the Wet theme (some of them actually keep their g-strings on), strutting up and down a runway-like stage while patrons look on from a small, dimly lit bar and seating area. These guys are a mixed bag (some hot, some not), and at times you may wonder what the prerequisite is for being a dancer here. The cover charge, good for entry to both clubs, is $5.

Upper Northeast DC (Map 5)

Long a favored gathering spot among the black community, *Delta Elite* (☎ 529-0626, 3734 10th St NE; Ⓜ *Brookland*) attracts a mostly local crowd. Doors open at midnight, but the Delta doesn't really get going until around 1 am, when partygoers from other nightspots migrate to this popular after-hours dance club and keep it bumping till 4 am. Friday is women's night, and Saturday pulls in a mostly male crowd. Open Friday and Saturday only; $5 cover.

THE HOT SPOT

(continued from page 200)

At **Odds** (☎ 296-8644, 1160 20th St NW; ⓜ Farragut West), starting at 9 pm Thursday to Saturday, are all-you-can-drink specials ($10) that make the place pretty crazy (since many GWU students don't have Friday classes, drinking starts a night early). Desperate? Come Tuesday, when Bud pitchers cost 25¢. Odds has lots of fun memorabilia, like baseball cards and movie posters, to focus on when your head is swimming. There's a dance club here, too (hip-hop, house). Closed Sunday.

If everyone in heaven were *really* well-dressed, it might look like **Dragonfly** (☎ 331-1775, 1215 Connecticut Ave NW; ⓜ Farragut North). Everything's white here – walls, tabletops, chairs – and lit with celestial radiance in a design scheme that architectural magazines have profiled. A showy crowd sips martinis, nibbles costly sushi, and occasionally deigns to watch the kung fu and Japanese anime screened on ethereal walls. Open till 1 am daily (1:45 am Friday and Saturday).

Come back down at **Fox & Hounds** (☎ 232-6307, 1533 17th St NW), a casual, divey bar attached to Trio Restaurant. Its huge patio is the main draw, especially for scoping the boys on 17th St on summer eves. Beer's the usual potable, but something called 'Winston Whirlie's World-Famous Whimwham' is poured too.

Buffalo Billiards (☎ 331-7665, 1330 19th St), one of DC's most popular places to play pool, runs 30 pool and snooker tables that pull college kids and yuppies into this bright, below-street-level cave. Tables are kind of costly – an arcane computerized system tallies the tab, but it's usually about $12 for two people playing for an hour. The wait's generally half an hour.

Displayed at **U-topia** (☎ 483-7669, 1418 U St NW; ⓜ U St-Cardozo), northeast of Dupont Circle proper near the Shaw district, is the work of local painters: usually big, frenetic canvases, all for sale. This narrow bar – which began life as a gallery – is a relaxed place attracting an eclectic crowd of bar-crawling youngsters, gay couples, and older urban homesteaders. It has an eclectic menu, too, leaning toward Cajun (gumbo, jambalaya). Happy hour (4:30 to 7:30 pm weeknights) offers dollar-off drinks. Live blues or jazz happens Thursday and Sunday.

On first thought, Arabic *arguilehs* (hookahs) and Andean food don't seem a felicitous combination. But **Chi Cha Lounge** (☎ 234-8400, 1624 U St NW; ⓜ U St-Cardozo), also near Shaw, makes it work. Curl into its velvet settees, nibble Ecuadorian tapas, and order a pipeful of Bahrainian fruit-and-honey-cured tobacco and a *chicha* (a fruity South American concoction guaranteed to knock you on your bottom). Ah, East and West *do* combine beautifully. Open till 1:30 am nightly (2:30 am Friday and Saturday). Hookahs are available Sunday to Tuesday.

Nearby **Stetson's** (☎ 667-6295, 1610 U St NW; ⓜ U St-Cardozo) has been around for 20 years and is the place to grab a brew and nosh for little cash. Amid the endearingly tacky decor (piñatas and neon), you can get $1.50 drafts, $5.50 pitchers, and pizza and chili. Thursday, come for $3.50 pitchers of Rolling Rock. There's an outdoor patio and two beat-up pool tables, too. The crowd's largely liberal yups who live near Dupont Circle. Open till 1 am daily.

Dance Clubs The place in DC where you're most likely to see an Icelandic beauty tangoing with a suave Pakistani subconsul, **MCCXXIII** (☎ 822-1800, 1223 Connecticut Ave NW; ⓜ Farragut North) heads a duo of clubs for DC's *internationalistas*, many of them Embassy Row staffers (and people hitting on them). In this beautifully designed club – the name is the street address, in Roman numerals – DJs come on at 11 to play worldbeat and techno, and patrons sip martinis before shimmying onto the dance floor. There's no cover charge. Nearby is **18th Street Lounge** (☎ 466-3922, 1212 18th St NW), at Thomas Jefferson Place, which proclaims its exclusivity by having no sign on its door (look for the street number). In a beautiful mansion that once housed Teddy Roosevelt, its sleek dance floors are ruled by trip-hop and dub. Cover charges vary with the night; closed Sunday. Both clubs are

ENTERTAINMENT

JOHN NEUBAUER

Cheap entertainment

famed for snobbish bouncers who leave less attractive patrons waiting in the cold. Via scrupulous field research, we've discovered that wearing teeny skirts helps.

Sesto Senso *(☎ 785-9525, 1214 18th St NW)* is a restaurant and club for people longing for Capri: comely Europeans and Middle Easterners, the boys in tight hip-hugging pants, the girls working little cellphones. Thursday to Saturday nights, the tanned beauties dance to a nonstop funk and techno mix amid swank decor. The same folks also drift into ***Rumors*** *(☎ 466-7378, 1900 M St NW;* Ⓜ *Farragut North),* along with yuppies and students. It's a renowned meat market, but its look is strictly Adirondacks – it's done up as a boathouse, complete with boat. A DJ plays dance music Tuesday to Sunday. There's a $2 cover charge on weekends.

Lulu's Club Mardi Gras *(☎ 861-5858;* Ⓜ *Foggy Bottom),* at 22nd and M Sts NW, tricked out in lacy N'awlins decor, is party central: eight rooms, two dance floors, seven bars, 26 TVs, and plenty of cheap booze ($3 drafts) to lubricate the shimmy of the mating-dance crowds. On weekends you get house and industrial on the downstairs floor, '70s and '80s retro upstairs. Lines start early here, and the patrons seem barely pubescent. The cover is $5; open till 3 am nightly.

If Latin dancing is your thing, go to ***Diversité*** *(☎ 234-5740, 1526 14th St NW),* on the edge of Shaw, where the music menu is like something planned by Simón Bolívar: salsa, merengue, Cuban jazz, tango, even Honduran *punta.* There are DJs and live acts, too, and you can take tango lessons on Monday evening. The cover is usually $10. Open till 11:30 pm Monday to Thursday, 4 am Friday and Saturday, 2 am Sunday. It's best to drive or take a cab here.

Live Music *The Garage (☎ 331-7123, 1214-B 18th St NW)* is a loud rock club with a good calendar of local talent. True to its name, it has an auto-shop motif: car parts on the wall and a garage door that clatters down over the stage. There's also a rooftop terrace and great sound system. Some shows are 18 and over – Thursday's 'Soul Camp' (hip-hop dance party) draws many teens.

Metro Cafe *(☎ 518-9109, 1522 14th St NW),* on the edge of Shaw, is a venue booking on-the-rise bands. With only 175 seats, it has an intimate (and smoky) ambience, and acts here play everything from country to punk. The cover is generally about $10, and shows are open to all ages. Nearby, ***New Vegas Lounge*** *(☎ 483-3971, 1415 P St NW)* is a Chicago-style blues club that has hosted greats like Wilson Pickett. It's crappy-looking on the outside and little better inside, with its plywood paneling and shaky tables, but the music's great. Friday and Saturday, the Out of Town Blues Band plays. Tuesday is an open-mike jam (bring your guitar, but note that most performers are very polished). On Thursday, enter free with a college ID. The cover charge is $8 or so. Closed Sunday and Monday.

Adams-Morgan (Map 9)

DC's most crowded club district surrounds the intersection of 18th St NW and Columbia Rd, where the dance clubs, dives, pool halls, and pubs are packed so closely that bar-crawling is a literal possibility. The scene is delightful: black, white, brown, straight, gay, in-between; friendlier than downtown's clubgoers; and more grown-up than Georgetown's barhoppers. Adams-Morgan is also beloved for its plethora of rooftop bars, a heaven-sent gift in summertime DC.

There's no direct Metro access here, unfortunately. You can get off at the Woodley Park-Zoo station and walk a few blocks or take a cab. Alternately, there's 'The Link' Metrobus (see Getting Around). The few paid parking lots max out early in the evening.

Bars A good place to start the stagger up 18th St is *Millie & Al's Bar* (☎ 387-8131, 2440 18th St NW), a comfortably worn dive with Monday dollar drafts and a constant stream of sports events on two TVs. The young, jock-ish crowd piles in for happy hour (4 to 7 pm Tuesday to Sunday), decent pizza, and Jell-O shots.

Asylum (☎ 319-9353, 2471 18th St NW) lures a very young slacker clientele into its dungeon-decorated downstairs confines. It's easy to miss – look for the rusted car-parts sculpture at its entrance. Shiner beers (there's a reason you've never heard of it) cost 25¢ at 6 pm Saturday, and the price increases 50¢ per hour thereafter. It has a little pool table and, for those in need of morning-after resuscitation, 'Liquid Brunch' at noon Sunday, with half-price Bloodies.

Kokopooli's (☎ 234-2306, 2305 18th St NW) is, as its name suggests, a pool bar (the name also refers to the Indian character painted on the entrance). It's got eight tables ($10 per hour); it's friendly; and the interesting paint job continues inside, including a mural of an octopus that looks ready to rack up with the patrons.

Want more pool? *Angles Bar & Billiards* (☎ 462-8100, 2339 18th St NW), over Fountain Café, has two tables (which seem in constant use) and Wednesday tournies. If you aren't good with a stick, 40 varieties of Scotch will keep your hands busy. The bar opens at 6 pm nightly, and the crowd's fratty. *Brass Monkey Bar & Billiards* (☎ 667-7800, 2317 18th St NW) has one of Adams-Morgan's best rooftop bars, a big patio overlooking 18th St. It offers cheapie specials (like $2 rail drinks) all week, and the patrons are young and arrive in big groups. The Monkey's over the Spaghetti Garden, in case you're hungry. Open till 2 am nightly.

King of the rooftop deck scene is *Perry's* (☎ 234-6218, 1811 Columbia Rd), a sushi-Southwestern-restaurant-bar whose top terrace, lit by twinkling lights and cooled by a fountain, offers a great view. You can't sit at the rooftop tables without a $15 minimum food purchase – you'll have to sit at the bar – so arrive hungry. The best time to come is Sunday, drag brunch day, when fabulous queens sashay around schmoozing and singing to the patrons. Open till 11:30 pm Monday to Thursday, 12:30 am Friday and Saturday, and 11 am to 3 pm Sunday.

If you just want a drink without attitude, try *Dan's Bar* (☎ 265-5241, 2315 18th St NW), a quintessential dive as plain as its name. This place focuses on beer – mostly domestic brews – and if you want to stare into your glass and mumble, that goes over just fine at ultra-relaxed Dan's. Open 7:30 pm to 3 am Wednesday to Saturday.

Little *Pharmacy Bar* (☎ 483-1200, 2337 18th St NW) sits in what used to be a drugstore. In remembrance, pills are embedded in the tabletops and old medicine jars decorate the walls of this cool, calming place, which young clubhoppers like for a quiet nightcap after dancing. There's a small café menu too. Open 5 pm till last call nightly.

The best coffeehouse in DC is nearby: *Tryst* (☎ 232-5500, 2459 18th St NW), a big Greenwich Village – style place with couches, armchairs, and bookshelves scattered about, lots of light flooding through streetside windows, and patrons so faithful they practically seem to pay rent. Liquor, beer, and wine flow along with caffeine, and there's a menu of waffles, muffins, and cake. It's a great place to meet people; everyone in the neighborhood, from old folks to toddlers, comes here eventually.

Slackers seeking their own off-the-beaten track bar head north of Adams-Morgan, scorning the yuppies in favor of Mount Pleasant. They roost at *Raven Grill* (☎ 387-9274, 3145 Mt Pleasant St; Ⓜ Columbia Heights), a beat-down dive that's been around practically forever – it got its liquor license back when Prohibition ended.

ENTERTAINMENT

Dance Clubs Chic, glittering *Cities* (☎ 328-7194, 2424 18th St NW) used to change its decor twice annually to mimic an international capital (Paris, Rome, etc); thus its name. It has settled on a fixed identity now: downstairs is an elegant bar and restaurant, and upstairs is the Privé dance club. Privé isn't particularly interesting, and you need reservations – so stay downstairs, order a Mediterranean appetizer and an aperitif ($5) and watch the en-vogue European and American patrons cruise one another. Open till 11 pm daily (2 am Friday and Saturday).

Felix (☎ 483-3549, 2406 18th St NW) is a somewhat self-conscious joint whose swinger mood and martini bar appeal to the yuppie and Euro crowd bored with Cities. Its three floors offer things like a restaurant, Wednesday Sinatra nights, nonstop 007 films, and a lounge pit in which to pose. The first two floors are dedicated to dancing, cigar-smoking, and sampling Bordeaux and gins, but the 3rd floor, where you can relax in a big settees and listen to live blues or jazz, is the nicest. Felix is a pretty good pick-up scene around 9 pm on weekends: you'll meet 30-ish professionals who've come from the suburbs in search of someone to debauch, or at least dance with. The cover charge is $5; open till 2:30 am Wednesday to Sunday.

Adams-Morgan is known for East African establishments, but *Bukom Café* (☎ 265-4600, 2442 18th St NW) taps the other side of the continent, drawing a stylishly dressed crowd of West Africans and black Americans to share its excellent cuisine and sexy late-night club scene, where bands play African and Caribbean music: reggae, highlife, funky jazz. There's hardly any room to dance, so everyone kind of stands in place, bounces to the music, and rubs against their neighbors. Open daily; live music starts at 9 pm weekdays, 10 pm Friday and Saturday. There's no cover!

A manic club for the barely-legal set, *Crush* (☎ 319-1111, 2323 18th St NW) is easily spotted: look for the lines. Some of DC's most-popular DJs work the long, narrow dance floor upstairs with a mix of funk, disco, and hip-hop. Patrons are generally under 25, and you can dance (but not drink) if you're 18. Beer is $1 on Thirsty Thursdays. Open till 2 am Wednesday and Thursday; dance till 3 am Friday and Saturday, with $2 rail drinks to help you out. Dress lightly, even in winter: the frenetic floor is a sauna.

Club Heaven and *Hell* (☎ 667-4355), both at 2327 18th St NW, also draw DC's youthful boogiers. Upstairs Heaven has three bars and painted cherubs on its walls. Its big draw is Thursday '80s night (moosh your hair up into a Howard Jones), but it has techno and house DJs most nights. Hell is the darker downstairs pub, and wee devils poke pitchforks at you from its walls. Here you can play pool and dress rumpled. You'll need neater clothes and $5 cover to get past the gatekeeper (St Peter?) at Heaven. Hell's open daily; Heaven's closed Sunday and Monday.

Elegant *Blue Room* (☎ 332-0800, 2321 18th St NW) has three floors – restaurant, dance floor, and lounge – and cool-blue artwork on its walls. The dance floor has a techno-oriented DJ, and the 3rd-floor bar is small, intimate, and open only Friday and Saturday. It has upscale clientele, and, for the neighborhood, relatively expensive drinks. *Tom Tom* (☎ 588-1300, 2333 18th St NW) is a chic bar and restaurant serving yummy brick-oven pizzas and wines to a professional crowd. Downstairs is a small bar; upstairs is a roomy roof terrace, a pool table, and another bar. Dance music is spun by DJs Thursday to Saturday.

Chief Ike's Mambo Room (☎ 332-2211, 1725 Columbia Rd NW) also attracts professionals. But ain't nobody getting dressed up here. The decor is Day of the Dead meets *Night of the Living Dead*, with blinking lights, monster comics laminated onto the tables, and voodoo critters on the walls. You can dance weekends and drink all week. Upstairs are two 'subclubs': Chaos, which plays punk, and Cosmo Lounge, with hip-hop DJs, plus live figure-drawing sessions ($7) 7:30 to 10 pm Tuesday and Wednesday. The comedy troupe Gross National Product performs at Ike's. Former Clinton advisor George Stephanopoulos used to hang here, which gave it 15 minutes of fame; now Ike's is less crowded and more fun. The weekend cover is $3 downstairs, $7 upstairs. Open till 2 am nightly.

Just next door is ***Latin Jazz Alley*** (☎ *238-6190, 1721 Columbia Rd NW*), above El Migueleño restaurant, a tiny place with mirrored walls open Wednesday to Saturday only. It's a club-slash-dance school: lessons are 7:30 to 9:30 pm and cost $5. Mambo's taught Thursday, salsa on the other nights. The crowd is young and mostly white. Once they've learned their steps, they go to ***Habana Village*** (☎ *462-6310, 1834 Columbia Rd NW*). DC's best Latin club. This old townhouse has a cosmopolitan bar and romantic back room where you can sip a mojito and nibble tapas in front of the fireplace. But after 10:30 pm the scene on the upstairs dance floor explodes as DJs and live bands play salsa, merengue, mambo, tango, and bossa nova to a mixed Latin and white crowd. Men (usually 30 to 50) pay a $5 cover. Women (significantly younger) enter free. You can learn to salsa here 7:30 to 9:30 pm Wednesday and 7 to 9 pm Thursday ($10). Closed Sunday to Tuesday.

Live Music Some of Adams-Morgan's most serious fun happens at the anagrammatic ***Madam's Organ*** (☎ *667-5370, 2461 18th St NW*). It's easy to find this blues and jazz club – look for the wall mural of the bodacious red-haired mama with the club's name painted across her overflowing decolletage. Inside it's more funky decor, with stuffed animals, bizarre paintings, and, upstairs, Daddy's Love Lounge & Pickup Joint (actually dedicated to pool-playing) and a deck. Redheaded women – natural or dyed – get half-price Rolling Rocks. Wednesday there's a fine bluegrass jam with much whoopin' and stompin'. Who says DC's got no soul? Open till 2:30 am daily.

Live blues and jazz are on the menu nightly at ***Columbia Station*** (☎ *462-6040, 2325 18th St NW*). Down-home local acts play here to a casual crowd noshing pizza and burgers, and streetside windows roll back to cool off the room. Open practically till dawn Friday and Saturday, and till 1:30 am other nights.

RICK GERHARTER

Shaw & the New U District (Map 10)

Years ago this district was 'Black Broadway,' the heart of DC's black music and theater scene, but the '68 riots put the kibosh on that. In the '90s, encouraged by cheap rents and easy subway access in this rough part of DC, entrepreneurs began snapping up unused spaces to house new-music clubs and funky bars. Now the area is emerging from the riots' ashes, and it has become DC's best place to hear home-grown musical talent, catch poetry slams, and meet locals ranging from angry white street punks to upscale black professionals.

U St-Cardozo or Shaw-Howard University Metro stations are near all places listed here. Also see Getting Around for details on 'The Link,' the Metrobus running between Adams-Morgan and U St each quarter-hour.

See the Dupont Circle section, earlier, for bars and clubs on 14th St and western U St.

Bars U St has several friendly, no-attitude bars that locals often use as rendezvous points before and after a night of music. A fine place to launch an evening, ***Polly's Cafe*** (☎ *265-8385, 1342 U St NW;* Ⓜ *U St-Cardozo*) is a basement-level, brick-walled café/bar that was a New U pioneer (it's been around for about a decade). It has a fireplace for raw weather and a patio for fair, plus reasonably priced pints and a menu of basic eats like salads and burgers. Pitchers of Rolling Rock go for $8.

Wind up the night at *King Pin* (☎ 588-5880, 917 U St NW; Ⓜ U St-Cardozo), a late-night slacker bar drawing spillover from Velvet Lounge and 9:30 Club (see Live Music, below). This small upstairs joint opens around 8 pm nightly and fills up after midnight; it's a friendly, low-key place to drink a last beer while your eardrums recover from a loud show.

Dance Clubs Techno and hip-hop rule *2:K:9* (☎ 667-7750, 2009 8th St NW; Ⓜ Shaw-Howard University), in a sleekly converted warehouse near the Howard campus. The club promotes itself as multicultural, and the under-30 crowd indeed seems equally drawn from white and black neighborhoods. Go-go dancers gyrate in cages elevated above the downstairs dance floor, which has a super-loud sound system. There's a $12 cover charge. Open till 2 am Thursday to Saturday.

Another hip club, particularly among upscale black couples, is *Republic Gardens* (☎ 232-2710, 1355 U St NW; Ⓜ U St-Cardozo), the reincarnation of a 1940s nightclub that stood on the same spot (Pearl Bailey waitressed here). Its five rooms and four bars are done up in lovely Renaissance-style furnishings, and hip-hop, dancehall, and R&B spin from the upstairs DJ booth. A raging pick-up scene goes on among the dressed-up patrons – if you don't feel like flirting, Republic's not for you. Downstairs, should you need fortification, its restaurant serves spicy Caribbean fare. The cover is $5 to $10, depending on the night.

With its lengthy vodka list, Russian food, and amusing Soviet-chic decoration – murals of Lenin and Rasputin glower from the walls and doors – *State of the Union* (☎ 588-8926, 1357 U St NW; Ⓜ U St-Cardozo) certainly isn't your average house and acid-jazz club. But that's what it is: live bands play here Monday, Thursday, and Saturday,

and other nights DJs spin house and hip-hop for one of DC's most ethnically diverse dance floors. The cover is $6 to $9. It's open every day of the year, should you want to dance on Christmas Day.

Bar Nun (☎ 667-6680, 1326 U St NW; Ⓜ U St-Cardozo) is a two-floor club that's been around a couple of years but hasn't hit its stride yet; it's kinda empty some nights. Like many clubs in the New U, it's got a scrambler of a calendar: Monday is open-mike poetry and performance art; Thursday is hip-hop; Friday is live jazz; Saturday a DJ spins dance music. Toothsome Ethiopian cuisine is served downstairs. Open till 2 am nightly (4 am Friday and Saturday).

Live Music The *9:30 Club* (☎ 265-0930, 815 V St NW; Ⓜ U St-Cardozo) has long been DC's premier live rock venue. In '96 it moved from its old, small downtown digs to its spankin' new home, which can fit 1200 patrons and has two levels and four bars. (If you've been in DC awhile, you'll recognize the basement bar, salvaged from 9:30's old home.) The calendar is thick with big names, from Yo La Tengo to Sonic Youth to Reverend Horton Heat to DC-raised wideneck Henry Rollins. Shows are standing-room-only on the main floor, but you can sit downstairs or in the 'Planet Lounge,' with its night-sky decor. The concert line (☎ 393-0930) gives you show dates and costs.

Black Cat (☎ 667-7960, 1831 14th St NW; Ⓜ U St-Cardozo), co-owned by Foo Fighter Dave Grohl, is current head kitty of DC's indie-rock clubs. Set in a beat-up old warehouse, it draws fans of grunge and industrial rock, mostly under 30, to listen to the likes of Girls Against Boys, the Zimmermans, and Jimmie's Chicken Shack. The club also supports a fine calendar of poetry and fiction readings. The cover charge varies with the band, but there's no cover in the Red Room bar where the beer – 12 on tap – is cheap and the kids are done up in urban street-rat gear (even if they're visiting from the 'burbs). Shows are open to all ages.

DC bands on their way up play *Velvet Lounge* (☎ 462-3213, 915 U St NW; Ⓜ U St-Cardozo), a tiny club with a big dedication to local talent. Emerging acts such as Glenmont Popes, Vanity Champ, Clare Quilty, et al, who can't draw a 9:30-size crowd play to grunge-music fans in the Velvet's upstairs hall; downstairs is a dark little pit of a bar. The cover is usually no more than $5. Occasional private events (featuring free beer and drinks) are held to 'road test' new bands – to attend, email freebeerdc@aol.com. Velvet issues great compilation CDs of the acts it books. Look for them, especially *(Lights Out Let's Go!)*, in local stores. Open nightly till 2 am (3 am Friday and Saturday).

The legendary jazz club **Bohemian Caverns** – where Miles Davis, John Coltrane, Ella Fitzgerald, and Duke Ellington once played – was, as of 2000, planning to reopen on U St. Felled by the 1968 riots, it's being upgraded with a pink granite bar and lots of stalactites and cave decor. Watch for listings.

Upper Northwest DC (Map 11)

Don't neglect far upper DC in your bar and club crawls – several worthy venues await you up here. **The Deck** *(☎ 337-9700, 2505 Wisconsin Ave NW)*, in the Savoy Suites, is a beautiful-people hangout and tiki bar where an outdoor barbecue fumes Thursday to Saturday evenings, serving burgers and chicken to offset the alcohol streaming from the palm-covered bar. The crowd is young, straight, white, and checking one another out.

In Cleveland Park is the large **Ireland's Four Provinces** *(☎ 244-0860, 3412 Connecticut Ave NW; ◍ Cleveland Park)*, a landmark Irish bar with live Celtic and folk music, 21 beers on tap, relentless emerald-shamrock decor, and a great, friendly scene of late-20s neighborhood professionals cruising and schmoozing. Come on a hot summer night to sit on the streetside patio, or during weekday happy hour for a $4 20oz Guinness. Watching the Four Ps' shenanigans from across the street is smaller **Nanny O'Brien's** *(☎ 686-9189, 3319 Connecticut Ave NW; ◍ Cleveland Park)*, which styles itself an 'authentic' Irish bar, and lives up to that billing – you'll hear more genuine brogues here than almost any other DC bar.

There's live Celtic music most nights, and an excellent Irish jam session on Monday.

There's a pronounced fascination with the 1950s in the mood of Cleveland Park's other bars. Exhibit A: **The Aroma Company Tobacco Shop & Lounge** *(☎ 244-7995, 3417 Connecticut Ave NW; ◍ Cleveland Park)*, a sleek retro club filled with those strange kidney-shaped '50s coffee tables and old sofas; the tiled bar serves up the Scotch and ciggies. Live jazz plays here Friday eve. A $3 cover is charged Thursday to Saturday. Up the way, **Atomic Billiards** *(☎ 363-7665, 3427 Connecticut Ave NW; ◍ Cleveland Park)* is a cozy downstairs pool hall with Jetsons-style lounge furniture, murals of spaceships, and beers costing about $5. Tables cost $8 per hour, and there are Monday-night tournies. It also has dozens of board games. Open till midnight nightly (2 am Friday and Saturday).

When you just can't take any more cuddly animals, ditch the kids at the National Zoo and head across the street to **Zoo Bar** *(☎ 232-4225, 3000 Connecticut Ave NW)*, also called the Oxford Tavern, a cozy neighborhood beer-drinkin' dive with live music Friday and Saturday and happy hour from 3 to 7 pm. There's a wee patio, too.

KENNEDY CENTER (MAP 3)

DC's main cultural jewel, the Kennedy Center *(☎ 467-4600, 800-444-1324, www.kennedy-center.org, 2700 F St NW; ◍ Foggy Bottom)*, is given most of the credit for transforming DC from a cultural backwater to an artistic contender in the late 20th century. The stately white-marble building overlooking the Potomac holds two big theaters, a theater lab (where new or experimental theater is staged), cinema, opera house, and concert hall (and the fine Roof Terrace Restaurant to boot; see Places to Eat). It's home to the National Symphony, National Opera, and Washington Ballet (see below). National theater companies perform here, too. Film festivals and cultural events are frequent highlights. About 3000 performances are held here annually.

Orchestra seats for theater cost about $60; $140 for opera; $40 for concerts. Inquire about half-price tickets, sometimes

ENTERTAINMENT

RICK GERHARTER

Kennedy Center

available on performance day. You can order tickets by phone (☎ 467-4600) and collect them at the will-call window.

Millennium Stage, a series of daily free music and dance performances, runs annually, usually starting in spring. It's a perfect opportunity to see first-class performances for *nada*. Shows start at 6 pm; check the Web site for a schedule. Some performances are also held at noon on the Capitol grounds.

A free shuttle bus runs between Foggy Bottom Metro station and the center every 15 minutes from 9:45 am to midnight Monday to Saturday and noon to 8 pm Sunday. There's parking at the center, but it's pricey and fills up fast.

THEATER

DC theater – to make a gross overgeneralization – can be divided into three camps. First, there's the Kennedy Center, presenting famed companies and productions; then there's a second string of big theaters, which often host Broadway national runs; and a third group of adventurous small stages, presenting cutting-edge works whose quality ranges from fabulous to sophomoric.

Among the big boys is the *National Theatre (Map 3;* ☎ *800-447-7400, 1321 Pennsylvania Ave NW;* Ⓜ *Federal Triangle).* Established in 1835 and renovated in 1984, it's Washington's oldest continually operating theater. This is where you'd catch *Les Misérables* and *Rent.* Its neighbor, the *Warner Theatre (Map 3;* ☎ *783-4000, 1299 Pennsylvania Ave NW;* Ⓜ *Federal Triangle),* also hosts national runs of Broadway musi-

cals. It's a beautifully restored 1924 Art Deco theater that stages headliner concerts, comedians, and shows like *Riverdance.* Tickets cost $25 to $55.

Nearby, *Ford's Theatre (Map 3;* ☎ *347-4833, 511 10th St NW;* Ⓜ *Gallery Place),* where John Wilkes Booth killed Abraham Lincoln, mostly stages works about American history, such as *Elmer Gantry* and musicals on Lincoln's life and times. Tickets cost $25 to $40.

For something edgier, there's the landmark regional theater *Arena Stage (Map 6;* ☎ *488-3300, 1101 6th St SW;* Ⓜ *Waterfront),* near the Washington Channel at Maine Ave SW. Actually three theaters, including a theater-in-the-round, it stages both classic and experimental works. It was DC's first racially integrated theater, and it's continued that progressive tradition through performances addressing African American history. It also does favorites such as *Our Town* and *The Miracle Worker.* Tickets cost $30 to $50 or more.

DC boasts two excellent Shakespeare theaters. The *Folger Shakespeare Theater (Map 4;* ☎ *544-7077, 210 E Capitol St SE;* Ⓜ *Capitol South),* a magnificent Globe-style theater attached to the Folger Shakespeare Library, stages classic and modern interpretations of the Bard's plays. Tickets cost $20 to $40. On 7th St NW's Gallery Row, the *Shakespeare Theatre (Map 3;* ☎ *547-1122, 450 7th St NW;* Ⓜ *Archives),* under artistic director Michael Kahn, has been called 'one of the world's three great Shakespearean theaters' by *The Economist,* and its home company stages a half-dozen works annually plus a free summer Shakespeare series in Rock Creek Park. Tickets for events at the theater cost $10 to $45.

The new-theater scene bubbles and boils east of Dupont Circle on 14th St NW between P and Q Sts. Here you'll find smaller repertory companies, alternative theater, and cheaper seats. Check listings for *Woolly Mammoth Theatre Co (Map 8;* ☎ *393-3939, 1401 Church St NW),* off 14th St; *Source Theatre Company (Map 10;* ☎ *462-1073, 1835 14th St NW;* Ⓜ *U St-Cardozo);* ***Church Street Theatre*** *(*☎ *265-3748; 1742 Church St*

NW; **○** *Dupont Circle)*, home to the Stanislavsky Theatre Studio; and **Studio Theatre** *(☎ 332-3300, 1333 P St NW)*. As of 2000, Woolly Mammoth was considering a move, so call ahead.

Over in Adams-Morgan is the art gallery/performance space **DC AC** *(Map 9; ☎ 462-7833, 2438 18th St NW; **○** Woodley Park-Zoo)*, where some performances are free; others cost around $10. It's a venue for all kinds of adventurous stuff written by young local playwrights. Recent sample: *Baked Baby*, a satire of yuppie life.

Other worthy venues to consider include the following:

Lincoln Theatre *(Map 10; ☎ 328-9177, 1215 U St NW; **○** U St-Cardozo)* – the center of the 1930s 'Black Broadway'; recently renovated to host music and theater.

Discovery Theatre *(☎ 357-1500; **○** Smithsonian)*, in the Smithsonian Arts & Industries Building (Map 3) – stages delightful productions, such as puppet shows, for kids.

Gala Hispanic Theatre *(☎ 234-7174, 1625 Park Rd NW; **○** Columbia Heights)* – has staged four major Spanish-language productions annually for a quarter-century.

Capitol Hill Arts Workshop *(☎ 547-6839, 545 7th St SE; **○** Eastern Market)* – small community theater staging theater, cinema, and musical events.

Theater J *(☎ 518-9400, 1529 16th St NW; **○** Dupont Circle)*, at the DC Jewish Community Center – stages plays addressing urban American Jewish experience, like Josh Kornbluth's *Red Diaper Baby*.

CINEMA

DC doesn't have many interesting movie houses, but the museums – both the Smithsonian and smaller museums – offer great cinema calendars, with many free or low-cost screenings of overseas works, classics, documentaries, and mega-screen IMAX crowd-pleasers (some even have popcorn!). Get calendars at museum information desks. Also check out the Library of Congress' offerings.

The Kennedy Center (see above) has a 250-seat theater that screens classics and hosts many premieres and film festivals

under the auspices of the **American Film Institute**. As of 2000, AFI was considering moving to Silver Spring, Maryland, so call the Center to check what's on in the cinema during your visit.

Among commercial houses, the Cineplex Odeon chain operates several cinemas that show a mixture of popular and art-house movies. (Call 333-FILM for information on any of them.) The queen of the chain is the **Uptown** *(Map 11; 3426 Connecticut Ave NW; **○** Cleveland Park)*, in Cleveland Park, an old movie palace with a balcony and big screen. There's also the **Foundry** *(Map 7; 1055 Thomas Jefferson St NW; **○** Foggy Bottom)*, near M St in Georgetown; the **Janus** *(Map 8; 1660 Connecticut Ave NW; **○** Dupont Circle)*, in Dupont Circle; and the **Outer Circle** *(Map 11; 4849 Wisconsin Ave NW; **○** Tenleytown-AU)*.

Fancy leather seats and liquor with your flick? Head up Wisconsin Ave NW to General Cinema's **Club Cinema**, atop Mazza Gallerie mall *(Map 11; **○** Friendship Heights)*. It'll cost you, though: $12 for the film, plus more for drinks.

A convenient chain gigaplex theater is downstairs in Union Station (Map 4), off the food court. It plays primarily action flicks and teen-friendly movies and thus pulls crowds of kids, so stay away if you're allergic to baggy jeans.

CLASSICAL MUSIC & OPERA

The National Symphony Orchestra, directed by Leonard Slatkin, and the Washington Chamber Symphony perform at the Kennedy Center. The symphony also holds summertime concerts at **Wolf Trap Farm Park** *(☎ 703-255-1860)*, a performing-arts center that's a 40-minute drive away in Vienna, Virginia (see Excursions).

In town, other classical performances take place at acoustically monumental venues such as the **National Gallery of Art**, **National Building Museum**, **Corcoran Gallery**, and **Library of Congress**, as well as at local universities and churches. A major university venue is **Lisner Auditorium** *(☎ 994-1500; **○** Foggy Bottom)*, on the GWU campus at 21st and H Sts NW.

ENTERTAINMENT

The Washington Opera (☎ 295-2400, 800-876-7372) is an emerging jewel. Famed tenor Placido Domingo became its conductor in 1996. The opera performs grand classics such as *Otello* and *Tosca* at the Kennedy Center, which has been its home for more than 25 years. Tickets are costly.

DANCE

Washington's premier dance venue is the Kennedy Center (see above), home of the *Washington Ballet*. The company hasn't been known for groundbreaking productions, although its reputation is changing as it explores the work of younger choreographers. The Center also hosts fine visiting groups: Merce Cunningham, Alvin Ailey, etc.

Although hidden in an obscure neighborhood, *Dance Place (Map 5;* ☎ *269-1600, 3225 8th St NE;* Ⓜ *Brookland)* is the only truly cutting-edge dance space in the capital. Run by five resident modern-dance companies offering a year-round calendar of new work, it also hosts the work of top-notch national companies such as the Joe Goode Performance Group. Tickets are usually around $15.

SPECTATOR SPORTS
Football

The *Redskins* are a populist religion in DC: whether they're winning or losing, 'Skins games empty the city, drawing streams of people into sports bars and living rooms to cheer the punting and the grunting. They play at Jack Kent Cook Stadium in Maryland. Tickets are impossible, unless you can schmooze your way up to a Congressman or local celebrity: the waiting list is thousands of names long. Absent friends in high places, check the *Post* classified ads for ticket resales (be prepared to pay through the nose), or go to Georgetown's Champions bar (see above) and watch the game from the comfort of a barstool.

Basketball

Michael Jordan recently became part owner of the *Washington Wizards*, lending a new aura of glamour and hope to a hapless team previously most noted for its cheerleaders' endearingly arrhythmic routines. His Airness hasn't alchemized them into a killer team, but they're still fun to watch at the MCI Center (Map 3; Ⓜ Gallery Place). The new women's team, the *Washington Mystics,* also play here. Buy tickets for both teams at the Center (☎ 628-3200) or charge by phone through Ticketmaster (☎ 432-7328); they range from $9.50 to $42.50. Games start around 7 pm.

Prefer college ball? The *Georgetown Hoyas* also play at the MCI Center, and tickets are pretty cheap. The University of Maryland *Terrapins* (☎ 800-462-8377) play at the Cole Field House out in College Park, Maryland; this fierce team's tickets go fast.

Other Sports

National Major League soccer champions *DC United*, a relatively new team, play at RFK Stadium (Map 4; Ⓜ Stadium-Armory). Call ☎ 703-478-6600 for game information; tickets can be charged at 202-432-7328. Costs are quite reasonable: $10 to $22.

DC's National Hockey League team, the *Capitols*, take the ice at MCI Center (see above). Tickets range from $19 to $60.

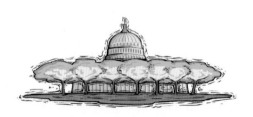

Shopping

The US capital is no shopping mecca – you won't find scads of unique Manhattan-style boutiques or hyper-funky secondhand shops here. Yet DC does excel in a few areas. Those with a taste for kitsch love the place – from rubber Nixon masks to FBI ballcaps to offbeat Americana (stars-and-stripes underpants, anyone?), DC shops sell the ultimate in tacky memorabilia. Less giddy shoppers, on the other hand, appreciate the plethora of museum stores, which offer truly unique books, jewelry, crafts, art, and souvenirs from across the US and around the world. And there are the classic souvenirs, too: stuffed pandas from the National Zoo, shredded money from the Bureau of Printing & Engraving, balsawood airplanes from the National Museum of Air & Space.

The main shopping neighborhoods are Georgetown and Adams-Morgan, both flooded with locals and suburbanites on weekends. Prices are comparable to those in most big US cities. Generally, stores are open 10 to 5 weekdays and Saturdays; some close on Sunday, but many are open noon to 5 pm. Sales tax is 5.75% in the District, 4.5% in Virginia, and 5% in Maryland.

Kid-oriented stores – including toy shops – are discussed in the Washington, DC for Kids section, earlier. See the Places to Eat chapter for information on farmers' markets.

WHERE TO SHOP

The **National Mall** (Map 3) is as much a shopping destination as a sightseeing one. All the museums here – even the US Holocaust Memorial Museum – operate gift and souvenir shops. (Highlights of these stores are discussed below, under Museum Stuff.) Federal agencies on the Mall's fringes also have shops, which sell publications and souvenirs related to their functions (like the hot bestseller *Getting to Know Soil* offered by the US Department of Agriculture store). Don't miss the vendor carts that set up on

the Mall's fringes along Constitution and Independence Aves, especially if you are looking for souvenirs: T-shirts with rude political jokes, Redskins hats, oversize Mylar balloons, funny sunglasses – these guys have got it all.

Downtown DC (Map 3) is a neighborhood in transition: stores and galleries are gradually returning to the area after many stagnant years. On 7th and 8th Sts NW are several art galleries, booksellers, and boutiques; a bit north, the MCI Center contains a cluster of shops, including the MCI Destination Store. Clustered around the Metro Center station are many chain stores, such as Banana Republic. Here, too, is Hecht's (☎ 628-6661), 1201 G St NW; it's roughly equivalent to New York's Macy's, a big department store selling a full range of mid-priced clothing, cosmetics, shoes, and housewares. Open daily.

In the National Press Building are the **Shops at National Place** (Map 3; ☎ 662-1250; Ⓜ Metro Center), 14th and F Sts NW, with a handful of (uninteresting) boutiques and an OK food court. It's a good place to rest your dogs, if nothing else. Better is the **Old Post Office Pavilion** (Map 3; ☎ 289-4224; Ⓜ Federal Triangle), with an extensive, tourist-crowded food court, souvenir shops, newsstands and sundries stores, and a gorgeous central atrium. If you're in the market for truly upscale shopping, go to the **Watergate** complex on the riverside in Foggy Bottom (Map 3), which has many couture boutiques.

South of the Mall is **L'Enfant Plaza** (Map 6), a subterranean shopping mall and food court that caters to Federal Rectangle work-a-day bureaucrats. This is a good place to stop for cheap film, newspapers, and snacks; it also has a few basic clothing stores.

East of the Mall, Capitol Hill has two major shopping destinations. **Union Station** (Map 4; ☎ 371-9441), 50 Massachusetts Ave NE, was restored in the 1980s to its former Beaux-Arts splendor. Now you'll find it sports a multiscreen cinema, an extensive food court with everything from sushi to barbecue, a dozen restaurants, and a variety of stores that include chains like Victoria's Secret and the Body Shop, and boutiques that sell toys, jewelry, and DC souvenirs. The National Zoo Store is here; so too is a B Dalton, the Great Train Store (selling train memorabilia and toys), and the Best of DC souvenir shop. Two-hour validated parking is available for shoppers.

Eastern Market (Map 4), on the Hill at 7th and C Sts SE, is DC's last historic public market. Its South Hall is open daily except Monday and has food and produce counters; its North Hall hosts local artists and craftspeople, and on weekends a farmers' market and flea market spill over the outdoor sidewalks. The market has fostered the growth of a surrounding small shopping district with jewelry and clothing shops, antique stores, and booksellers.

The teeming anthill of local commerce is, of course, **Georgetown** (Map 7). From the intersection of Wisconsin Ave and M St NW radiate block after block of clothing boutiques, antique dealers, galleries, gourmet-food shops, bookstores, and salons. Although the neighborhood's swank, many stores are moderately priced to attract tourists and Georgetown University students. There are plenty of chains, too, such as Urban Outfitters and Banana Republic. It's all anchored by **Georgetown Park** (Map 7; ☎ 298-5577), an elegantly designed upscale mall on the north bank of the C&O Canal, right at Wisconsin and M. It has a nice downstairs food court (with splashing fountains) and more than 100 shops: FAO Schwarz, J Crew, Victoria's Secret, etc. Here too is 250-year-old Caswell-Massey, an apothecary that once sold soaps and toiletries to George Washington. There's no Metro stop in Georgetown, so walk here from Foggy Bottom station (don't drive, because finding parking on these crowded, narrow streets is a fool's errand).

Shoppers in search of less preppy stores go to **Adams-Morgan** (Map 9). Its main drag, 18th St NW, is lined with old townhouses that hold great vintage and modern clothing boutiques, music stores, and funky thrift shops full of retro treasures. Ethnic markets and omnibus discount stores yield votive candles, frilly *quinceñera* dresses, cheap housewares, Latin food items, and even CDs and videos. The **New U** area (Map 10), around U and 14th Sts NW, has a much smaller but similar collection of shops, several of which specialize in African items such as masks and wooden carvings.

WHAT TO BUY
Museum Stuff

The Smithsonian's museums all have gift shops selling items related to their collections; shop profits feed back into museum programming. Find information about them at www.si.edu/info/shop.htm. Most have a product range from 25¢ postcards to $5000 reproductions, so there's something here for most everyone. Don't overlook DC's plethora of small museum shops, either, many of which sell find-it-nowhere-else treasures that large museums don't carry. Shops listed below generally have the same hours as the museums themselves; see the Things to See & Do chapter for details and location and contact information.

The **National Air & Space Museum**'s gift shop is more like a gift mall: it's a three-floor emporium offering books, toys, posters, model aircraft, and such iconic DC souvenirs as freeze-dried Astronaut Ice Cream (tasting like cotton candy squished by a steamroller). It has an incomparable selection of books on all aspects of aviation – you won't find such a collection of aircraft history, pilot manuals, etc, in almost any other US bookstore. All kinds of kites roost here too, from classic diamond shapes to neon butterflies.

The **National Museum of Natural History** has another big gift emporium, heavy on field guides, jewelry, ethnic crafts, wee rubber dinosaurs, and stuffed animals, including those long-armed monkeys that are hell to cram into overhead luggage bins. Its Gem & Mineral Shop sells moderately priced mineral samples.

Asian art posters, crafts, lovely pottery, and books – including many scholarly tomes – are across the Mall in the **Freer** and

Smithsonian Craft Show

Collectors of American crafts should visit DC in spring, when the Smithsonian's extraordinary craft show (www.si.edu/craftshow) takes over the National Building Museum (Map 3; Ⓜ Judiciary Square), 401 F St NW, with displays, a juried exhibition, talks, and auctions, all featuring artists who have elevated American craft traditions into the realm of exceptional creative art. It's usually held in late April, and leading American potters, furniture-makers, metalsmiths, glass, paper and textile artists, and jewelry creators display their work.

Sackler shops. If you're in the market for art posters, browse the elongated shops lining the underground corridors linking the **National Gallery of Art**'s East and West Buildings. The collection here is quite extensive, with framed and unframed reproductions of the museum's best-known works (some as cheap as $2), plus cards and general and scholarly art books. For books on modern art, cross the Mall to the **Hirshhorn Museum**'s small but excellent store, on the 1st floor. Most DC art museums sell exhibition catalogs, which are the perfect souvenir, enabling you to re-experience exhibits you loved during your time here and to share them with others.

Philatelists go to the **National Postal Museum** for current US stamps and poster-size blowups of unique historical stamps. The **Anacostia Museum**'s small shop has a thoughtful collection of African and African American toys, books, and crafts. African art – textiles, baskets, musical instruments, dolls – can also be found at the **National Museum of African Art**. The **National Museum of American History** shop has reproductions of old war posters (Revolutionary War onward), crafts, mobiles, toys, regional American foods from Vermont maple syrup to stone-ground Carolina grits, and Indian crafts such as Navajo pottery and Inuit statues. It has the Smithsonian's

largest book and video collection, too, on all aspects of American history and culture.

The **Renwick Gallery**, near the White House, has DC's best museum shop. Handmade textiles and hand-dyed silks are available, as is glasswork, woodwork, and unique jewelry, much of it quite affordable (a pair of hand-blown ruby-glass earrings cost $12). Its excellent choice of books includes how-to manuals on jewelry- and fabric-making, ceramics, glassblowing, and cabinetry, many appropriate for kids. In this store, you can learn as well as buy; it feels like an organic extension of the crafts museum upstairs, not a vending kiosk tacked on as an afterthought.

The Smithsonian's **National Zoological Park** has several shops on its grounds that sell toys and products featuring all manner of charismatic megafauna: ostriches, seals, tigers, wolves, elephants, and the inevitable pandas. (Bring home a plastic hyena for less-beloved relatives.) It also has the Zoo Bookstore, in the Education Building on the Connecticut Ave NW side, which has a pretty good natural-history and field-guide section.

Among DC's non-Smithsonian museums, the **National Building Museum** shop is an

Get the Poop

The National Zoo's animals collectively produce hundreds of pounds of manure every day. Most is trucked off to the dump, but some is made into DC's most unusual souvenir: ZooDoo fertilizer. Composted animal dung (only from plant-eating beasties) is mixed with wood chips, straw, and leaves and sold in buckets decorated with little drawings of animal butts. Buy ZooDoo at any zoo information booth, or order it from Friends of the National Zoo (☎ 673-4989); a 1lb bucket costs about $5. The zoo uses it on its own beautiful grounds, so you can see how well it works – and you'll probably be the only person on your block with genuine zebra poop in your zinnias.

amateur architect's dream, with small furniture pieces, rich coffee-table books, paper models of famed buildings, and a collection of books on American and international architecture. In Kalorama, the **Textile Museum**'s lovely little shop sells original handmade fabrics, rugs, tapestries, jewelry, and books from around the world; items range from $4 bead bracelets to thousand-dollar kilims.

Nearby, the **Phillips Collection** shop has a good collection of posters, pop and scholarly art books, and knickknacks imprinted with famous paintings: umbrellas sporting Renoir's *Luncheon of the Boating Party*, Monet water-lily mugs, etc.

The **B'nai B'rith Klutznick Museum** store sells all manner of Judaica, from books, mezuzahs, and beautiful menorahs to handmade yarmulkes and Passover china. There are some surprises here, too, such as hand-painted Limoges porcelain dreidels ($110) and a playful, near-life-size stuffed rabbi doll ($1500).

The **National Museum of Women in the Arts**, a unique institution dedicated to women artists, has an equally unique shop: a small room left of the museum entrance, it holds books, prints, posters, jewelry, and handicrafts – all made by women.

The Historical Society of Washington, DC's **Heurich House** has a small shop selling books on DC history – including small-press publications available nowhere else – and tchotchkes such as wreaths, ornaments, and dolls made by DC artisans. The Dept of the Interior's **Indian Craft Shop** (☎ 208-4056), which is actually just crowded little room No 1023 on the 1st floor of the department's C St NW headquarters, sells gorgeous but costly basketry, weavings, and jewelry made by Native Americans. It's open 8:30 am to 4:30 pm weekdays, plus the third Saturday of each month. Show picture ID to enter the building.

Books

DC's bookstores are more than simply places to buy books and magazines. Several house cafés that encourage casual meetings and conversations; others sponsor readings and open-mike events, and some stay open late, straddling the line between store and club. Many museum shops have unique book sections selling titles related to their collections, too – from space exploration to local birds. DC's think tanks and federal agencies often feature their own shops, which are open to the public, so you can buy those tomes on fiscal policy and Third World agroforestry that you've looked for everywhere else.

Secondhand Idle Time Books (☎ 232-4774; Ⓜ Woodley Park-Zoo), 2410 18th St NW, in the heart of Adams-Morgan, has three creaky wood floors stuffed with used literature and nonfiction, including the best secondhand political and history collection in the city. Its sci-fi, sports, and humor sections are also topnotch. It's open till 10 pm nightly and has a good newsstand in its front window. A sweet-tempered old cat patrols its upper floors.

Second Story Books & Antiques (☎ 659-8884; Ⓜ Dupont Circle), 2000 P St NW, up to its eyeballs in dusty used tomes, is a Dupont Circle fixture that also offers used LPs and CDs and a small stock of Asian antiques. It's a good place to stop on your way to the local cafés, and an impromptu pick-up scene flourishes among its shelves. It's such a beloved DC institution that Defense Secretary William Cohen wrote a cheesy poem in its honor ('Hieroglyphics heaped/in deep layers of ink....'). Open daily.

Kulturas (☎ 462-2541; Ⓜ Dupont Circle), 1608 20th St NW, has a great selection of used nonfiction and fiction; among its specialties are philosophy, poetry, and history. Open daily. Over in Georgetown, the Antiquarian Bookshop (☎ 338-8272; Ⓜ Foggy Bottom), 1222 31st St NW, sells rare tomes and scholarly works, and the charming Old Forest Bookshop (☎ 965-3842), 3145 Dumbarton St NW, focuses on used literature and history and is open daily. Also check out Lantern Bryn Mawr Bookshop (☎ 333-3222), 3241 P St NW, which sells only donated books; proceeds support Bryn Mawr women's college. Open daily.

New Dupont Circle has a fabulous selection of bookstores. Queen among them is Kramerbooks (☎ 387-1400; Ⓜ Dupont Circle), 1517 Connecticut Ave NW, with the Afterwords café and bar behind its shop. Open 24 hours on weekends, it's as much a spot for schmoozing as for shopping: you can listen to live bands, drink a pint, check email for free on its public terminal, nosh, and flirt with comely strangers (the store is a fabled pick-up spot for straights and gays). This flagship independent – which leapt into First Amendment history when it firmly refused to release Lewinsky's book-buying list to Starr's snoops – features fine current literature, travel, and politics sections.

Just up the way is Lambda Rising (☎ 462-6969), 1625 Connecticut Ave NW, a shop that's a major landmark in gay and lesbian DC. It sells CDs and videos as well as books, and the flyers and free giveaways near its door are a good way to learn about happenings in gay DC. Open daily. Nearby, Lammas (☎ 775-8218), 1607 17th St NW, is a women's bookstore with a good stock of lesbian, feminist, and spiritual titles. Open daily.

South of the circle is Olsson's (☎ 785-1133), 1307 19th St NW, offering both books and music. It's part of a chain but has an indie mood, with book-obsessed staff full of great recommendations. Other convenient Olsson's are at 418 7th St NW (☎ 638-7610; Ⓜ Gallery Place) and 1200 F St NW (☎ 347-3686; Ⓜ Metro Center). The 7th St branch has the friendly Footnotes café and a nice selection of jazz and blues CDs. All are open daily.

MysteryBooks (☎ 483-1600; Ⓜ Dupont Circle), 1715 Connecticut Ave NW, is sacred ground for DC mystery-lovers; on the scene for almost two decades, it has a huge selection of current and classic mysteries and thrillers (Chandler to Grafton) and a hopping calendar of readings. Its interior, dark green with wood trim, conjures up a drawing room in an Agatha Christie tale: too bad there's no brandy to sip. Open daily.

The International Language Center (☎ 332-2894) and Newsroom (☎ 332-1489) feature books and periodicals in 100 lan-guages; both are at 1753 Connecticut Ave NW near S St. Fans of Vertigo, the leftist-politics bookstore that once anchored Dupont Circle's south side, should note that it has moved to College Park, Maryland.

Way up in northwest DC is a key literary nexus, Politics & Prose bookstore and cof-feehouse (☎ 364-1919; Metrobus Nos L1 or L2), 5015 Connecticut Ave NW. This active independent has an excellent selection of literary fiction and nonfiction – it's fiercely supportive of local authors – plus dedicated staff, high-profile readings, and a staggering total of 15 active book clubs. Open daily. Also in upper northwest DC, Travel Books & Language Center (☎ 237-1322, Ⓜ Tenley-town), 4437 Wisconsin Ave NW, sells a gar-gantuan selection of guidebooks, maps, and foreign-language publications. Open daily.

Downtown's best bookstore is Chapters (☎ 347-5495; Ⓜ McPherson Square), 1512 K St NW, a friendly shop dedicated almost ex-clusively to literary fiction; it has one of the liveliest reading calendars in town. It's just blocks from the White House, too, which makes it a favorite of white-collars as well as tourists. Its book club meets at the shop monthly. Closed Sunday.

On Capitol Hill, you can stop by the Gov-ernment Printing Office & Bookstore (☎ 512-0132; Ⓜ Union Station), 710 N Capitol St between G and H Sts (open 8 am to 4 pm weekdays only), which sells 15,000 titles published by the US government, in-cluding the blockbusters *Selling to the Mili-tary* and *Nest Boxes for Wood Ducks*. Near the Capitol, the two-level Trover Shop (☎ 547-2665; Ⓜ Eastern Market), 221 Penn-sylvania Ave SE, is a DC institution for books, cards, and gifts. It also has a wide se-lection of books-on-tape, which are rentable. Unsurprisingly, given its location, its current-politics section is great. Closed Sunday.

Clothing

Vintage & Recycled DC is a good town for secondhand shopping – its plethora of wealthy folks who attend lots of fancy recep-tions and parties means that well-stocked consignment shops are in ready supply.

Shoppin' in the Suburbs: Local Malls

Several big malls on DC's outskirts draw shoppers in search of chain stores and bargains. Many are easily reached via Metro; all are open daily.

Pentagon City (☎ 703-415-2400), 1100 S Hayes St, Arlington, has its own subway stop on the Blue Line in Virginia. It houses 160 shops, including Macy's, Nordstrom, Banana Republic, Gap, the Disney Store, a cinema, and a big food court. It's not distinguished by anything, but this was the place that Monica Lewinsky got busted by Ken Starr's troopers back in '98.

Farther north in Virginia, just west of the Beltway, is gigantic **Tysons Corner** (☎ 703-893-9400), 1961 Chain Bridge Rd, McLean, a shopping complex that has, over the years, metastasized into its own strange, sidewalk-less suburban Edge City. With about 250 stores, there are few human needs Tysons can't fill: it has over 20 restaurants, big department stores from Bloomie's to Nordstrom, and smaller shops from Abercrombie & Fitch to Georgetown Tobacco. The adjacent, swanker Fairfax Square complex has Louis Vuitton, Gucci, Fendi, Chanel, and Hermés. You'll need to drive here.

On the Red Line at the DC-Bethesda border is upscale **Mazza Gallerie** (☎ 966-6114; Ⓜ Friendship Heights), 5300 Wisconsin Ave NW, anchored by Neiman-Marcus and patronized by matrons in search of the perfect cocktail dress. The mall has a variety of costly boutiques focusing on women's fashion and jewelry, plus a Williams-Sonoma. Downstairs is a seven-screen movie theater, but there's no food court. There's a Hecht's department store just across Western Ave from the mall.

The fire-breathing monster of mid-Atlantic outlet malls is just a half-hour drive south of DC: **Potomac Mills** (☎ 703-490-5948), Woodbridge, Virginia, which features about 250 discount shops: Ikea, Saks, Marshall's, and Spiegel, among others. This place now draws more tourists and tour buses (about 24 million per year) than Williamsburg or Virginia's other historic sites, which might say something about Americans' priorities. Take Exit 158-B off I-95.

One such shop is Secondi (☎ 667-1122; Ⓜ Dupont Circle), 1702 Connecticut Ave NW, which markets high-end used clothing for men and women, including formalwear – a $200 Vera Wang on the rack here probably cost its Kalorama-matron first owner a few thousand. Open daily.

Another fine consignment shop – this one mostly for women – is Inga's Once Is Not Enough (☎ 337-3072), 4830 MacArthur Blvd NW, with many items coming in from residents of its chi-chi upper northwest neighborhood. Inga herself, who is a fashion consultant for the local Fox channel, takes her customers firmly in hand, showing them what they really want to buy in her very crowded shop, which is thick with designer labels (Prada, Armani, etc). It's easiest to drive here. Closed Sunday.

Secondhand Rose (☎ 333-6635), 1516 Wisconsin Ave NW, is a somewhat pricier shop, offering consignment women's clothing that's no more than two years old. This isn't a place for bargain-hunters – no $10 dresses here – but this Georgetown store has fast turnover and all items are in good condition. Closed Sunday.

It's hard to resist a place named Meeps Fashionette (☎ 265-6546; Ⓜ U St-Cardozo), 1520 U St NW. This vintage clothier appeals to both boy and girl denizens of the New U club district with its 1950s and '60s swinger-style clothes: puffy skirts for dancing, suede-lapelled blazers, and accessories like funky hats and beaded purses. Items are moderately priced (dresses around $30) and in decent shape. Open daily.

Want some vintage jeans? Deja Blue (☎ 337-7100; Ⓜ Foggy Bottom), 3005 M St NW, has stacks of 'em, plus salespeople who can take one glance at you and throw you several pair that fit like they were tailored for your booty alone. They usually run between $30 and $40, but they're worth it. Open daily.

If you're into serious savings, go down to Capitol Hill to the American Rescue Workers' Thrift Store (☎ 547-9701; Ⓜ Eastern Market), 745 8th St SE near the Marine Barracks, a no-frills operation selling everything from women's wear to baby dresses to furniture. Nothing is in great shape, but the clothes are extremely cheap, usually just a few bucks. Closed Sunday.

New DC has lots of the usual American chain stores: Gap, Banana Republic, Ann Taylor, Abercrombie & Fitch, etc, many in suburban malls (see the 'Shoppin' in the Suburbs' boxed text, earlier). It doesn't have many unique clothing stores, but some of the more interesting ones are mentioned here.

Shake Your Booty, at 2324 18th St NW in Adams-Morgan (☎ 518-8205; Ⓜ Woodley Park-Zoo) and 3225 M St NW in Georgetown (☎ 333-6524; Ⓜ Foggy Bottom), purveys Ecstasy-bright kiddie clubwear; look no farther for flower-topped plastic slides and embroidered cropped jeans. Its focus is on shoes. Open daily. Up 18th St is Betty (☎ 234-2389), No 2439, a little shop that sells stylish women's clothing, much of it by local designers. The pieces are sexy, elegant, and reasonably priced. Closed Tuesday.

Every city needs a great hat shop, and DC's is the Proper Topper (☎ 842-3055; Ⓜ Dupont Circle), 1350 Connecticut Ave NW, selling to both men and women. Fedoras, floppy-brimmed picture hats, berets – if it sits on your head, this shop has got it. Open daily. If you're looking for a Stetson, however, Red River (☎ 546-5566; Ⓜ Eastern Market), on Pennsylvania Ave between 6th and 7th Sts SE, is the place for you and all sorts of other displaced cowboys lonely for the prairie. It sells fancy boots, big-buckled belts, silver accessories, and other things you need for riding the range (or, more likely, the Metro). Closed Sunday and Monday.

Commander Salamander (☎ 337-2265; Ⓜ Foggy Bottom), 1420 Wisconsin Ave NW,

is a Georgetown institution that's been a friend to street punks and wannabes for decades – back when Friday night in Georgetown meant seeing *Rocky Horror* at the Key Theatre, this was the place everyone stopped off for black lipstick and handcuffs. It now sells funky makeup, all colors of hair dye, Gothwear, and baggy clothes from Moschino, Hook-Ups, etc. Open daily. For a wider selection of hip gear in Georgetown, check out the chain stores Diesel (☎ 625-2780), 1249 Wisconsin Ave NW, and Urban Outfitters (☎ 342-1012), 3111 M St NW, both open daily.

For jewelry, scarves, and even clothing, Eastern Market on Capitol Hill is a great resource (see Where to Shop, earlier in the chapter, and the Things to See & Do chapter). On weekends, vendors set up tables outdoors with flotillas of handmade items, most well within even a budget traveler's grasp: dangly earrings, Andean sweaters, floppy sundresses, straw hats, you name it. Summer is the best time to shop here.

DENNIS JOHNSON

Furniture, Antiques & Other Interesting Junk

Brass Knob (☎ 332-3370; Ⓜ Woodley Park-Zoo), 2311 18th St NW, Adams-Morgan, is a unique two-floor shop selling salvage 'rescues' from old buildings and homes: fixtures, lamps, tiles, stained glass, mantelpieces, keyplates, mirrors, etc. Its selection ranges from 'ehh' to fantastic, and its owners are knowledgeable and helpful. Open daily.

Also in Adams-Morgan is Skynear (☎ 797-7160), 1800 Wyoming Ave NW, which is actually two shops in one. Upstairs (for grownups) are extremely reasonably priced stylish new furniture and jewelry: big 'distressed' armoires, funky sofas, and the like go for hundreds less here than at comparable shops. Downstairs (for kids starting out), more basic items like futons are cheaper still. Open daily.

Farther north is the incredibly crowded antique/junk shop, Logan's Antiques (☎ 483-2428; Ⓜ Columbia Heights), 3118 Mount Pleasant St, stuffed to its rafters with old housewares and furniture, some of it beat, some in great shape. While away a rainy afternoon picking through the place. Closed Sunday. Miss Pixie's Furnishings & Whatnot (☎ 232-8171), 1810 Adams Mill Rd NW, is a whimsical little joint purveying old housewares, furniture, and doodads, all cheap and presided over by Miss Pixie herself. Open Thursday to Sunday.

If you're in the market for housewares but are sick of Pottery-Barn-style homogeneity, visit Home Rule (☎ 797-5544; Ⓜ U St-Cardozo), 1807 14th St NW, which sells amusingly original items like frog-shaped toothbrush holders with sucker feet for sticking on the wall, brightly colored martini glasses, animal-shaped salt-and-pepper sets, and rugs and linens, too. The mosaic decorating the front counter symbolizes the U St district's revitalization – it's made up of smashed glass from the 1968 riots. Closed Monday and Tuesday.

Those with more spending green enjoy sleek Apartment Zero (☎ 628-4067; Ⓜ Archives), 406 7th St NW. Its clean-lined modern furniture and home accessories, which look like something George Jetson

RICK GERHARTER

Galleries at R St and Florida Ave

might buy if he was into Danish Modern, pride themselves on their functionality – many items are modular or foldable. Sample prices: chairs start at around $200; lamps at $100, funky clocks at $40. Closed Monday and Tuesday.

Artwork

Art galleries cluster in three areas in DC: in the streets around Dupont Circle, especially at R St and Florida Ave NW; downtown along 7th St NW; and in Georgetown. Many close on Sunday and Monday, so call ahead.

The Dupont gang, which tends to be the most affordable, includes Burdick Gallery (☎ 986-5682; Ⓜ Dupont Circle), 2114 R St NW, specializing in Inuit carvings and prints. You can find inexpensive pieces here, such as a silky stone bear for $150. Next door at Affrica (☎ 745-7272), 2010½ R St NW, are traditional African sculptures, masks, and textiles; its neighbor Gallery K (☎ 234-0339), No 2010, is a topnotch two-floor showcase for contemporary international artists' work.

Studio Gallery (☎ 232-8734), a 30-artist cooperative downstairs at 2108 R St NW, has modern canvases and sculpture. Its upstairs neighbor, Anton Gallery (☎ 328-0828), specializes in contemporary realist and abstract canvases; shows change monthly. The Troyer Gallery (☎ 328-7189), 1710 Connecticut Ave NW, is among DC's better-known spaces, hosting frequently changing shows by emerging local artists. Its focus is on abstract art, including photography, painting, and sculpture. Dupont Circle galleries host a collective 'open house' on the first Friday of every month, staying open till 8 pm.

The 7th St galleries, all easily accessible from the Archives Metro, include Numark Gallery (☎ 628-3810), No 406, specializing in fine prints, many by locals. At the same address is Touchstone Gallery (☎ 347-2787), which offers impressive shows of photography and modern canvases. For a free gallery crawl downtown, show up at the MCI Center's Discovery Channel Store at 6:30 pm on the third Thursday of the month; local artists will show you around.

Interesting Georgetown galleries include the big Creighton-Davis Gallery (☎ 333-3050), 3222 M St NW in Georgetown Park, a sort of catchall for 20th-century works from Picasso to Hockney. The Old Print Gallery (☎ 965-1818), 1220 31st St NW, sells antique maps, prints of cowboys and duckhunters, and landscapes. For something more up-to-date, Parish Gallery (☎ 944-2310), 1054 31st St NW, features the work of African Americans and other minority artists, with many locals represented.

Eats & Drinks

Eastern Market's South Hall is the closest DC gets to foodie heaven: in its friendly confines are a bakery, dairy, fish counter, poultry counter, butcher, produce vendors, and flower stands. Put together a real Southern feast here – the Southern Maryland Seafood Company serves up the blue crabs and shrimp; over at Union Meat Company are fresh chitterlings, pigs' trotters, and all kinds of sausage and steak. To get it all blessed, stop by Calomiris, the Greek produce stand,

RICK GERHARTER

Galleries along 7th St

RICK GERHARTER

and Mexican and Salvadoran desserts and snacks. A bit farther south is Casa Peña (☎ 462-2222; Ⓜ Dupont Circle), 1636 17th St NW, which sells, among other items, five different brands of *yerba maté*. Open daily.

A Cleveland Park neighborhood favorite is Vace Italian (☎ 363-1999; Ⓜ Cleveland Park), 3315 Connecticut Ave NW, a deli offering fresh pastas, cheeses, gnocchi, and Italian sweets. Closed Sunday.

Up in Tenleytown is one of DC's odder food shops, Rodman's (☎ 363-3466; Ⓜ Tenleytown), 5100 Wisconsin Ave NW. It sells low-priced exotic condiments (Thai spices, Indian pickles), pastas, chocolates, pâtés, and other foodstuffs in a discount-dimestore atmosphere: with its crowded, dusty aisles, it feels like the junkshop of gourmet markets. Open daily.

For something sweet, go up the street to Krön Chocolatier (☎ 966-4946; Ⓜ Friendship Heights), 5300 Wisconsin Ave NW in Mazza Gallerie, known for hand-dipped truffles and amusing novelties like edible chocolate baskets and milk-chocolate telephones and cars.

The New York gourmet chain Dean & DeLuca has its main DC shop (☎ 342-2500; Ⓜ Foggy Bottom) at 3276 M St NW in the middle of Georgetown: the big brick hall has produce, meat, and bakery counters (all costly; this is a place for Black Angus beef and caviar), and outside is a lovely canopied dining area for noshing on its ready-made sandwiches and pastries. Open daily.

For a libation to complete your gourmet feast, go to the elegantly designed, pale-wood-trimmed GrapeFinds (☎ 387-3146; Ⓜ Dupont Circle), 1643 Connecticut Ave NW. The shop's arranged by taste categories (sweet, fruity, bold, etc) rather than by type and so is helpful for vino novices, particularly since lots of bottles are under $15. The shelves display fun little wine facts, too, like a Renaissance pope's desire to have his corpse washed in Orvieto. If you prefer caffeine to alcohol, stop at Teaism (☎ 638-7740), 400 8th St NW: it sells more than 30 varieties of loose teas and herb drinks, plus elegant Asian tGwares. Open daily.

which sells Orthodox icons among its cucumbers and oranges. Market hours are 8 am to 6 pm Saturday, 8 am to 4 pm Sunday, 10 am to 6 pm Tuesday to Friday.

Merkato Market (☎ 483-9499; Ⓜ Woodley Park-Zoo), 2116 18th St NW in Adams-Morgan, sells Ethiopian spices, flours, , and *halal* meats; its deli offers ready-to-eat veggie and meat dishes. Staff seem used to confused shoppers and will help you with cooking tips. Its bulletin board is a good place to check out happenings in the local East African community. Up the street at 2202 18th St NW is Addisu Gebeya (☎ 986-6013), a similar Ethiopian food shop. Both are open daily.

Adams-Morgan and neighboring Mount Pleasant can be considered ground zero for Latin-American groceries, bodegas, and specialty shops: stroll down Columbia Rd or Mount Pleasant St to find dozens of places selling chiles, South American spices,

Music

DC has all the usual nationwide music stores, such as Tower, but a mere handful of interesting independents. One of the most convenient places to shop is the local Olsson's chain (see Bookstores, above), which sells a thoughtful – albeit fairly small – selection of new CDs.

Adams-Morgan's 18th St drag sports a fine selection of little music stores, all crowded with youth doing the click-click-click through racks of discs. The best is DC CD (☎ 588-1810; Ⓜ Woodley Park-Zoo), No 2343, which showcases Washington talent, putting the work of local labels and bands front and center. It has new and used CDs, plus stacks of vinyl, and you can listen to anything before buying it. It's open late daily. Across the street, Flying Saucer (☎ 265-3472), No 2318, is another good used-CD shop, with enthusiastic staff. For an eclectic mix of new pan-African music, stop at Ethio Sound (☎ 232-0076), up the street at No 2409.

Melody Record Shop (☎ 232-4002; Ⓜ Dupont Circle), 1623 Connecticut Ave NW, has been serving Dupont Circle its daily CD and vinyl requirements for nearly 30 years. The deceptively small storefront hides a very wide range of discs. It's open till 10 pm daily (11 pm weekends).

Although it's over a Hardee's and is about the size of a phone booth, the Guitar Shop (☎ 331-7333; Ⓜ Dupont Circle), 1216 Connecticut Ave NW, is DC's most impressive instrument retailer and repairer. Springsteen and Dylan have shopped here, and the store's been around since 1922. The dedicated staff help musicians – be they novice or star – find what they really need in an incredibly dense collection ranging from top-of-the-line Martins to off-brand cheapies. Closed Sunday.

Another DC-area landmark for fine instruments is the House of Musical Traditions (☎ 301-270-9090; Ⓜ Takoma), just over the Maryland border at 7040 Carroll Ave in Takoma Park. These guys sell things you've never heard of – doumbeks, djembe drums, hurdy-gurdys, psalteries – plus beautiful guitars, accordions, and banjos, plus acoustic-music CDs. Open daily.

Tattoos & Bodily Decorations

These days, even DC lobbyists get roses inked onto their ankles and delicate rings inserted into their schnozzes. Many of them were decorated at Fatty's Custom Tattooz (☎ 452-0999; Ⓜ Dupont Circle), 1333 Connecticut Ave NW, 3rd floor, a clean, friendly place that does both tattoos and piercing (on almost any body part you care to proffer). They have a huge selection of ready-made designs, but they're happy to ink your own design on you, too. Prices start around $50. Open daily.

Grafixx Tattoos & Body Piercings (☎ 628-9556; Ⓜ Metro Center), 1340 G St NW, will put holes just about anywhere (noses, navels, tongues, even naughty bits) for prices starting at $40. Tattoos start around $50; the shop artists do nice cartoon, tribal, and

Asian work and will help you create personal designs. Closed Sunday.

Sex Shops

The Pleasure Place (☎ 483-3297; Ⓜ Dupont Circle), 1710 Connecticut Ave NW, sells lots of giggle gifts (T-shirts with naughty sayings, flavored body oils, windup jumping genitals) along with a more thoughtful selection of lingerie and things that go 'whirr' in the night. It's aimed at both men and women. Open daily (till midnight weekends). Across the way is the Leather Rack (☎ 797-7401), 1723 Connecticut Ave NW, which has restraints, toys, condoms, and leather clothes, primarily for gay men. It's been around for 25 years, has a good reputation, and is a comfortable, friendly place to shop. Open till 11 pm daily.

Dream Dresser (☎ 625-0373; Ⓜ Foggy Bottom), Georgetown's S&M shop at 1042 Wisconsin Ave NW, sells everything a well-kept dungeon requires, including chain-mail skivvies and latex corsets, plus tall boots and maid's costumes. It's mostly for straights. Closed Sunday.

Other Interesting Shops

Wanna-be G-men go to the Counter Spy Shop (☎ 887-1717; Ⓜ Farragut North), 1027 Connecticut Ave NW, which purveys surveillance and countersurveillance gear. Some patrons seem to be here for a laugh, but others are very serious indeed. Pick up Predator VI night-vision goggles, Air Tasers, line-bug detection devices, and everything your paranoid little heart desires. It's closed Sunday (due to some conspiracy, no doubt).

Up in Adams-Morgan, Yemaya Botanica (☎ 462-1803; Ⓜ Woodley Park-Zoo), 2441 18th St NW, sells Santería and Vodou goods like herbs, amulets, icons, *santos* (religious statues), and a huge variety of prayer candles, not to mention Jinx Removing air freshener and Go Away Evil cologne (neither available at Counter Spy, by the way). Staff do shell readings in Spanish and English, too. Closed Sunday.

Feeling stressed by your travels? Go to Georgetown's Better Botanicals (☎ 888-224-3727; Ⓜ Foggy Bottom), 3066 M St NW,

which prepares custom-made Ayurvedic herbal products (oils, soaps, shampoos, scents); their service and knowledge have been recommended by readers. The stuff costs ($15 for 8oz of lotion), but staff are dedicated and give you helpful tips. Open daily. Farther down, at 3065 M St, is Sephora (☎ 338-5644), a two-floor cosmetics-and-scents shop that's a lot of fun: upstairs are huge racks of pencils, liners, and powders in all colors of the rainbow, and downstairs the walls are lined with nearly every perfume imaginable. There's lots of cheap picks (like teeny eyeliners for $3). Open daily.

Backstage (☎ 775-1488; Ⓜ Dupont Circle), 2101 P St NW, is a costume and theatrical store that caters to both the drag crowd and government types in search of fancy dress for parties. It rents outfits, and you can buy funky face paints, wigs, and masks. Closed Sunday.

Wake Up Little Suzie (☎ 244-0700; Ⓜ Cleveland Park), 3409 Connecticut Ave NW, is a funny and original gift shop selling stuff like neon clocks, bright chunky metal-and-ceramic jewelry, polka-dotted pottery, cards, and T-shirts. If you're jonesing for an *Invasion of the Monster Women* lunchbox or boxing-rabbi windup doll, Suzie's your woman. Open daily.

Bead junkies enjoy Beadazzled (☎ 265-2323; Ⓜ Dupont Circle), 1507 Connecticut Ave NW, which specializes in all things small and stringable – from 5¢ clay doohickeys to expensive pearls – with a selection from round the world and helpful staff to tell you how to put them together. Open daily.

For one-of-a-kind ceramics, woodwork, and jewelry, Appalachian Spring (☎ 682-0505), in Union Station's East Hall, is the place. Prices are pretty reasonable – you can find beautiful mugs for around $10 – and it also sells quilts and metalwork. Open daily.

Excursions

Virginia

Visitors taking a first glance at Washington's Virginia suburbs can be forgiven for thinking of them as simply a huge dormitory for the workers of Washington, DC. But among the suburbs, malls, and crowded highways and airports of Northern Virginia are a wealth of historic sites that reveal much about American history, particularly the cataclysm of the Civil War and the days of plantations and slavery. Arlington National Cemetery, the Pentagon, and Mount Vernon are other fascinating attractions. Whether you're interested in exploring colonial-era towns or just spending a day hiking in the woods or browsing antique shops, an excursion west of the Potomac is well worthwhile.

ARLINGTON

Both Arlington and its southern neighbor, Alexandria, can be considered extensions of Washington itself. In fact, they *were* part of the city until 1847, when DC ceded its land west of the Potomac back to Virginia. During the Civil War, the Potomac waters became a symbolic borderline between North and South – to the north, the capital of the Union; to the south, the Confederate heartland, with General Robert E Lee's mansion commanding the riverside heights. Now, however, with Metro links and four bridges, the divide between DC and Virginia is hardly noticeable. Dense with fascinating historic and federal sites, including Arlington National Cemetery and the Pentagon, Arlington is only a quick jaunt away for visitors to the capital.

Orientation & Information

Arlington is a collection of neighborhoods – Rosslyn in the north, Crystal City and Pentagon City in the south, Clarendon and Ballston in the west. Arlington's eastern boundary is the Potomac, crossed by the Key, Theodore Roosevelt, Arlington Memorial, and 14th St (I-395) Bridges. Southeast is Alexandria, reached by US-1 (Jefferson Davis Hwy) and the George Washington Memorial Parkway.

The Arlington Visitor Information Center (☎ 703-228-5720, www.co.arlington.va.us; Ⓜ Pentagon City), 735 S 18th St, is near I-395 exit 9. The staff here can help you make hotel reservations. Open 9 am to 5 pm daily.

Arlington National Cemetery

The 612 acres and 245,000 graves of this national cemetery (☎ 703-607-8052, www .arlingtoncemetery.com) are a somber counterpoint to the soaring monuments to US history just across the Potomac. It's the burial ground for military personnel and their families, the dead of every war the US has fought since the Revolution, and American leaders such as JFK, Oliver Wendell Holmes, and Medgar Evers.

The cemetery, west of the Lincoln Memorial, has its own Metro station. From the Metro, turn west and follow signs to the visitors' center, where maps, books, and Tourmobile (☎ 888-868-7707) tours are available. Tourmobile charges $4.75/$2.75 adults/kids.

Nearby, at the end of Memorial Drive, the first site you'll see is the **Women in Military Service for America Memorial**, honoring women who have served in the armed forces in times of war and peace, from the Revolution onward. The memorial includes an education center and theater.

On the slopes above are the **Kennedy gravesites**. Near the eternal flame that

LEE FOSTER

The eternal flame at John F Kennedy's grave

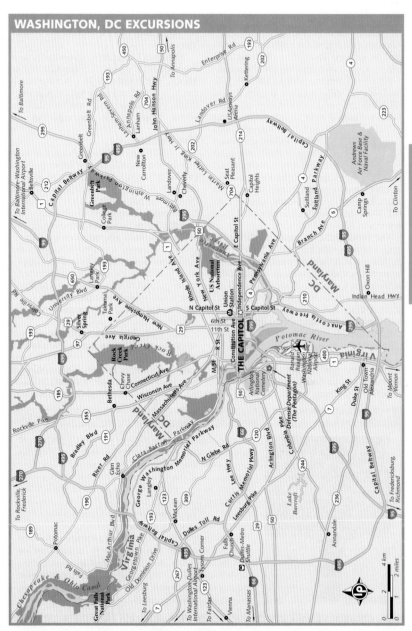

WASHINGTON, DC EXCURSIONS

EXCURSIONS

marks the grave of John F Kennedy lie gravestones for Robert Kennedy, Jacqueline Kennedy Onassis, and her two children who died in infancy. The site is one that JFK admired just days before his assassination.

Nearby **Arlington House** (☎ 703-557-0613) is the former home of Robert E Lee. His home and part of his 1100-acre property were confiscated after he left to command the Confederate Army of Virginia, and Union dead were buried around the house to spite him. After the war, the family sued the federal government for reimbursement. The government paid off the Lees, and Arlington Cemetery was born on their old lands. Eventually, the historic house (circa 1817) opened for public tours. Open 9:30 am to 4:30 pm daily; free.

The **Tomb of the Unknown Soldier** holds unidentified bodies from WWI, WWII, and the Korean War. Soldiers march before it 24 hours a day, and visitors come to watch the changing of the guard. Mid-March to September, the guard changes every half-hour; at other times, it changes hourly.

Other notable memorials include the Confederate Monument, the tomb of Pierre L'Enfant, the mast of the battleship USS *Maine*, the *Challenger* memorial, and the Nurses' Memorial. The **Iwo Jima Memorial**, dedicated to the Marine Corps, is on the cemetery's northern fringes. You can also check out the graves of boxer Joe Louis, explorer Richard Byrd, and President William Taft.

Arlington Cemetery is free and opens at 8 am daily. It closes at 5 pm October to March, 7 pm April to September. Parking is available for $1 per hour for the first three hours. Funerals are still held here daily, so visitors should be quiet and respectful.

The Pentagon

The US Dept of Defense is housed in what may be the world's biggest office building (☎ 703-695-1776), built in just 16 months during WWII. About 25,000 people work in this massive polygon, which has more than a dozen miles of corridors. Its five sides surround a 5-acre courtyard. The ominousness of its appearance has provoked amusing responses – during the 1967 March on the Pentagon, Abbie Hoffman and the Yippies tried to levitate the building to exorcise its 'demons,' and Norman Mailer wrote that it resembled 'some plastic plug coming out of the hole made in flesh by an unmentionable operation.'

Free guided tours show you portions of the Pentagon. They're tightly disciplined – you must stay with the group and keep quiet (which is for the best; if you got lost in here you'd never find the way out). You also see a short film. Tours run on the hour from

LEE FOSTER

The Known Unknown

For several years after the Vietnam War, the US government had no 'unknown' Vietnam War soldier to inter in Arlington's Tomb of the Unknown Soldier. All recovered remains were identified, albeit slowly, via new forensic techniques. Finally, in 1984, an appropriately anonymous set of remains was located, and Defense Secretary Caspar Weinberger approved their burial in the tomb. The remains joined those of WWI, WWII, and Korean War unknowns.

But in 1998, the family of Michael J Blassie, an Air Force lieutenant shot down near An Loc in 1972, discovered via DNA testing that the corpse was that of their lost relative. Blassie was removed in the first-ever Unknowns disinterment and reburied in Missouri. The Vietnam crypt at Arlington, meanwhile, stands permanently empty.

Raising the flag at the Iwo Jima Memorial

9 am to 3 pm weekdays only. Adults need photo ID; overseas visitors must bring passports. Show up early, as tours fill up fast.

Take the Metro to Pentagon station. At the top of the escalator, you'll see the tour window.

Newseum

The Freedom Forum – a nonpartisan, international foundation dedicated to preserving a free press – operates the state-of-the art Newseum (☎ 888-639-7386; Ⓜ Rosslyn), 1101 Wilson Blvd, which offers a fascinating, hands-on look at how the news is reported, produced, spun, and consumed. In one hall, a block-long screen displays breaking news; the day's front pages from the world's top newspapers are displayed below it. The interactive newsroom and broadcast studio allow visitors to create and tape their own broadcasts and write their own news stories. Thoughtful exhibits examine journalistic ethics, and the News History gallery traces historic events and the journalists who covered them.

Outside in the museum's **Freedom Park**, a memorial honors journalists killed on the job. Icons from political struggles around the world are displayed, including Berlin Wall chunks.

As of 2000, the Newseum was planning to move to a prime location at Pennsylvania Ave and 6th St NW in downtown DC – call ahead to check on the museum's moving dates. Open 10 am to 5 pm Tuesday to Sunday; free.

Theodore Roosevelt Island

This 91-acre wooded island (☎ 703-285-2598), in the Potomac off Rosslyn, is a wilderness preserve honoring the conservation-minded 26th US president. A large memorial plaza and statue of Teddy dominate the island's center, and trails and boardwalks snake around the shorelines. The island's swampy fringes shelter birds, raccoons, and other small animals. A fine place for a hike, it offers great views of the Kennedy Center across the river. The mood is surprisingly rural, despite jets slamming down into nearby National Airport, cruising so low that you can practically read their engines' serial numbers.

From DC, cross the Potomac on the Theodore Roosevelt Memorial Bridge (I-66) and exit northbound onto George Washington Memorial Parkway. You'll spot the small parking lot on the road's east side; from here, walk across the pedestrian bridge to the island. Better yet, take the Metro to Rosslyn and walk three blocks east to the footbridge.

The Mount Vernon Trail (see below) runs past the island on the Potomac's west bank, so the island is a convenient stop on a long bike ride or jog. Note that bikes aren't permitted on the island itself; lock them up in the parking lot.

George Washington Memorial Parkway

The 25-mile Virginia portion of this highway, honoring the first US president, winds past recreation areas and memorials all the

DENNIS JOHNSON

EXCURSIONS

One Place You Can't Tour

The FBI lets tourists wander its halls. Even the Pentagon welcomes visitors, and shows them cheerful videos about national defense. So, many tourists wonder, can we visit the Central Intelligence Agency, too?

No way, friends. The CIA is among the world's most secure facilities. In Langley, Virginia, between Chain Bridge Rd and the George Washington Memorial Parkway, it offers no tours, bars civilians, and doesn't let anyone without security clearance in the door. Its main building, the George Bush Center for Intelligence (ahem), has its own power plant and double walls to protect against attack. Even the precise number of its employees is classified. If you drive up to the complex (as we blithely did), stern military policemen question you before sending you firmly on your way. But check out the agency's Web site (www.odci.gov/cia/information/tour/tour.html) for a highly selective virtual tour.

way south to his old estate, Mount Vernon. A national parkland, it's lined with remnants of Washington's life and works, such as his old Patowmack Company canal (in Great Falls National Park) and parks that were once part of his farmlands (Riverside Park, Fort Hunt Park, etc). For modern visitors, the road is a pleasant alternative to the traffic-choked highway arteries farther away from the river.

North of Arlington in **Turkey Run Park**, you can access the riverside Potomac Heritage National Scenic Trail. The 18½-mile **Mount Vernon Trail** parallels the parkway from Key Bridge to Mount Vernon – it's paved and perfect for biking.

In Arlington itself, stop at **Lady Bird Johnson Park**, named for the First Lady who tried to beautify the capital via greenery-planting campaigns. The small Lyndon Baines Johnson Memorial Grove is here, too.

Gravelly Point, just east of the parkway and north of National Airport, has public ballfields and the Roaches Run Waterfowl Sanctuary, a good birdwatching area.

Washington & Old Dominion Trail

Despite its dense suburbs, northern Virginia is laced with hiking and biking trails. In addition to the Mount Vernon Trail (see above), the 45-mile, paved Washington & Old Dominion Trail (W&OD; ☎ 703-729-0596) follows an old railway bed from Shirlington, in southern Arlington, to Purcellville, in Virginia's Allegheny foothills. From here, it's a short jump to the Appalachian Trail and its 2000 miles of trail south to Georgia and north to Maine.

Horseback riding is permitted on the W&OD from Vienna to Purcellville. Find the southern trailhead just west of I-395 near the intersection of Shirlington Rd and S Four Mile Run Drive. It's also easy to pick up the trail at the Dunn Loring and East Falls Church Metro stations.

Places to Stay

A comfortable bed in Arlington (there are over 30 hotels and motels) costs much less than one in DC. Some are near Metro stops, but for many you'll need a car. Virginia room tax is usually about 10%.

Econo Lodge National Airport (☎ 703-979-4100, 2485 S Glebe Rd), 3 miles southwest of the 14th St Bridge and west of I-395, charges $60 to $120 year-round. ***Econo Lodge Metro*** (☎ 703-538-5300, 6800 Lee Hwy; Ⓜ East Falls Church) has singles and doubles for $70 to $100 in low season (about $10 more in high). Kids under 18 stay free with parents at both hotels.

Other mid-range places include ***Best Western Pentagon*** (☎ 703-979-4400, 2480 S Glebe Rd), with comfortable singles and doubles for $72 to $100 (kids under 18 free); and ***Cherry Blossom Travelodge*** (☎ 703-521-5570, 3030 Columbia Pike), with clean, well-maintained singles and doubles for $59 to $79.

Slightly more expensive are ***Days Inn Crystal City*** (☎ 703-920-8600, 2000 Jefferson Davis Hwy; Ⓜ Crystal City), 1.3 miles southwest of the 14th St Bridge on US-1, with singles and doubles for $100 in low season, $10 to $20 more in high; and **Holiday Inn National Airport** (☎ 703-684-7200, 2650 Jefferson Davis Hwy), which includes transportation to the airport in rates that start at $100/120 low/high season.

Comfort Inn Ballston (☎ 703-247-3399, 1211 N Glebe Rd; Ⓜ Ballston) has spacious doubles that cost about $72 weekends, $125 weekdays. **Holiday Inn Arlington at Ballston** (☎ 703-243-9800, 4610 N Fairfax Drive; Ⓜ Ballston), I-66 exit 71, has a pool, sauna, exercise room, and singles and doubles for $80 weekends, $140 weekdays.

Expensive choices, with all the luxuries you expect for the price, are the **Ritz-Carlton Pentagon City** (☎ 703-415-5000, 1250 S Hayes St; Ⓜ Pentagon City), where doubles start at about $140 weekends, $220 weekdays; and the **Crystal City Marriott** (☎ 703-413-5500, 1999 Jefferson Davis Hwy; Ⓜ Crystal City), with weekend specials for $74 to $135 and weekday singles/doubles starting at $189/209.

Places to Eat

Arlington sports several vibrant restaurant enclaves. You'll find good choices in Shirlington, Crystal City, Rosslyn, Clarendon, and near the Court House Metro station. The brewpubs mentioned under Entertainment, below, also serve meals. The **food court** at the Pentagon City mall (Ⓜ Pentagon City) has just about every sort of fast food imaginable and is open daily.

Shirlington Shirlington Village, a shopping district on S 28th St just west of I-395 (southbound exit 7, northbound exit 6) has good meal choices, including lots of hearty American food.

Bistro Bistro (☎ 703-379-0300, 4021 S 28th St) serves innovative American cuisine, including four kinds of yummy burgers (lamb, turkey, etc) and veal meatloaf. Entrées cost $8 to $18. If you're lucky with the weather, eat at a sidewalk table. **Carlyle Grand Café** (☎ 703-931-0777, 4000 S 28th St) is a lively bistro with great rotisserie and grilled meats (dinner entrées run $14 to $20). It's also a good spot for a quick coffee

and dessert – its 'Best Buns' bakery serves good muffins and breads.

For Asian, try **Charlie Chiang's** (☎ 703-671-4900, 4060 S 28th St), specializing in Hunan and Szechuan dishes. Charlie's just creeps into the moderate bracket, with main courses for $8 to $20.

Crystal City Crystal City, a business hub of towering office complexes, is a place to go for expensive dinners with great views of downtown DC. It doesn't have Arlington's most interesting cuisine, however. Use the Crystal City Metro station to reach these restaurants.

Two miles southwest of the 14th St Bridge, **Ruth's Chris Steak House** (☎ 703-979-7275, 2231 Crystal Drive), on the 11th floor of Crystal Park building No 3, is a carnivore's delight and an upscale place where you should dress up to eat. As you dine, you get magnificent views of the DC skyline. A meal for two is well over $60, as entrées cost $16 to $30 apiece.

For more fine views of DC by night, try **Penthouse Restaurant** (☎ 703-416-4100, 300 Army Navy Drive), serving Continental cuisine on the 14th floor of the Doubletree Hotel (be warned, entrées cost $20 to $40), and the revolving **Skydome Lounge** above. **Stars Restaurant** (☎ 703-521-1900), in the Sheraton National Hotel at Columbia Pike and Washington Blvd, also has great views.

If you don't care about views and are hungering for great Vietnamese at low prices, try **Saigon Crystal** (☎ 703-920-3822, 536 S 23rd St), where entrées start at $10. Try the seafood hot pots.

Rosslyn The Rosslyn Metro station is convenient to these places. Stop by **Atomic Grounds** (☎ 703-524-2157, 1555 Wilson Blvd), an upscale 'cyberlounge' open at 6:30 am daily.

Red Hot & Blue (☎ 703-276-7427, 1600 Wilson Blvd), at N Pierce St, open daily for lunch and dinner, gets rave reviews from everyone. Sample Memphis-style wet and dry ribs, chicken, smoked ham, and all the Southern sides you could wish for; entrées cost $7 to $15.

EXCURSIONS

Other Rosslyn delights are **Star of Siam** (☎ *703-524-1208, 1735 N Lynn St*), with a fabulous selection of Thai curries and seafood dishes, and **Tivoli** (☎ *703-524-8900, 1700 N Moore St*), right above the Rosslyn Metro, an upscale place serving delectable northern Italian cuisine. The 'Tiv' is expensive: entrées such as linguine Saracena cost about $25.

Clarendon The area around the Clarendon Metro station is the heart of Arlington's 'Little Saigon,' an enclave of Vietnamese restaurants and other businesses. You can eat yourself silly in this neck of the woods.

Good choices for inexpensive, sumptuous Vietnamese feasts include **Queen Bee** (☎ *703-527-3444, 3181 Wilson Blvd*) – with sugarcane shrimp to die for – **Nam Viet** (☎ *703-522-7110, 1127 N Hudson St*), and **Cafe Dalat** (☎ *703-276-0935, 3143 Wilson Blvd*).

Hard Times Café (☎ *703-528-2233, 3028 Wilson Blvd*) features four kinds of chili: Texas, Cincinnati, Terlingua, and vegetarian. They all come two-, three-, or four-way, depending on the toppings you want. The house root beer's great. **Sagebrush Grill** (☎ *703-524-1432, 1345 N Courthouse Rd*) is an inexpensive Tex-Mex place with the most economical lunch specials you're likely to taste.

A clone of the branch in DC's Dupont Circle, **Xando** (☎ *703-522-0300, 2050 Wilson Blvd*) is the classiest of coffeehouses, with every treatment of the holy bean imaginable, and plain coffee, too; it turns into a bar after dark.

Entertainment
Nightlife in Arlington is sleepier and more of a locals' scene than in DC. Yet you'll find comfortable, welcoming bars and clubs throughout the city, especially in Clarendon.

Try **Whitlow's on Wilson** (☎ *703-276-9693, 2854 Wilson Blvd;* Ⓜ *Clarendon*), with 12 brews on tap, a pool table, jukebox, live music, and an amiable, scuffed-up atmosphere. Nearby, **Galaxy Hut** (☎ *703-525-8646, 2711 Wilson Blvd*) has passable American pub grub and a well-stocked 14-tap bar. **Iota**

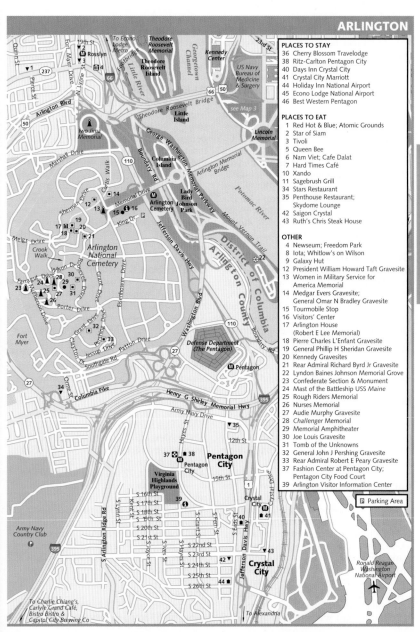

EXCURSIONS

PLACES TO STAY
36 Cherry Blossom Travelodge
38 Ritz-Carlton Pentagon City
40 Days Inn Crystal City
41 Crystal City Marriott
44 Holiday Inn National Airport
45 Econo Lodge National Airport
46 Best Western Pentagon

PLACES TO EAT
1 Red Hot & Blue; Atomic Grounds
2 Star of Siam
3 Tivoli
5 Queen Bee
6 Nam Viet; Cafe Dalat
7 Hard Times Café
10 Xando
11 Sagebrush Grill
34 Stars Restaurant
35 Penthouse Restaurant;
   Skydome Lounge
42 Saigon Crystal
43 Ruth's Chris Steak House

OTHER
4 Newseum; Freedom Park
8 Iota; Whitlow's on Wilson
9 Galaxy Hut
12 President William Howard Taft Gravesite
13 Women in Military Service for
   America Memorial
14 Medgar Evers Gravesite;
   General Omar N Bradley Gravesite
15 Tourmobile Stop
16 Visitors' Center
17 Arlington House
   (Robert E Lee Memorial)
18 Pierre Charles L'Enfant Gravesite
19 General Phillip H Sheridan Gravesite
20 Kennedy Gravesites
21 Rear Admiral Richard Byrd Jr Gravesite
22 Lyndon Baines Johnson Memorial Grove
23 Confederate Section & Monument
24 Mast of the Battleship USS *Maine*
25 Rough Riders Memorial
26 Nurses Memorial
27 Audie Murphy Gravesite
28 *Challenger* Memorial
29 Memorial Amphitheater
30 Joe Louis Gravesite
31 Tomb of the Unknowns
32 General John J Pershing Gravesite
33 Rear Admiral Robert E Peary Gravesite
37 Fashion Center at Pentagon City;
   Pentagon City Food Court
39 Arlington Visitor Information Center

🅿 Parking Area

(☎ 703-522-8340, 2832 Wilson Blvd) is the best place to see live local rock bands. It also has a restaurant, but you're better off ordering food at the bar. There's a poetry series every second Sunday ($5 cover).

Over in Shirlington, a friendly place is the ever-popular *Capitol City Brewing Company (☎ 703-578-3888, 2700 S Quincy St)*, sister to the one on Capitol Hill, with the same menu of microbrews and burgers-and-chicken fare.

Arlington boasts more than a half-dozen professional drama companies. *Washington Shakespeare Company (☎ 703-418-4807, 601 S Clark St)* tweaks the Bard's whiskers with nontraditional performances like *The Taming of the Shrew* with an all-female cast. *Classika Theatre (☎ 703-824-6200, 4041 S 28th St)* stages Russian works.

Getting There & Away

Metrorail Three Metrorail lines link downtown DC to northern Virginia. The Orange Line runs through Rosslyn west to Vienna; the Blue Line runs through Rosslyn south to Franconia-Springfield (stopping at Arlington Cemetery, the Pentagon, Pentagon City, Crystal City, and National Airport). The Yellow Line travels to Alexandria and south to Huntington. For information on the Metro, see the Getting Around chapter.

Bus Arlington lacks its own bus system but is well served by DC Metrobuses (☎ 202-637-7000), which stop at its Metro stations. Greyhound/Trailways (☎ 800-231-2222) buses also pass through Arlington on their way to/from DC.

Car & Motorcycle Driving within the Beltway can be a headache: traffic congestion is often maddening, and once you reach a destination, parking is extremely limited. Nonetheless, driving is pretty much a necessity if your destination isn't near a Metro station – most areas aren't walkable.

Interstate 95 splits into the I-495 Beltway around the DC area. A feeder freeway, I-395, cuts north-south through Alexandria and Arlington to reconnect with I-95 South. US-50 runs east-west through Arlington

and Falls Church; I-66 leads west to the Shenandoah Valley. US-1 is a slower, more relaxed alternative to the north-south I-95 (and offers access to many historic attractions, such as Mount Vernon).

ALEXANDRIA

Once a bustling port city that rivaled New York and Boston, Alexandria was founded in 1699, well predating Washington itself. It became a part of the capital in 1791 but returned to Virginia's control in 1847. Now its old buildings and port warehouses hold upscale restaurants, pubs, shops, and hostelries, especially in the restored Old Town district. The pre-Revolutionary kitsch can get a bit thick, but Alexandria's beautiful 18th-century houses and colonial sites, most open to the public, make it a charming day-trip destination.

Orientation & Information

The main streets dividing Alexandria are north-south Washington St (George Washington Memorial Parkway) and east-west King St. Addresses are numbered by the 100 system – eg, Cameron to Queen is the 200 block north.

The historic area, **Old Town**, is a square bounded by the King St Metro to the west, Slaters Lane to the north, the Potomac River to the east, and the Beltway to the south. Most historic sights lie east of Washington St, and King St is the best station from which to reach them.

The Alexandria Convention and Visitors Association (☎ 800-388-9119, www.FunSide.com) is in Ramsay House, 221 King St, Alexandria, VA 22314; open 9 am to 5 pm daily. It's the best place to start a walking tour, and you can pick up a free 24-hour parking permit here. The association sells a Market Square block ticket ($9/5 adults/kids) for entry to three Alexandria attractions: the Stabler-Leadbeater Apothecary Museum, Carlyle House, and Gadsby's Tavern Museum.

Torpedo Factory

This complex at 105 N Union St was built during WWI to manufacture torpedo parts (and was reused during WWII as a munitions factory). Today, it is the centerpiece of a revamped waterfront with a marina, shops, parks, walkways, residences, offices, and restaurants. The **Torpedo Factory Art Center** (☎ 703-838-4565) houses nearly 200 artists and craftspeople who sell their creations directly from their studios. Open 10 am to 5 pm daily; free.

Also in this complex (Studio 327) is the **Alexandria Archaeology Center** (☎ 703-838-4399), where archaeologists engaged in a number of local urban digs clean and catalog the artifacts they've unearthed. You can watch their work and view informative videos. Open 10 am to 3 pm Tuesday to Friday, 10 am to 5 pm Saturday, 1 to 5 pm Sunday; free.

Fort Ward Museum & Historic Site

Fort Ward (☎ 703-838-4848), 4301 W Braddock Rd, is the best-restored of the 162 Civil War fortifications known as the Defenses of Washington. The Northwest Bastion of the fort has been completely restored, and the remaining earthwork walls give you a good sense of the defenses' original appearance. The on-site museum contains interpretative displays and features exhibits on Civil War topics. Tours, lectures, and living-history programs are offered, too.

The museum is open 9 am to 5 pm Tuesday to Saturday, noon to 5 pm Sunday; the historic site is open 9 am to sunset. Both are free.

Gadsby's Tavern Museum

This museum (☎ 703-838-4242), 134 N Royal St, consists of two tavern buildings built in 1752 and 1792 and named after John Gadsby, who operated them from 1796 to 1808. As the center of political, business, and social life in early Alexandria, they were visited by George Washington and Thomas Jefferson. Lafayette stayed here in 1824, and Washington's last two birthday celebrations were held in the tavern ballroom. Its rooms are restored to their 18th-century appearance. Look for the gravestone of the 'female stranger' who died here in October 1816.

April through September, it's open 10 am to 5 pm Tuesday to Saturday, 1 to 5 pm Sunday (11 am to 4 pm Tuesday to Saturday and 1 to 4 pm Sunday other months); $4/2 adults/kids over 10.

The Lyceum

The Lyceum (☎ 703-838-4994), 201 S Washington St, is Alexandria's history museum, housed in a Greek Revival building that was restored in the 1970s. The exhibits focus on Alexandria since its founding and include prints, photographs, ceramics, silver, and Civil War memorabilia. Open 10 am to 5 pm Monday to Saturday, 1 to 5 pm Sunday; free.

Stabler-Leadbeater Apothecary Museum

This museum (☎ 703-836-3713), 105–7 S Fairfax St, is an 18th-century apothecary shop, founded in 1792 by Quaker pharmacist Edward Stabler. Its shelves are lined with 900 beautiful handblown apothecary bottles and strange old items like 'Martha Washington's Scouring Compound.' It's a fascinating collection. Historical fun fact: It was here, on October 17, 1859, that Robert E Lee received orders to quash John Brown's abolitionist insurrection in Harpers Ferry. Open 10 am to 4 pm Monday to Saturday, 1 to 5 pm Sunday; $2.50/2 adults/kids over 10.

Prince Street

The 100 block of Prince St, called **Captain's Row**, is one of two remaining cobblestone streets in Alexandria. The cobblestones served as the ballast of English ships, and the street was possibly laid by Hessian prisoners of war. It's lined with lovely private homes, many built for sea captains. One was owned by a Captain John Harper, whose wife, it is said, died in self-defense after the birth of her 15th child.

Gentry Row is the 200 block of Prince St, named after the number of imposing private dwellings. The rosy-colored **Athenaeum** (☎ 703-548-0035), a Greek Revival building at No 201, is a fine-arts museum, open 10 am to 4 pm Tuesday to Saturday, 1 to 4 pm Sunday; free. Hours are erratic, so call ahead to make sure it's open.

EXCURSIONS

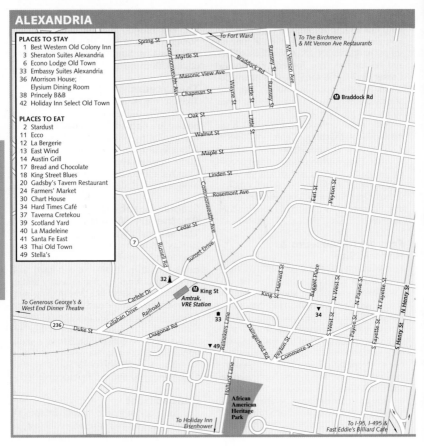

ALEXANDRIA

PLACES TO STAY
1 Best Western Old Colony Inn
3 Sheraton Suites Alexandria
6 Econo Lodge Old Town
33 Embassy Suites Alexandria
36 Morrison House;
   Elysium Dining Room
38 Princely B&B
42 Holiday Inn Select Old Town

PLACES TO EAT
2 Stardust
11 Ecco
12 La Bergerie
13 East Wind
14 Austin Grill
17 Bread and Chocolate
18 King Street Blues
20 Gadsby's Tavern Restaurant
24 Farmers' Market
30 Chart House
34 Hard Times Café
37 Taverna Cretekou
39 Scotland Yard
40 La Madeleine
41 Santa Fe East
43 Thai Old Town
49 Stella's

EXCURSIONS

Black History Resource Center

This center (☎ 703-838-4356), 638 N Alfred St (entrance on Wythe St), displays paintings, photographs, books, and other memorabilia documenting the black experience in Alexandria and Virginia from 1749 to the present. Here you can pick up a brochure for self-guided walking tours of important Alexandria black-history sites. Open 10 am to 4 pm Tuesday to Saturday; free.

In the next-door annex, the **Watson Reading Room** has a wealth of books and documents on African American topics. Operated by the museum, the **African American Heritage Park**, along Holland Lane, is worth a stop to see headstones from a 19th-century black cemetery.

Christ Church

This red-brick Georgian-style church (☎ 703-549-1450), at the corner of N Washington and Cameron Sts, has been in use since 1773. George Washington, who had a townhouse in Alexandria, purchased a pew here. Robert E Lee was confirmed here, and the interesting churchyard cemetery contains the mass grave of Confederate soldiers. Open 9 am to 4 pm Monday to Saturday, 2

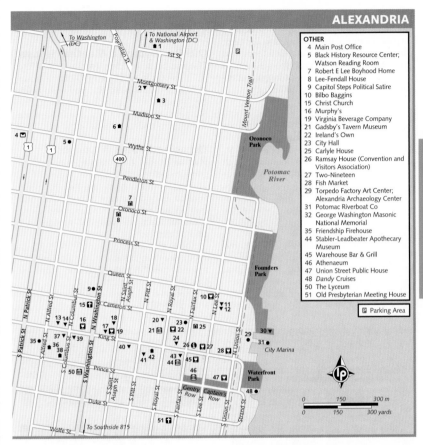

ALEXANDRIA

OTHER
4 Main Post Office
5 Black History Resource Center;
   Watson Reading Room
7 Robert E Lee Boyhood Home
8 Lee-Fendall House
9 Capitol Steps Political Satire
10 Bilbo Baggins
15 Christ Church
16 Murphy's
19 Virginia Beverage Company
21 Gadsby's Tavern Museum
22 Ireland's Own
23 City Hall
25 Carlyle House
26 Ramsay House (Convention and
   Visitors Association)
27 Two-Nineteen
28 Fish Market
29 Torpedo Factory Art Center;
   Alexandria Archaeology Center
31 Potomac Riverboat Co
32 George Washington Masonic
   National Memorial
35 Friendship Firehouse
44 Stabler-Leadbeater Apothecary
   Museum
45 Warehouse Bar & Grill
46 Athenaeum
47 Union Street Public House
48 *Dandy* Cruises
50 The Lyceum
51 Old Presbyterian Meeting House

Parking Area

EXCURSIONS

to 4:30 pm Sunday; free. Docent-led tours are offered Sunday.

George Washington Masonic National Memorial

Alexandria's most prominent landmark, this neoclassical monstrosity (☎ 703-683-2007), 101 Callahan Drive at King St, features a fine view from its 333-foot tower, where you can see the Capitol, Mount Vernon, and the Potomac River. Washington, initiated into the Masons in Fredericksburg in 1752, later became Worshipful Master of Alexandria Lodge No 22. There are tours on the half-

hour in the morning, on the hour in afternoon, and lots of parking. Open 9 am to 4 pm daily; free.

Robert E Lee Boyhood Home

Built in 1795, this Georgian-style townhouse (☎ 703-548-8454), 607 Oronoco St, was the general's home from the age of five. Lee's father, Henry, a Revolutionary War commander and governor of Virginia from 1792 to 1795, moved his family here in 1810. Open 10 am to 4 pm Monday to Saturday, 1 to 4 pm Sunday from February to December; $4/2 adults/kids over 10.

Across the street, the 1785 **Lee-Fendall House** (☎ 703-548-1789), 614 Oronoco St, displays furniture that belonged to the Lees, plus a neat collection of miniatures and dollhouses that kids like. Open 10 am to 3:45 pm Tuesday to Saturday, noon to 3:45 pm Sunday; $4/2 adults/kids.

Carlyle House

Near the corner of Fairfax and Cameron Sts is the imposing, Georgian-style Carlyle House (☎ 703-549-2997), 121 N Fairfax St, built by Scottish merchant John Carlyle in 1753. Guided tours run on the half-hour from 10 am to 4:30 pm Tuesday to Saturday, noon to 4:30 pm Sunday; $4/2 adults/kids over 10 years old.

Friendship Firehouse

This 1855 Italianate firehouse, 107 S Alfred St, displays historic firefighting gear – a great draw for kids. Local legend has it that George Washington helped found this volunteer fire company, served as its captain, and even paid for a new fire engine. Open

10 am to 4 pm Friday and Saturday, 1 to 4 pm Sunday; free.

Old Presbyterian Meeting House

The red-brick building (☎ 703-549-6670), 321 S Fairfax St, was built in 1775 by a group of Calvinist dissenters. The graveyard holds the Tomb of the Unknown Soldier of the Revolutionary War. Open 9 am to 5 pm weekdays; free.

Organized Tours & Cruises

Ramsay House (see Information, earlier) conducts informative walking tours of Old Town Alexandria from late March to November. They commence at noon daily and cost $8 per person. There are also ghost tours at 9 pm on weekend nights; $4/3 adults/children.

The Potomac Riverboat Co (☎ 703-548-9000) docks its boats at the city marina behind the Torpedo Factory. April to October, its boats cruise the Potomac from Georgetown to Mount Vernon; prices range from $7 to $22.

Alexandria has many beautiful historic houses.

PHILIP GAME

The *Dandy* (☎ 703-683-6076), departing from the foot of Prince St, is a restaurant/cruise ship renowned for its food and service. On weekdays, lunch costs $26; Sunday champagne brunch costs $32; midnight dance cruises start at $23.

Places to Stay

Econo Lodge Old Town (☎ 703-836-5100, 702 N Washington St) is the best close-to-town bet for the budget traveler; doubles cost $70 to $80. *Econo Lodge Mount Vernon* (☎ 703-780-0300, 8849 Richmond Hwy), 7½ miles south of the I-95/I-495 Beltway, is a similar cheapie; rooms cost $65 to $75. There are dives along this strip, so beware.

Holiday Inn Eisenhower (☎ 703-960-3400, 2460 Eisenhower Ave; Ⓜ Eisenhower Ave), just north of I-95/I-495, has a heated indoor pool and an exercise room. Singles cost $69 to $119, doubles $79 to $129.

Best Western Old Colony Inn (☎ 703-739-2222, 615 1st St), on George Washington Memorial Parkway, includes a free breakfast in its year-round rate of $69. *Sheraton Suites Alexandria* (☎ 703-836-4700, 801 N Saint Asaph St), a block east of N Washington St, has doubles starting at $115/135 low/high season.

Princely B&B (☎ 800-470-5588, 819 Prince St) rents rooms in 30 houses in and around Old Town; expect to pay about $70/80 single/double. Alexandria & Arlington B&B Network (☎ 888-549-3415, www.aabbn.com) is a booking service.

Embassy Suites Alexandria (☎ 703-684-5900, 1900 Diagonal Rd), adjacent to the King St Metro and the Amtrak/VRE terminal, is a trusted favorite, offering all the facilities – indoor pool, sauna, sundeck, exercise room, and restaurant. Rooms cost $154 to $204 year-round.

Holiday Inn Select Old Town (☎ 703-549-6080, 480 King St) has a restaurant and gift shop and arranges transport to Metro and the airports. Some rooms have a balcony overlooking a central courtyard. All rooms cost $169.

Morrison House (☎ 703-838-8000, 116 S Alfred St) is one of the most expensive choices, but it's worth the cost if you can

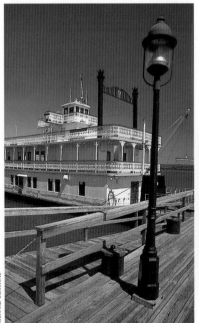

RICHARD CUMMINS

Riverboat at the marina

afford it. This four-star, boutique-style hotel includes two excellent restaurants (see Places to Eat) and a library where afternoon tea is served. The rooms, furnished with Federal-style reproductions, have marble baths, include the aid of a butler, and start at $175/200 single/double. Suites cost $350/550. There's a sweet resident house dog, named Spot.

Places to Eat

Alexandria is thick with eateries, many of them concentrated in Old Town.

For a taste of the South, try *Southside 815* (☎ 703-836-6222, 815 S Washington St), with moderately priced, heavily caloric dishes like biscuits and gravy, succotash, and po'boys. *Stardust* (☎ 703-548-9864, 608 Montgomery St), with a star-strewn interior decor, serves delightful new American and fusion dishes, with an emphasis on seafood; entrées start around $12.

EXCURSIONS

Short on cash? Stock up at the Saturday *farmers' market* (☎ 703-370-8723, 301 King St) in front of City Hall; cheap fresh produce, baked goods, and meats are sold. *Bread and Chocolate* (☎ 703-548-0992, 611 King St) has wonderful sandwiches plus desserts to keep any sweet tooth satisfied. A hearty breakfast costs $3.50 to $6.50.

The inexpensive and casual *Hard Times Café* (☎ 703-683-5340, 1404 King St) focuses on chili (see the listing under Arlington, earlier). *Stella's* (☎ 703-519-1946, 1725 Duke St), where the decor harks back to the 1940s, wins our prize for the best Sunday brunch, with unlimited champagne and a diverse breakfast selection from 11 am to 2:30 pm ($12.95). There's an adjoining beer garden.

East Wind (☎ 703-836-1515, 809 King St), several thousand miles away in terms of flavor, is a good choice for Vietnamese vegetarian lunches (around $7) or steaming *pho*. Other lunch possibilities are *La Madeleine* (☎ 703-739-9494, 500 King St), a French bakery/café concocting fresh breads and pastries in its wood-burning oven, and *King Street Blues* (☎ 703-836-8800, 112 N Saint Asaph St), a Southern 'roadhouse' diner serving beef stew and garlic potatoes, hot salad, and yummy chicken. Lunch specials cost only $5.

Thai Old Town (☎ 703-684-6503, 300 King St) testifies to the growing number of Southeast Asian immigrants in the DC area and the popularity of their cuisine. Pad Thai here costs less than $10, sweet-and-sour soups less than $5.

Taverna Cretekou (☎ 703-548-8688, 818 King St) is a delightful eatery – it has an outside grapevine arbor, waiters spontaneously dance à la Zorba after supper, and Sunday brunch is legendary. You'll pay $20 to $25 for a full meal.

Santa Fe East (☎ 703-548-6900, 110 S Pitt St) and *Austin Grill* (☎ 703-684-8969, 801 King St) both have fireplaces and offer good Tex-Mex food for a reasonable price. Lunch costs $7 to $14, dinner $12 to $20.

La Bergerie (☎ 703-683-1007, 218 N Lee St), in the Crilley shops, is Alexandria's best dining choice. A full dinner of classic French or Basque cuisine costs $35. Closed Sunday.

Neighboring *Ecco* (☎ 703-684-0321, 220 N Lee St) serves delicious Italian pizzas, pastas, and sauces (generous servings) accompanied by hearty salads. Entrées cost $8 to $15.

Gadsby's Tavern Restaurant (☎ 703-548-1288, 138 N Royal St) tries hard to emulate an 18th-century hostelry but errs on the side of kitsch. But its history makes it worth a visit. *Scotland Yard* (☎ 703-683-1742, 728 King St) serves, yes, Scottish cuisine (no haggis). At dinner, the lace curtains, Highland menu, and cozy atmosphere (plus tasty 'Bramble Mist' dessert) echo the glens.

Chart House (☎ 703-684-5080, 1 Cameron St), on the waterfront, offers views that justify the considerable cost. Entrées cost $16 to $25, Sunday champagne brunch (11 am to 2:30 pm) around $18.

Elysium Dining Room (☎ 703-838-8000), a multiaward winner in Morrison House (see Places to Stay), is bloody expensive, but by all reports, it's well worth the hefty check. It's open daily for breakfast and dinner, Sunday for brunch.

Kids enjoy *Generous George's Positive Pizza & Pasta Place* (☎ 703-370-4303, 3006 Duke St), west of Old Town, with its big, crispy-crusted pies going for about $14 for a large. Pasta, oddly, is also served on pizza crust. It's a crowded, happy place.

Away from Old Town, a clutch of mid-priced, interesting multiethnic restaurants is springing up along Mt Vernon Ave. Try *Po Siam* (☎ 703-548-3925, 3802 Mt Vernon Ave); *Evening Star Café* (☎ 703-549-5051, 2000 Mt Vernon Ave), serving Cajun-inspired dishes; or *Bombay Curry Company* (☎ 703-836-6363, 3110 Mt Vernon Ave).

Entertainment

For quiet beers, try *Union Street Public House* (☎ 703-548-1785, 121 S Union St), easily spotted by the big gas lamps out front; *Warehouse Bar & Grill* (☎ 703-683-6868, 214 King St), with great crabcakes and humorous caricatures adorning its walls; *Virginia Beverage Company* (☎ 703-684-5397, 607 King St), with 13 taps, homemade root beer, and huge steaks; and *Fast Eddie's Billiard Cafe* (☎ 703-660-9444, 6220 Richmond Hwy), south of the Beltway,

Come to King St for live music.

rises at 8 pm; there are matinees Wednesday and Sunday.

Capitol Steps Political Satire (☎ 703-683-8330, 210 N Washington St) is a DC tradition, a comedy troupe that pokes satiric bipartisan fun at sinning presidents and erring members of Congress.

Getting There & Around

From Union Station in DC, you can catch the Metro to Arlington, Alexandria, and points beyond in northern Virginia. The King St Metro station, the closest to Old Town, doubles as the Amtrak station (Amtrak passes through Arlington on its East Coast route). Other Arlington Metro stations, connected to the Yellow and Blue Lines, are Braddock Rd and Eisenhower Ave.

Alexandria's bus system, DASH (☎ 703-370-3274), operates daily; 85¢ for a four-hour pass. From King St station, you can take Metrobuses and the DASH bus AT-5 directly to the Alexandria visitors' center.

Visitors can park free at any two-hour parking meter in the city by picking up a pass from the visitors' center.

FAIRFAX

Fairfax, just south of I-66 and west of the Beltway, is of interest to visitors chiefly for its variety of mid-priced lodgings; you can usually get rooms for under $100. Try ***Hampton Inn – Fairfax*** (☎ 703-385-2600), at the intersection of US-50 and US-29; ***Holiday Inn Fairfax City*** (☎ 703-591-5500), on Route 123; and ***Comfort Inn University Center*** (☎ 703-591-5900, 11180 Main St), on US-50. On Route 123, you'll find ***Bailiwick Inn*** (☎ 703-691-2266), a fine restored 19th-century residence. Its comforts are not cheap: singles and doubles cost $130 to $295.

George Mason University Center for the Arts (☎ 703-993-8788, 4400 University Drive) hosts symphonies, dance companies, chamber-music groups, and jazz artists and has an adjoining professional theater. The center is open September to May.

Fairfax is near the end of the Metro's Orange Line, and two stations (Vienna and Dunn Loring) are on its northern fringe. But a car is definitely a necessity out here.

with 26 Brunswick pool tables. ***Bilbo Baggins*** (☎ 703-683-0300, 208 Queen St) is known not for hobbits but for an extensive wine bar (over 200 varieties).

The DC area's premier venue for folk, country, Celtic, and bluegrass music is ***The Birchmere*** (☎ 703-549-7500, 3701 Mt Vernon Ave), south of Glebe Rd. Other live-music venues are along or near King St: ***Murphy's*** (☎ 703-548-1717, 713 King St) and ***Ireland's Own*** (☎ 703-549-4535, 132 N Royal St) both have live Irish entertainment nightly, lubricated by buckets of Guinness. ***Two-Nineteen*** (☎ 703-549-1141, 219 King St), a Creole/New Orleans–flavored place, features jazz nightly.

Fish Market (☎ 703-836-5676, 103 King St), serving reliable seafood meals and providing good music, suits the more mature crowd.

West End Dinner Theatre (☎ 703-370-2500, 4615 Duke St) boasts the area's largest dinner-theater stage, featuring Broadway musicals and comedies ($30 to $35). Tuesday to Sunday, dinner is at 6 pm and the curtain

EXCURSIONS

RICHARD CUMMINS

EXCURSIONS

Happiness Is a Warm Blunderbuss

Do you dream of Charlton Heston? Will they have to pry your sidearm out of your cold, dead hand? Then the NRA National Firearms Museum (☎ 703-267-1600), at NRA headquarters, 11250 Waples Mill Rd in Fairfax, is the place for you. Two thousand guns, going all the way back to the 1300s, trace the glorious history of firearms from muskets to semiautomatics. The museum includes a replica of the St Louis shop where the Hawken rifle, used by mountain men in the 19th century, was created; a Coney Island shooting gallery; and Wild West firearms. There are also interactive displays, photos, and plenty of NRA agit-prop to take to folks back home. It's free, open daily, and brooks no pacifists.

VIENNA & RESTON

The principal attraction in Vienna, a sizable suburban city between Dulles Airport and DC, is **Wolf Trap Farm Park for the Performing Arts** (☎ 703-255-1860), 1624 Trap Rd, the country's first national performing-arts park. Year-round dance, theater, music, and children's performances take place at this beautiful 130-acre park. The best time to visit is summer, when performances are staged in the centuries-old Barns of Wolf Trap, outdoor Filene Center amphitheater, and children's outdoor Theatre-in-the-Woods. (Why the name Wolf Trap? Back in the 1600s, wolves caused damage in the area, so farmers paid local wolf-trappers with tobacco bundles. The nickname stuck.)

Order tickets by phone through Tickets .com (☎ 800-955-5566) or online (www .wolf-trap.org). In-house shows start at $25, lawn picnic spaces at $17.50. The Filene Center is at 1551 Trap Rd, the Barns at No 1635. From Beltway exit 12, take the Dulles Toll Rd to the Wolf Trap exit. Alternately, a shuttle bus runs from the West Falls Church Metro station.

Reston, one of the country's first planned communities, was built in 1964. It holds **Terraset**, 11411 Ridge Heights Rd, the country's first earth-sheltered school, and an interesting town center. Built during the oil crisis in the 1970s, the school is built partially into the hillside to conserve energy. Also in Reston is the **US Geological Survey** (☎ 703-648-4748), 12201 Sunrise Valley Drive, where data on minerals and land and water resources are collected and distributed; tours run Monday, Tuesday, and Thursday.

GREAT FALLS NATIONAL PARK

This scenic 800-acre park (☎ 703-285-2966) protects the area where the Potomac, generally a placid river, becomes raging whitewater as it descends from the rocky Piedmont to the flatter Coastal Plain. Several miles of trails wind through the woods and along the falls. In 1785, George Washington's Patowmack Company built a canal here to circumvent the falls – a three-quarter-mile stretch of it remains, and you can explore what's left on foot. You can also hike among the ruins of **Matildaville**, a trading town that died in the 1820s as canal business declined.

Park grounds are open 7 am until dusk daily; entrance costs $4/2 vehicles/pedestrians. The visitors' center, open 10 am to 5 pm daily, conducts historical programs. From I-495, take exit 13 to Georgetown Pike and drive 4 miles to Old Dominion Drive. Turn right to enter the park.

Across the river is the **C&O Canal National Historic Park** (see the Maryland section). Your entrance fee permits access to both parks for three days.

In the town of Great Falls is a restaurant worth a splurge: **L'Auberge Chez Francois** *(☎ 703-759-3800, 332 Springvale Rd)*, which is among the Washington area's best restaurants. Presided over by François Haeringer, it serves widely acclaimed French Alsatian cuisine. Prix-fixe menus begin at $32. Dinner is served dailed except Monday; there's also Sunday brunch.

LEESBURG

Near the Maryland border on Route 7, northwest of Dulles Airport, Leesburg is among Northern Virginia's oldest towns. Its colonial-era buildings, quaint antique shops and hostelries, and nearby plantations make for a delightful day trip. It's also on the **W&OD Trail** (see Arlington), and a night here is a welcome break on a bike trip.

Leesburg has a rich military and political history – a British staging ground during the French and Indian War, it served the same role for the colonials in the Revolution. The Declaration of Independence and Constitution were secreted here after the British torched Washington in 1814. At nearby Oak Hill, President James Monroe penned the Monroe Doctrine in 1823. In 1861, a major Civil War battle was fought at nearby Ball's Bluff. The Confederates forced the Union troops back across the Potomac, and houses on Leesburg's King St were used as hospitals. One patient was the young Oliver Wendell Holmes, later a Supreme Court justice.

The Leesburg tourist office (☎ 703-777-2420, www.leesburgva.org), in Market Station at 108-D South St, is open 9 am to 5 pm daily.

Loudoun Museum

Exhibits and artifacts at this museum (☎ 703-777-7427), 16 Loudoun St, narrate northern Virginia's history from Native American times to the present. It's of interest to non-Virginian visitors because of its attention to the Civil War and slavery. The museum is also the starting point of an interesting self-guided walking tour. Open 10 am to 5 pm Monday to Saturday, 1 to 5 pm Sunday; $1/50¢ adults/children.

Morven Park

A mile north of Leesburg on Old Waterford Rd is a 1500-acre historic property (☎ 703-777-2414) that was once the home of Virginia Governor Westmoreland Davis. The Greek Revival mansion, with its manicured boxwood gardens, resembles a transplanted White House, and its antique carriage museum includes more than 100 horse-drawn vehicles. Open noon to 5 pm daily except Monday, from April through October; $6/3 adults/kids.

Oatlands Plantation

This circa-1803 National Historic Trust plantation (☎ 703-777-3174), on Route 15, 6 miles south of Leesburg, was established by a great-grandson of Robert 'King' Carter, the wealthy pre-Revolutionary planter. The carefully restored Greek Revival–style mansion is surrounded by lovely gardens and neat fields that feature in local hunt events such as the Loudoun Hunt Point-to-Point in April (☎ 540-338-2578). More interesting are the Sheep Dog Trials in May (☎ 703-777-3174), featuring search-and-rescue dogs. Open 10 am to 4:30 pm Monday to Saturday, 1 to 4:30 pm Sunday from April to December; $8/7 adults/kids 12 and over.

Animal Park

Formerly in Reston, this park (☎ 703-433-0002), 19270 James Monroe Hwy, is a children's zoo with all kinds of domestic and exotic animals. Kids can ride ponies, bottle-feed lambs, and pet and watch other fluffy beasties. In spring, it's open 10 am to 5 pm Friday to Sunday; mid-June to Labor Day, it's open 10 am to 5 pm Wednesday to Sunday; $6/4 adults/kids 12 and under.

Places to Stay

Leesburg is a romantic-getaway, fancy-inn kind of town. There are few budget accommodations, so visit weekdays, when prices drop.

Reliable B&Bs include the renovated, red-brick 1760 **Norris House Inn** (☎ 703-777-1806, 108 Loudoun St SW), with doubles for $100 (weekdays) to $150 (weekends). **Colonial Inn** (☎ 800-392-1332, 19 S King St), attached to Bella Luna Ristorante (see Places to Eat), offers singles and doubles for $99 to $175.

The 1766 **Laurel Brigade Inn** (☎ 703-777-1010, 20 W Market St) is popular and always requires advance booking. (It's named for a Confederate brigade led by a local colonel.) It features lovely gardens, a restaurant for lunch and dinner, and pleasantly furnished rooms (without phones). Doubles cost $65 to $90, making the Laurel Brigade one of the town's best deals.

Price no object? Consider **Landsdowne Resort** (☎ *800-541-4801, 44050 Woodbridge Parkway*), nestled on the Potomac banks. With its Trent Jones–designed golf course, tennis courts, pools, and two posh restaurants, it caters to older, wealthy guests and charges $200 to $290 for high-season doubles (about $40 less in low season).

Places to Eat

Lightfoot (☎ *703-771-2233, 11 N King St*) is a progressive American bistro with an à la carte seasonal menu and freshly baked breads. **Laurel Brigade Inn** features steak and seafood dishes; lunch entrées start at $10, and fixed-price dinner costs $14. **Bella Luna Ristorante**, in the Colonial Inn, is a cozy place with classic mid-range Italian dishes.

Tuscarora Mill (☎ *703-771-9300*), Market Station, occupies the upper level of a 19th-century mill. Hearty lunches average about $12 and are worth it; dinner features innovative New American entrées, and Sunday brunch is popular.

MOUNT VERNON

Fascinating Mount Vernon (☎ 703-780-2000, www.mountvernon.org), George Washington's home, is a Virginia must-see. Among historic houses, it ranks second only to the White House in popularity. The country estate of this quintessential country gentleman has been meticulously restored and affords a glimpse of rural gentility as it was when Washington 'took to the farm.' All is not ostentation, however – there are many remnants of the farm's working past, plus regular living-history presentations.

Situated on the Potomac banks, Mount Vernon includes immaculate gardens, a preserved 19-room mansion, and several outbuildings. Work on the main building commenced in 1754, on land that the family had owned for 80 years. George and his wife, Martha, lived here from 1759 to 1775, when George assumed command of the Continental Army. After his eight years as president, he retired here in 1797.

Both George and Martha are buried in an enclosure on the house's south side. (George died here in his four-poster on December 14, 1799.) The entrance to the family vault bears the legend 'Within this enclosure rest the remains of General George Washington.' The two sarcophagi are simply inscribed: 'Washington' and 'Martha, Consort of Washington' (what, 'wife' wouldn't do?).

The colonnaded facade of the main building faces the Potomac; the kitchen and slaves' and workers' quarters are detached. In the main reception room is the key to the Bastille, presented to Washington by Thomas Paine on behalf of Lafayette (it has left the building just once, flown to Paris for the bicentennial of the storming of the Bastille). The library, with its ornate fireplace, globe, and revolving chair and secretary desk, exudes an air befitting the nation's first president. An adjoining museum displays the results of an archaeological dig on the blacksmith's shop and slaves' quarters.

The estate is open 9 am to 5 pm daily in March, September, and October; 8 am to 5 pm April to August; otherwise, 9 am to 4 pm. Admission costs $9/4.50 adults/children six to 11. In summer, go early – there are usually long lines.

Mount Vernon is 16 miles south of DC on the George Washington Memorial Parkway. On public transit, take a Yellow Line Metro train to Huntington, then board Fairfax Connector (☎ 703-339-7200) bus No 101 to the estate. You can also bike down here along the riverside **Mount Vernon Trail**.

Mount Vernon Inn (☎ *703-780-0011*), a colonial-style restaurant on the estate, serves lunch (around $7.50) daily and candlelight dinner Monday to Saturday ($12 to $20). For the inappropriately dressed, a snack bar is near the estate entrance.

AROUND MOUNT VERNON
Woodlawn Plantation

In the town of Mount Vernon, Woodlawn (☎ 703-780-4000), 9000 Richmond Hwy, features two very different houses that are both splendid examples of their architectural times. The plantation home itself once

Manassas National Battlefield Park

North of the town of Manassas and 26 miles from DC, this Civil War battlefield is a must-visit for amateur historians. Two cataclysmic, seesawing battles between the Union and Confederacy raged here in July 1861 and August 1862, killing more than 4000 men. The battles are called Bull Run in the North, Manassas in the South. The smaller 1861 battle – the war's first major engagement – was won by the Confederates, led by General Stonewall Jackson. In 1862, advantage again fell to the South, as troops commanded by Jackson and Robert E Lee forced the Northerners back toward DC.

A good self-guided tour commences from the park's visitors' center (☎ 703-361-1339). The center also features exhibits, a captivating video, and a free pamphlet showing all points of interest. In August, the park stages reenactments of the battles.

The park is open daylight to dusk daily, the visitors' center 8:30 am to 5 pm daily; $2. Kids enter free. Take I-66W to Route 234 exit 47B; the battlefield is a half-mile along this road.

EXCURSIONS

belonged to Eleanor 'Nelly' Custis, granddaughter of Martha Washington, and her husband, Major Lawrence Lewis, George Washington's nephew. William Thornton (the Capitol's first architect) built it between 1800 and 1805 on Mount Vernon acreage that George Washington gave the couple. You can tour the house to see its period antiques and the gardens to see a stunning rose collection.

Frank Lloyd Wright's **Pope-Leighey House** – a 1940s middle-class Usonian dwelling of cypress, brick, and glass – is also on Woodlawn's grounds. (Originally intended as low-cost houses for the middle class, Wright's Usonian dwellings featured aesthetically elegant designs yet used durable, inexpensive materials.) It was moved here in 1964 from Falls Church to rescue it from destruction. Furnished with Wright pieces, the house is utilitarian in structure but quite beautiful.

Both houses are open 10 am to 5 pm daily from March to December; $6/4 adults/kids. From DC, reach Woodlawn along the George Washington Memorial Parkway. Bear right just before Mount Vernon itself, onto Route 235 S; take it 3 miles to the intersection with US-1, where you'll see Woodlawn's entrance.

Gunston Hall

This brick home (☎ 703-550-9220) belonged to George Mason, a contemporary of Wash-

ington. Mason penned the lines 'all men are by nature equally free and independent, and have certain inherent rights' – words adapted by Thomas Jefferson for the Declaration of Independence.

Among the key framers of the Constitution, Mason later refused to support the document because it didn't include a bill of rights or provide a checks-and-balances system to curb the federal government's power. He wrote the Virginia Declaration of Rights in May 1776, which later became the basis of the Bill of Rights. But, unlike Jefferson and Washington, Mason deliberately avoided political office, preferring to remain at home with his family at Gunston Hall.

Gunston Hall, which dates from 1755, is an architectural masterpiece with elegantly carved wooden interiors. Meticulously kept formal gardens with boxwood hedges surround the home. Open 9:30 am to 5 pm daily; $5/1.50 adults/kids. Gunston Hall is on a bend in the Potomac River, about a 15-minute drive from Mount Vernon via Route 235, US-1, and Route 242.

A couple of riverfront parks are near Gunston Hall. Among them is **Mason Neck State Park** (☎ 703-550-0960), 7 miles northeast of Woodbridge on Route 242, which offers a range of outdoor activities and programs. Many birdwatchers come to the adjacent wildlife refuge for the weekend bald-eagle counts.

Maryland

Maryland, which surrounds three sides of DC, is a little state that somehow manages to cram everything from soulless suburbs (near the Beltway), mountainous wilderness (western Maryland), industrial towns (Baltimore), and placid estuaries (along the Chesapeake) into its boundaries. A daytripper from DC can hike along the C&O Canal, visit key Civil War battlefields, and explore a host of historic sites scattered around the capital. Annapolis, Maryland's yachting capital, and Baltimore, with its vibrant waterfront and great aquarium, are other great trips – see Lonely Planet's *Virginia & the Capital Region* for details on those two cities.

BETHESDA

Once a pokey rural town, Bethesda has grown into one of America's wealthiest and most influential suburbs. It's dominated by corporate skyscrapers and the large campuses of the National Institutes of Health and the National Naval Medical Center (where US presidents go to see the doctor). Day-trippers like the town for its plethora of ethnic restaurants.

Orientation & Information

Downtown Bethesda is centered on the intersection of Wisconsin Ave (running south to Georgetown) and Old Georgetown Rd. The Metro station here makes Bethesda a convenient destination – visitors can walk to restaurants, clubs, bookstores, and boutiques within a compact zone near the station. But the coolest way to reach Bethesda is on the **Capital Crescent Trail**, which runs 11 miles from Georgetown right through downtown Bethesda. See Activities in the Things to See & Do chapter for more details.

The Conference & Visitors Bureau of Montgomery County (☎ 800-925-0880) provides information about Bethesda and most of DC's northern suburbs.

National Institutes of Health

NIH (Ⓜ Medical Center), along Wisconsin Ave north of downtown Bethesda, is a 316-acre, 20,000-employee research metropolis. It funnels billions of dollars to biomedical research enterprises around the country and performs groundbreaking work on AIDS, cancer, and other scourges at its Bethesda headquarters. Visitors can see the huge **National Library of Medicine** or stop by the visitors' center (☎ 301-496-1776) to learn about NIH's work and take free weekday tours.

Places to Stay

Downtown Bethesda lodgings cater to business travelers and are only slightly cheaper than those in downtown DC. Rooms start at $100 on weekdays and are discounted by a third or more on weekends.

American Inn (☎ 800-323-7081, 8130 Wisconsin Ave), a decent older motel, is within walking distance of the Metro. Doubles cost $150 weekdays, $84 weekends, including breakfast and Internet access. Kids under 18 stay free. Newer motel chains downtown include Ramada and Residence Inn by Marriott.

The deluxe, 11-floor *Hyatt Regency Bethesda* (☎ 301-657-1234, 1 Bethesda Metro Center), above the Metro station, features an atrium lobby and glass-enclosed penthouse pool. Rooms start at $270 weekdays, $109 weekends. A business center, babysitting, and currency exchange are available.

Places to Eat

Bethesda is a burgeoning gourmet ghetto, with a variety of cuisines to rival what you'll find in DC's Adams-Morgan. All the following selections are near the Metro.

Tastee Diner (☎ 301-652-3970, 7731 Woodmont Ave) is a beloved icon of old Bethesda, a 24-hour chrome-fronted joint staffed by waitresses with tall hair who don't mind serving you fries-with-gravy at 4 am. A burger costs $2.25. *Bethesda Crab House* (☎ 301-652-3382, 4958 Bethesda Ave) is another taste of pre-suburban Maryland. Blue-collar workers and oldtimers rub elbows with yuppies around paper-lined picnic tables, hammering away at the sweet crustaceans doused in Old Bay seasoning and served with hush puppies and brew.

Faryab (☎ *301-951-3484, 4917 Cordell Ave*) is among the best Afghan restaurants going – its juicy lamb kebabs and meat-topped *aushak* noodles are a carnivore's dream. Entrées run $10 to $16. Closed Monday. Nearby, acclaimed *Cesco Trattoria* (☎ *301-654-8333, 4871 Cordell*) serves up-scale Italian; start with a warm octopus salad and move to classic *osso buco*. Entrées start at $10.

Bethesda's answer to Tex-Mex, *Cotton-wood Cafe* (☎ *301-656-4844, 4844 Cordell*) serves high-end Southwestern specialties (fajitas cost $10) in a fancy but un-stuffy atmosphere. *Tara Thai* (☎ *301-657-0488, 4828 Bethesda Ave*) is a wonderful mid-priced seafood restaurant, serving things like chili-spiked mussels for $8.

Getting There & Around
In addition to the main Metro station, Bethesda is served by Metrobuses No 32, 34, and 36, running along Wisconsin Ave from Georgetown. Griffin Cycle (☎ 301-656-6188), 4949 Bethesda Ave, two blocks from the Capital Crescent Trail, rents bicycles for $15 a day.

TAKOMA PARK
Straddling DC's northeastern boundary, Takoma Park was DC's first commuter suburb (founded in 1883). Today this funky little town – nuclear-free! – is home to an alternative community that's worth visiting for its bohemian shops and serious obsession with music. The Metro's Red Line Takoma Park station makes access from downtown easy.

Takoma Park Co-op (☎ 301-891-2667), 201 Ethan Allan Ave, serves as an alternative cultural center, selling smudge sticks, fair-trade coffee, and organic produce and offering handbills and posters rallying residents to political action. It's a good place to find out about local cultural events, too. Open 9 am to 9 pm daily.

Acoustic and folk music are a big deal in Takoma Park (the great guitarist John Fahey grew up here). The **House of Musical Traditions** (☎ 301-270-9090, 800-540-9090), 7040 Carroll Ave, carries an impressive array of acoustic instruments from around the world, including harps, concertinas, drums, dulcimers, and flutes. Inquire about Friday-evening jam sessions and other concerts. Other Takoma shops include a bookstore, Tibetan-imports store, and a great international beads shop.

The town hosts an annual **folk festival** (☎ 301-589-3717), highlighting local talent, in mid-September.

Takoma Park offers several accommodations that are a nice alternative to staying in downtown DC. The lively hostel *India House Too* (☎ *202-291-1195, 300 Carroll St*), just over the DC border, is described in the Places to Stay chapter. Also consider *Davis Warner Inn* (☎ *301-408-3989, 8114 Carroll Ave*), a B&B in the town's oldest home. A beautiful mansion with finely landscaped gardens, it features three rooms sharing a bath ($75) and a fourth with private bath and Jacuzzi ($125). The owners have dogs. Full breakfast is served, and there's a bus link to the Takoma Park Metro.

Within sight of the Metro, *Takoma Station* (☎ *202-829-1999, 6914 4th St NW*) is a great tavern with some of the DC's area's best blues, jazz, and reggae. The comfortable, spacious club hosts live music nightly.

LOWER POTOMAC CORRIDOR
The Potomac's lower stretches are hemmed in by the burgeoning suburbs of Maryland and Virginia, but the Maryland shore is protected by the C&O Canal National Historic Park and dotted with historic attractions. A hike or bike ride here makes a fine day trip.

Glen Echo Park
On the banks of the Potomac several miles north of DC, visitors stumble upon Glen Echo Park (☎ 301-492-6229), a former amusement park where an old arcade, bumper-car pavilion, and carousel are scattered among other architectural oddities, including a stone tower, yurts, and a Spanish-style ballroom. In this ghostly, lost-in-time fantasyland off MacArthur Blvd, the National Park Service runs a unique arts-and-crafts center.

EXCURSIONS

Glen Echo began life in 1891 as a Chautauqua retreat center, one of several established in the 19th century to 'promote liberal and practical education, especially among the masses.' The center promptly failed and an amusement park took over the site, linked to DC by a trolley line. The park flourished until the '60s, then declined, due in part to tensions over desegregation. The federal government bought the site in 1971.

Now the park is again an educational center, this one promoting the arts. Stop at the NPS office in the Arcade for information on park programs; it's open 9 am to 5 pm daily.

Also in the Arcade is **Adventure Theater** (☎ 301-320-5331), which stages children's plays; the stone tower houses a bookstore and art gallery. Artists work in the Mongolian-style yurts, and the Spanish Ballroom hosts folk and swing dances and the **Puppet Company Theater** (☎ 301-320-6668). Music, arts, dance, and photography classes are offered year-round. The lovely historic **Dentzel Carousel** remains the park's centerpiece – you can ride it May through September, 11:30 am to 6 pm weekends and 10 am to 2 pm Wednesday and Thursday; 50¢.

Discovery Creek Children's Museum (☎ 202-364-3111), set in Glen Echo's old stable, is a children's ecological museum offering exhibits and activities (nature hikes, craft workshops) for kids two to 11. Open 10 am to 3 pm weekends; admission is free for adults, $4 per kid.

Just north of the Glen Echo parking lot is the **Clara Barton National Historic Site** (☎ 301-492-6245), the house where the founder of the American Red Cross lived from 1891 until her death in 1912. It's open 10 am to 5 pm daily for free guided tours.

It's easiest to reach Glen Echo by car. From DC, follow Massachusetts Ave NW to Goldsboro Rd, turn west, and drive a half-mile to MacArthur Blvd, where you'll see the Glen Echo parking lot. Alternately, take the Montgomery County Ride-On (☎ 240-777-7433) No 29 bus from the Friendship Heights Metro station. It departs every half-hour; the fare is $1.10 during rush hours, 90¢ at other times.

The park is open daily, but the best time to visit is weekends, when most buildings are open to the public and most performances are held.

C&O Canal National Historic Park

The historic C&O Canal runs 184½ miles alongside the Potomac from Georgetown to Cumberland, in western Maryland. Begun in 1828, the canal was envisioned as a trade route through the rugged Appalachians to the Ohio Valley beyond. But by 1850, new railroads had already rendered it obsolete, and construction was eventually abandoned. During its short heyday, however, the canal made an enduring mark on Maryland, as trading and industrial towns grew up alongside it and Civil War battles were fought along its length. Romantic legends of the barge trade and boatsmen still persist, along with ghostly remnants of lockhouses, aqueducts, and canalside inns.

Today, the scenic canal corridor is a national park, and the 12-foot-wide gravel **towpath** alongside the canal is perfect for daylong hiking and biking excursions. If you feel really ambitious, follow the path all the way up to **Harpers Ferry**, West Virginia (where John Brown staged his 1859 abolitionist raid) or **Antietam Battlefield** (where the bloodiest day of the Civil War occurred on September 17, 1862). Rent bikes at Swains Lock (17.2 miles from Georgetown), Whites Ferry (35 miles), Harpers Ferry (approximately 60 miles), and Williamsport (100 miles). For bicycle rentals in DC, see the Things to See & Do chapter.

The National Park Service operates visitors' centers at Georgetown, Great Falls Tavern, Williamsport, Hancock, and Cumberland. For maps and excursion guides listing campsites, bike-repair shops, and other resources along the route, contact park headquarters at ☎ 301-739-4200 or write to Box 4, Sharpsburg, MD 21782. Get a copy of Mike High's *C&O Canal Companion*, sold in local bookstores, for a mile-by-mile guide.

Great Falls (Maryland Side)

Fourteen miles upriver from Georgetown, where the central Piedmont meets the

Coastal Plain, the Potomac cascades 77 feet down a series of beautiful, treacherous rapids known as Great Falls. The C&O Canal was constructed to allow barges to bypass the falls. Today, Great Falls' Maryland side is part of the C&O park, and it's a popular spot for viewing the falls, hiking, biking, picknicking, and riding historic canal barges.

The park's entrance is in the sprawling, wealthy suburb of Potomac, at the end of MacArthur Blvd. Park admission costs $4 per car, $2 for pedestrians or bicyclists, but the gate is staffed only at peak periods.

The park's visitors' center is the canalside **Great Falls Tavern** (☎ 301-299-3613), built in 1828 as a lockhouse and open 9 am to 5 pm daily. Exhibits here demonstrate how the locks work. April to October, barge rides start here several times daily from Wednesday to Sunday; $7.50/4 adults/kids under 14.

From the tavern, a half-mile walk down the towpath and across a series of bridges to Olmstead Island leads to the **falls overlook**, which offers a beautiful view of rugged rock and roaring rapids. (The whitewater is dangerous, so keep kids clear.) For serious scramblers, the 2-mile **Billy Goat Trail** traverses mountainous rock crags, and the towpath provides an easy loop back. Other easy loop trails lead through the woods past the remains of gold-mine diggings, prospector's trenches, and overgrown Civil War earthworks. Inquire at the tavern about whitewater paddling and licensed outfitters. No bike or boat rentals are available at this park.

A small snack bar is open seasonally in the park, but the best place to eat is *Old Angler's Inn* (☎ *301-299-9097, 10801 MacArthur Blvd*), established in 1860 off the towpath at the park's southern tip. It's French and it's expensive, but the lovely patio and gracious service are deserved luxuries after the Billy Goat Trail or a long bike ride. It's open for lunch and dinner Tuesday to Sunday year-round. A dinner of Scottish salmon costs $26.

Note that **Great Falls National Park**, also administered by the NPS, is across the river in Virginia (see the Virginia section, earlier).

Admission paid at either side permits access to either park for three days.

Swains Lock

Seventeen miles north of Georgetown, Swains Lock was operated by the Swain family for generations. Jesse Swain was lock-tender from 1907 until the lock closed in 1924. Today, his grandson Fred runs **Swains Boathouse** (☎ 301-299-9006), which rents bicycles ($5.55 per hour, $13 all day), canoes, kayaks, and boats ($8.50 per hour, $19 all day). He also sells fishing tackle and bait and oversees a hiker/biker campground for towpath through-travelers. There's a small refreshment stand. From the Beltway, you can reach Swains by exiting onto River Rd and driving north to Swains Lock Rd.

White's Ferry

Once operated by Confederate Colonel EV White, this ferry (☎ 301-349-5200), 35 miles upriver from Georgetown, is the last of the many ferries that once plied the Potomac. It's a nice way to hop from the Maryland to the Virginia shore, particularly if you're headed for historic Leesburg (see Virginia, earlier).

The ferry runs 5 am to 11 pm daily year-round. Cars are charged $3/5 one way/roundtrip; bicyclists pay 50¢. From late April through October, the ferry operator also rents canoes and provides canoeists with shuttle service upriver. The ferry's seasonal store sells groceries and bait.

OTHER MARYLAND ATTRACTIONS
Paul E Garber Facility

The Garber Facility (☎ 202-357-1400), 3904 Old Silver Hill Rd, Suitland, is the Smithsonian Air and Space Museum's restoration and storage workshop. Its 150 restored craft include the *Enola Gay* (the B-29 that dropped the atomic bomb on Hiroshima), warbirds from WWI and WWII, and spacecraft. Housed in dozens of huge metal sheds, Garber is a haunting place – an odd combination of an aircraft cemetery and Dr Frankenstein's lab.

EXCURSIONS

Tours last three hours. The sheds are un-heated, and there are no restrooms or drinking water along the way. Since much information included in the tour is highly technical, visits by children under 14 are discouraged. The free tours start at 10 am weekdays, 10 am and 1 pm weekends. Call two weeks ahead to reserve a spot.

The collection will eventually be moved to the museum's new Dulles Airport facility, in Virginia, due to open in 2003, so call before your visit.

Surratt House

This nondescript former tavern and post office (☎ 301-868-1121), 9118 Brandywine Rd in Clinton, is an infamous place. A 'safe-house' for the Confederate Underground during the Civil War, it was owned by Mary Surratt, whose son John hatched the Lincoln assassination conspiracy with John Wilkes Booth. After Booth killed Lincoln at Ford's Theatre in Washington in April 1865, the assassin fled to Surratt's house to retrieve weapons and supplies stored here. Mary Surratt was judged an accomplice, and a military court ordered her hung at DC's Fort McNair on July 7, 1865. She was the first woman executed in the US. Curiously, John Surratt himself escaped execution.

The house now offers exhibits on 19th-century farm life and the assassination. Costumed docents guide you on tours that examine whether Mary was actually guilty of conspiracy (the evidence is uncertain). It's open March to mid-December from 11 am to 3 pm Thursday and Friday, noon to 4 pm weekends; $3/1 adults/kids. The house runs the rollicking John Wilkes Booth Escape Tour several times yearly ($45) – it lasts 12 hours and retraces the assassin's flight from Ford's Theatre to Virginia, where he was shot down.

From I-95, take exit 7 and drive south on Route 5 (Branch Ave) to Route 223W (Woodyard Rd). Turn right, drive 1 mile to Brandywine Rd, turn left, and you'll see the house on your left.

Fort Washington

Military-history buffs enjoy visiting this restored fort (☎ 301-763-4600) at the confluence of the Potomac and Piscataway Creek. Established in 1808 to guard the southern approach to DC, demolished by its own troops in 1814 to keep it out of British hands, and later rebuilt, the fort has been parkland since 1946.

Here you can see remnants of several stages of its life, from earthworks to concrete batteries, and watch living-history demonstrations showing how Civil War–era soldiers lived and worked. It's also a lovely place to picnic. From the Beltway, take Hwy 210 (Indian Head Hwy) to Fort Washington Rd. Turn right to reach the fort.

LONELY PLANET

You already know that Lonely Planet produces more than this one guidebook, but you might not be aware of the other products we have on this region. Here is a selection of titles which you may want to check out as well:

Virginia & the Capital Region
ISBN 0 86442 769 7
US$21.99 • UK£13.99 • 159FF

USA
ISBN 0 86442 513 9
US$24.95 • UK£14.99 • 180FF

New York City
ISBN 1 86450 180 4
US$16.99 • UK£10.99 • 129FF

Washington DC map
ISBN 1 86450 078 6
US$5.95 • UK£3.99 • 39FF

Available wherever books are sold.

Index

Bold indicates maps.

Boxed Text

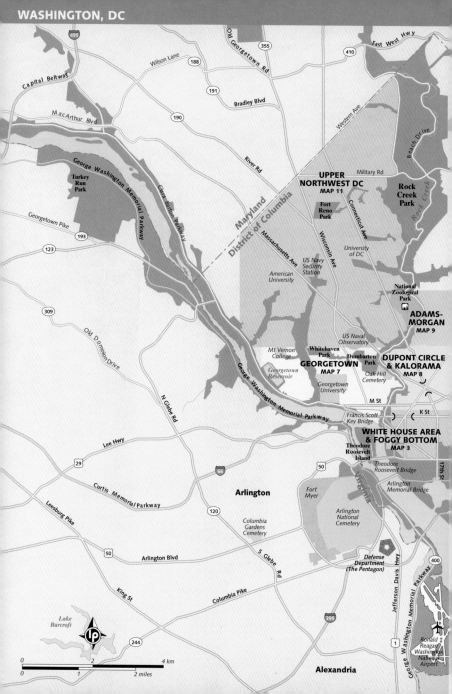

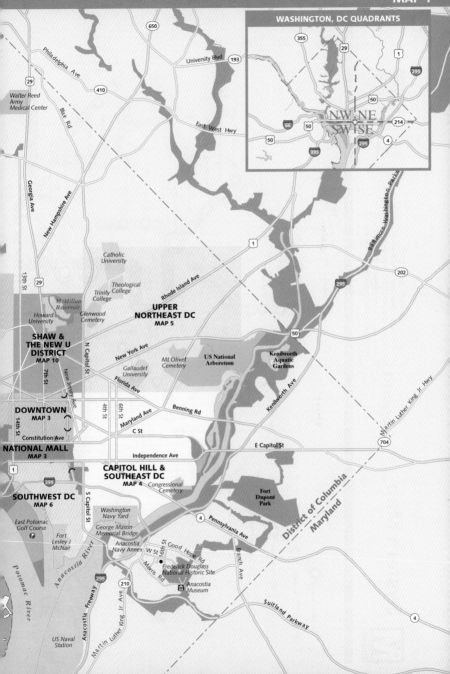

MAP 1

WASHINGTON, DC QUADRANTS

355
29
1
295
50
214
66
50
NW NE
SW SE
50
395
295
4

650
University Blvd
193
Philadelphia Ave
29
410
Walter Reed
Army
Medical Center
Blair Rd
East West Hwy
Baltimore-Washington Parkway

Georgia Ave
New Hampshire Ave
1
202
295

Catholic
University
13th St
29
Theological
College
Rhode Island Ave
Trinity
College
McMillan
Reservoir
**UPPER
NORTHEAST DC
MAP 5**
Howard
University
Glenwood
Cemetery
50
Kenilworth
Aquatic
Gardens

**SHAW &
THE NEW U
DISTRICT
MAP 10**
N Capital St
New York Ave
Mt Olivet
Cemetery
US National
Arboretum
7th St
New Jersey Ave
Gallaudet
University
Florida Ave
Kenilworth Ave

**DOWNTOWN
MAP 3**
4th St
6th St
Maryland Ave
Benning Rd
14th St
C St
Martin Luther King Jr Hwy

**NATIONAL MALL
MAP 3**
Constitution Ave
Independence Ave
E Capital St
704

1
**CAPITOL HILL &
SOUTHEAST DC
MAP 4**
Congressional
Cemetery
395
S Capital St
Fort
Dupont
Park
District of Columbia
Maryland

**SOUTHWEST DC
MAP 6**
Washington
Navy Yard
Pennsylvania Ave
4

East Potomac
Golf Course
George Mason
Memorial Bridge
Fort
Lesley J
McNair
Anacostia
Navy Annex
US Good Hope Rd
W St
Morris Rd
Frederick Douglass
National Historic Site
Branch Ave

Potomac River
Anacostia River
295
210
Anacostia
Museum

US Naval
Station
Martin Luther King Jr Ave
Anacostia Freeway
Suitland Parkway
4

Potomac River

METRORAIL SYSTEM

System Map

Legend

● Red Line • Glenmont/Shady Grove
● Orange Line • New Carrollton/Vienna/Fairfax-GMU
● Blue Line • Addison Road/Franconia-Springfield
● Green Line • Branch Avenue/Greenbelt
● Yellow Line • Huntington/Mt. Vernon Sq-UDC

Transfer Station
Parking
Future Station

Commuter Rail
MARC
Virginia Railway Express

Station in Service

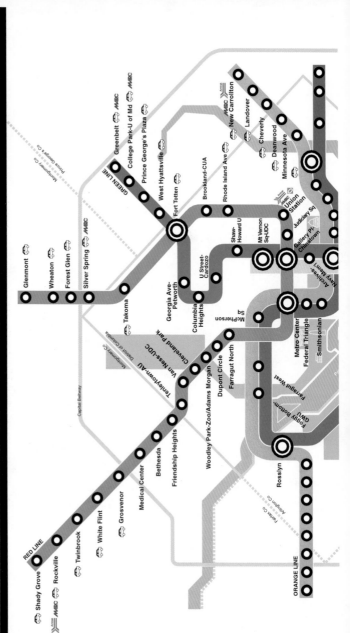

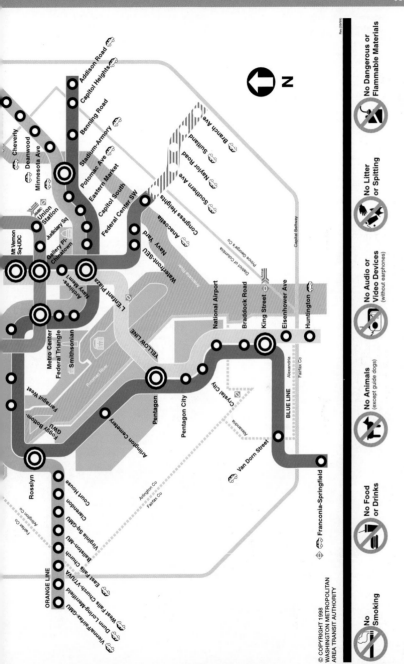

MAP 2

N

© COPYRIGHT 1998
WASHINGTON METROPOLITAN
AREA TRANSIT AUTHORITY

Rev.(09/99)

No Dangerous or
Flammable Materials

No Litter
or Spitting

No Audio or
Video Devices
(without earphones)

No Animals
(except guide dogs)

No Food
or Drinks

No
Smoking

Addison Road
Capitol Heights
Benning Road
Stadium-Armory
Potomac Ave
Eastern Market
Capitol South
Federal Center SW

Cheverly
Deanwood
Minnesota Ave

Branch Ave
Suitland
Naylor Road
Southern Ave
Congress Heights
Anacostia

Mt Vernon
Sq-UDC
Union
Station
Judiciary Sq
Gallery Pl-
Chinatown
Archives-
Navy Mem'l
L'Enfant Plaza
Navy Yard
Waterfront-SEU

Metro Center
Federal Triangle
Smithsonian
Farragut West

National Airport
Braddock Road
King Street
Eisenhower Ave
Huntington

YELLOW LINE

BLUE LINE

Pentagon
Pentagon City
Arlington Cemetery
Crystal City

Foggy Bottom-
GWU

Rosslyn
Court House
Clarendon
Virginia Sq-GMU
Ballston-MU
East Falls Church-VT/UVA
West Falls Church-
Dunn Loring-Merrifield
Vienna/Fairfax-GMU

ORANGE LINE

Van Dorn Street
Franconia-Springfield

Potomac River
Anacostia River

District of Columbia
Prince George's Co

Capital Beltway

Alexandria
Fairfax Co

Alexandria
Arlington Co
Fairfax Co

Fairfax Co
Arlington Co

NATIONAL MALL, DOWNTOWN, WHITE HOUSE AREA & FOGGY BOTTOM

Georgetown

see MAP 7

Rock Creek Park

Dupont Circle & Kalorama

see MAP 8

Dupont Circle

P St
Twining Court
Hopkins St
O St
Newport Rd
N St
Sunderland Pl
Jefferson Pl

Massachusetts Ave

Scott Circle

Rock Creek & Potomac Parkway

Rock Creek

M St

Ward Pl

New Hampshire Ave
22nd St
21st St
20th St
19th St
18th St
17th St
16th St
15th St

De Sales Pl

Rhode Island Ave

Connecticut Ave

Vermont Ave

1
2
3
4
5
6
7

10
11
8
9
12
13
14
15
16
17

L St

8th
9th

Farragut North

29

K St

Washington Circle

Foggy Bottom

29
30
31
32
33
34
35
36
37
38
39
40
41
42
43
44
45
46
47
48
49
50
51
52
53
54
55
56
57
58
59
60
61
62
63

Pennsylvania Ave

I St

Farragut West

Farragut Square

McPherson Square

McPherson Square

25th St
24th St
23rd St
26th St

71
72
73
74

H St

Foggy Bottom/GWU

George Washington University

World Bank

76
75

77
78
79
80

Lafayette Square

Treasury Annex

The Watergate

70

Juarez Circle

Kennedy Center

G St

F St

114
115

E St

Old Executive Office Building

Pennsylvania Ave (ped mall)

Treasury Building

104

White House

Executive Ave

105

120
121

Pershing Park

White House Area

116

New York Ave

Corcoran Gallery

US Navy Bureau of Medicine & Surgery

State Department

Rawlins Park

Interior Department

Red Cross

DAR Hall

147
148
149
150

Constitution Hall

Organization of American States

The Ellipse

117
118

Department of Commerce Building

National Academy of Sciences

Federal Reserve

146

Virginia Ave

22nd St

C St

D St

151
152

50

To Arlington

50

Rock Creek & Potomac Pkwy

NW
SW

166

Lincoln Memorial

169

Henry Bacon Drive

Vietnam Veterans Memorial

167

Constitution Gardens

168

Reflecting Pool

Rainbow Pool

172
173

Washington Monument

Arlington Memorial Bridge

Daniel French Drive

West Potomac Park

170
171

ALT 50

Kutz Bridge

Ohio Drive

Franklin Delano Roosevelt Memorial Park

West Basin Drive

Cherry Blossom Promenade

Tidal Basin

Potomac River

ALT 50

Rock Creek Potomac Pkwy

0   250   500 m
0   250   500 yards

MAP 3

Logan Circle

Columbia St

P St

see MAP 10

O St

N St

Shaw & the New U District

New Jersey Ave

Ridge St

M St

7th St

29

12th St

11th St

10th St

13th St

Thomas Circle

14th St

Eckington Pl

9th St

8th St

6th St

5th St

Mt Vernon Square/UDC

ALT 50

Pierce St

395

19 ▼

21 ■

24 ■

L St

27 ▼ 28 ▪

New Convention Center

18 ▪ 20 ■

22 ▪ 23 ▪ 25 ▪

26 ▪

Mt Vernon Square

K St

3rd St

2nd St

1st St

Tunnel

New Jersey Ave

66 ▼

68 ▪

69 ●

I St

Downtown

Government Printing Office

Franklin Square

67 ●

Zei Alley

64 ▪

65 ▼

New York Ave

Washington Convention Center

89

91 ●
92 ▼ 93
94 ▼

Chinatown
95
96 ▼ 97 ▼
98 ●

H St

102 ▪

Massachusetts Ave

Capitol Hill & Southeast DC

103 ▪

Georgetown Law School

81 ●

82 ●

85 ●

86 ●

87 ●

88 ●

90 ▪

99 ● 100 ●

101 ▪

G St

110 ▼
108 109
107 ▼

111 ●

112 ●

National Museum of American Art & National Portrait Gallery

Gallery Place/ Chinatown

MCI Center

113 ●

National Building Museum (Old Pension Building)

144 ▲

see MAP 4

106 ●

131 ●

130 ●

132

133 ●

129 ●

125
126 ▼

142 ▼ 143 ●

Judiciary Square

145 ▪

122 ●

123 ●
124

127 ▼

128 ■

Pennsylvania Ave
Freedom Plaza

Old Post Office Pavilion

Federal Bureau of Investigation

134 ▼ ▼ 141
135
136 ● 140 ▲
137 ▼ 138 139 ▼

Judiciary Square

50

D St

Louisiana Ave

119 ▪

153 ●

Ronald Reagan Building/ International Trade Center

154 ▪

Federal Triangle

Pennsylvania Ave

157 ▼
156 ▲ 158 ●
155 ▼

159 ▲

160 ▲ 161 ●

Indiana Ave

C St

Department of Labor

165 ▪

Union Station Plaza

Interstate Commerce Commission

Constitution Ave

50 1

National Archives

Archives/ Navy Memorial

Indiana Plaza
162 ●
163 ▼
164 ▪

John Marshall Park

National Museum of American History

National Museum of Natural History

National Sculpture Garden & Ice Rink

National Gallery of Art, West Building

National Gallery of Art, East Building

US Capitol

Madison Drive

Capitol Reflecting Pool

(ped mall)

National Mall

1

Jefferson Drive

The Castle
178 179 ●
174 180 ✿
176 177

Smithsonian

Freer Gallery of Art

Arts & Industries Building

Hirshhorn Museum

National Air & Space Museum

181 ●

US Botanic Garden

US Department of Agriculture

Independence Ave

United States Holocaust Memorial Museum

Forrestal Building

US Postal Service

Department of Energy

FAA Building

Maryland Ave

Health & Human Services Department

Rayburn House Office Building

L'Enfant Promenade

Hancock Park

L'Enfant Plaza

Southwest DC

see MAP 6

Canal St

ALT 50

C St

National Bureau of Printing & Engraving

D St

14th St

L'Enfant Plaza

12th St

9th St

7th St

School St

6th St

4th St

Virginia Ave

3rd St

Federal Center SW

395

NATIONAL MALL

WHITE HOUSE AREA & FOGGY BOTTOM

DENNIS JOHNSON

DOWNTOWN

JOHN NEUBAUER

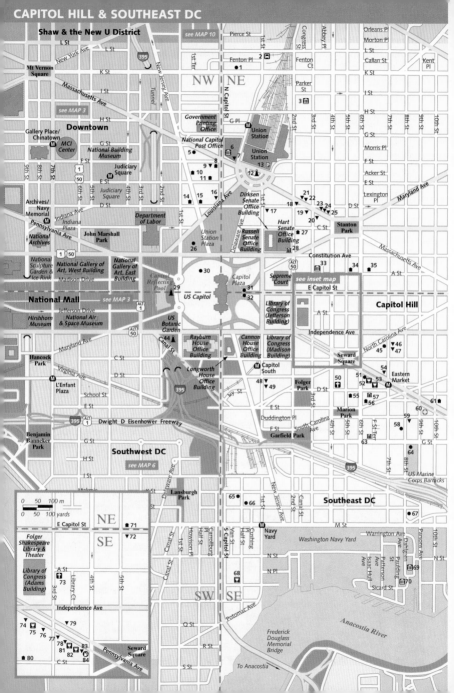

CAPITOL HILL & SOUTHEAST DC

Shaw & the New U District

see MAP 10

NW NE

Downtown

Gallery Place/Chinatown

National Building Museum

Judiciary Square

Archives/Navy Memorial

National Archives

John Marshall Park

Department of Labor

National Sculpture Garden & Ice Rink

National Gallery of Art, West Building

National Gallery of Art, East Building

National Mall

see MAP 3

Hirshhorn Museum

National Air & Space Museum

US Botanic Garden

Rayburn House Office Building

Cannon House Office Building

Longworth House Office Building

Hancock Park

L'Enfant Plaza

Benjamin Banneker Park

Southwest DC

see MAP 6

Government Printing Office

National Capitol Post Office

Union Station

Union Station

Dirksen Senate Office Building

Hart Senate Office Building

Russell Senate Office Building

Union Station Plaza

Capitol Reflecting Pool

US Capitol

Capitol Plaza

Supreme Court

Library of Congress (Jefferson Building)

Library of Congress (Madison Building)

Capitol South

Folger Park

Stanton Park

see inset map

Capitol Hill

Seward Square

Eastern Market

Marion Park

Garfield Park

US Marine Corps Barracks

Southeast DC

Navy Yard

Washington Navy Yard

Lansburgh Park

Frederick Douglass Memorial Bridge

Anacostia River

To Anacostia

Folger Shakespeare Library & Theater

Library of Congress (Adams Building)

Seward Square

MAP 4

Upper Northeast DC

see MAP 5

Langston Golf Course

Kenilworth Aquatic Gardens

Lincoln Park

Potomac Ave

Congressional Cemetery

Anacostia Park

John Phillip Sousa Bridge

Wells Memorial Bridge

11th St Bridge

Stadium/Armory

PLACES TO EAT
4 French's Fine Southern Cuisine
7 Capitol City Brewing Company
9 Kelly's Irish Times
16 La Colline
17 The Monocle
18 Red River Grill
19 La Brasserie
20 White Tiger
21 Neil's Deli
22 Armand's Chicago Pizzeria
23 La Loma
24 2 Quail
25 Cafe Berlin
46 Misha's Deli
47 Tunnicliff's Tavern
48 Tortilla Coast
49 Bullfeathers
54 Bread & Chocolate
59 Banana Café & Piano Bar
72 Jimmy T's
74 Barolo
76 Sherrill's Restaurant & Bakery
77 Xando Café & Bar
78 Thai Roma; Conrad's Pub
79 La Lomita Dos
83 Tune Inn

BARS & CLUBS
52 Remington's
53 The Little Pub
58 Phase 1
65 The Nation
66 Wet
67 Bachelor's Mill
68 Ziegfeld's/Secrets
75 Capitol Lounge
81 PoliTiki
82 Hawk & Dove

OTHER
1 Dept of Motor Vehicles/
   Adjudication Services
2 Greyhound Terminal
3 Capital Children's Museum
5 Budget Rent-A-Car
6 National Postal Museum
12 Columbia Memorial Fountain
13 Paid Parking Lot
26 Taft Memorial Carillon
28 Sewall-Belmont House
29 Ulysses S Grant Monument
30 Grotto
31 US Capitol Self-Guided Tours Line
32 US Capitol Guided Tours Line
33 Frederick Douglass Museum
36 Emancipation Memorial
37 Mary McLeod Bethune Memorial
38 Car Barn (Private)
39 1111-1119 E Capitol St NE Houses
   (Private)
40 Philadelphia Row (Private)
42 Armory
43 RFK Stadium
44 Bartholdi Fountain
45 Eastern Market; Market Lunch
50 Ebenezer United Methodist Church
51 Capitol Hill Fax Service
57 Friendship House Settlement
60 Old Naval Hospital
62 DC General Hospital
63 John Phillip Sousa Birthplace (Private)
64 Marine Commandant's House
69 Marine Corps Museum
70 Navy Museum
73 St Marks Episcopal Church
84 Capitol Hill Exxon

PLACES TO STAY
8 Phoenix Park Hotel; Dubliner
10 Washington Court
11 Hotel George; Bis
14 Hyatt Regency
15 Holiday Inn on the Hill
27 Thompson-Markward Hall
34 Bull Moose B&B
35 B&B on A
41 A Capitol Place
55 Maison Orleans Bed 'N
   Breakfast
56 Hereford House
61 The White's House
71 Doolittle Guest House
80 Capitol Hill Suites

0   .5   1 km
0   .25   .5 mile

UPPER NORTHEAST DC

To Rock Creek
Cemetery

Scale Gate Rd

Upper Hospital Rd
Lower Hospital Rd
Harwood Rd

Catholic
University

Arnold Drive

Pershing Drive

NW | NE

National
Shrine
of the
Immaculate
Conception

Michigan Ave

CUA/
Brookland

3

Bunker Hill Rd

Quincy St
Perry Pl
10th St

Brookland

4

Theological
College

7th St
8th St
9th St

5

10th St

Hawthorne Drive

Germain Dr

Trinity
College

4th St

6

Michigan Ave

Girard
St

McMillan
Reservoir

Girard St
Franklin St

Girard St
Franklin St

Evarts St

Evarts St

Girard St

6th St
4th St
1st St

Franklin
St

Evarts
St

Glenwood
Cemetery

Douglas St
Cromwell Terr
Channing St

29

Howard
University

Banneker
Recreation
Center

McMillan Drive

Douglas St

Channing St

Bryant St

McMillan
Park

Bryant St
Ascot Pl
Adams St

Rhode
Island Ave

College St

Bryant St

Adams St

Prospect
Hill
Cemetery

St Marys
Cemetery

W St

V St

1

Rhode Island Ave

W 5th St
4th St
3rd St
2nd St

Oakdale Pl
Elm St

U St

Thomas St

T St

W St

V St

U St

Todd Pl

U St

2nd St
3rd St
4th St

W St

V St

10

V St

T St

**Shaw & the
New U District**
see MAP 10

Porter St
Winberger St

29

1

Shaw/
Howard
University

Florida Ave

New Jersey Ave

Seaton Pl

S St

Randolph Pl

R St

Quincy Pl

Seaton Pl

S St

Randolph Pl

Eckington Rd

13

14

Brentwood
Park

Penn Ave

6th St

Brentwood Parkway

Miriam St

Warner
St

Q St

Franklin St

Bates St

Porter St

P St

Kennedy
Playground

1

9th St
8th St
7th St
6th St
5th St

Emmanuel
Ct

Ridge St

O St

ALT
1
50

N St

New York Ave

Patterson St

M St

Neal Pl

Morse St

6th St

Lincoln Circle W

Lincoln Circle N

Mt Vernon
Square/
UDC

Pierce St

1st Terr

1st St

Pierce St

1st St

Congress St

Abbey Pl

Orleans Pl
Morton St

Lincoln Circle

Kent
Pl

L St

Downtown
see MAP 3

Fenton Pl

K St

1st Terr

L St

2nd St
3rd St

Callan St

5th St
6th St
7th St
8th St

Mt Vernon
Square

395

Thomas St

Channing St

Douglas St

Adams St

MAP 5

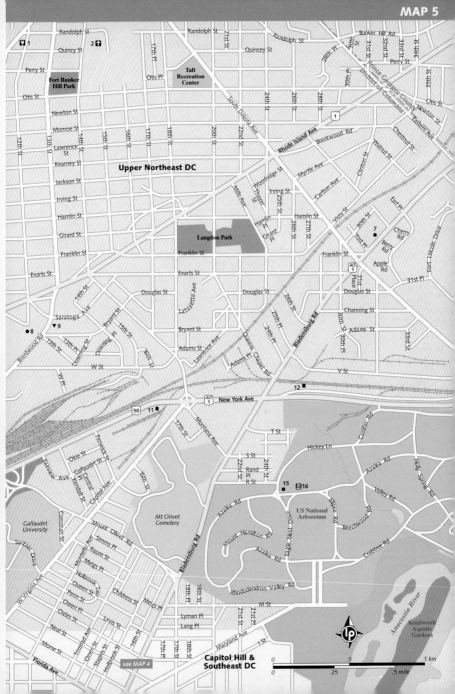

Randolph St
Quincy St
Randolph St 21st St
Quincey St
Randolph St
Bunker Hill Rd
28th Pl
30th St
31st St
32nd St
33rd St
34th St
Perry St
35th St

Perry St
Fort Bunker Hill Park
Otis Pl
Taft Recreation Center
Prince Georges County
District of Columbia
Eastern Ave
Newton St

Otis St
Newton St
South Dakota Ave
24th St
26th St
28th St
30th Pl
Rhode Island Ave
Brentwood Rd
1
Newton St
Chestnut St

Monroe St
Lawrence St
Kearney St
12th St
13th St
15th St
17th St
18th St
20th St
22nd St

Upper Northeast DC

Jackson St
Woodridge St
Myrtle Ave
Clinton St
Walnut St

Irving St
Hamlin St
Mills Ave
Thayer St
25th St
Irving St
Carlton Ave

Girard St
Hamlin
Pl
Hamlin St
Hamlin St
Vista St
30th St
York Pl
7
Berry Rd
Cherry Rd

Franklin St
Langdon Park
Girard Pl
26th St
27th St
Franklin St
Apple Rd

Franklin St
Evarts St
ALT 1
31st Place
31st Pl

Evarts St
Evarts St
Douglas St
Douglas St
25th Pl
26th St
Douglas St
Channing St
33rd St

14th St
Douglas St
Lafayette Ave
24th St
Bladensburg Rd
30th St
30th Pl
Adams St

Saratoga Ave
Bryant St
15th St
Bryant St
Queens Chapel Rd
V St

8
9
13th St
13th Pl
Downing Pl
Downing St
Adams St
Lawrence Ave
Adams Pl
Adams Chapel Rd

Brentwood Rd
W St
18th St
W Pl

50
11
17th St
Montana Ave
ALT 1
New York Ave
12

T St
Hickey Ln
Coulter Rd

Okie St
Fenwick St
S St
24th St
Azalea Rd
Holly Spring Rd

Fairview Ave
Gallaudet St
Central Ave
15th St
Rand Pl
R St
15
16
US National Arboretum
Valley Rd

Kendall St
Capitol Ave
Mt Olivet Cemetery
Azalea Rd
Beechwood Rd

Gallaudet University
Corcoran St
Mount Olivet Rd
Simms Pl
Bladensburg Rd
Ellipse Dr
Eagle Nest Rd
Crabtree Rd

Switzer Drive
Montello Ave
Raum St
Meigs Pl
Mount Hamilton Rd
Azalea Rd

W Virginia Ave
Holbrook St
Queen St
Penn St
Childress St
Meigs Pl
18th Pl
Rhododendron Valley Rd

Owen Pl
Oates St
Levis St
16th St
17th St
M St
Anacostia River

Neal St
Morse St
Immaculate Ave
Orren St
Staples St
Holbrook St
Lyman Pl
Lang Pl
21st St
21st Pl
Kenilworth Aquatic Gardens

Florida Ave
see MAP 4
Maryland Ave
1st St
18th St
17th St
18th Pl

Capitol Hill & Southeast DC

0   5   1 km
0   .25   .5 mile

SOUTHWEST DC

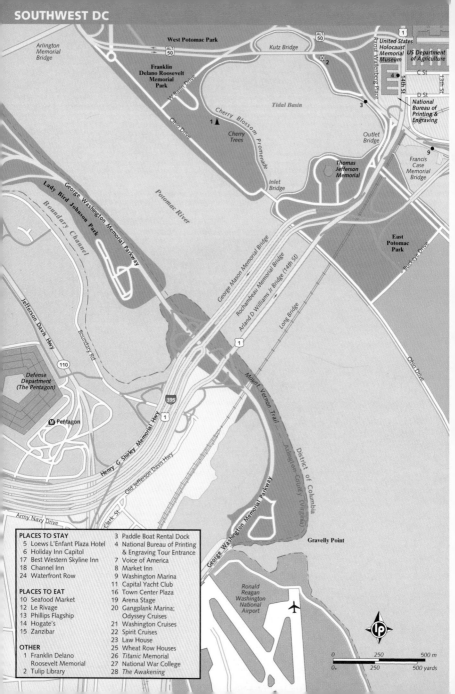

Arlington Memorial Bridge

West Potomac Park

Kutz Bridge

United States Holocaust Memorial Museum

US Department of Agriculture

ALT 50

Raoul Wallenberg Place

14th St

13th St

C St

Franklin Delano Roosevelt Memorial Park

W Basin Drive

Ohio Drive

Cherry Blossom Promenade

Tidal Basin

National Bureau of Printing & Engraving

D St

4

3

1

Cherry Trees

Outlet Bridge

Thomas Jefferson Memorial

Francis Case Memorial Bridge

Inlet Bridge

9

George Washington Memorial Parkway

Lady Bird Johnson Park

Boundary Channel

Potomac River

East Potomac Park

Rock Creek Drive

Jefferson Davis Hwy

Boundary Rd

George Mason Memorial Bridge

Rochambeau Memorial Bridge

Arland D Williams Jr Bridge (14th St)

Long Bridge

Ohio Drive

110

1

Defense Department (The Pentagon)

Mount Vernon Trail

395

Arlington County (Virginia)

District of Columbia

M Pentagon

Henry G Shirley Memorial Hwy

Old Jefferson Davis Hwy

Clark St

1

Gravelly Point

Army Navy Drive

George Washington Memorial Parkway

Ronald Reagan Washington National Airport

PLACES TO STAY
5 Loews L'Enfant Plaza Hotel
6 Holiday Inn Capitol
17 Best Western Skyline Inn
18 Channel Inn
24 Waterfront Row

PLACES TO EAT
10 Seafood Market
12 Le Rivage
13 Phillips Flagship
14 Hogate's
15 Zanzibar

OTHER
1 Franklin Delano Roosevelt Memorial
2 Tulip Library

3 Paddle Boat Rental Dock
4 National Bureau of Printing & Engraving Tour Entrance
7 Voice of America
8 Market Inn
9 Washington Marina
11 Capital Yacht Club
16 Town Center Plaza
19 Arena Stage
20 Gangplank Marina; Odyssey Cruises
21 Washington Cruises
22 Spirit Cruises
23 Law House
25 Wheat Row Houses
26 *Titanic* Memorial
27 National War College
28 *The Awakening*

0   250   500 m
0   250   500 yards

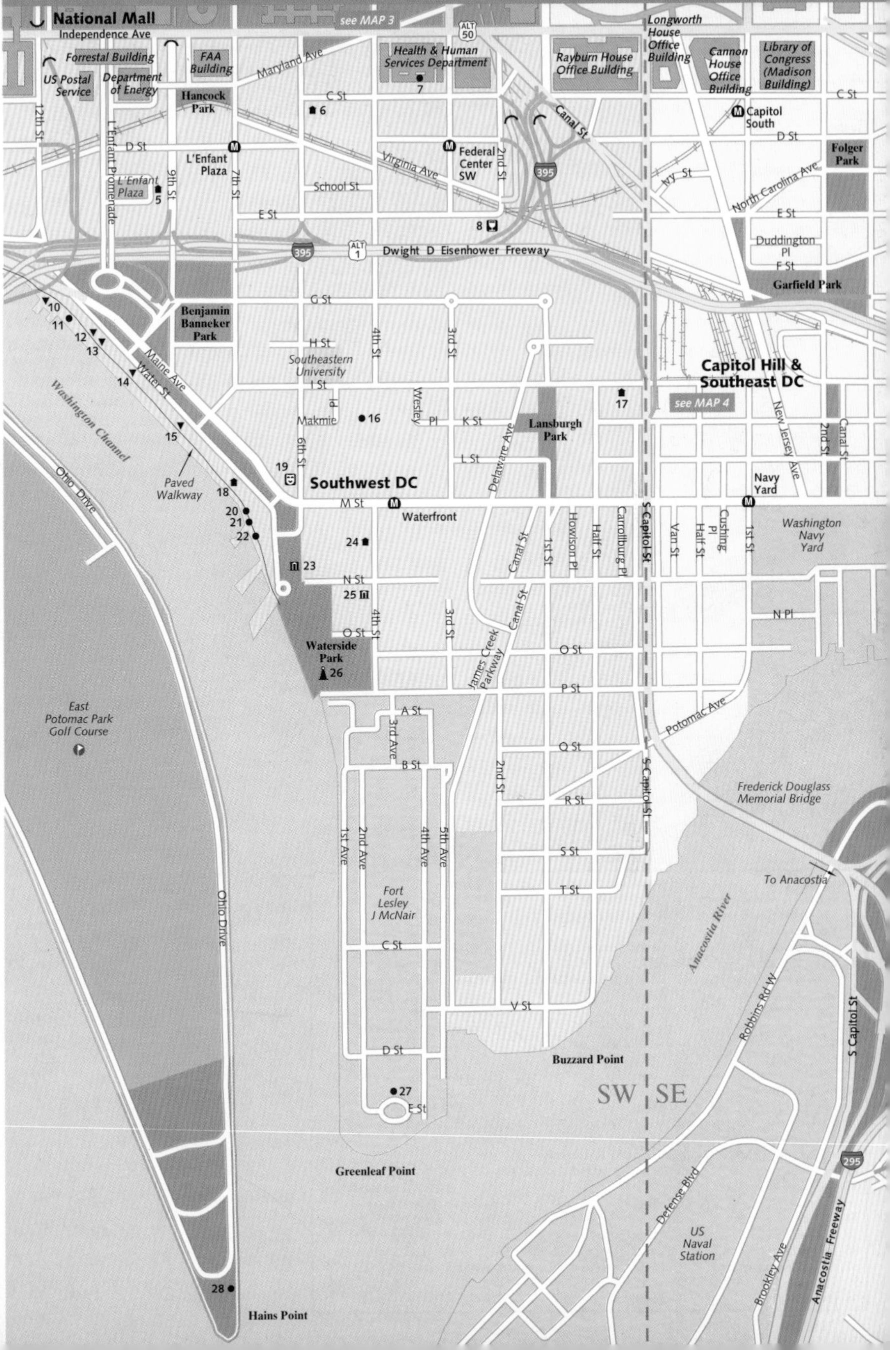

MAP 6

National Mall
Independence Ave
Forrestal Building
US Postal Service
Department of Energy
FAA Building
Hancock Park
L'Enfant Plaza
L'Enfant Promenade
L'Enfant Plaza
D St
12th St
9th St
7th St

see MAP 3
Maryland Ave
C St
6
Health & Human Services Department
7
Virginia Ave
Federal Center SW
School St
2nd St
E St

Longworth House Office Building
Rayburn House Office Building
Cannon House Office Building
Library of Congress (Madison Building)
Canal St
1st St
Ivy St
Capitol South
C St
D St
Folger Park
North Carolina Ave
Duddington Pl
E St
F St
Garfield Park

395
8

ALT 50
ALT 1
395
Dwight D Eisenhower Freeway

10
11
12
13
14
Maine Ave
Water St
Benjamin Banneker Park
G St
H St
Southeastern University
I St
Makmie
4th St
Wesley Pl
16
K St
Delaware Ave
Lansburgh Park
L St

Capitol Hill & Southeast DC
see MAP 4
17
New Jersey Ave
2nd St
Canal St
1st St

15
Paved Walkway
18
19
20
21
22
23
Southwest DC
6th St
M St
Waterfront
24
3rd St
N St
25
O St
Waterside Park
26
James Creek Parkway
Canal St
Howison Pl
Carrollburg Pl
Half St
Van St
Cushing Pl
Half St
S Capitol St
Navy Yard
Washington Navy Yard
N Pl

Washington Channel
Ohio Drive

East Potomac Park Golf Course

A St
B St
3rd Ave
4th Ave
5th Ave
2nd St
P St
Q St
R St
S St
T St
Potomac Ave
Frederick Douglass Memorial Bridge
To Anacostia
Anacostia River
Robbins Rd

1st Ave
2nd Ave
Fort Lesley J McNair
C St
V St
D St
Buzzard Point
SW SE

27
E St
Greenleaf Point

US Naval Station
Defense Blvd
Brackley Ave
295
S Capitol St
Anacostia Freeway

28
Hains Point

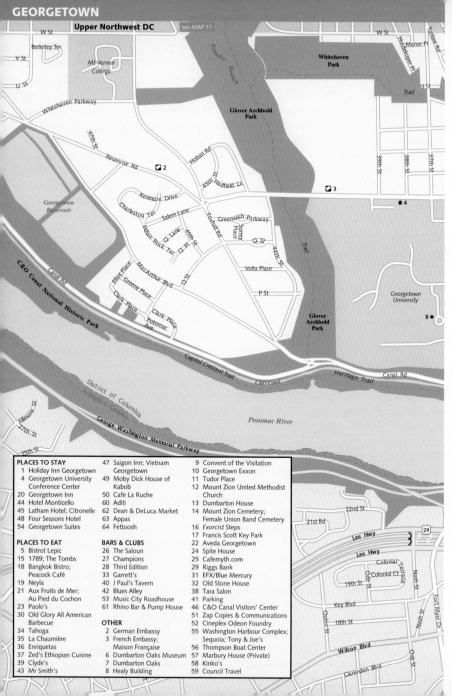

GEORGETOWN

Whitehaven
Park

Glover Archbold
Park

Mt Vernon
College

Berkeley Ter

W St

V St

U St

Whitehaven Parkway

W St

Manor Pl
Huidekoper Pl

Trail

39th St
38th St
37th St

47th St

Reservoir Rd

Hoban Rd

2

45th St
Hadfield Ln

3

4

Georgetown
Reservoir

Kenmore Drive

Charleston Ter

Salem Lane

Indian Rock Ter

Greenwich Parkway

Foxhall Rd

Surrey
Place

Q St

47th St

Trail

Georgetown
University

C&O Canal

Canal Rd

C&O Canal National Historic Park

Elliott Place

Greene Place

MacArthur Blvd

Q St

Q St

Volta Place

P St

Glover
Archbold
Park

8

Clark Place

Clark Place
Potomac
Ave

Capitol Crescent Trail

C&O Canal

Heritage Trail

Canal Rd

District of Columbia
Arlington County

Fillmore St

27th St

George Washington Memorial Parkway

Potomac River

25th St

PLACES TO STAY
1   Holiday Inn Georgetown
4   Georgetown University
    Conference Center
20 Georgetown Inn
44 Hotel Monticello
45 Latham Hotel; Citronelle
48 Four Seasons Hotel
54 Georgetown Suites

PLACES TO EAT
5   Bistrot Lepic
15 1789; The Tombs
18 Bangkok Bistro;
    Peacock Café
19 Neyla
21 Aux Fruits de Mer;
    Au Pied du Cochon
23 Paolo's
30 Old Glory All American
    Barbecue
34 Tahoga
35 La Chaumière
36 Enriquetas
37 Zed's Ethiopian Cuisine
39 Clyde's
43 Mr Smith's

47 Saigon Inn; Vietnam
    Georgetown
49 Moby Dick House of
    Kabob
50 Cafe La Ruche
60 Aditi
62 Dean & DeLuca Market
63 Appas
64 Fettoosh

BARS & CLUBS
26 The Saloun
27 Champions
28 Third Edition
33 Garrett's
40 J Paul's Tavern
42 Blues Alley
53 Music City Roadhouse
61 Rhino Bar & Pump House

OTHER
2   German Embassy
3   French Embassy;
    Maison Française
6   Dumbarton Oaks Museum
7   Dumbarton Oaks
8   Healy Building

9   Convent of the Visitation
10 Georgetown Exxon
11 Tudor Place
12 Mount Zion United Methodist
    Church
13 Dumbarton House
14 Mount Zion Cemetery;
    Female Union Band Cemetery
16 *Exorcist* Steps
17 Francis Scott Key Park
22 Aveda Georgetown
24 Spite House
25 Cafemyth.com
29 Riggs Bank
31 EFX/Blue Mercury
32 Old Stone House
38 Tara Salon
41 Parking
46 C&O Canal Visitors' Center
51 Zap Copies & Communications
52 Cineplex Odeon Foundry
55 Washington Harbour Complex;
    Sequoia; Tony & Joe's
56 Thompson Boat Center
57 Marbury House (Private)
58 Kinko's
59 Council Travel

22nd St

21st Rd

Lee Hwy

Lee Hwy

29

Colonial

Colonial Ct

O St

Nash St

Fort Myer Dr

19th St

Key Blvd

18th St

Quinn St

Wilson Blvd

Clarendon Blvd

Oak St

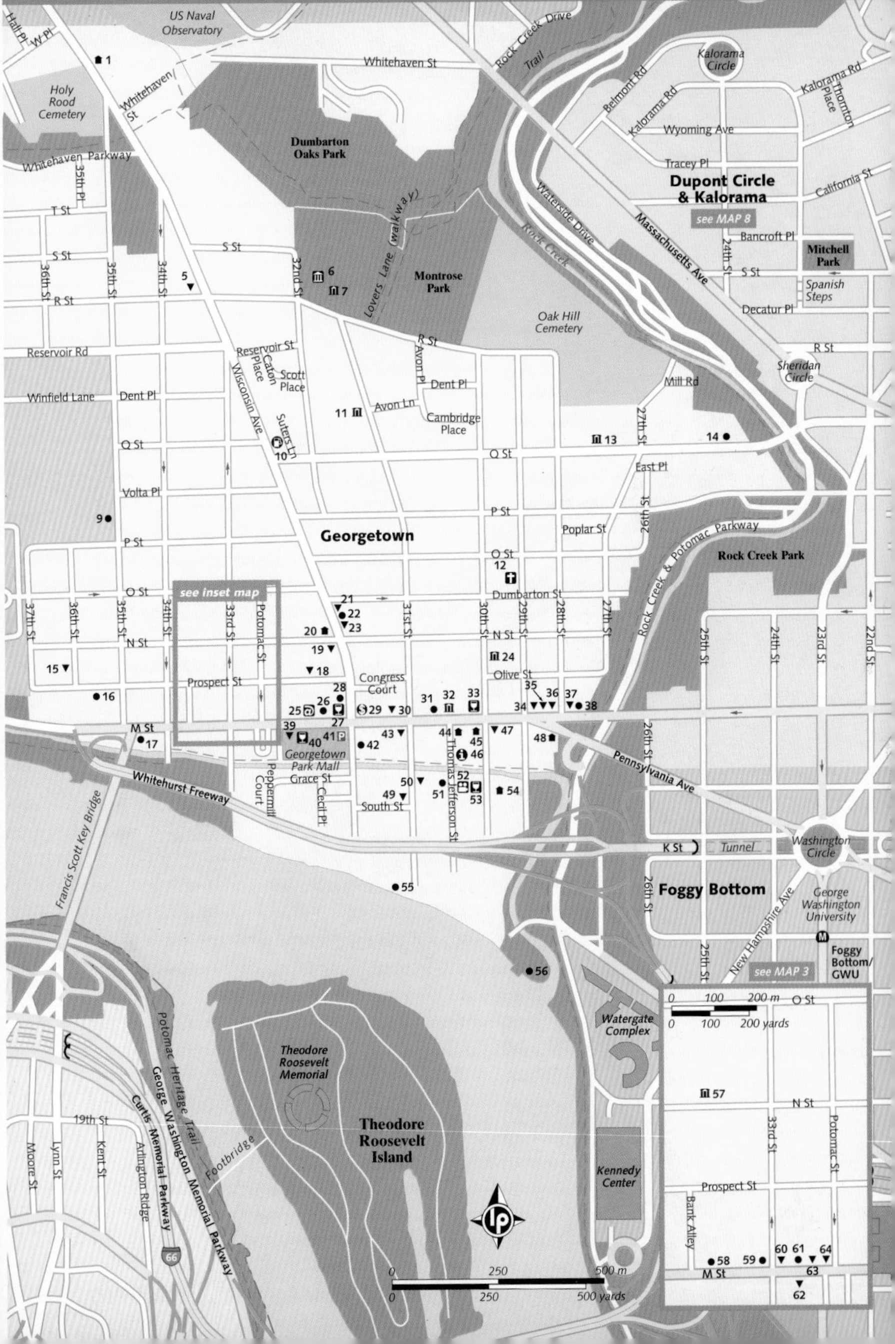

MAP 7

US Naval Observatory

W Pl
Hall Pl

■ 1

Whitehaven St

Rock Creek Drive
Trail

Kalorama
Circle

Holy
Rood
Cemetery

Whitehaven St

Belmont Rd

Kalorama Rd
Kalorama Rd

Tracey Pl
Wyoming Ave

Thornton
Place

Kalorama
California St

Whitehaven Parkway

35th Pl

Dumbarton
Oaks Park

Waterside Drive

Dupont Circle
& Kalorama

see MAP 8

T St

S St

S St

34th St

32nd St

River Creek

24th St

Bancroft Pl

Mitchell
Park

S St

S St
36th St

R St

5 ▼

Lovers' Lane (walkway)

6 ■
7 ■

Montrose
Park

Oak Hill
Cemetery

Decatur Pl

Spanish
Steps

Sheridan
Circle

Reservoir Rd

Reservoir St

R St
Dent Pl

R St

Avon Pl

Dent Pl

Mill Rd

Winfield Lane

Dent Pl

Scott
Place

11 ■

Avon Ln

Cambridge
Place

Q St

13 ■

14 ●

Wisconsin Ave

Suters Ln

Q St
10 ■

East Pl

Volta Pl

P St

9 ●

P St

P St

Poplar St

O St
12

Rock Creek Park

Georgetown

O St

Rock Creek & Potomac Parkway

37th St

36th St

35th St

see inset map

33rd St

Potomac St

21 ▼
22 ▼
23 ▼

31st St

30th St

29th St

28th St

27th St

Dumbarton St

N St

20 ●
19 ▼
18 ▼

N St

25th St

24th St

23rd St

22nd St

Prospect St

Congress
Court

24 ■

Olive St

15 ▼

16 ●

28
26 ■
25 ■ 27

31 ▼ 32 33
29 ▼ 30 ▼ ■

35
34 ▼ 36 37
▼ ▼ ▼ ▼ 38

Pennsylvania Ave

M St

17 ●

39 ▼
40 41 ▼
▼

43 ▼
42 ●

44 ▼

45
46

47 ▼

48 ■

26th St

Georgetown
Park Mall
Grace St

Pepperill
Court

Cecil Pl

50 ▼
49 ▼

Thomas Jefferson St

51 ▼

52
53

54 ■

South St

Whitehurst Freeway

55 ●

K St Tunnel

Washington
Circle

Foggy Bottom

George
Washington
University

25th St

New Hampshire Ave

Foggy
Bottom/
GWU

see MAP 3

56 ●

Watergate
Complex

Q St

0   100   200 m
0   100   200 yards

57 ■

N St

33rd St

Potomac St

Theodore
Roosevelt
Memorial

Theodore
Roosevelt
Island

Kennedy
Center

Prospect St

Francis Scott Key Bridge

Potomac Heritage Trail

George Washington Memorial Parkway

Curtis-Arlington Ridge

Footbridge

19th St

Lynn St

Moore St

Kent St

66

Bank Alley

58 ● 59 ●

60 ▼ 61 ▼ 64 ▼
63 ▼
62 ▼

M St

0   250   500 m
0   250   500 yards

DUPONT CIRCLE & KALORAMA

Upper
Northwest DC
see MAP 11

Rock Creek St

Trail

Kalorama
Circle

Kalorama

5 ▪

Kalorama Rd   6 ▪

8 ▪

Belmont Rd

3 ▪   Kalorama Rd   4 ▪

2 ▪

Wyoming Ave   7 ▪

Connecticut Ave

Columbia Rd

1 ▪

Wyoming Ave

Tracey Pl

California St

17 ▪

Waterside Drive

18 ▪   19 ▪

Phelps Pl

Leroy Pl

24th St

23rd St

Massachusetts Ave

Bancroft Pl

**Mitchell
Park**

S St

26 ▪   ▪ 27

22nd St

*Spanish
Steps*

28 ▪

29 ▪

Decatur Pl

▼ 38

21st St

37 ▼   39 ▼

36 ▼

**Oak Hill
Cemetery**

30 ▪

31 ▪

R St   ▼ 34   35 ▼

▼ 33

32 ● ●   53 ▪

Florida Ave

Mill Rd

*Sheridan
Circle*

▪ 49

Hillyer
Court

Hillyer Pl

54 ▼

55 ▪

48 ▪

50 ▪

▪ 51   52 ▪

27th St

Q St

71 ▪   75 ▪

72

Georgetown

East Pl

see MAP 7

▪ 67

74 ▪

26th St

15th St

69

P St

68 ▪ ▪   ▪ 70

▼ 73

92 ▼

93 ▼

Poplar St

90 ●

91 ▪

Twining
Court

Hopkins St

Rock Creek & Potomac Parkway

O St   95 ▪

30th St

29th St

28th St

27th St

N St

Rock Creek Park

Newport Rd

Olive St

N St

New Hampshire Ave

West End

Ward Pl

120 ▪   ▪ 121

▼ 124   125 ▼

123 ▼   M St

21st St

122 ▪

26th St

25th St

24th St

23rd St

22nd St

● 136

135 ▼   137 ▪

Foggy Bottom

0   100   200 m

0   100   200 yards

Rock Creek

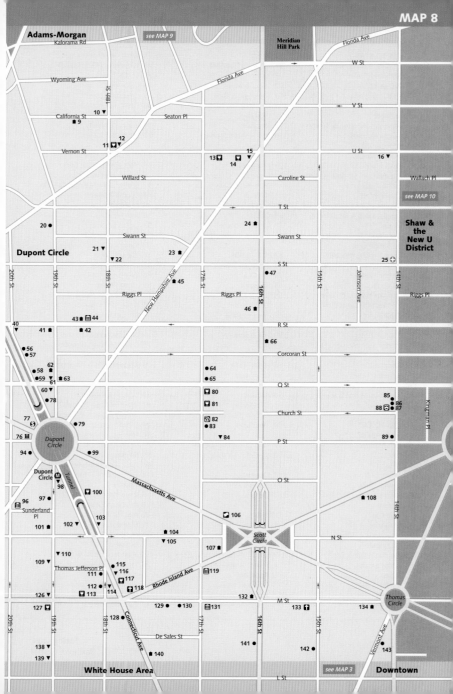

PLACES TO STAY
6 Windsor Park Hotel
7 Normandy Inn
8 Taft Bridge Inn
9 1836 California
18 Washington Courtyard by Marriott
19 Washington Hilton & Towers
23 Swann House
24 Windsor Inn
41 Shalom House
42 Davis House
43 International Student House
45 Carlyle Suites
46 The Brenton
62 Dupont at the Circle
63 Simpkins Bed & Breakfast & Hostel
66 Embassy Inn
67 Brickskellar Inn
70 Radisson Barceló Hotel Washington
72 Westin Fairfax
75 Hilton Embassy Row
95 The Mansion on O Street
101 The Inn at Dupont Circle
104 Tabard Inn
107 Governor's House
108 Braxton Hotel
120 Washington Monarch Hotel
121 Park Hyatt; Melrose
122 Ritz-Carlton
132 Jefferson Hotel
134 Wyndham Washington
140 Renaissance Mayflower Hotel

PLACES TO EAT
10 Addis Ababa
12 El Tamarindo
15 Julio's
16 U-topia
21 Straits of Malaya
22 Lauriol Plaza
34 Restaurant Nora
35 Teaism
36 Thai Chef
37 Timberlakes
38 City Lights of China
39 La Tomate
40 Xando Coffee & Bar
54 Zorba's Cafe
60 Raku
61 Firehook Bakery
73 Obelisk
84 Café Luna
92 Pesce
93 Johnny's Half Shell
98 Xando Coffee & Bar
102 Sticks & Bowls
103 Luna Grill & Diner
105 Iron Gate
109 I Ricchi
110 The Palm
114 Bertucci's Brick Oven Pizzeria
116 Julia's Empanadas
123 Asia Nora
124 Lulu's New Orleans Cafe; Club Mardi Gras
125 Meiwah
126 Sam & Harry's
135 Galileo
138 Oodles Noodles
139 Smith & Wollensky

BARS & CLUBS
11 Common Share
13 Chi Cha Lounge
14 Stetson's
55 Childe Harold
65 Club Chaos
68 The Fireplace
69 Mr P's; The Loft
80 Fox & Hounds
81 JR's
85 Diversité
86 Metro Cafe
87 Lizard Lounge
89 New Vegas Lounge
90 Badlands
91 Omega DC
97 Buffalo Billiards
100 The Big Hunt
111 Sesto Senso; The Garage
112 18th Street Lounge
113 Sign of the Whale
115 MCCXXIII
117 Dragonfly
127 Rumors
137 Odds

OTHER
1 Islamic Center
2 Icelandic Ambassador's Residence
3 The Lindens (Private)
4 French Ambassador's Residence
5 Chinese Embassy
17 Japanese Embassy
20 Italian-American Foundation
25 Whitman-Walker Clinic
26 Woodrow Wilson House
27 Textile Museum
28 Cameroon Embassy
29 Croatian Embassy
30 Pakistani Embassy (Moran House)
31 Haitian Embassy
32 Fondo del Sol Visual Arts Center
33 R St Gallery Row
44 National Museum of American Jewish Military History
47 Scottish Rite Masonic Temple
48 Turkish Embassy
49 Letelier Plaque
50 Irish Embassy
51 Indian Embassy
52 Phillips Collection
53 Cineplex Odeon Janus
56 The Left Bank
57 Lambda Rising
58 Women in the Life
59 Moto-Photo
64 Lammas
71 Anderson House (Society of the Cincinnati)
74 Indonesian Embassy (Walsh-McLean House)
76 Blaine Mansion (Private)
77 Riggs Bank
78 Kramerbooks & Afterwords Café
79 Washington Club
82 cyberSTOP Café
83 Washtub Laundromat
88 Woolly Mammoth Theatre Co
94 CVS Pharmacy
96 Historical Society of Washington, DC
99 Sulgrave Club
106 Australian Embassy
118 Cathedral of St Matthew the Apostle
119 B'nai B'rith Klutznick Museum
128 American Express
129 Avis Rent-A-Car
130 Mail Boxes Etc
131 National Geographic Society; Explorers' Hall
133 Metropolitan AME Church
136 Japanese Embassy Information & Culture Center
141 Planned Parenthood
142 Washington Post
143 CVS Pharmacy

Facing page:
Bartholdi Garden
water lilies

ADAMS-MORGAN

PLACES TO STAY
5 Adams Inn
14 Kalorama Guest House
31 Washington International
  Backpackers

PLACES TO EAT
1 Heller's Bakery
2 Don Juan's
4 Pupuseria San Miguel
11 Mama Ayesha's
16 Astor
17 Cashion's Eat Place
18 Rocky's Café
19 Perry's
22 Red Sea
23 Belmont Kitchen
24 Felix
25 New Orleans
27 Meskerem
28 I Matti
30 Bukom Café
32 Rumba
33 Mobay
34 La Fourchette
40 Roxanne; Peyote Grill

BARS & CLUBS
3 Raven Grill
7 Chief Ike's Mambo Room
8 Latin Jazz Alley
21 Asylum
26 Cities
35 Angles Bar & Billiards
36 Pharmacy Bar
37 Tom Tom
38 Club Heaven & Club Hell
39 Crush
41 Kokopooli's

OTHER
6 Evers Laundry
9 Church of Jesus Christ of
  Latter-day Saints
10 Mexican Cultural Institute
12 City Bikes
13 Pink Palace
20 Crestar Bank; Saturday
  Farmers' Market
29 DC AC
42 Meridian International Center

Rock Creek Park

Porter St

Williamsburg Lane

Piney Branch Pkwy

Beach Drive

Trail

Rosemont Ave

Pierce Mill Rd

Kalmia Rd

Kingle Rd

Adams Mill Rd

Olmsted Walk

Valley Trail

National Zoological Park

Rock Creek

Trail

Hawthorne St

Cathedral Ave

27th St

Woodley Pl

Cathedral Ave

Garfield St

Woodley Rd

Woodley Park-Zoo
M

Upper Northwest DC

see MAP 11

Cleveland Ave

Calvert St

24th St

Connecticut Ave

Duke Ellington Memorial Bridge

▼ 11

Normanstone Lane

Woodland Drive

Trail

McGill Terrace

28th St

Biltmore St

Allen Place

29th St

23rd St

Edgevale Terrace

Normanstone Drive

Rock Creek Drive

Trail

Rock Creek & Potomac Parkway

Taft Bridge

Belmont Rd

Wyoming Ave

Belmont Rd

Kalorama Rd

Ashmeade Place

Rock Creek Park

IP

0   250   500 m
0   250   500 yards

MAP 9

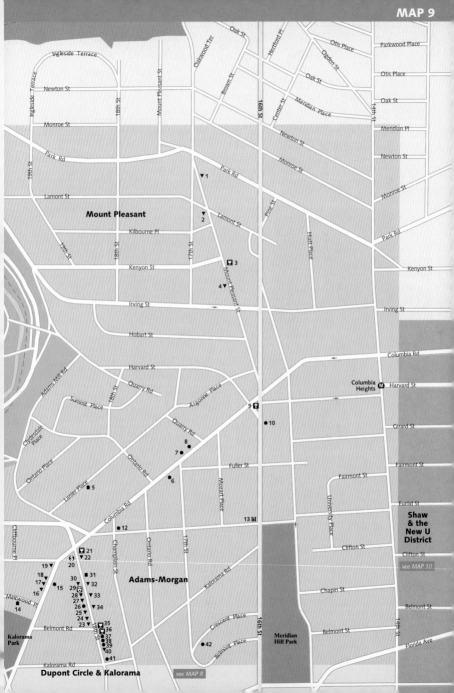

Ingleside Terrace
Ingleside Terrace
Newton St
Monroe St
Park Rd
19th St
Lamont St
Mount Pleasant
19th St
18th St
Kilbourne Pl
Kenyon St
17th St
Irving St
Hobart St
Harvard St
Adams Mill Rd
Summit Place
18th St
Quarry Rd
Argonne Place
Clydesdale Place
Quarry Rd
Ontario Place
Lanier Place
Ontario Rd
Columbia Rd
Cliffbourne Pl
Champlain St
Ontario Rd
17th St
Kalorama Rd
Adams-Morgan
Mintwood Pl
Belmont Rd
Kalorama
Park
Kalorama Rd
Dupont Circle & Kalorama

Oak St
Oakwood Ter
Brown St
Hertford Pl
Center St
16th St
Oak St
Meridian Place
Newton St
Monroe St
Pine St
Lamont St
Park Rd
Hiatt Place
Irving St
Columbia Rd
Harvard St
Girard St
Fuller St
Mozart Place
Fairmont St
University Place
Clifton St
Chapin St
Crescent Place
Belmont Place
16th St
Meridian
Hill Park
Belmont St

Otis Place
Parkwood Place
Ogden St
Otis Place
14th St
Oak St
Meridian Pl
Newton St
Monroe St
Park Rd
Kenyon St
Columbia
Heights
Fairmont St
Euclid St
Shaw
& the
New U
District
Clifton St

see MAP 10

Belmont St
14th St
Florida Ave

see MAP 8

▼1
▼2
▼3
4▼
9 ▮
● 10
8 ●
7 ▼
● 6
● 5
● 12
13 ▥
▣ 21
▼ 22
20
19 ▼
18 ▼
17 ▼
16
30 ■ 31
29 ▼ 32
28 ▼ 33
27 ▼ 34
26 ●
25 ▼
24 ▼
23 ▼ 35
▼ 36
● 37
● 38
● 39
●40
●41
● 42
14 ■
15 ●

see MAP 8

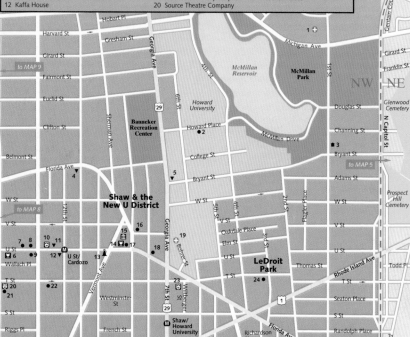